PRENDERGAST: LEGAL VILLAIN?

T0308053

PRENDERGAST: LEGAL VILLAIN?

Grant Morris

VICTORIA UNIVERSITY PRESS

TE WHARE WĀNANGA O TE ŪPOKO O TE IKA A MĀUI

VICTORIA
UNIVERSITY OF WELLINGTON

VICTORIA UNIVERSITY PRESS
Victoria University of Wellington
PO Box 600 Wellington
vup.victoria.ac.nz

National Library of New Zealand Cataloguing-in-Publication Data
Morris, Grant, 1974-
Prendergast : legal villain? / Grant Morris.
Includes bibliographical references and index.
ISBN 978-0-86473-937-7
1. Prendergast, James, 1826-1921.
2. Judges—New Zealand—Biography. I. Title.
347.93014092—dc 23

Printed by Printlink, Wellington

This book was published with the assistance of
the New Zealand Law Foundation.

To Olivia, Chloe and Imogen

CONTENTS

List of illustrations   viii

Acknowledgements   x

1   Introduction   1

2.   The creation of a colonial imperialist – The upbringing, education   5
     and experience of James Prendergast in England, 1826–1862

3.   Colonial beginnings – Experiences in Victoria, Australia, 1852–1855   22

4.   Return to the colonies – Experiences in Dunedin, 1862–1867   32

5.   Prendergast as Attorney-General, 1865–1875   44

6.   Chief Justice Prendergast, 1875–1899   88

7.   The Barton affair, 1876–1878   138

8.   The Treaty is a simple nullity – Prendergast and *Wi Parata v The*   154
     Bishop of Wellington

9.   Prendergast as 'Acting Governor', 1875–1899   172

10. 'Retirement', 1899–1921   188

11. Conclusion   197

Notes   203

Bibliography   232

Index   247

ILLUSTRATIONS

Between pages 180 and 181

1. One of only five pictures of Prendergast that remain (excepting group photos). This photograph was taken in approximately 1880. Ref: 1/2-079213-F. Alexander Turnbull Library, Wellington, New Zealand. http://natlib.govt.nz/records/23175340

2. Caroline Prendergast, mother of James Prendergast. Painted by Caroline's brother, the prominent portrait artist George Dawe R.A. Hall Collection. Photographed by Pete Nikolaison.

3. Michael Prendergast QC, James Prendergast's father. Pencil portrait by Thomas Wright, associate of George Dawe R.A. Hall Collection. Photographed by Pete Nikolaison.

4. London's Central Criminal Court, the 'Old Bailey', one of the many professional locations in which Michael Prendergast QC worked. James may have appeared here as a barrister. *Illustrated London News*, 4 March 1843. Kent State University Libraries. Special Collections and Archives.

5. The goldrush to the Ballarat goldfields during the mid-1850s, which included the Prendergast brothers. Painting by Samuel Thomas Gill (1872). Courtesy of the National Library of Australia.

6. Dunedin in 1868. Prendergast was a leading figure of this boomtown from 1862 to 1867. Ref: 0518_01_010A. Hocken Collections, University of Otago Library, Dunedin, New Zealand.

7. Lambton Quay, Wellington, in 1873, showing, from left, the Athenaeum, St Andrew's Church and the Supreme Courthouse. Prendergast appeared in this court as Attorney-General and during his early years as Chief Justice. Ref: 1/4-010013-F. Alexander Turnbull Library, Wellington, New Zealand. http://natlib.govt.nz/records/23213072

8. The next Wellington Supreme Court, built in 1881 and Prendergast's professional residence from 1881 to 1899. Ref: 1/2-011634-G. Alexander Turnbull Library, Wellington, New Zealand. http://natlib.govt.nz/records/22775418

9. George E. Barton, the gifted but erratic barrister, and Prendergast's arch-nemesis. Reproduced with the permission of the Victorian Parliamentary Library, Australia.

10. Prendergast's mansion on Bolton Street, built during the late 1860s, was one of the most prominent landmarks in Wellington. Prendergast lived in the house for over 50 years. Ref: NegE748/37. Hocken Collections, University of Otago Library, Dunedin, New Zealand.

11. Christopher William Richmond in 1888, Prendergast's good friend and closest colleague. Ref: 1/1-013502-G. Alexander Turnbull Library, Wellington, New Zealand. http://natlib.govt.nz/records/22719131

12. Richmond was a regular visitor at Prendergast's Bolton Street mansion. During one visit in 1879, he sketched this picture of Thorndon. Ref: E-284-040. Alexander Turnbull Library, Wellington, New Zealand. http://natlib.govt.nz/records/23131426

13. Wiremu Parata, Ngati Toa leader and the plaintiff in Prendergast's most infamous case. Ref: PA2-2577. Alexander Turnbull Library, Wellington, New Zealand. http://natlib.govt.nz/records/23013231

14. The iconic settlement of Parihaka at the time of the November 1881 invasion for which Prendergast was partly responsible. Ref: PA1-q-183-18. Alexander Turnbull Library, Wellington, New Zealand. http://natlib.govt.nz/records/23014599

15. Government House, Prendergast's residence during the many times when he acted as Administrator for the colony. Ref: 1/2-140327-G. Alexander Turnbull Library, Wellington, New Zealand. http://natlib.govt.nz/records/23013231

16. Cartoon of Prendergast during his retirement in 1907, from the *Free Lance*, a publication covering Wellington's social scene. *New Zealand Free Lance*, Vol. VII, 30 March 1907. Courtesy of Papers Past, National Library of New Zealand.

17. Prendergast (seated, far left) was the New Zealand delegate to the Imperial Court of Appeal Conference in London. *Illustrated London News*, 20 July 1901. Hocken Collection, University of Otago Library, Dunedin, New Zealand.

18. The Court of Appeal in 1903, featuring some of Prendergast's former colleagues and his replacement (left to right): Cooper, Conolly, Williams JJ, Stout CJ, Denniston, Edwards JJ. Ref: 2075_01_001A.jpg. Hocken Collections, University of Otago Library, Dunedin, New Zealand.

19. The author visited Prendergast's gravesite in 1998 and found it completely overgrown and unrecognisable. This is perhaps symbolic of Prendergast's fall from leading colonial figure to legal villain. Morris Collection.

20. James Nairn's portrait of Prendergast which hangs in the Wellington High Court, unveiled in 1899. Courtesy of the Wellington High Court.

ACKNOWLEDGEMENTS

The completion of this book has been supported by a range of individuals, institutions and organisations. Firstly, I would like to thank the team at Victoria University Press, and in particular, managing editor Fergus Barrowman and production editor Kyleigh Hodgson, for their support and advice throughout the publishing process. VUP has been, and continues to be, the leading supporter of legal biography in New Zealand. Secondly, I would like to thank the librarians of all the research institutions that I have worked in while completing this work. These include: the Victoria University of Wellington and University of Waikato libraries, the Alexander Turnbull Library and Archives New Zealand, the Hocken Library, the State Library of Victoria, the British Library, the Inns of Court Libraries and the National Archives, London.

Financial support for this research was provided by a number of organisations. In 2013 the Law Foundation provided generous funding for research and publication costs. From 2002, the Victoria University of Wellington Law Faculty has helped to fund conference leave to present papers about Prendergast and also provided funding to cover research assistance. This book is derived from my doctoral thesis. For the period 1998–2000 I extend my thanks to the Department of History at the University of Waikato for the opportunity to work as a Doctoral Assistant, and the Ryoichi Sasakawa Foundation for their generous scholarship, and in particular, for making the British research trip possible.

I would like to give special thanks to my two doctoral supervisors, Dr Douglas Simes and Professor Peter Spiller. Their advice and encouragement throughout the postgraduate process and beyond was invaluable. My mentor, Professor Simon Burrows, was also a great support during this time. Since joining Victoria in 2002 I have had the opportunity to discuss Prendergast with many accomplished legal historians in many different fora. In particular, I would like to thank Professor David Williams, Professor Richard Boast, Professor Jeremy Finn, Associate Professor Jacinta Ruru and Professor Philip Girard.

The Australian and New Zealand Law and History Society has played a key role in facilitating my legal history career. The annual conference provides an excellent testing ground for ideas and arguments and a ready-made network of high quality legal historians. I discussed Prendergast at several conferences, even as far afield as the American Society for Legal History and British Legal History conferences. In the later stages of the research process I am indebted to my two research assistants, Sarah Lamb and Tessa McKeown. Thanks also to the Hobbs and Knight families for their assistance and support throughout the project.

On a more personal note, I would like to thank my family. During the PhD process, the success of the vital Wellington archival trips was partly due to the support of my late grandmother, Merle Morris, who provided accommodation, meals and fascinating historical discussions during the evenings. Finally, I would like to thank three people who played an integral role in supporting me during the long period in which this work was completed: my wife, Olivia Fraser-Morris, and my parents, David and Lindsay Morris. Olivia has been my friend and confidant throughout the ups and downs of postgraduate and academic research. My thanks to my parents are not only for this book, but for all the academic studies leading up to the completion of the thesis.

1

INTRODUCTION

James Prendergast is a well-known name to those who study New Zealand's legal history. During his life, Prendergast was a respected judge and pillar of the colonial establishment. In recent years, he has been vilified for a statement made in 1877 referring to the Treaty of Waitangi as 'a simple nullity'. Despite his influential career and impact on the development of the New Zealand legal system, it is for this statement that most remember James Prendergast today.

There were only four Chief Justices of New Zealand during the nineteenth century; Prendergast was the third. As the head of the judiciary, the Chief Justice plays a pivotal role in the legal system. The first Chief Justice, William Martin, is reasonably well covered in New Zealand historiography, as is the fourth, Robert Stout. Both have biographies and are the subjects of various journal articles,[1] although Stout's relatively strong coverage is primarily due to his political, rather than legal, career. The second Chief Justice, George Arney, was competent but kept a low profile. Prendergast served as Chief Justice for 24 years, making a number of pivotal decisions and adjudicating in many controversial cases. This followed ten years as Attorney-General during the later stages of the New Zealand Wars, and before that, several years as a prosperous barrister in gold-rush Dunedin. With such a strong connection with the development of the New Zealand legal system it is somewhat surprising that Prendergast has never been the subject of a biography. Pen-portraits have provided the outline of his life in G. H. Scholefield's *A Dictionary of New Zealand Biography* (1940), *The Dictionary of New Zealand Biography* (1990), and David Williams' *A Simple Nullity? The* Wi Parata *case in New Zealand law and history* (2011), but beyond this very brief treatment, Prendergast's life remains largely untouched.

The *Wi Parata* decision, in which Prendergast made his infamous statement (in a joint decision with Christopher William Richmond), has been discussed by scholars at length, but while treating the case they have virtually ignored the man. Therefore, a biography of Prendergast's life and career was waiting to be written. An impressive number of political biographies appear in New Zealand's more recent historiography, including Raewyn Dalziel's *Julius Vogel*, Judith Bassett's *Sir Harry Atkinson*, Jeanine Graham's *Frederick Weld*, Ray Fargher's biography of Donald McLean and Edmund Bohan's works on George Grey and Edward Stafford. Yet few academic legal biographies exist.[2] Peter Spiller's *The Chapman Legal Family*,

Alex Frame's *Salmond: Southern Jurist* and Janet November's biography of Ethel Benjamin are the few comprehensive models available to the legal historian. The Chapman family, Salmond and Benjamin are legal figures widely admired by the present generation. Prendergast's present reputation is largely negative, posing a different challenge to the legal biographer.

Legal history in general has been lightly covered in New Zealand's historical literature. *A New Zealand Legal History* (1995, 2001), by Peter Spiller, Richard Boast and Jeremy Finn, filled an important gap, but much work remains to be done. Previous to *A New Zealand Legal History*, only Robin Cooke's *Portrait of a Profession* (1969) stood as a broad New Zealand legal history. *Portrait of a Profession*, along with the vast majority of early legal history, is more a celebration of the legal profession, written by lawyers, than a critical academic book. Perhaps this relative scarcity of New Zealand legal history is due to the technical nature of the research. The principal tools of the legal historian are law reports and statutes. A competent knowledge of case analysis and statutory interpretation is therefore usually required to do justice to legal history. Not surprisingly, most New Zealand legal biographies have been produced by academics associated with law schools.

The lawyer and the historian both rely on the key skills of research, analysis and writing. While law requires a certain technical knowledge, the approaches taken in both disciplines share more similarities than differences. Legal history in New Zealand is not an overcrowded field of study. In terms of time periods, New Zealand legal historians are essentially limited to three main areas of study: Maori legal history before European settlement, nineteenth-century legal history and twentieth-century or modern legal history. The primary themes running through nineteenth-century New Zealand legal history are the cultural encounter between colonial settlers and Maori and implementation of the English legal system in New Zealand.

Perhaps the reason a biography of Prendergast has not been written in recent years is the infamy now attached to his name. But the study of history demands that all subjects be explored, not only those popular or attractive in any given era. If only the 'safe' subjects were written about, history would become greatly distorted. Also, it is impossible to know the nature of a subject until extensive research has been carried out.

Therefore, the reasons for writing a legal biography of James Prendergast are clear. Firstly, Prendergast was an extremely influential figure in nineteenth-century New Zealand history, and in particular, legal history. Secondly, New Zealand legal history is an area requiring more comprehensive research. Thirdly, a balance is needed in recent New Zealand historiography. 'Unpopular' subjects such as James Prendergast need to be addressed to provide a full picture of New Zealand's development. Currently, Prendergast is a two-dimensional figure in New Zealand history. This book seeks to provide a third dimension.

Thus the reasons for this biography are closely linked to the aims. The primary aim of this biography is to explore the role and influence of James Prendergast in the administration of New Zealand colonial justice. The book also seeks to explore the enduring relationship between the English and the New Zealand legal systems. Another key aim is to challenge the reduction of a number of prominent historical figures to mere stereotypes. Prendergast was more than the archetypal colonial imperialist.

The focus of this book is the life and career of James Prendergast. The work could be located in the genre of legal historical biography. Prendergast lived an exciting, eventful and controversial life. His English background forms the focus of Chapter 2. This background is vital in understanding Prendergast's views and later actions and also in examining the close connections between the English legal system and the New Zealand colonial legal system. Chapter 3 explores Prendergast's first colonial experience in the colony of Victoria. A comparison is provided between this experience and Prendergast's later successes in the colony of New Zealand. Chapter 4 focuses on Prendergast's beginnings in New Zealand. Starting as a barrister in Dunedin, Prendergast quickly worked his way up the New Zealand legal ladder. An exploration of the high-profile Dunedin Bar during the 1860s provides a range of insights into the foundations of New Zealand's legal profession.

Chapter 5 focuses on Prendergast's time as Attorney-General. After the Chief Justiceship, it is this role in which Prendergast left his most enduring legacy. Through his legislation, legal opinions, court advocacy, and administrative skills, Prendergast dominated the governmental legal environment for ten years. Studying the development of the legal system during such a formative period provides insights into the administration of New Zealand colonial justice. The largest and most important chapter of this book, Chapter 6, explores Prendergast's role as Chief Justice from 1875 to 1899. The focus is primarily on his judicial decisions, but attention is also paid to his administrative duties as Chief Justice. The length of this chapter also reflects the length of Prendergast's term as Chief Justice, an impressive 24 years of judicial service.

Chapter 7 presents a case study in which Prendergast's very career is threatened through a feud with the renegade barrister George Barton. Through this case study the nature of the New Zealand legal profession at that time can be explored. Chapter 8 explores Prendergast's role in the *Wi Parata* decision. This chapter forms a vital part of the biography, as without the infamy resulting from the *Wi Parata* decision, Prendergast would probably remain as unknown as his predecessor, Arney. Modern New Zealand legal scholarship has become fixated by Prendergast's view on the Treaty of Waitangi. Chapter 9 discusses Prendergast's role as Administrator of New Zealand, and in particular, his controversial involvement in the 1881 invasion of Parihaka. Chapter 10 looks at the final 21 years of Prendergast's long life, after his retirement from the bench.

A traditional methodological approach has been taken in this biography. The available archival material relating to the life and career of James Prendergast was explored. This material is primarily located in law reports, statutes, newspapers (primarily accessed through Papers Past), Department of Justice archives in Archives NZ, and personal papers in the Alexander Turnbull Library and Hocken Library. Other sources included law journals and official government publications such as the Appendices to Journals of the House of Representatives and New Zealand Parliamentary Debates. Research was carried out in New Zealand, Australia and England. By researching and visiting the key locations in Prendergast's life, a feeling for his journey was obtained. For the sections dealing with the New Zealand Wars, the Treaty of Waitangi and native title, secondary literature has been surveyed at length to provide an appropriate historiographical context. The broad structure of the book is chronological, but within each chapter, themes are used as a framework to a greater degree than chronology.

The first biography of James Prendergast has been a long time coming. Admired during his lifetime, forgotten after his death and vilified in the present day, Prendergast's reputation has moved from one extreme to the other. His legacy remains, but questions have been raised as to whether this legacy is positive or negative. Different interpretations on the life of Prendergast will continue to emerge. His historical actions are so near the heart of key New Zealand issues, such as race relations, land and heritage, that he will always be relevant in New Zealand historiography.

The actions and events of colonial New Zealand form the basis of this book. The personalities, problems, conflicts and triumphs provide the themes and issues. James Prendergast was a prominent figure in the story of colonial New Zealand for over a half a century. In 1826, Aotearoa–New Zealand was controlled by Maori, with a few vulnerable European settlements dotted around the coastline. In 1826, London was the centre of the growing British Empire. In 1826, James Prendergast was born in London. Eventually, he would play a large and controversial part in transforming New Zealand from the home of Maori to a prosperous colonial outpost of the British Empire.

2

THE CREATION OF A COLONIAL IMPERIALIST

The upbringing, education and experience of James Prendergast in England, 1826–1862

While Prendergast is known as a long-serving and controversial New Zealand judge, he was in many ways a product of Victorian England. Prendergast's privileged English background is the context within which we must judge this judge. The opportunities Prendergast enjoyed in England were largely a result of the successful legal career of his father, Michael Prendergast QC. Prendergast senior played a pivotal role in directing the life of James. Born in the heart of London in 1826, James found himself literally at the centre of the huge British Empire. Education was a high priority in the Prendergast family, and James attended the elite St Paul's School. From St Paul's he took the natural step to the University of Cambridge. James was an able student but not entirely sure as to which career he would pursue. After completing his B.A. and spending a year as a school teacher, Prendergast decided to follow his father into the legal profession.

After a brief adventure in Victoria, Australia, James returned to London to begin his career in the law. In the shadow of his high-profile and controversial father, James did not achieve prominence as quickly as hoped. Eventually, an overcrowded legal profession and the death of his father would convince James to leave the centre of the Empire and travel to its farthest reaches. The background of James Prendergast has much in common with other leading New Zealand figures during the late nineteenth century who were born into the English elite, but not able to achieve the prominence they desired in England. The upbringing and schooling Prendergast received is reflected in his legal judgments and political actions while in New Zealand. Created by Imperial Britain, Prendergast sought to recreate Britain in New Zealand.

1. Early years

James Prendergast was born on 10 December 1826 in the parish of St Bartholomew the Great in the City of London.[1] Prendergast's birthplace of Holborn is within the sound of Bow Bells, technically making James a 'cockney'. The Prendergast family had lived in the shadow of St Bartholomew's for several generations and James' grandfather, Michael, was the local draper. James' father, Michael (1795–1859), is described as "a gentleman who had risen, by his own industry and talent, from a humble origin to a high position at the English Bar, without the aid of influential friends and patronage."[2] In a clear example of nineteenth-century social mobility, Michael was a working-class boy who became a successful middle-class professional through educational opportunities. Despite his "humble origin", Michael Prendergast QC became a leading legal figure in London, while his brother, Joseph, achieved renown as a classical scholar.[3] Therefore, while James had a privileged upbringing, his generation of Prendergasts was the first to enjoy this opportunity.

While the Prendergast family may not have enjoyed an illustrious genealogy, James' mother's family were well-known to the English elite. Caroline Prendergast née Dawe was the sister of George Dawe R.A., one of the foremost English portrait artists of his time.[4] Caroline's father, Phillip Dawe, was also a well-known artist and engraver. Caroline Prendergast gave birth to three sons and one daughter, of whom James was the third child. Born to an ambitious, successful father and cultured mother, the future prospects for young James were bright.

In 1836, at the age of nine, James began his education at St Paul's School. James' elder brother, Philip, had already spent two years at the school when James arrived.[5] In 1836, St Paul's School, founded by John Colet in 1509, had already educated some of England's most famous sons, including John Milton, Samuel Pepys and John Churchill. The school stood across the street from Christopher Wren's masterpiece and was closely connected with the cathedral. It has long been considered one of England's most elite public schools. When James began his time at the school, John Sleath was finishing his time as headmaster. Herbert Kynaston replaced Sleath in 1838.[6] The historian of St Paul's writes, "there is virtual unanimity that Kynaston was kindly, charming, urbane and almost completely ineffectual . . . . whatever his short-comings, he could inspire scholarship in those of his pupils capable of it."[7] Kynaston was an important figure in English educational and cultural life during the mid-1900s.

The school curriculum was dominated by Latin and Greek, preparing many of its scholars for the Universities of Oxford and Cambridge. All 153 boys were taught in one large room with strict discipline and traditional teaching methods.[8] The school building was cramped and gloomy, described by one old Pauline as presenting "more the appearance of a prison than a school for happy boys."[9] St Paul's was closely associated with its rival and fellow day-school, Merchant Taylors' School. James' brother Michael (junior) and his father Michael (senior) both attended Merchant Taylors'.[10]

Prendergast was a successful pupil and left St Paul's in 1845 as a Pauline Exhibitioner, a much sought-after academic honour with financial benefits.[11] The traditional nature of St Paul's curriculum is exemplified by Prendergast's speech at the 1844 Winter Speeches.[12] The speech was taken from Plautus' *Captivi*. Whatever its limitations, St Paul's had equipped James well for his next educational step, the University of Cambridge. Through his schooling, James received strong parental support but was subject to high expectations. In c1844, Michael wrote to his wife Caroline: "I hope James is now head boy, let him remember the prize and the desk, the approbation of his father and mother and the respect of his master and schoolfellows."[13]

2. A Cambridge education

It was at the University of Cambridge that James began to demonstrate a somewhat restless nature. Admitted as a pensioner (fee paying student) to Caius College on 12 May 1845, Prendergast resided there only one term before migrating to Queens' College on 18 December 1845.[14] His reasons for migration were varied and at first he was unsure as to which new college to enter: "I am going to migrate to Trinity unless they let me have my dinner at 4 o'clock, they have the impudence to say that the Freshmen are (to) dine after the others at 5 o'clock".[15] One reason which may have determined his move to Queens' was the greater availability of fellowships.[16]

A collection of letters from James to his father and mother during c1845 provide further insights into the personality of James, aged 18 to 19. James showed frustration with his mother as a correspondent: "It is now 6 o'clock and it is Thursday evening, at 7 o'clock on Thursday last, I sent you a letter I have had no answer what do you mean by it, I shall not write any more now".[17] Caroline Prendergast was in low spirits during the early 1840s, probably due to the death of her daughter, the continual absence of her husband and poor health. Caroline died in February 1846, during James' second year at Cambridge.

In his letters, James describes his studies and academic interests. For a man who would make his name dispensing very practical judgments in the colonies, his education was of a traditional academic nature. Even while at St Paul's, Prendergast's education focussed on the classic texts, though not all his time was spent studying, "I have begun the Prometheus and have read the whole of the second book of Euclid . . . . I shall walk up to Lords after tea to see the finish of the match between our School and Kings College."[18] The reference to Prometheus is almost certainly Aeschylus' *Prometheus Bound* in Greek. The other reference is to Euclid's *Elements*, also in Greek. Prendergast also mentions studying Homer and Horace. During his first year at Cambridge he continued reading Euclid and also attended lectures on Latin and Greek composition.[19] James' main subject of interest was mathematics,[20] which may partly account for his problem-solving, logical approach to the practice of law. This was a common path for Cambridge scholars given the dominance of the mathematical tripos. A schooling in the classics was common amongst many members of New Zealand's elite during the nineteenth century and helped to provide Prendergast with intellectual credibility amongst this elite group.

Cambridge was hugely influential in mathematical developments during the nineteenth century and Prendergast would have been taught by some of the best mathematicians in the world. The Cambridge School of Mathematical Physics was flourishing by the 1840s. The School produced such figures as Lord Kelvin, Arthur Cayley, James Clerk Maxwell and Isaac Todhunter. Prendergast entertained hopes of gaining high enough grades to be named a 'wrangler' (top mathematics student) which could result in the offer of a college fellowship.[21] Despite the confident tone in Prendergast's letters to his father, he failed to shine as a mathematician and could not compete with the elite Cambridge cohort of the late 1840s. There is no indication from Prendergast's letters as to whether he was tutored by William Hopkins, the prominent mathematician and geologist, who also found fame as 'senior-wrangler maker'. Hopkins was the inspirational tutor of many Cambridge mathematics students. An interesting comparison can be made between Prendergast and his future colleague, Joshua Williams. Williams was 11 years younger than Prendergast and also attended Cambridge (L.L.M., M.A.). Unlike Prendergast, Williams was a star student, placing high in class and winning academic prizes.[22] Despite this, Williams found himself struggling to establish himself as a London lawyer at the same time as Prendergast (1859–1861).

James kept in close touch with his two brothers while at Cambridge, and they provided him with a support network in his early days of university study. The correspondence between the Prendergast family demonstrates a closeknit unit, while also highlighting the difficulties caused by distance and separation. The young James Prendergast was close to his mother, father and both elder brothers. The loss of his family by the early 1860s would have altered his outlook on life and made him a more independent and solitary man. No letters written by James at Cambridge remain after January 1846, possibly due to the death of his mother soon after that date. The last surviving letter from James to his mother is dated 27 December 1845, "I have now become a loyal member of a royal College [Queens'], I hope your knee is much better by this time . . . . I must finish with a hope that this will find you much better than when I left you."[23]

James graduated with an Ordinary B.A. degree in Mathematics in 1849. While he successfully completed his degree at Cambridge, he did not shine as a scholar in the way he had at St Paul's. With a position of 85th out of 115, James can hardly be said to be a leading Cambridge student.[24] During this period of English legal history, it was not necessary to obtain an L.L.B. degree before becoming a lawyer. Therefore, James could study mathematics at university and then proceed to the Inns of Court for training as a barrister. All the Prendergasts were 'Cambridge Men'. James' paternal uncle, Joseph Prendergast, left Queens' with a Doctorate of Divinity and became a leading classical scholar. Michael senior left Pembroke with a law degree, while Michael junior completed his legal degree at Trinity Hall. Philip was admitted to Caius, stayed, and completed a B.A. For many well-to-do young men, the ancient universities opened up career opportunities not accessible to others. During his brief time in Victoria, Australia, James would inform his father by letter of 'Cambridge Men' he had met in the distant colonies. Attending Cambridge for four years would provide Prendergast with an influential network of acquaintances for later life.

After completing his degree in 1849, James Prendergast was admitted to the Middle Temple in central London.[25] James' elder brother, Michael, had been admitted to Middle Temple six years earlier but would only be called to the bar in November 1849. James' journey to the bar was even slower. Whether this was due to a reluctance to enter the legal profession or the lack of legal jobs available is not clear. Much had changed in Prendergast's personal life, with the death of his mother in February 1846.[26]

3. School teaching in Somerset

After his admission to the Middle Temple in 1849, Prendergast abruptly left and took the unexpected step of becoming a school teacher. The school was a small private institution run by the Reverend William Routledge and located at Bishop's Hull, a small rural community south-west of Taunton, Somerset. Far from the bustling activity of London, Prendergast began in paid employment. From his own accounts it seems that James was unsure about his decision: "When I first came down [to Bishop's Hull] of course the school was new to me and I did not much like it".[27] His father supported him in what was seen by both as a temporary measure:

> I assure you all your friends here greatly commend your prudence in taking your present position and your uncle Joseph who knows something of such matters thinks you are very fortunate. I know you will listen to your father . . . . I hope you will not imagine you are not forwarding yourself in the world. You are doing so.[28]

The experience of teaching in rural Somerset must have allowed Prendergast to see a different way of life from urban London. The students numbered 28 and were aged from seven to sixteen.[29] Most were preparing for a career in the army.[30] Prendergast lived at the school with Reverend Routledge, his family and a young teacher of French.[31] After settling in at the school, Prendergast began to enjoy the experience more, finding time for walking and reading.[32] Prendergast's career as a school teacher was brief and in late 1851, he returned to London.

In 1852, Prendergast married Mary Jane Hall, a Cambridgeshire woman.[33] The two probably met while Prendergast was living in Cambridge. On 17 June 1852, five days after his marriage, Prendergast set sail for the Victorian goldfields in Australia. James intended Mary to join him after he struck gold. School teaching had provided James with a valuable experience and an income for a short time, but he was restless for adventure and prestige. The story of his adventures in Australia is recounted in Chapter 3.

4. Beginnings as a lawyer

It was not until 30 April 1856, when James had recently returned from Victoria, that he was finally called to the bar and began practice as a lawyer. The bulk of James' training at Middle Temple must have taken place between his brief teaching career and his departure for Victoria in 1852 or on his return from Victoria in 1855, with perhaps some brief training in 1849.

For six years, Prendergast worked as a special pleader in the London courts before setting off for the colony of New Zealand in 1862. The role of a special pleader was to organise pleas and "develop the point in controversy between parties" resulting in a more efficient judicial process.[34] In practice, the art of special pleading was complex and confusing. One critic from the time described the frustrations of special pleading: "enough to make a horse laugh; a drizzling mass of empirical inventions, circuitous procedure, and unintelligible fiction, calculated for no purpose but to fortify monopoly and wrap justice in deceit and mystery."[35] Special pleading had experienced a revival after the drawing up of the 1834 'Hilary Rules'. The purpose of the rules was to "strike a balance between the extreme precision of special pleading and the extreme vagueness of the general issue" and enable the plaintiff to "be told as clearly as possible what defence he will have to meet, and to be informed what facts the defence admits, and what facts it disputes."[36] Unfortunately the practical result was to introduce a precision and rigidity which further complicated court procedure. From the 1850s to the 1870s the English legal system struggled to contain the negative effects of special pleading.[37]

A few reports remain commenting upon Prendergast's performance as a special pleader. In Sir James' obituary, the *Dominion* recounted a well-known Prendergast anecdote:

> Frequently he conducted cases before his father, who was very short-sighted. On one occasion the learned Judge failed to observe that his son was engaged in an important case. At tea he declared that a young pleader in the suit in question had done remarkably well for a junior. Great was the surprise when informed that the subject of his eulogy was his own son![38]

Despite these favourable comments on Prendergast, the English legal profession was seriously overcrowded during the mid-nineteenth century. Barely a year after Prendergast had begun practising, a Royal Commission was created to investigate the professions, hoping to discover the reasons why many educated middle-class sons were failing to gain adequate professional work.[39]

Official reports of Prendergast's performance as a special pleader are limited. The name Prendergast appears in the English Reports, as a lawyer, from the period

1856–1862, but it is unclear whether this is James Prendergast or another.[40] A collection of letters from 1862 shows James dealing with Philip's declining health and attending to cases, but these sources are limited in their scope.[41] What can be said about the legal careers of James and Philip Prendergast in London from 1859 to 1862 is that, at the end of the period, James left London permanently and Philip had a mental breakdown. Neither of the brothers received any recorded public acclaim for their work.

Prendergast lived in and worked from Sergeants' Inn, Fleet Street, in the heart of legal London. During the nineteenth century the title of Sergeant was bestowed upon a barrister who was to be appointed as a judge.[42] The society of Sergeants provided accommodation to London barristers in the society inn. At the time of Prendergast's career as a London lawyer, his father would have been a Sergeant and was living in Sergeants' Inn with James.[43]

Prendergast served his legal apprenticeship in the legal offices of Thomas Chitty. Chitty was an associate of Michael Prendergast QC and family connections enabled James to study under this eminent legal figure. Chitty had supported Michael Prendergast's application for Judge of the Sheriff's Court in London.[44] Chitty wrote a glowing testimony for James:

> with much pleasure I can forward . . . testimony to you being in every respect well fitted for the post which you are a candidate for. You were my pupil for some time . . . you . . . exhibited every thing expected . . . [of] . . . a sound lawyer [and] swift-minded man.[45]

During the early 1830s, Chitty was a leading special pleader in the Courts of King's Bench, Common Pleas and Exchequer of Pleas. Chitty had a comprehensive knowledge of the forms of proceedings used in these courts.[46] The first edition of Chitty's classic work, *Forms of Practical Proceedings in the Courts of King's Bench, Common Pleas and Exchequer of Pleas*, was published in 1834 during a time of reform and change in the English legal system:

> The inspiration for the conception, construction, compilation, presentation and publication of this work was doubtless attributable to the extraordinary ferment then prevailing for the reform of civil procedure, engendered very largely by the celebrated speech on Law Reform delivered in the House of Commons in 1828 by Henry Brougham, an ardent and articulate disciple of Jeremy Bentham.[47]

Chitty supplied vital information to common law practitioners in a rapidly changing environment.

Prendergast began his apprenticeship with Chitty in 1855 or 1856, the time at which Chitty was preparing to publish the seventh edition of his now established work.[48] Working under a master of English common law would have provided Prendergast with a knowledge base which he could use in administering the New Zealand legal system during the latter half of the nineteenth century.

The influence of Michael Prendergast and Thomas Chitty would have aided James in gathering enough work to continue in practice. With his father's death in 1859, James would have lost his primary mentor and benefactor in the London legal world. But other options were available to young professional men, namely, change in one's career or travel to the colonies. Thus in 1862, James Prendergast abandoned his legal career in England and set off to try his luck in New Zealand. In only three years Prendergast would rise from a little-known special pleader in the London courts to Attorney-General of New Zealand.

5. The influence of Michael Prendergast QC

The rise of James Prendergast as a legal leader was partly due to the influence of his father, Michael Prendergast QC. Michael Prendergast senior was from a relatively ordinary background, although his father made one particularly wise property investment in central London. Through assertiveness and perseverance, Michael rose to prominence, first as a barrister and then as a judge. Michael attended Merchant Taylors' School and obtained a prestigious Parkyn Exhibition to progress to Pembroke College at the University of Cambridge.[49] Studying specifically for an L.L.B. degree, Michael was certain of his desire to lift himself up into the legal profession. After being admitted into Lincoln's Inn in 1816, Michael was eventually called to the bar in 1820[50] and graduated with his L.L.B. in 1821.[51] From this moment, life moved fast for young Michael Prendergast. He made an advantageous marriage to Caroline Dawe, the daughter of a successful artist, in 1821.[52] Their first son, Michael junior, was born the following year, with a second son, Philip, following in 1824.

Born and bred in the City of London, Michael Prendergast set out to make a name for himself in the capital of the growing British Empire. From 1821 to 1842, Michael appeared as counsel in a number of high-profile cases[53] and succeeded in establishing himself as a leading London advocate. Michael's third son, James, was born in 1826, followed by a daughter, Caroline, in 1829. Tragedy befell the young lawyer when his daughter died in c1840, aged approximately 11 years.[54]

In 1848, he transferred to the county of Norwich, taking the position of Recorder, after the murder of the previous Recorder for that city. During the sensational and high-profile trial of the murderer, Michael Prendergast had acted as one of the successful prosecutors.[55] In 1850, Michael was appointed Queen's Counsel.[56] Michael Prendergast served in several other important legal-political positions, but it was his appointment as Judge of the Sheriff's Court in London in 1856 that brought him widespread fame, or infamy.

The list of criticisms, both contemporary and recent, concerning Michael Prendergast in the later stages of his career is very long indeed. Michael's performance as a London judge has been described as "mediocre"[57] and "eccentric".[58] Matters came to a head when, in 1858, Prendergast was accused of incompetency, bias and discourteous conduct towards certain barristers and hauled before the Court of Common Council.[59]

George Henry Lewis, a London barrister, made a number of serious complaints about Prendergast's ability as a judge. Lewis claimed Prendergast had desired to ask questions of his client, the defendant, before Lewis had actually called the defendant as a witness. When Lewis complained of a breach of proper procedure, Prendergast apparently ignored him. While questioning the defendant, Lewis claimed that Prendergast repeated the defendant's answers incorrectly. After Lewis complained again, Prendergast and Lewis argued in front of the court. After a short but bitter exchange, Lewis was committed by Prendergast for one hour. Two decades later, Chief Justice James Prendergast would make legal history by committing a barrister for contempt.

While Judge Prendergast was absolved of blame in the 1858 enquiry, his reputation as a lawyer also seems to have been the subject of controversy and debate. Anecdotes tell of Michael Prendergast QC arguing with judges, juries and coroners and assaulting a cab driver in central London while drunk.[60] James Prendergast would also be the subject of much controversy as a judge, while Michael junior's career would be ruined by alcoholism. The leading barrister, Ballantine, described Michael Prendergast:

> Slovenly as his dress was, his mind was more so: with a greater fund of general knowledge than most people, it seemed mixed so inextricably in his brain that it was next to useless. He rarely had any but the smallest cases from the dirtiest of clients.[61]

A favourite Prendergast anecdote was when the lawyer lost his brief in court. Looking in his pockets, Prendergast produced a piece of toast, before finally locating "the single greasy sheet that constituted his instructions".[62] These anecdotes appear exaggerated and somewhat dubious given Prendergast's professional success, which was the result of hard work and natural talent.

Like his career as a judge, Prendergast's appearance and organisation were condemned, while his integrity was supported by some:

> Mr. Prendergast, is in the Crown Court, a Titon among the minnows . . . . He has a peculiar penchant for fact . . . . A well-thumbed bundle of leaves, once perhaps a perfect copy of Archbold's Criminal Law, constitutes the whole of his library in Court . . . . To the honour of Mr. Prendergast it must also be said, that he is equally dauntless in the defence of his clients as for the liberties of his own profession . . . There are few men at the Criminal Bar of this country, more powerful advocates for the acquittal or fair trial of a prisoner, than Mr. Prendergast.[63]

The commentaries on Michael Prendergast occasionally praise his sense of justice[64] and it seems he was a very eccentric and outspoken, rather than corrupt, judge. His quick temper and authoritarian approach was passed onto his son James, although the younger Prendergast mellowed somewhat in his later years. Michael Prendergast was a loyal advocate and a fearless opponent, but did not pay homage to rules and procedures.

Despite Michael Prendergast's apparent shortcomings, he acted as a dedicated advisor and mentor to his son, James. An analysis of the life and character of James Prendergast could lead one to believe he partly modelled himself on his father, but was more diligent and conservative in personality. Letters between father and son show common interests and fatherly guidance. Though Michael had many enemies, he also had powerful friends in the City who could aid James in his early years as a barrister. Michael Prendergast died in 1859 after a short illness, leaving approximately 3000 pounds; a respectable, if not particularly large, amount for a self-made man and a high-profile London judge and lawyer.[65] Three years later, James Prendergast left London, the long-time home of the Prendergast family.

A collection of letters from the late 1830s written by Michael Prendergast to his wife, Caroline, provides insights into Prendergast family life. This decade was perhaps the happiest for the Prendergast family, with four growing children and a fairly stable marriage. While the career of Michael Prendergast did not really flourish until the 1840s, that decade was marred by the death of his daughter and wife. The 1850s saw Michael Prendergast achieve even more professional prominence, but the decade was dominated by the ultimately ill-fated Australian adventure undertaken by his three sons. The end of the 1860s saw only James still active in public and private life.

During the 1830s, Michael was often away from the Prendergast family home in London. Attempting to procure work as a special pleader on the Norfolk circuit, Michael travelled to towns such as Bury St Edmunds, Ipswich, Norwich, King's Lynn and Cambridge.[66] While Michael's career was struggling at this point, his keen interest in his family demonstrates the strong family bonds that continued throughout the nineteenth century:

> The weather has got milder but I am sure Michael must keep to his room. Philip must rest himself . . . and his muscular affection will speedily [heal] . . . . I hope James will find the business of school exhausts enough of his animal spirit to prevent any further annoyance to you by their overflow . . . . Pray answer by return of post and tell me how you are.[67]

The Norfolk circuit was competitive and cut-throat:

> I have had no business hitherto and as you may suppose am in not very good spirits, my heart too is occasionally troublesome. At Huntingdon, I presume, I was very near having a brief, the waiter told me, at dinner time a gentleman wished to speak to me outside the door, I went but the gentleman had vanished, having, I suppose been . . . [taken] . . . by the superior merits of some other barrister, to me this was a grievous disappointment, I however must imitate the

conduct of the patient angler who having caught no fish, contented himself with
the thought that he has had a glorious nibble.[68]

Michael's fortitude is evident and can later be seen in the personality of his son,
James.

By 1839, Michael Prendergast's frustration at the slow progression of his career
is evident, "I am not at all pleased with my situation on the circuit, it is neither
respectable nor comfortable."[69] Tragedy struck soon after, with the death of young
Caroline Prendergast:

> I can assure you I have many disappointments to bear up against besides the
> never-ending sorrow, which is renewed by almost every event. Again I beg of
> you to keep up your spirits and to remember that duty demands us to interest
> ourselves in . . . life.[70]

Only a few short years after the death of his daughter, Michael lost his wife,
reversing the fortunes of the Prendergast family.

With the death of James Prendergast in 1921, the family of Michael Prendergast
QC came to an end. James had only one 'blood' nephew, Michael, who did not
marry and predeceased his uncle. While James was brought up in a nuclear family,
members of the extended Prendergast family also had some influence during his
formative years.

One of James' paternal aunts married Charles Manning, who became close
friends with his brother-in-law, Michael Prendergast QC. Charles Manning and
his sons, Charles junior and Henry, played an important role in the life of James
Prendergast, looking after his affairs in England after 1862. Manning senior was
also a trustee of the controversial estate belonging to James' grandfather, Michael
Prendergast. When James decided to send his nephew to Oxford during the late
1870s, the Mannings took care of him. Though not particularly popular with
other members of the Prendergast extended family, the Mannings were trusted
friends of James. Henry Manning was in charge of a lunatic asylum and cared for
Philip Prendergast when he became ill during the 1860s.[71]

Despite having a fairly large extended family, Prendergast left his impressive
fortune to his wife's nephews and nieces. Perhaps James decided these Australasian-
based relatives by marriage were closer to him that any relations in England. By the
end of his life, James had become an 'English New Zealander', detached from his
former life in England.

6. Prendergast and the links between the New Zealand and English legal systems during the nineteenth century

A variety of aspects of the English legal system were brought to New Zealand
by settlers, including the structure of the legal system, the English constitutional
framework, substantive law, English legal procedure, dress, formalities, training

methods and prejudices. Also transported to the colony was an intense focus on property rights and land ownership. James Prendergast was heavily influenced by the English legal system, especially during the period before he travelled to New Zealand in 1862. Practising law on the other side of the world from 1862 onwards weakened the influence slightly, but in the statutes and legal decisions created by James Prendergast from 1865 to 1899, the English influence is clearly evident.

To a large extent, men such as Prendergast who constructed the New Zealand colonial legal system sought to recreate the environment they left behind in the 'mother country'. Yet the affluent English, Anglican background of James Prendergast was not the only heritage integral in building New Zealand's legal system. New Zealand was settled primary by English, Scottish and Irish immigrants, each country having its own individual system of law. Christopher William Richmond, Supreme Court Judge, had a similar background to that of Prendergast. Both men were born in London during the 1820s. Both had fathers who were barristers. Both received their legal education at the Middle Temple and then struggled to find work in England.[72] Not surprisingly, Prendergast and Richmond became close colleagues and good friends.

In contrast to Prendergast, Chief Justice Robert Stout was a Presbyterian Scot born into a merchant family on the wind-swept Shetland Islands. He left Scotland for New Zealand as a teenager. Like Prendergast, Stout had a short spell as an educator. Stout spent several years school teaching in Dunedin before commencing his practical training as a lawyer in the New Zealand legal environment.[73] Prendergast's nemesis, George Elliott Barton, was a Protestant Irishman who began his career in Dublin and then practised in Melbourne after leaving Ireland due to controversial political involvement.[74] All these men brought a different view of life and law to the New Zealand environment, but it was the English legal system that was the model for the New Zealand system. Scottish and Irish lawyers were plentiful in the colony but were required to practice 'English' law.

The legal–historical background to James Prendergast's experiences in England provides an important context for the historian. From this background we can gain some understanding of the cultural influences that helped to formulate Prendergast's world view. In Europe, the period from Napoleon's defeat at Waterloo in 1815 to the outbreak of World War I in 1914, was one of relative peace. After defeating the French in the Napoleonic Wars, Britain was effectively the most powerful nation in the world. Although Britain found itself engaged in a number of colonial wars, including the New Zealand Wars and the Boer War, and one continental war, the Crimean War, these conflicts did not greatly alter Britain's powerful geo–political position. Imperial Britain had spread across the globe, including its colonies in British North America (Canada), Australia, New Zealand, India and Southern Africa. Queen Victoria ruled at the height of Britain's power from 1837 to 1901.

Prendergast was an imperialist and in a cultural sense, is also clearly identifiable as a 'Victorian'.

The main military conflict to affect Britain from 1826 to 1862 was the Crimean War (1854–1855). This war was fought primarily on Russian soil. For some of this time, Prendergast was in Victoria, searching unsuccessfully for his fortune in gold. Therefore, when Prendergast came to New Zealand in 1862 during the New Zealand Wars, he found himself in the midst of war for the first time. Though in Dunedin until 1865, Prendergast played an important role in the later stages of the New Zealand Wars.

Politically and constitutionally, Britain was undergoing great change between 1826 and 1862. The Reform Act 1832, passed by the Whig Government, extended the franchise to a greater number of male voters. Though Prendergast leaned towards the 'Conservatives' such as Atkinson and Hall in New Zealand, it is unclear whether he was a Conservative/Tory or a Liberal/Whig when voting in Britain. Michael Prendergast QC had limited contact with several key political figures, including the famous Whig Lord Chancellor and legal reformer, Henry Brougham.

The period 1826–1862 was dominated by the continuing industrial revolution in Britain. Technology improved dramatically as Britain became 'the workshop of the world'. This period of economic growth and liberalisation of trade also resulted in appalling social conditions for workers in the new industrial cities. Low wages, child labour, poor health and government apathy were all important social problems during the mid-nineteenth century. As a Londoner, Prendergast would have seen this suffering, but, having a privileged upbringing, he would not have experienced it personally.

Intellectual, scientific and philosophical thought underwent a revolution with the ideas of Charles Darwin, Herbert Spencer, Jeremy Bentham, John Austin and John Stuart Mill. These men, along with others such as John Ruskin, Cardinal Newman, Thomas Carlyle, Thomas Macaulay and Charles Dickens, provided the intellectual framework for the industrial age.[75] This was the intellectual climate in which Prendergast developed his world view.

The English legal system underwent far-reaching changes during the nineteenth century. Michael Prendergast QC, in particular, would have been greatly affected by these developments. The practice of law was fiercely competitive[76] and young lawyers struggled to secure briefs and reputations at the bar. When W. S. Gilbert satirised the English legal system in 1875, his lyrics had more than a little truth in them. For example, a corrupt judge speaks of his early years as an English barrister:

> When I, good friends, was called to the bar,
> I'd an appetite fresh and hearty.
> But I was, as many young barristers are,
> An impecunious party

. . . .

> At Westminster Hall I danced a dance,
> Like a semi-despondent fury;
> For I thought I never should hit on a chance
> Of addressing a British Jury –
> But I soon got tired of third-class journeys,
> And dinners of bread and water;
> So I fell in love with a rich attorney's
> Elderly, ugly daughter.[77]

This oversupply of lawyers would provide difficulties for Michael Prendergast during his early years as a barrister and lead to his sons, Michael and James, permanently emigrating to the colonies to secure adequate work.

London was the centre of legal action in the British Empire during the nineteenth century and Michael Prendergast eventually became a prominent figure in that environment. Michael ended his career as a judge of the Central Criminal Court at the Old Bailey, located next to the infamous Newgate Prison. The English legal system in the years before the Judicature Acts of 1873 and 1875 was exceedingly complex. From 1856 to 1862, when James Prendergast was practising in London, the courts included: Queen's Bench, Chancery, Probate, Divorce, Exchequer, Admiralty and Common Pleas. The systems of law and equity were separate and practised in different courts. While the New Zealand legal system was to be more streamlined than its English counterpart, Prendergast would help to ensure that New Zealand closely followed English developments in statute and case law. The increasing dominance of statute law in England, reflecting the positivist views of Bentham and Austin, who saw the State as an appropriate vehicle for law reform, influenced Prendergast during his time as an English barrister. The codification of much English criminal law in 1861 would be followed by Prendergast in New Zealand only six years later.[78]

Intellectually, Prendergast's formative years began with his student years at Cambridge in 1845. From 1849 to 1852, Prendergast continued to read widely,[79] but lacked the focused study experienced at university. Only on his return to London in 1855, did Prendergast begin his study of the law in earnest. At Cambridge, Prendergast studied primarily in mathematics, though he was able to take other subjects as well. In placing Prendergast in an intellectual and jurisprudential context, the historian must explore the key philosophical ideas dominating in Britain during the mid-nineteenth century. For the study of James Prendergast, the most important ideas are those of a legal, political nature and those focusing on race and culture.

In 1859, Charles Darwin (1809–1882) published his seminal work, *On the Origin of Species by Means of Natural Selection*. While Darwin's ideas were primarily focused on different species, other writers applied his theories to race and political life.

Herbert Spencer (1820-1903), inspired by Darwin, coined the phrase 'survival of the fittest' when applying evolution to human experience. During the early 1860s he published several important works arguing his theses. Prendergast would have been a practising lawyer during the time Darwin and Spencer achieved widespread renown, and would have been exposed to their views. Prendergast's views on race, for example, the idea of Maori as 'primitive barbarians' who had not reached the stage of having an established legal system,[80] fit into the paradigms of evolution and natural selection and can also be used as an example of stadial theory.[81] Little mention of religion is found in any personal material relating to Prendergast and his family but there are references to members of the family attending Anglican churches and taking some interest in the theological position of church ministers. By all accounts the family was solidly Anglican.

The philosophy most evident in Prendergast's jurisprudential approach is that of legal positivism. Leading scholars in this field included Jeremy Bentham (1748-1832) and John Austin (1790-1859). Bentham's *Introduction to the Principles of Morals and Legislation* (1789), and Austin's *The Province of Jurisprudence Determined* (1832) were pivotal influences in nineteenth-century legal thought, and evidence of positivistic legal thought can be seen in the judgments of Prendergast. Blackstone's *Commentaries on the Laws of England* also influenced Prendergast. As with many colonial legal figures, Prendergast could rely on Blackstone while implementing English law abroad.[82] While Prendergast was in Victoria, Michael Prendergast senior offered to send him a copy of Henry John Stephen's re-working of the *Commentaries*.[83]

The concepts of legal objectivity and parliamentary supremacy were prevalent in nineteenth-century England and would have influenced Prendergast while studying. The Whig view of history, which stressed the inevitable progression towards parliamentary government and constitutional improvement, could also have inspired Prendergast's legal and judicial thought. The triumph of the English system of government was celebrated in Macaulay's *History of England* (1849, 1855), which was published to wide acclaim during the 1850s, when Prendergast was working in London. Prendergast had his own personal copy of Macaulay's work.[84] Prendergast did not openly discuss philosophy in his personal correspondences, but close analysis of his judgments and legal opinions provide insights into his intellectual approach and legal background.

7. Prendergast's experiences in England and his role in nineteenth-century New Zealand history

While the influence of James Prendergast in English society was minor, his influence in New Zealand was very significant. From 1865 to 1899, Prendergast played a key role in establishing an English-inspired legal system in New

Zealand. Analysis of Prendergast's life in England sheds light upon his actions in New Zealand. Prendergast had all the educational opportunities necessary to prepare him for his meteoric rise in New Zealand society. Educated at leading English institutions such as St Paul's School, the University of Cambridge and Middle Temple, Prendergast met and associated with the elite. As a learned man, Prendergast therefore had credibility when working with other university-educated New Zealand leaders such as Frederick Weld (educated in Germany), William Fox (Oxford), Edward Stafford (Trinity Dublin), Alfred Domett (Oxford), William Rolleston (Cambridge), George Arney (Oxford), and Joshua Williams (Cambridge).[85] In fact, Prendergast's Cambridge degree would have made him one of the most impressively educated members of New Zealand's ruling class. Most did not have Oxbridge degrees, although the first three Chief Justices were all Oxbridge graduates. To say Prendergast moved from being 'a small fish in a big pond' to 'a big fish in a small pond' is to simplify matters, but there would still be truth in the statement.

The experience of school teaching would have allowed Prendergast to see a non-legal environment but also made him realise that his ambitious nature would not be satisfied by the teaching profession. After his travels in Australia and failure as a goldminer and adventurer, Prendergast returned to practice law in London. It was only when James left London for Dunedin that his ambitions were finally realised. The trials and lessons of these early years allowed James to move quickly up the New Zealand legal ladder.

Prendergast came from a closeknit family which experienced tragedy during the 1840s while James was obtaining his education. The loss of his mother and sister would have affected Prendergast's outlook on life. While James had the support of an extended family, with the death of his father in 1859 he decided his familial ties were weak enough to leave England permanently. Prendergast took his intellectual background with him to the colonies and with him came ideas of legal reform, positivism and English superiority. Prendergast did not greatly adapt his jurisprudential approach, obtained in London, to suit the new colonial environment of New Zealand.

Prendergast was fortunate to be guided by capable mentors throughout his formative years. His uncles Joseph Prendergast and Henry Dawe, the Reverend William Routledge and the eminent lawyer Thomas Chitty all played important roles in the life of James Prendergast. His immediate family was also pivotal during his youth. Prendergast was close to his mother, who struggled with illness and tragedy, and also to his brothers, whom he lived, studied and travelled with over a period of 30 years. But it was his father, Michael, who had the most influence over the young man. The temperamental, controversial lawyer and judge dominated the youth of his three sons and all attempted to follow in his legal footsteps. Michael junior and Philip were unable to emulate their father's success, but James surpassed his father by successfully transferring his talent and ability to the New Zealand environment. By the time James Prendergast arrived in New Zealand his mentors had gone and he was a man in control of his own destiny.

The colonial imperialist was educated and trained to command others and be dedicated to serving a higher body, in this case, the British Empire. Many of the beliefs and prejudices of Victorian England can be found in the personality of James Prendergast. Prendergast entered the English elite at a young age and was schooled in the classical traditions at ancient places of learning. Growing up in the heart of Imperial Britain, Prendergast became a strong supporter and advocate of its values. As a young man, Prendergast was ambitious, but not completely sure of where to channel these ambitions. As a student, Prendergast was diligent and bright but not exceptional. As a school teacher, he was restless. As a goldminer he was a disaster and as a London lawyer, one of a large crowd. Both inspired and protected by his influential and controversial father, James Prendergast did not really flourish until he left his homeland and family behind him for a new life in New Zealand.

The family of Michael Prendergast, while full of potential during the 1830s, suffered after this time. Michael's career flourished near its end, but under a cloud of controversy and criticism. The London of Michael and James Prendergast was a city of change, overcrowding, social problems and tradition. This was the environment which created James Prendergast and from which he gained his views on law, politics, religion, race and class. His family background, training and intellectual outlook was English but his success was colonial. While leaving England may have been the making of the man, at 36 Prendergast could not change his outlook on the world, which had become firm and inflexible. The influence of James Prendergast on New Zealand history shows a man who left his country but never abandoned its values.

3

COLONIAL BEGINNINGS

Experiences in Victoria, Australia, 1852–1855

The experience of James Prendergast in colonial New Zealand was a resounding personal triumph. His experience in colonial Australia was a different story altogether. The young man left his budding legal career in London for the adventure and risk of the Victorian goldfields in 1852. The adventure quickly turned sour and Prendergast transformed himself from a goldminer into a clerk. This administrative experience would prove useful to Prendergast in New Zealand. While the Australian experience was not an obvious success, it provided Prendergast with the training that would enable him to rise quickly in New Zealand society during the 1860s. Throughout Prendergast's career the influence of the Australian period can be seen.

Prendergast had a habit of turning up in colonial lands during traumatic national events. During the early 1850s in Victoria, miner resentment towards bureaucratic authority reached breaking point at the Eureka Stockade. While Prendergast was in New Zealand during the 1860s, Maori resentment towards British authority also reached breaking point in the form of the New Zealand Wars.

The Australian adventure engaged not only James Prendergast, but also his brothers, Philip and Michael. Placed in difficult circumstances, the different personalities of the three brothers became evident. Philip arrived in Victoria with James and stayed briefly after James' departure. Michael came in 1853 and stayed on to become a member of the Victorian Parliament. Unfortunately, Michael's colonial experience was to end in tragedy. The Victorian gold rushes of the 1850s form the historical background for this period of Prendergast's life and provide interesting insights about 'Englishmen abroad'. The conflict between the English gentleman and the harsh colonial frontier is apparent.

1. Prendergast as colonial adventurer: Gold-mining 1852–1853

On 17 June 1852, James, his brother Philip, his cousin, Thomas Jeffrey and his friend, Frederick Cropp, set sail from Portsmouth aboard the brand new clipper, *Francis Henty*.[1] The young men were drawn to the colonial frontier by the promises of adventure and wealth. Prendergast had recently married, but left his wife, Mary, in England. The *Francis Henty* carried 135 passengers and was dominated by English adult males.[2] With only 17 adult females and 15 non-English passengers, this was a homogeneous group of young English men voyaging to seek their fortune on the Victorian goldfields.[3]

After a relatively speedy 77-day passage from Land's End, the young men landed at Portland Bay, Victoria.[4] They reached Melbourne's Port Phillip in September 1852.[5] The voyage had been relatively safe and successful, with only one infant death.[6] James had found the trip somewhat mundane:

> I cannot imagine a more uninteresting voyage than that of England to Australia; even the pursuit of Gold did not seem to enliven us: there was not one on board who seemed to be possessed of the spirit of adventure.[7]

The pride of the Prendergasts was insulted at one point during the voyage, providing insights into the different 'categories' of passengers onboard, "They [Ship's Owners] next attempted to reduce us to the state of Government Emigrants requiring us to sweep & wash the cabins & otherwise to wait upon ourselves but this also they eventually abandoned."[8] Despite this indignity, the Prendergasts were comparatively lucky to be aboard the *Henty*. On arriving at Victoria, Philip spoke of:

> one [ship] in quarantine that left England with upwards of four hundred persons but arrived here with less than three hundred the rest having perished by the yellow fever which broke out I suppose in consequence of the overcrowded state of the ship.[9]

The first impression of Victoria that struck the Prendergast brothers was the high price of goods and services.[10] The group camped for a brief time at Liardet's Point, Port Phillip before travelling to the diggings. The young men had the opportunity of viewing the bustling infant city of Melbourne, "Melbourne is increasing most rapidly; but the buildings, particularly the shops, are anything but handsome. . . . No pavements – little light – oil of course, dangerous to be on the streets after dark = the country much safer than Town."[11] In 1852, Philip estimated the population of Melbourne to be at least 100,000, with the pre-rush population being 10,000.[12] The actual figures are approximately 40,000 in 1852, which was an increase from 25,000 in pre-rush Melbourne.[13] Like James, Philip was struck by the high rate of crime, especially the danger of highwaymen robbing diggers and:

> one in particular who rides single well armed & well mounted to whom they have given the title of Captain his deeds are very astonishing. But we intend to go in spite of them all even of the great Captain himself.[14]

The extraordinary amount of men flooding into Victoria is apparent in Thomas Jeffrey's letters, "there are thousands of people going to the diggins from all parts of the world, ships are coming in 2 & 3 daily, and altogether things are in a pretty fix".[15] James now found himself in a group of eight, with all the men intending to set off for the Bendigo goldfields: the two Prendergast brothers, James (aged 26) and Philip (28), Thomas Jeffrey (26), Frederick Cropp (20), and a William Simons (35), his wife, Ann (34) and their two children, Sarah (11) and Maria (10), whom they had met on the boat voyage to Victoria.[16] The Simons family was a recent and interesting addition to the original group of four young men. After poor reports from Bendigo, the group of diggers decided to travel to the rich Ovens diggings instead. Unfortunately, just before the intended departure, Simons left the group to care for his family and Jeffrey deserted after a bitter argument with James, which came to blows.[17] This is another example of James' temper. It is not clear what started this brawl, but a pattern of behaviour can be seen throughout Prendergast's life. While he managed to work well with most people, he also managed to have vicious feuds with certain men.

Eventually the Prendergast brothers and Frederick Cropp reached the Eureka diggings at Ballarat and by January 1853 were working a rich 'hole'.[18] April of 1853 saw the three men still digging at Eureka, though their rich 'hole' had failed to yield the amount of gold expected. James' writings speak of the hardship of the diggings and he advises friends in England not to travel to Victoria in search of fortune.[19] During this period the tenacity and mind-set of James becomes clearer:

> Success I am persuaded must eventually be the end sooner or later to the man who will give himself wholly up to the work. What he will chiefly stand in need of is power of Endurance without he can do nothing. . . . Pluck is the one thing needful. Any man from any class who can bear disappointments and hard fare will make a good gold digger.[20]

Prendergast's attitude reflected the 'Victorian Frame of Mind', especially in his dedication to hard work and his stubbornly optimistic outlook.[21] Unfortunately for James and Philip, endurance and pluck were not enough to ward off dysentery. Both young men became extremely ill and came close to death. It was at this time, in late 1853, that the eldest Prendergast brother, Michael, arrived in Melbourne. Quickly establishing himself as a barrister in the city, Michael had the funds to bring his younger brothers to Melbourne and care for them:

> Philip and James arrived in Melbourne in the very extremity of starvation and distress. If it had not been for the lucky accident that brought me out at the right time they must have died the death so many gentlemen have met with out here.[22]

Many years later, in dramatic circumstances, James would return the favour he owed to his brother Michael. The gold-digging experience had been a failure and almost fatal. James and Philip, in debt, now looked to other occupations to make their fortunes in the fledgling Victorian state.

2. Prendergast as colonial administrator: Clerical work in Victoria 1854–1855

On 30 December 1853, James Prendergast was appointed Clerk of Petty Sessions at Elephant Bridge, Western Victoria.[23] Working from the local hotel, James had his first real experience with administrative work. In January of 1854, James described his surroundings:

> I am at this moment sitting in a room at the Public House at Elephant Bridge a Township 80 or 90 miles from Geelong. I am appointed Clerk of Petty Sessions at a salary of 250 pounds and an allowance of 62 pounds per annum for House-rent. There is no Bench at present; nor are there any constables: nor is there a lock-up.[24]

While not entirely happy with his new position, James was optimistic: "In a few years perhaps things will change. Till then I will hope on and work on."[25] Perseverance and patience brought James through the summer of 1854 and in May 1854 he wrote to his father stating that he may return to England soon.[26] James managed to make himself useful in the small Elephant Bridge community, and aside from his clerical position acted as administrator for the Public Pound.

James found living at the Public House disagreeable and, with the imminent arrival of his wife, began looking for other positions.[27] As Philip writes, "James is not quite contented with his place of course he cannot he having nobody to speak to no books & nothing to do."[28] James received his wish and was removed from Elephant Bridge to a clerical position at Carisbrook, a new town experiencing a rush of diggers.[29] While James was happy with his performance at Carisbrook, others were not: "After all my labour which was very great an objection was made to my writing and that I was slow."[30] Disgusted by his treatment, James blamed an Irish barrister and contemplated his revenge. After visiting Melbourne in an unsuccessful bid to retain his position, James met his wife, who had just arrived aboard the *Blackwell*, and began a new job in Maryborough, just west of Carisbrook. James was not the only disgruntled Victorian settler. During these later months of 1854, miner agitation was rising against the authoritarian Victorian governor, Charles Hotham. On 3 December 1854, Government troops and police attacked a miner's stockade at the Eureka diggings. Approximately thirty diggers and five soldiers were killed.[31]

Three months after losing his position at Carisbrook, James decided to leave Victoria with his wife and return to London.[32] After little more than two years of colonial life, James returned to his homeland, somewhat bitter but definitely wiser. His brother Philip wrote:

> when he [James] arrives in England [he] will be one of the best men there as he was here the best. He will tell you how he has been treated here by the

scoundrelly Irish. If he goes to the bar he will have a great superiority over his rivals from his enlarged knowledge of the world and his own natural ability and his success I think will be certain. . . . In discharging him the Government of the Colony has lost an able and honourable man.[33]

Michael also blamed the Irish for James' premature departure: "his removal from the Government service is solely attributable to the malice and jobbery of the detestable Irish Orange set that are the curse of the Colony."[34]

Reports of Prendergast's movements between October 1854 and April 1856 are sketchy. In the *New Zealand Dictionary of Biography*, Bassett and Hannan state, "In 1856 another Londoner, the young Julius Vogel, set up shop next to Prendergast's office on the Dunolly field, near Maryborough. Vogel and Prendergast began what was to be a long and mutually beneficial association."[35] Dalziel states that, "Vogel set up shop for the first time [in Dunolly] by himself, sandwiched between a general store and the legal offices of J. Prendergast."[36] Scholefield states that, "At the request of his father, he [James] and his wife returned to London by the 'Anglesea' in 1856."[37] All these statements are incorrect.

The supposed Prendergast/Vogel connection stems from a mistaken interpretation of a Dunolly sketch map. The map shows Julius Vogel's shop located next to an L. Prendergast (Solicitor).[38] One could suspect a spelling error with 'L' substituted for 'J'. In fact, this solicitor was not James Prendergast, but almost certainly Leonard Prendergast who was admitted to the Victorian Bar in 1854 and practiced in Dunolly throughout the rest of the decade.[39] James was not admitted to practice until April 1856[40] and therefore could not practice before this date. Also, he returned to London in early 1855, making it impossible for him to meet Julius Vogel at Dunolly in 1856.[41] This finding has implications for an analysis of Prendergast's later career, as James was closely involved with Vogel in New Zealand. In fact, Vogel assisted Prendergast's rise to legal power in New Zealand. The relationship between the two leading figures cannot be seen in the light of a shared Victorian experience, as it is probable that the two men did not know of each other until they met in Dunedin.

Scholefield's claim that James and his wife returned to London by the *Anglesea* in 1856 is also inaccurate. No primary evidence exists to support James Prendergast being in Victoria during mid to late 1855. In fact, the letters written by the Prendergast brothers during their Victoria experience state that James was on his way back to London at the time of the first 'Eureka trials', which took place in January and February 1855.[42] The date of Philip's letter stating that James was in the process of returning to London aboard the *Anglesea* is 27 January 1855, and according to another of Philip's letters, James was still in Victoria as at 7 January 1855. James did leave Victoria in early 1855 and his poor wife Mary would have spent only three months in the colony before having to face another three-month ship journey back to London.

3. The Prendergast brothers: Family relationships in Victoria

While both James and Michael Prendergast attempted assertively to adapt to the colonial environment, Philip Prendergast found life in Victoria difficult and frustrating. After the ill-fated goldmining episode at Eureka with James, Philip spent some months in Melbourne recovering his health. From his letters, Philip seems to be a man of many ideas, but with an inability to put the ideas into practice.[43]

After failing to secure a long-term position, Philip began to despair for his future in Victoria:

> If I fail the failure will not affect me for I am now callous to disappointments. But if successful? I cannot tell how I shall bear that for success is a thing most of us are strangers to out here.[44]

Much of Philip's bitterness was directed against Irish settlers holding positions of importance:

> Englishmen of education are at a discount here. The places under Government filled from top to bottom with wild Irish imported from their bogs expressly for the places & places made expressly for them . . . . Englishmen cannot be kept down long by any and least of all can it be expected the Irish dogs shall have the rule . . . . There is neither law nor order here at least on the Government part. Our Legislative assembly is an assembly of ignorance and cowardice that neither know it's [sic] power nor has the courage to hold it. The country is bankrupt and the people are starving and our two papers the most lying journals under the sun.[45]

Michael Prendergast concluded in 1855 that his two younger brothers were both "miserable colonists".[46] After successive failures, Philip Prendergast left Victoria to return to London in 1856. Three years later Philip was admitted to the Middle Temple.[47]

Unlike Philip and James, Michael Prendergast flourished in the Victorian colonial environment. With no intention of becoming a goldminer like his younger brothers, Michael arrived in Melbourne in July of 1853 and was admitted to the Victorian Bar on 20 October 1853.[48] While at first Michael located his offices in Melbourne, he also travelled to country sessions and circuits. From 1856 to 1858 he based himself at Maryborough.[49] This knowledge of the Victorian hinterland aided his attempts at being elected as a member for the Victorian Legislative Assembly.

Michael's work brought him into personal contact with some of Victoria's most powerful men, including Chief Justice Sir Redmond Barry, Henry Chapman and W. C. Haines. Michael enjoyed colonial society:

> I like the Colony very well and the independent way of living. But a voyage of 16 thousand miles and a life more like that of a knight errant than any thing you can imagine . . . have combined to excite in my mind rather than allay a strong desire of going forth in search of further adventures.[50]

On 28 November 1855, Michael married Jane Smyth, whom he had met during his voyage from London to Melbourne.[51] Jane was a frank and forthright woman who was not shy to express her views, "God ordained very wisely when he peopled it [Australia] with a tribe of ugly black savages, and I think the English acted very foolishly in coming to inhabit a country that was not made for them."[52] A son, Michael, was born to Michael and Jane Prendergast soon after marriage. This son would play an important role in James Prendergast's later life.

Michael had his first major opportunity for public prominence during the trials following the Eureka tragedy. As counsel for one of the prisoners, he received high praise.[53] But by most accounts, Michael's brief time as a member of the Legislative Assembly was not a resounding success. In 1860, he accompanied a fellow member of the Legislative Assembly by the name of George Barton on a political tour of the mining districts. Ironically, 18 years later in the nearby colony of New Zealand, Barton would attempt to destroy the judicial career of James Prendergast in controversial fashion. Michael Prendergast and Barton were heavily criticised by *The Argus* during their tour:

> Listen to the language of the intemperate advocate of temperance, and mark well the unseemly exhibitions of itinerant stump orators; and, after that, don't complain if you find English journalists confounding the Legislative Assembly of Victoria with an asylum for the reception of "drunken lawyers" and gibbering idiots.[54]

Michael stood for re-election in Maryborough in 1861 and lost.[55]

After losing his seat in the Victorian Legislative Assembly, Michael left Victoria for the gold rush in southern New Zealand. He spent approximately seven years practising law in Dunedin before returning to Victoria in c1868.[56] Upon his return to Victoria, Michael floundered. In May 1870 the Wedderburn correspondent for the *Inglewood Advertiser* told of Michael's pathetic downfall:

> It appears that he [Michael] left Wedderburn late in the evening of Thursday the 12th inst., to walk to Kingower, but in his present weak and imbecile state of mind, he had mistaken the road, and wandered into the bush, where he continued to wander about, exposed to the cold and heavy rains, without food or shelter, for five days, when he was accidently found.[57]

Fortunately, Michael was found by a local farmer before he perished. Brought before magistrates on charges of vagrancy, the broken man was discharged and taken to Inglewood Hospital for medical treatment.[58]

Alcoholism led to the disintegration of Michael's career, and eventually the loss of his wife and his health, as described in the following account by English settler James Bodell:

> This Gentleman [Michael] as I approached the House was on the footpath with only Trousers and Shirt on, smashing the front Windows of his house. I

could see in a moment what was the Matter. He was heavy drinker, and he was suffering from an attack of delirium tremens. . . . His Wife was about as fine a looking Woman as there was in Victoria but she had to leave him.[59]

4. The impact of the Australian experience on James Prendergast's future career

Although James spent only 28 months in Victoria, his experience there had an obvious effect upon his career. When he arrived in Dunedin in 1862 during the Otago gold rush, he could draw on his experiences in Victoria. The administrative skills James acquired at Elephant Bridge and Carisbrook were put to use in a New Zealand context. A more wary approach to people, politics and power was also a result of the Australian episode. In Dunedin, instead of attempting to become a miner himself and make a quick fortune, James set up a legal practice to support the mining community. After two years in Victoria, he was poor and disillusioned. After two years in Dunedin, he was on the verge of becoming Attorney-General of New Zealand.

The different personalities of the three brothers became evident during the trials and tribulations of the Victorian experience. Luckily, the brothers kept in contact with their father in London through letters. These letters have survived and provide the historian with a rich source of primary material. James appears as a conscientious, hard-working young man, though with a quick temper. Michael, the eldest brother, seems to be more inspired and emotional. Compared with James, Michael's personality is more volatile, eventually leading to alcoholism and mental illness. Philip described the essential difference between his two brothers:

> Unlike Michael who has a distinct and different genius he [James] will apply himself assiduously to the drudgery of his profession and so will be sure of securing first the confidence of the Attornies and eventually the favour of the Public . . . You know him to be a good son and I know him to be an excellent brother and a tried friend.[60]

The experience of the Prendergast brothers in Victoria provides the historian with insights into the class structure of the 1850s. Whether onboard the *Francis Henty* or on the goldfields, the Prendergasts are very aware of their role as gentlemen and the treatment to which they are entitled. Cultural encounter is also apparent, for example, in the disparaging attitude of the Prendergast brothers towards the Irish Protestant settlers in Victoria. Jane Prendergast's dismissive comments about indigenous Australians also highlight the ethnocentric view of many European colonists.

The Prendergast story also provides insight into the beginnings of Melbourne city. In the Prendergast letters, the fledgling city is described in detail, with especial reference to rapid population growth, crime and architecture. The Victorian goldfields are detailed as a place of both hardship and opportunity, where qualities such as perseverance and stamina are more important than class and breeding. If gentlemen did not adapt to the colonial frontier they were faced with two choices: return home or perish. The experiences of the three brothers provide a case study which sheds light on major events such as the Victorian gold rush, the Eureka Stockade and the development of the Victorian Legislative Assembly. In particular, Michael Prendergast played an important role in all of these historical events.

When comparing James Prendergast's experience in Dunedin with that of Victoria, the question arises: why was Dunedin so successful and Victoria a relative failure? The first answer would be that Victoria was a training ground for Dunedin. The naive young man who landed at Port Phillip in 1852 was not the same man who arrived at Port Chalmers ten years later. Another reason was James' decision to undertake only professional work in Dunedin instead of trying his hand once more at goldmining. With the added advantages of a formal law qualification and courtroom experience, James could flourish at the Dunedin Bar.

The first colonial adventure of James Prendergast nearly resulted in his early death. The fact that Prendergast returned to Australasia a decade later for a second colonial adventure demonstrated his tenacity and faith in the opportunities offered by the colonial frontier. The Victorian adventure was to be the last time that the three Prendergast brothers would be together. Each brother took away different lessons from Victoria. James used the experience to become a colonial leader. Philip returned to England to practice as a London lawyer and presumably, learned that the colonies were not for him. Michael had high hopes of colonial success, but alcohol combined with a turbulent personality to break his spirit and destroy his career.

While James discovered that he was an indifferent goldminer and adventurer, he also discovered a penchant for administrative work. If Prendergast had persevered in Victoria it is possible that he could have risen to high station. His quietly determined and stoic nature was well suited to the colonial environment. In a world of quick fortunes, heart-breaking tragedy and rough politics, James Prendergast survived with confidence and health intact. Others, such as the Prendergasts' friend, Dawson, were not so fortunate (as Michael describes):

> You may have heard of poor Dawsons sad calamity. Having suffered reverses and vicissitudes of all sorts at the Taron diggings and having failed at the Bar at Sydney he arrived here 18 months ago with nothing but a wig and gown and a few pounds in his pocket. He was just in the right time. It took him a marvellously short time to establish a reputation which up to this time has gone on increasing both as an orator and lawyer . . . . As soon as he saw his way he wrote for his wife and family to come over and was anxiously expecting an answer. None however arrived till a month ago when he heard they had taken places on board the John Taylor – and shortly after the report of the shipwreck arrived.

It was a melancholy thing to see the poor fellow walking up to the Flagstaff to get the final confirmation or refutation of the report – at last bit by bit the worst was confirmed. The suspense had worn him out already and the extinction of all hopes has altogether altered him. He has given up the profession and has gone to Ballarat with what object no one knows.[61]

4

RETURN TO THE COLONIES
Experiences in Dunedin, 1862–1867

The experience of James Prendergast in Otago was pivotal to his eventual career success and place in history. In approximately three years, Prendergast transformed himself from an unknown immigrant to a leader in the fledgling New Zealand legal profession. Prendergast arrived in Dunedin during a boom time, the Otago gold rush. He immediately established a reputation as a capable and competent lawyer. This reputation and helpful personal contacts led to Prendergast being offered a succession of important official legal positions, namely, Acting Provincial Solicitor for Otago, Crown Solicitor for Otago, Legislative Councillor, and Attorney-General of New Zealand.

The success of Prendergast in Dunedin must be seen in the context of broader New Zealand legal history. During the early and mid 1860s, Otago experienced a phenomenal economic boom and became the most flourishing centre in the New Zealand colony. The opportunities for young lawyers were many and varied. This period of New Zealand legal history, centred in Dunedin, could well be titled 'The Golden Age'. Many of the leading names in nineteenth-century law and politics furthered their careers in gold-rush Dunedin, including Julius Vogel, George E. Barton, William Richmond and Robert Stout. Dunedin provided the springboard for the success of James Prendergast and had a huge and lasting impact on his future life.

1. Arrival in Dunedin and beginnings in practice

The Otago gold rush began with the discovery of a huge deposit at Tuapeka in 1861 by Gabriel Read. Dunedin soon became New Zealand's largest town. James Prendergast arrived with his wife, Mary, at Port Chalmers on 30 November 1862 aboard the *Chile*. The *Otago Daily Times* described the voyage:

> Throughout the voyage all the passengers were very healthy, and the ship as usual, arrived cleanly and in good order. To Captain Turnbull, on arrival, warmly expressed addresses were addressed complimenting him on his skill and attention, and from the shore as the vessel reached the Port, he was saluted from Mr Taylor's battery, the salute being returned by the discharge of two guns on board. The majority of the passengers remain by the vessel until Friday.[1]

Prendergast had been inspired to leave London for Dunedin by his elder brother, Michael. Michael Prendergast had settled in the Otago region in c1861[2] with his wife and son and was establishing himself in the Dunedin legal profession. Shortly before leaving Victoria for Otago, Michael had tried to convince James to return to colonial life:

> I hope you will all other advantages being equal if you leave England come here [Victoria]. I am sure you will make more money than you expect – Though of course not so much as at Bombay or Calcutta. I will send you one of my parliamentary speeches and Examiners article thereon . . . . If you come mind to learn the science drawing acts of parliament. I will get you profitable employment at once.[3]

> I should certainly recommend you if you leave England to come to Melbourne. From this port is the best method of reaching Queensland and New Zealand. As you see from the papers the Rush to New Zealand is something frightful. But I should recommend you to come here before you go there . . . . Mind what I told you about drafting Parliamentary Bills.[4]

Michael Prendergast was just one of a number of relatively young immigrant lawyers who were furthering their careers in the early Otago gold rush. Capital was flowing into the area to finance the economic boom and professionals were enjoying the fruits of this commercial action.

Upon arriving in Dunedin, Prendergast would have discovered a small, rugged town, bustling with activity and trade. It would have been a world away from the city of London, but Prendergast had experienced this kind of abrupt change of scene before, namely in Melbourne during the early 1850s. Prendergast was admitted to the Dunedin Bar in December, almost immediately after his arrival in 1862.[5] Other leading figures in New Zealand legal history were also admitted to the Dunedin Bar during 1862, including William Richmond and Bryan Cecil Haggitt. Also admitted in 1862 were Prendergast's brother Michael and James' future partner, Edmund Pell Kenyon.[6]

Prendergast's first Dunedin case was *R v SG Isaacs and Daniel Campbell* on 12 December 1862 before Gresson J.[7] The first defendant wrote a letter to the *Otago Daily Times* which was claimed to be in contempt of court. The second defendant, Campbell, was the newspaper publisher/printer. Prendergast acted for the second defendant and successfully argued for the contempt charge against him to be dropped. Gresson was impressed by Prendergast's first New Zealand performance, noting: "that upon this the first opportunity of your appearing before me, I am happy to be able to compliment you on the way in which you have conducted the argument".[8] It has been claimed that Prendergast's first client was Julius Vogel.[9] This is not accurate but Vogel was helping to run the *Otago Daily Times* at the time Prendergast was representing Campbell.

References to Prendergast's professional relationship with Vogel in Dunedin are confused. Prendergast played a role in two cases involving Vogel, the 1862 *Campbell* case and the 1864 *New Zealand Banking Corporation* case. In 1863, James Grant was charged with criminal libel against Vogel. Contrary to Dalziel's statements, there is no evidence that Prendergast was involved in this case. He was not Crown Prosecutor at this time and the accused was undefended.[10]

Another of Prendergast's most well-known performances as a Dunedin barrister involved arguing against Vogel. There was a spate of high-profile defamation cases during the latter half of the nineteenth century in New Zealand and in 1864 the *Otago Daily Times* was facing a criminal libel charge brought by the New Zealand Banking Corporation.[11] Prendergast represented the plaintiff and was aided by his future nemesis, George E. Barton. Vogel was editor of the *Otago Daily Times* and implicated in the charge. The law reports show Prendergast making a methodical and logical argument. The jury awarded damages of 500 pounds, much less than was sought by the plaintiff, but still a victory for Prendergast's client.[12] The case was unsuccessfully appealed on specific points of law.[13] This episode does not seem to have harmed the future relationship between Prendergast and Vogel.

Prendergast became a leading figure at the Dunedin Bar. He started up and became a senior partner in the firm of Prendergast, Kenyon and Maddock, and during his time in Dunedin commanded a substantial share of bar practice.[14] The firm was located in central Dunedin at the Victoria Chambers on Manse Street.[15] Prendergast's firm became Kenyon and Hosking after his departure in February 1867 and then Hosking and Cook in 1907.[16]

Prendergast had the support of efficient and capable clerks. On 6 February 1864, William Downie Stewart, the future New Zealand politician, became the articled clerk of Prendergast.[17] On 7 December 1864, Hanson Turton became Prendergast's clerk.[18] Turton would rise to a high position at the Dunedin Bar. It was common in Dunedin during the 1860s for articled clerks of leading barristers eventually to become leading barristers themselves in a relatively short space of time. For example, Downie Stewart was articled to Prendergast, and Robert Stout was articled to Downie Stewart in Dunedin.[19]

Various opinions exist as to Prendergast's talent as an advocate. The Colonial Law Journal in 1875 described him in the following terms:

> As a pleader, his reputation stood very high, and probably no member of the Bar was more consulted on pleadings than he was. In an equal measure had he the preference, by the unanimous voice of the profession, in legal arguments in *Banco*. At *Nisi Prius*, he had probably not the same weight, as his method of handling cases was a little too technical, and too lawyer-like. His examination of witnesses was always singularly careful and judicious; and, when fairly roused, his addresses were pointed and effective, and thoroughly in earnest . . . . he was, as somebody said of Lord Campbell, a safe verdict-getter if he only had a chance. Scorning any attempt at well-rounded periods, or even figures of speech for the mere purpose of display, he would hammer and hammer away, at

the most telling points of his case, until success seemed assured. But, whatever may be said concerning his successes with juries, the reports show that in *Banco* and the Court of Appeal, he was practically invincible.[20]

Robert Stout remembered Prendergast as, "the best special pleader at a time when special pleading was of great consequence. He was also a great Banco lawyer."[21] Common observances on Prendergast's advocacy stress his steadfastness, reliability and lack of showmanship. While Prendergast may not have been a flamboyant advocate, his talents were obviously observed and appreciated, as his meteoric rise up the professional ladder would suggest.

The Macassey Law Reports (1861–1872) include a number of cases in which Prendergast was counsel. These cases were heard from December 1862 to February 1867 in the Dunedin Supreme Court before Richmond and Chapman JJ. From his first appearances as a Dunedin lawyer, Prendergast's career was intertwined with that of William Richmond. In 1875, Richmond and Prendergast would begin adjudicating together on the Wellington Supreme Court Bench. The Macassey Reports are brief and supply little information on Prendergast as an advocate. From the limited information available, Prendergast appears as an organised, methodical and persistent advocate. He often appeared in court with other leading lawyers, including George E. Barton and Thomas Gillies. Sometimes, he would appear against these prominent practitioners. Prendergast received more than his share of work at the Dunedin Bar.[22]

This claim is supported by trial reports in the *Otago Daily Times* and *Otago Witness*. Prendergast appeared in 209 cases reported in either newspapers or Macassey's Reports from December 1862 to December 1865, including 133 in Dunedin's ultimate boom year, 1864. Of these cases, 39 per cent were criminal, including 23 per cent involving stealing, while 61 per cent were civil matters, including 15 per cent involving contract disputes.

While Prendergast had obtained an impressive array of official positions, he did not take a particularly active part in Dunedin social life. Upon Prendergast's death, Robert Stout commented that:

> He never took any prominent position in what may be termed the hurly-hurly of our social life. I can remember on one occasion his appearance on a public platform at a meeting which was held to protest against the leasing of the great recreation reserve of Dunedin, the Town Belt, but I am not aware of him appearing in any social or political discussion.[23]

As his life progressed, Prendergast became more involved in community institutions but he was never a socialite or high-profile social figure. He also took a very low-key approach to political issues and controversies.

2. Official positions: Acting Provincial Solicitor and Crown Solicitor

Prendergast's success at the Dunedin Bar prompted offers of official station. In a new settler society, able men were needed to take positions of responsibility and power. With a limited pool of talent and experience to draw upon, relatively young men with limited experience could rise quickly to high stations.[24] Prendergast was an example of this phenomenon. On 31 August 1863, less than two years after arriving in Otago, Prendergast was created Acting Provincial Solicitor for the Province of Otago.[25] This administrative position opened up a range of opportunities for Prendergast.

Two years later, Prendergast was appointed Crown Solicitor in Otago by Frederick Weld's Government.[26] This governmental position gave Prendergast authority to prosecute on behalf of the Attorney-General and was often referred to as Crown Prosecutor. When Prendergast resigned as Acting Provincial Solicitor in 1865, the position went to Bryan Cecil Haggitt.[27] These two positions allowed Prendergast to represent Otago society at a high level and gave him the necessary experience to become Attorney-General of New Zealand. In addition to the post of Crown Solicitor, Prendergast was also appointed Conveyancing Counsel to examine titles under the Land Registry Act 1860.[28]

Early in 1865, Prendergast played a key role in the high-profile case of William Jarvey.[29] Jarvey was accused of murdering his pregnant wife in Dunedin. Poison had been used to kill Catherine Jarvey and the case captured the imagination of colonial New Zealand. The analysis of Catherine's dead body was conducted by Dr John Macadam in Melbourne. Prendergast conducted the prosecution for the Crown at the trial on 15 March, along with James Howorth and his son, Henry. Spectators had to be turned away at the door. Chapman J presided over the court. Macadam had travelled from Melbourne to be at the trial and testified that Catherine Jarvey had indeed been poisoned. After 40 hours the jury still could not reach a decision so a second trial was arranged for June and eventually began on 11 September before Richmond J. Unfortunately, Macadam died on his way to the second trial. Prendergast again conducted the prosecution, this time with his partner, Kenyon.[30] Prendergast was successful and Jarvey was the first man hanged in Otago.[31]

On 10 July 1865, Prendergast was called to the Legislative Council of New Zealand.[32] From this point onwards, Prendergast's career began to focus on Wellington rather than Dunedin. Despite representing the Otago province in the Legislative Council, Prendergast would be required to relinquish his legal practice in Dunedin and his position of Crown Solicitor only two years after this appointment to the Council. The meteoric rise of Prendergast is summed up in the Colonial Law Journal of 1875:

> Mr. Prendergast received his first official appointment from Mr. J. H. Harris,
> Superintendent of Otago, as Acting Provincial Solicitor, on the retirement

of Mr. T. B. Gillies from that post. He subsequently received the further appointment of Crown Solicitor or Prosecutor for the Province. In 1865 he was, upon the suggestion of Mr. Sewell, invited to the Legislative Council, with a place in the Weld Administration, as Solicitor-General. He was sworn in as a member of the Upper House; but we believe that ere he took the oath of office as Solicitor-General, Mr. Weld resigned. Mr. Stafford succeeded Mr. Weld, and one of his first overtures was to Mr. Prendergast to become Attorney-General. This offer he accepted, and the appointment was formally announced on the 20th October, 1865.[33]

3. The Dunedin Profession 1862–1867

The Dunedin Bar of the period 1862 to 1867 was a kaleidoscope of talent. The bar grew alongside Dunedin town:

> In 1864 the population of Otago was 49,019 of which 15,790 lived in Dunedin, which was at that time the leading town in New Zealand. In the early 1860s its population had quadrupled with the discovery of payable goldfields and the consequent inrush of immigrants, communications between the coast and the interior had been established, and agriculture had been stimulated by the new local demand for foodstuffs.[34]

Analysis of the rolls at the time of Prendergast's legal career (and until 1871) in Dunedin reveals the following names: William Richmond, Bryan Cecil Haggitt, George E. Barton, George Cook, Michael Prendergast, Edmund Pell Kenyon, Thomas Gillies, Wilson Gray, James Macassey, Robert Stout, William Downie Stewart and Frederick R. Chapman.[35]

The Law Practitioners Act 1861 had required every Supreme Court Registrar to keep separate rolls for the admission of barristers and solicitors. Judges were to control admission and conduct legal examinations.[36] The Act was implemented in January 1862 and 33 lawyers were admitted in Otago that year, including Prendergast. By the end of 1866 the list had grown to 53.[37] At the end of the decade the Otago Bar was undoubtedly the strongest in New Zealand, as William Richmond commented:

> I have no doubt there is by far the best bar here, altho' individuals in other places are good lawyers. There is not Whitaker's match here as an advocate, but on the other hand there are several good men in Gillies, Prendergast, Barton, Wilson Gray, Cook – and a shoal of solicitors of various degrees of efficiency.[38]

The overwhelming majority of the lawyers had come originally from Britain and Ireland. Several, such as the Prendergast brothers and George E. Barton, had experience in Australia. This relatively small group of men created firms that would dominate Otago law in years to come and many of their number would rise to high office, for example, Prendergast (Chief Justice), Robert Stout (Chief Justice, Premier), Frederick Chapman (Supreme Court Judge), Thomas Gillies

(Supreme Court Judge). This was the 'golden age' of New Zealand law and the age was centred in Dunedin. Paul Kavanagh[39] described the period, "All of us have learnt to regard Dunedin as the nursery of our profession . . . . Here, too, from the earliest days, have practised some of the greatest men who have adorned the Bench and Bar of New Zealand."[40]

In his eulogy to Prendergast, Robert Stout, who had practised in Dunedin in the 1870s, recalled the wealth of talent of those early days:

> He is the last of the great barristers who practised in Otago in the early 'sixties. Every one of these barristers had a specialty. Mr James Howorth was an English barrister who practised at the Old Bailey in London, and was an able Crown Prosecutor. Mr T. B. Gillies . . . was an all-round advocate, who had had considerable business experience. Mr James Smith was noted for his power of cross-examination and his summing-up of evidence. Mr G. E. Barton was a brilliant advocate. Mr B. C. Haggitt was an able and careful lawyer. Mr Macassey was the ablest case lawyer in New Zealand.[41]

The Dunedin Bar, with some exceptions, saw themselves as a homogeneous club which both worked and played closely together. In c1866 a lawyers' cricket match was organised, featuring many of the key legal figures of the time: "According to arrangement, a match was played on the Dunedin Cricket Ground, on Saturday last, between two elevens selected from the members of the legal profession and their employees."[42] Prendergast collected three wickets, two of those clean-bowled, but was more disappointing with the bat, scoring a meagre two runs. At the day's end, "the wickets were drawn, as many of Mr. Turton's team were leaving the ground, and among others, the well recognised forms of Messrs Prendergast and Macgregor were visible. Taking all things into account, the day was most agreeably spent."[43]

While the lawyers mentioned in this chapter were leaders of the Dunedin Bar, all was not well with the Dunedin profession as a whole: "in 1864 there were a number of letters to the newspapers concerning the sham lawyers rampant on the diggings. The public and the profession were anxious the former should not be imposed upon (and the latter competed with)."[44] In 1867, Dunedin lawyer Thomas Parsons attempted to convince Attorney-General Prendergast to form "a properly disciplined bar in New Zealand along the lines of the English Inns of Court".[45] In 1869 the New Zealand Law Society's Act became law, but it did not immediately create an ordered and accountable legal profession.[46] The creation of national and regional law societies would be a central issue facing the profession from the 1860s onwards and an issue with which Prendergast would be closely involved.

Two notable figures at the Dunedin Bar during the 1860s were Michael Prendergast and George E. Barton. Michael, who had originally persuaded James to travel to Dunedin, was "a well-known member of the Bar in Otago"[47] from 1862 to the mid 1860s, at which point he disappears from the legal records. Newspaper reports mention Michael appearing before the Resident Magistrates Court and in a few Supreme Court trials, including one case in which he appeared opposite his younger brother.[48] He seems to have built up a modest legal practice from 1862 to 1864. Michael did not make the impression that his brother James did in Dunedin, possibly due to alcoholism and his increasingly fragile mental state. By 1865, James was Attorney-General of the colony while Michael's career seems to have come to an abrupt halt.

The future nemesis of James Prendergast was also working as a lawyer in Dunedin during the 1860s. George E. Barton arrived in Dunedin in c1861[49] with his wife and three young children.[50] Barton began a successful partnership with George Howorth before eventually being elected to the Otago Provincial Council in 1871.[51] During 1873 to 1876, Barton's whereabouts is uncertain, but an apposite anecdote could untangle this mystery:

> disaster suddenly fell upon him, through an action for slander in which he was mulcted to the extent of many thousand pounds for accusing a fellow solicitor of stealing a document that had been left in Court. To his dying day, G.E.B. maintained that he had seen the theft being committed as he came back accidentally to the court room where the various lawyers had left their papers on their tables . . . . When the verdict was given against him, he fled the country after transferring all that he had into the name of a friend, E. Ff Ward.[52]

Barton soon returned to New Zealand, re-appearing in Wellington in 1876. In 1877 he was counsel for Wiremu Parata in the now famous case heard by Prendergast and Richmond. In 1878 he was imprisoned by Prendergast for contempt of court. Barton had worked alongside Prendergast in many cases, including the 1864 *Otago Daily Times* libel case, and he had also been a close political ally of Michael Prendergast in the Victorian Parliament during the late 1850s and early 1860s. From 1864 to 1877 the relationship between Barton and James Prendergast deteriorated from comradeship to mutual hatred.

In his time as a lawyer in Dunedin, Prendergast had the opportunity of practicing before several of the leading judges in New Zealand legal history. One of these judges, William Richmond, was to play a pivotal role in Prendergast's later career and in the *Wi Parata* case for which Prendergast is chiefly remembered. Richmond was a high profile politician before resigning his seat in 1862. Deeply implicated in the outbreak of the Taranaki War, Richmond found New Zealand politics, "too strong for the men – at least too strong for me".[53] Moving to Dunedin from the North Island, Richmond entered into a successful practice with Thomas B. Gillies; both men would eventually become Supreme Court judges. Offered the position of Supreme Court judge in Otago in 1862, Richmond happily accepted and there he remained until 1867. In 1873, Richmond took a Supreme Court judgeship in Wellington and sat with Prendergast from 1875 until Richmond's death in 1895.

Prendergast appeared many times before his future brother judge from 1862 to 1867, and the Macassey Law Reports demonstrate a mutual respect between judge and barrister.

Henry Samuel Chapman joined Richmond on the Dunedin Bench in 1864.[54] Before his move to Otago, Chapman had already enjoyed an impressive career as a journalist, judge and politician in various locations in the vast British Empire.[55] Prendergast greatly admired Chapman as a judge, crediting him with "great ability, great perseverance, great patience, and great painstaking".[56] This respect was returned by the next generation of Chapmans. Henry Chapman's son, Frederick, rose to the Supreme Court Bench and rated Prendergast highly as a legal mind.[57]

Henry Chapman had been in Victoria, Australia from late 1854 through to 1864. Prendergast left Victoria in early 1855, and no records remain to prove that the two men knew each other at this point in their careers. Chapman was known to James' elder brother, Michael, as both served in the Victorian Legislative Assembly during the same period. In a letter from Michael to his father, he states "They [the Victorians] want a leader very badly. Chapman was tried and failed. If you were here you could not make less than 12000 twelve thousand a year. Chapman makes 8 failure though he is."[58] In early 1855, "Chapman joined leading members of the Victorian bar in agreeing to appear gratuitously in defence of the [Eureka] prisoners."[59] Michael Prendergast also increased his public profile by taking part in this defence resulting from the Eureka Stockade incident. No other direct references can be found linking Michael Prendergast and Henry Chapman, but the relationship between the Prendergast and Chapman legal families was one that stretched over several decades.

The romance and turmoil of a gold-rush society is reflected in the early beginnings of the Dunedin Bar. Friendships and feuds dominated the legal arena, and many leading lawyers used Dunedin as a springboard to future success. While the Dunedin Bar dominated the legal scene in New Zealand throughout the 1860s and most of the 1870s, the focus was soon to move to the newly named capital city, Wellington, along with many Dunedin lawyers, including Prendergast, Richmond and Barton.

4. The impact of the Otago experience on James Prendergast's future career

The Otago experience helped to equip Prendergast with the knowledge and skills which would make him leader of the bar and leader of the bench in New Zealand. Prendergast's experience as barrister at the Dunedin Bar improved his advocacy skills and prepared him for his role as Attorney-General. The qualities of persistence, stamina and strong argument can be seen in both Prendergast the barrister and Prendergast the Attorney-General. As Attorney-General, Prendergast was the leader of the legal profession, and the understanding of a lawyer's life gained in Dunedin was necessary for credibility. Working as a barrister also enabled Prendergast to analyse the role of a judge from the other side of the bench. By observing leading judges such as Chapman and Richmond, Prendergast could develop his own approach to judicial decision-making.

The official positions held by Prendergast while in Otago – Acting Provincial Solicitor and Crown Solicitor – provided administrative experience to a lawyer who would become a leading administrator of law in New Zealand. Working with the Otago Provincial Council and the New Zealand Government from Dunedin was the beginning of Prendergast's long involvement in colonial politics. These official positions also brought Prendergast to the attention of leading politicians in Wellington, for example, Henry Sewell and Edward Stafford, who would aid Prendergast in his rise to the top of the New Zealand legal profession.

Being in Dunedin during the 1860s was extremely advantageous for 'networking', and Prendergast made a number of key contacts there. One of Prendergast's first contacts, Julius Vogel, would eventually appoint Prendergast Chief Justice in 1875. William Richmond, the Otago Supreme Court judge before whom Prendergast practised, would become a close and powerful legal ally of Prendergast in Wellington. But not all contacts proved beneficial in future times. George E. Barton, who worked closely with Prendergast in Dunedin, would attempt to destroy his career when they met again in Wellington.

The Dunedin experience was a far greater success than the Victorian experience for a number of reasons, some obvious. First, Dunedin was his second attempt at colonial life and Prendergast was a shrewd man who learned from past mistakes. The disorganisation and poor management evident in Australia did not occur in Dunedin a decade later. This time, Prendergast knew that deriving income from goldminers' needs was often more financially beneficial than actually being a goldminer. Secondly, Prendergast was a qualified lawyer with experience when he arrived in Dunedin and found himself in the midst of a flourishing bar. When in Victoria, he could not legally practice law and struggled to find suitable administrative work, while his brother Michael, who was legally trained, conducted a successful practice in Melbourne. Thirdly, the Scottish environment of Dunedin seemed more to Prendergast's liking than what he perceived to be the Irish-dominated society in Victoria. Lastly, Prendergast was very lucky to be in the right place at the right time and to meet the right people.

Therefore, a combination of skills, experience and contacts allowed Prendergast to progress through the ranks of New Zealand lawyers with exceptional speed. Prendergast was a man who could seize opportunities, and settler New Zealand was full of potential for such men. In personality, Prendergast was diligent and capable but did not like to challenge established authority directly. Therefore, he could be relied upon to support those in power, especially those to whom he was indebted for his own positions. Prendergast was not alone in the speed of his career success. Peers such as Robert Stout and William Richmond also quickly rose to prominence in the colonial legal arena.

Prendergast was without doubt a successful barrister in Dunedin. His well-known practice and official recognition attest to this fact. While not a showman or great orator, Prendergast achieved results for his clients and was widely respected. In his official positions, Prendergast was successful enough to be considered for Attorney-General in 1865. There are no references found that comment on Prendergast's domestic life in Dunedin, for example, his relationship with his wife or his brother, Michael.

The Otago gold rush was a pivotal event not only in New Zealand legal history, but in New Zealand history generally. A huge influx of dynamic young people entered the colony and many continued to contribute to the building of settler New Zealand long after the gold rush was over. For British and Irish lawyers suffering from an overcrowded profession back 'home', Dunedin provided a host of opportunities. Invigorated by a flourishing town and inspired by the surrounding talent, the men of Dunedin law form an excellent case study of colonial enterprise and energy. There have been other gold rushes in New Zealand history, and times of economic boom, but from a legal perspective it is hard to find a period to rival Dunedin during the 1860s in terms of concentration of talent and achievement.

In the wider context of colonial legal history, the Dunedin gold rush can be compared to the Victorian gold rush of the 1850s. Apart from the fact that a number of lawyers participated in both experiences, there are several other similarities. Both gold rushes led to a rapid influx of lawyers who proceeded to engage in a dynamic legal environment. In both experiences, strong friendships were formed and bitter feuds erupted in a short space of time. Partnerships and practices were rapidly established and some just as rapidly collapsed. In both Dunedin and Melbourne, most present-day firms, and the legal profession as a whole, rest upon the foundations created in a gold-rush era.

In 1865, the New Zealand capital moved from Auckland to Wellington and the New Zealand Government became increasingly centralised. As Wellington grew, Dunedin became less and less the centre of the New Zealand legal profession. Therefore, though Dunedin had provided Prendergast with a springboard for success, his time there was short and it was to Wellington that he moved to further his career.

The Dunedin Bar provides the historian with an insight into the beginnings of the New Zealand legal profession. Exploring the early careers of leading legal figures helps the biographer to appreciate their later success in context. Prendergast made a number of long-lasting and influential contacts in Dunedin, including Richmond, Chapman and Vogel. The success of Prendergast and eventual failure of his brother Michael, who also practised in gold-rush Dunedin, was primarily due to personality differences. James was solid, reliable and knew when to follow orders. Michael was unpredictable, short-tempered and an alcoholic. The homogeneous club of white, male Dunedin lawyers could be extremely helpful to a young lawyer's career, but if one was not accepted by this club the results could be detrimental. That said, when the Barton-Prendergast feud erupted in 1878, the Dunedin Bar petitioned for an inquiry, supporting Barton, rather than Prendergast.[60]

Dunedin was vital to the success of James Prendergast in New Zealand. While it did not prepare him for the Maori–Pakeha conflict in the North Island, the Otago experience equipped him with vital skills, experience and contacts. In the minds of some, Prendergast always remained a Dunedin barrister, groomed in the nursery of the New Zealand legal profession.

5

PRENDERGAST AS ATTORNEY-GENERAL, 1865–1875

James Prendergast is primarily remembered for his contribution in two public roles, Attorney-General (1865–75) and Chief Justice (1875–99). Prendergast was appointed Attorney-General of New Zealand only three years after arriving in the colony, and he held that position for ten years. The nature of the position at that time was different from its nature in the present day. These differences directly affected the influence and actions of Prendergast.

During the first two years of Prendergast's career as Attorney-General he was also a member of the Legislative Council. Prendergast's speeches and political movements during these two years provide insights into his political views and key historical issues that were occuring during the 1860s. The issues facing the Legislative Council at this time included Maori political representation, the New Zealand Wars and regulation of the legal profession. Prendergast was also a pivotal figure in the controversial political debate pitting provincialists against centralists.

Another role of the Attorney-General was to provide legal opinions to the Government. Prendergast's opinions were influential and provide insights into his approach to race, politics and law. For example, Prendergast's hard-line approach to Maori affairs is clearly demonstrated during this era. Prendergast's legal opinions demonstrate his breadth of knowledge and also his reliance on English law and traditions.

Perhaps Prendergast's greatest contribution to New Zealand legal history while Attorney-General was overseeing the drafting and administration of a large body of legislation. The period 1865–75 was a fruitful time for new legislation, often directly reflecting developments in the English legal system. Prendergast's statutes were a key contribution to the New Zealand legal system, especially his codification of criminal law.

One of the key roles of Attorney-General was to appear on behalf of the Government in the New Zealand courts, and Prendergast played a leading role in several major trials. Throughout his time as Attorney-General, Prendergast personally advocated for the Crown in the Supreme Court and, in particular, the Court of Appeal. An analysis of his advocacy sheds light on his development as a litigator and also on his contributions to the New Zealand legal system.

In all of these four roles, Prendergast was faced with issues arising out of the later stages of the New Zealand Wars. Prendergast's actions as Attorney-General were crucial in the Government's waging of war against Maori from 1865 to 1870. His actions span the three branches of government: political and non-political Attorney-General (executive); Legislative Councillor (legislature); and Prosecutor (courts).

In a fifth role, Prendergast as Attorney-General served as the leader of New Zealand's lawyers. Thus, when the New Zealand Law Society was created in 1869, Prendergast became its first President. The formation and regulation of the practice of law in New Zealand is an important theme during the period 1865–75, with ground-breaking legislation being introduced, such as the Law Practitioners' Amendment Act 1866.

New Zealand politics during the time Prendergast was Attorney-General was dominated by three men: Edward Stafford, William Fox and Julius Vogel. Prendergast's relationships with these leading political figures affected his future career and influence in New Zealand society. The personal life of James Prendergast while Attorney-General was dynamic and changing. Prendergast moved from Dunedin to Wellington, built a house, bought land in the Manawatu and made a new circle of elite friends. He also witnessed the decline of his two brothers, Michael and Philip. Prendergast used the position of Attorney-General as a stepping stone for the Chief Justiceship, but this ten-year period marked the division between Prendergast the relatively unknown lawyer and Prendergast the important pillar of the New Zealand settler establishment.

1. The nature of the Attorney-General role

As with many aspects of Prendergast's life and career, the secondary material available is contradictory and confusing. Terms such as 'Solicitor-General' and 'Attorney-General' become interchangeable, with little description provided as to what these roles entailed. At the beginning of 1865, Prendergast was practising as a lawyer in Dunedin and by August he would fill the role of Crown Solicitor for Otago. On 10 July 1865, Prendergast became a member of the Legislative Council, 'representing' Otago.[1] Members of the Legislative Council were appointed by the Governor, and Prendergast's appointment states that "he shall [hold] his seat therein for the term of his life subject to the provisions of the said Act contained for vacating the same". Prendergast was appointed by Governor Grey (on the advice of responsible ministers), who was empowered to "summon to the said Legislative Council from time to time such person or persons as he the said Sir George Grey shall deem to be prudent and discreet men".[2]

Prendergast's work as a leading lawyer in Dunedin had brought him to the attention of politicians in Wellington, and Henry Sewell, the Attorney-General in Frederick Weld's 1865 Ministry, arranged for Prendergast's appointment as

Legislative Councillor. Henry Sewell was known for his fierce attacks on opponents in Parliament and he later referred to Stafford's Ministry, of which Prendergast was a key part, as a group of "respectable dummies".[3] When Weld's Ministry fell soon after Prendergast's appointment, Sewell attempted to retain personal power by undermining Prendergast's position.[4] Prendergast did not have the slightest intention of stepping aside for Sewell. Sewell was not seriously considered for inclusion in the Government of his rival, Edward Stafford. Prendergast was intent on cementing his position in the New Zealand political and legal establishment, a position he would hold until his retirement in 1899.

In the *New Zealand Gazette* and Parliamentary Debates, Prendergast is recorded as holding the post of Attorney-General from 20 October 1865.[5] The Weld Ministry ended on 16 October 1865, meaning that Prendergast took his post during Stafford's time as Premier. Before 16 October, the Attorney-Generalship was held by Prendergast's benefactor, Sewell. The Stafford Ministry of 1865 has been described in unflattering terms. "The Ministry he patched up was a strange one: Colonel A. H. Russell from Napier and James Prendergast, the Otago lawyer, both Legislative Councillors, Colonel Haultain from Auckland and James Paterson from Otago."[6] One of the members of Stafford's Ministry was John Hall, who would work closely with Prendergast in 1881 during the Parihaka invasion. Being a part of the New Zealand Parliament at that time also exposed Prendergast to other influential figures in his future career, including John Bryce, Donald McLean, Julius Vogel (whom Prendergast knew from Dunedin) and Frederick Whitaker.[7]

Sir John McGrath has written:

> The first initiative in New Zealand to separate the Law Officer role from membership of the Ministry holding office concerned the appointment of James Prendergast as Attorney-General in October 1865 . . . . Prendergast was appointed as Attorney-General but not to the Executive Council. Unlike his predecessors since 1856, he was not a Minister.[8]

Despite this, Prendergast was usually referred to as being part of the 'Stafford Ministry'.

Despite some claims from secondary sources that Prendergast first served as Solicitor-General, no Solicitor-General for Weld's Ministry appears in the official records, and this may be explained by a contemporary report.

> In 1865 he [Prendergast] was, upon the suggestion of Mr. Sewell, invited to the Legislative Council, with a place in the Weld Administration, as Solicitor-General. He was sworn in as a member of the Upper House; but we believe that ere [before] he took the oath of office as Solicitor-General, Mr. Weld resigned.[9]

Yet in a parliamentary debate on 25 August 1865, Prendergast is referred to as the Solicitor-General.[10] This claim is supported by recent historiography.[11] It is unclear as to whether Prendergast was gradually being positioned to serve as a political

Solicitor-General, similar to the way the role worked in Britain at the time, but it is certain that he never actually took up this role.

Prendergast served as political Attorney-General for less than two years. In 1866 the Attorney-General's Act was passed, making the post non-political (outside Parliament) and vested with life tenure. This Act came into effect in March 1867, resulting in Prendergast leaving his seat in the Legislative Council and giving up his Dunedin practice and position as Crown Solicitor of Otago. Prendergast's brief career as a politician was at an end, but his influence in Wellington's power elite would continue to grow. In offering Prendergast the permanent position in 1866, Stafford suggested an annual salary of 1200 pounds and assistance with removal costs from Dunedin to Wellington. Stafford was intent on a fast process: "I have to request that you will come to Wellington as soon as possible."[12] Stafford also offered Prendergast the first "vacancy occurring in the office of Judge of the Supreme Court in the Colony".[13] Prendergast was unsure about Stafford's ability to bind future governments, and, sure enough, in 1870 William Fox qualified Stafford's earlier statement:

> The late Government [Stafford's] seems to have exceeded its power in attempting to bind a future Government . . . But . . . the present Government will be prepared to offer to you the first puisne judgeship which may fall vacant during your tenancy of the non-political office of Attorney-General, and their own tenure of office as a Ministry. In case of the Chief Justiceship falling vacant, the Government would hold itself free from all previous pledges.[14]

The Chief Justiceship was one of several judicial positions to fall vacant in 1875. By this stage, Vogel had replaced Fox and offered Prendergast the coveted position of head of the judiciary.

Prendergast was not impressed with the frenetic and ever-changing nature of the Attorney-Generalship. On 3 October 1866, during the passage of the Attorney-General's Bill, Prendergast wrote a detailed, and somewhat self-serving, opinion on the matter to the Colonial Secretary. Prendergast argued that the Bill should remain in its present shape, "with an amendment excluding the officer only from the House of Representatives, and also, I am disposed to think from practising as a Solicitor, except in Crown business. I think the chief permanent officer should be termed Attorney General."[15] Prendergast also argued for the creation of a new political position, one suitable for non-practising lawyers, such as Sewell or Fox: "These persons would more properly hold an office to be termed 'Minister of Justice'."[16]

Prendergast's seat in the Legislative Council, which would be taken away by the Act, was very dear to the ambitious lawyer. Prendergast used his familiar strategy of appealing to British precedent: "I do not think it necessary to exclude the officer from the Legislative Council. In all Acts of the Imperial Parliament applying to permanent officers the officers are excluded only from the House of Commons."[17] The successful Dunedin practice held by Prendergast would also be lost under the new Act, with Prendergast reluctant to experience a drop in income:

> [T]he officer should be excluded from practising as a Solicitor except for the Crown, but not as a Barrister . . . as the salary allotted is insufficient to remunerate such a person as ought to fill the office, he ought to conduct the Crown Prosecutions in Wellington and be paid in addition for that.[18]

Prendergast argued for a more secure and lucrative political office, but most of his suggestions were not accepted. From the nature of some of the cases reported in the *Evening Post* (1865–1875) it does appear that Prendergast kept a private practice of sorts.

Prendergast's position as Attorney-General was akin to the present non-political role of Solicitor-General, and, with the Assistant Law Officer, they effectively comprised the Attorney-General's Department, which was responsible for routine legal work. On administrative matters, the Attorney-General liaised with the Judicial Branch of the Colonial Secretary's Department. When the Attorney-General became non-political, he reported to the Colonial Secretary. The Judicial Branch was changed to the Department of Justice in 1872 under the control of a new Minister of Justice. Also in 1872, the Attorney-General's Department was transformed into the Crown Law Office.

By this time some politicians were calling for the disestablishment of the constitutionally awkward non-political post of Attorney-General. The problem was resolved when Prendergast moved to the bench in 1875. One year later the Attorney-General's Act 1876 was passed, making the position political again, as it is to this day. The position of non-political Solicitor-General was introduced to replace Prendergast.

While Prendergast was appointed to the Legislative Council in July 1865, he did not become part of a ministry until appointed Attorney-General in Stafford's Ministry during October. New Zealand politics, from the time of responsible government in 1856 to the Liberals' victory in 1891, was fluid, ever-changing and based more on personality and local interests than on party loyalty.[19] Parliamentary politics during this period were markedly different to those of more recent times.[20] The first Premier of New Zealand was Henry Sewell, whose office lasted only a few weeks, during 1856. From 1856 to 1861, the Premier was Edward Stafford, who must rank as New Zealand's most powerful parliamentary politician from 1856 to the early 1870s, at which point Julius Vogel began to dominate Parliament. Beyond Parliament was the pivotal figure of Governor George Grey, who eventually entered Parliament as a member in the 1870s. The New Zealand Wars which raged throughout the early 1860s saw a succession of brief ministries led by William Fox, Alfred Domett, Frederick Whitaker and Frederick Weld.

It was Weld's Ministry of 24 November 1864 to 16 October 1865 that provided Prendergast with his political opening.

When Weld's Ministry collapsed on 16 October 1865, Edward Stafford, with experience and influence, was the obvious choice for Premier. Stafford's Ministry of relatively unknown politicians lasted until 28 June 1869, an impressive length by the standards of mid-to-late nineteenth-century New Zealand politics. Prendergast owed his newly founded position of power to Henry Sewell and Edward Stafford, but he eventually angered both men. By enabling Prendergast's rise to power, Sewell effectively created a rival who would replace him.

Prendergast's relationship with Stafford was harmonious until Stafford lost power in 1869. Stafford was pleased with his choice as Attorney-General, "who, although new, 'has won golden opinions from all who have come in contact with him', and his legal opinions were received with a respect and influence which Sewell never could acquire".[21] But in 1869, Stafford attempted to obtain the house currently occupied by the Governor. Stafford had leased the house as Colonial Secretary but was now demanding it as a private citizen.

> He [Fox] would get the Attorney General [Prendergast] to scrutinize the lease and other papers. The comedy lasted a fortnight. Attorney General Prendergast ruled that Stafford had signed the lease as Colonial Secretary and had no rights as a private citizen to claim Clifford's house from the Governor . . . Stafford finally refused to accept the Attorney General's ruling . . . He was patently in the wrong.[22]

The matter was laid before both Houses of the General Assembly in a battle of wills between Fox and Stafford.[23] As non-political Attorney-General, Prendergast was in the difficult position of having to be totally neutral. His opinion was brief and blunt: Stafford was totally in the wrong.[24] While in situations such as the invasion of Parihaka in 1881, Prendergast provided strong support for dubious political action, the Stafford incident demonstrates political integrity, with Prendergast willing to risk offending the dominant political figure of the time, who was attempting to abuse his power.

New Zealand politics during the late nineteenth century did not feature obvious political parties or labels such as 'conservative' and 'liberal'. During 1865 and 1866, when Prendergast served in the Stafford Ministry, a key debate was 'centralism' versus 'provincialism'. The capital city had been permanently transferred from Auckland to Wellington in 1865 and moves were afoot to dismantle the provincial system set up by Grey's 1852 Constitution. Wellington, as the most central New Zealand city, was the best site for a central government, despite its proclivity for earthquakes. Stafford was an outspoken centrist, and Prendergast's speeches in the Legislative Council reveal him to be a supporter of strong central government. During the early days of Prendergast's Attorney-Generalship, New Zealand was recovering from the wars between Maori and Pakeha based in the Taranaki and Waikato regions. While armed resistance continued from the Hauhau, Te Kooti, Titokowaru and others, the open warfare period was at an end by 1865 and Maori were suffering under the weight of drastic land confiscations.

During the latter half of Prendergast's term as Attorney-General, the borrowing schemes of Julius Vogel dominated the political scene. Vast amounts of overseas money were borrowed to finance immigration and the large-scale building of a national infrastructure. The early 1870s was a boom time for New Zealand settler society and during this period Prendergast finally cemented his position of power by 'rising' from Attorney-General to Chief Justice. Prendergast's beginnings in Wellington though, were relatively reserved and restrained.

In 1865, the Government Ministry consisted of seven portfolios: Premier, Colonial Secretary, Colonial Treasurer, Attorney-General, Postmaster-General, Minister for Colonial Defence and Minister for Native Affairs. In Stafford's Ministry, Prendergast took the position of Attorney-General, while Theodore Haultain received Colonial Defence and Andrew Russell, Native Affairs. Stafford took the other four portfolios, an impressive achievement for one man. Prendergast was a new and little-known political quantity, in a ministry dominated completely by Edward Stafford. By late August 1866, the Stafford Ministry was almost completely changed, but Prendergast remained. A new appointment, James Crowe Richmond as Commissioner of Customs, further strengthened Prendergast's connection with the Richmond-Atkinson families and the conservative elements in New Zealand politics. As Chief Justice, Prendergast would be a close and loyal ally of Richmond's elder brother, William.

In 1869 the legal profession moved towards effective regulation with the introduction of the New Zealand Law Society's Act, based on the English Law Society Charter of 1845. It was not welcomed by Auckland practitioners, who claimed that they had not been adequately consulted, and the passing of the Bill was principally due to the efforts of the Wellington and Christchurch legal communities.[25] The first Council was appointed by Governor George Bowen, and Prendergast, as Attorney-General, was the obvious choice for President. Other members of the first Council included Bryan Cecil Haggitt of Dunedin and William Travers of Wellington.[26] At the time, the New Zealand legal profession was still small (numbering only 225 in 1876),[27] and it took a while for the Law Society to become fully established; at least until Francis Bell became President in 1901. Between 1875 and 1897, records do not even mention any President,[28] and during Prendergast's five-year term in the role (1870–1875), the Council achieved little except monitoring issues of discipline. Prendergast's attention was focused on his role as Attorney-General, leaving him little time to attend to strengthening the Law Society.

2. Prendergast in the Legislative Council

The New Zealand Legislative Council was abolished in 1950. At that point in history, it had long been an anachronism. After Harry Atkinson and then the Liberal Party politically 'stacked' the Council during the 1890s to strengthen their respective political positions, the Council ceased to play an integral role in New Zealand's constitutional framework. Before the 1890s, the Council was an effective check on the House of Representatives and a forum for important discussions.

Prendergast's service as a Legislative Councillor lasted from July 1865 to October 1866. Prendergast was considered by several commentators to be a poor public speaker[29] and did not distinguish himself as a political orator. But his speeches in the Council were succinct and lucid, and generally treated with respect by his peers. Most nineteenth-century New Zealand politicians were effectively 'part-timers' with other occupations and independent incomes. This meant that Parliament could only sit for part of the year, as the rest of the time was needed to attend to private business interests. The parliamentary term began in late June and ended in early October, a period of little more than three months. During the 1865 term Prendergast delivered nine recorded speeches, and during the 1866 term, 15 recorded speeches.[30] Most of Prendergast's speeches were legal comments on legislation under consideration. This legislation ranged from land issues to parliamentary dissolution to codification of the criminal law. By analysing the New Zealand Parliamentary Debates of 1865–66, the nature of Prendergast's political involvement can be gauged.

A. Maori issues

The first recorded parliamentary speech made by the Honourable James Prendergast, Otago, was on 1 August 1865, approximately one month after he entered the Council. James Crowe Richmond, Colonial Secretary and younger brother of Richmond J, opened the debate, which concerned Maori representation in Parliament. After outlining the Weld Ministry's achievements up to August 1865, Richmond introduced the issue of Maori representation, arguing that his Ministry fully supported it:

> [T]he present movement was a corollary to the Native Lands Act. The two were essentially the abandonment of the system of protectorate, or dry-nursing. The Colonial and Home Governments confessed alike that they had failed. They were throwing the Maori on the world to take his lot with other subjects, and they must remove all disabilities . . . there was certainly a sense of wrong existing in their minds which we should remove. Now was the time, when we were getting the upper hand of them, to do it, and thus show them that we had none but friendly intentions towards them.[31]

James Menzies, from Southland, took a less approving view of Maori enfranchisement:

[H]e saw very grave objections to the passing of any clause which would provide any different qualification for Maori electors or members from that of the European population. He apprehended that it was absolutely necessary for us to maintain a power over the Maoris. They had but a very imperfect acquaintance with our laws, and paid but an extremely imperfect obedience to them.[32]

Another South Islander, Henry Tancred, believed Maori would be more effectively represented by their own political structure:

He wished to give the Natives a voice, but was opposed to so far amalgamating the two races as to allow them a seat in Parliament. Everybody must recognize that the Maoris and the Europeans were two distinct races, and therefore he thought that the only system would be to organize the former as a separate body, and not have half the House composed of Natives and the other half of Europeans.[33]

Prendergast stated simply:

[T]here could be no doubt that, in the minds of all our friends at Home, the Natives have an inborn right, as British subjects, to the privileges of this country. If it was a fact that according to the Constitution Act no alien could have a seat in the Legislative Council, he thought such an important working objection should be removed. Such a law was contrary to the rights of the Natives, who were the largest landholders in the colony, and he considered it was unjust that they should exist under such disabilities. [Prendergast] had no hesitation in saying in fact that he believed the objectionable words had crept into the Act by accident.[34]

Prendergast argued that Maori should have parliamentary representation, a view that appears at odds with his general dismissive attitude towards Maori. His argument that Maori were British subjects clearly corresponds with Article Three of the Treaty of Waitangi.

B. The New Zealand Wars

On 28 August 1866, the New Zealand Wars dominated debate in the Legislative Council. An Indemnity Bill, drawn up by Prendergast, was about to have its second reading. When passed, the long title of the Act read: "An Act for indemnifying persons acting in the suppression of the Native Insurrection."[35] Walter Mantell, an outspoken supporter of Maori, attempted to prevent the second reading, arguing that the Bill was poorly written and that Parliament should not protect leading military leaders such as Major-General Chute and Colonel Whitmore from answering for their actions during the Wanganui expedition. Mantell cited a list of accusations against the British army:

friendly Natives being pillaged of their horses, which were afterwards sold at Taranaki; the forcing of a number of friendly Natives to act as guides, and marching them in front of the column without arms and without rations, to attack their own friends . . . a spear which was taken from the body of a chief, and which a soldier – to use the language of the letter accompanying the gift – "had pierced through fifteen dead Maori bodies, to be certain that life was quite extinct."[36]

The military men residing in the Legislative Council leapt to the defence of the British Army, including Major Coote, Colonel Whitmore, Colonel Peacocke and Colonel Russell. Whitmore argued that the abuse of "friendly Natives" was unavoidable:

> It was difficult to distinguish a friendly from a hostile Native: his (Colonel Whitmore's) experience had taught him that most Natives were enemies when possible, and many friends when they dared not be enemies. At any rate, it was so in India and the Cape of Good Hope.[37]

Prendergast also defended his legislation. He refused to comment on the "[n]ative part of the Hon. Mr. Mantell's argument, but at what he thought he had wished to be considered the funny part".[38] Many of Prendergast's speeches in the Legislative Council displayed an avoidance of controversy and support of the majority. Prendergast continued to taunt Mantell, challenging him to write a better piece of legislation if he could. Mantell was unsuccessful in his bid to prevent the Bill from passing.

Two days later, Mantell sought revenge for Prendergast's dismissive treatment of his views. After Prendergast moved to introduce the Innkeeper's Liability Bill, based on a recent Imperial Act, Mantell criticised Prendergast's speech, the only voice raised against it.[39] Mantell continued to upset the Council with his calls for justice regarding Maori. On 18 September 1866, Prendergast sided with the conservative majority in the Council to question Mantell's inquiry into the legitimacy of certain Crown grants, a position consistent with his judgment in *Wi Parata*, 11 years later.[40] Prendergast, along with other Councillors such as Alfred Domett and Colonel Whitmore, repeatedly found himself in opposition to Mantell on other matters too,[41] although he was not always successful in his challenges to Mantell. On 5 October 1866, Mantell successfully moved to decline entertaining any more Bills for that session, other than those introduced by the colonial government. Prendergast protested vehemently, but the Hon. Dr Menzies "thought that the objection of the Hon. the Attorney-General had no weight with it".[42] The Council agreed.

C. English law

In the debate focused upon the Leases and Sales of Settled Estates Bill, Prendergast was responsible for the Bill and had based it completely on an English model:

> The Bill he was now asking them to read a second time was a transcript of a Bill introduced in the House of Lords by Lord Cranworth . . . The Council might

rely on it that the Bill was as perfect as legal skill could make it . . . Bill read a
second time, and passed through all its remaining stages without amendment.[43]

The successful passing of this Bill demonstrated Prendergast's heavy reliance upon
English statute law and the faith shown in him by the Council. Prendergast later
demonstrated this reliance on English law in his judgments as Chief Justice from
1875 to 1899.

Prendergast had only been in New Zealand for three years before entering
Parliament. This meant that he had more recent experience with English legal
developments than many other politician-lawyers such as Henry Sewell, Frederick
Whitaker or William Fox, who had been in New Zealand since the earlier days of
settlement. When introducing the Printing and Publishing Regulation Bill on 22
August 1865, Prendergast again referred to English legislative precedents, stating
that "a number of provisions with respect to publishing existed in England, but
it was doubtful whether the law was in force in the colony".[44] Although he often
followed English developments, Prendergast was occasionally willing to argue for
an independent path, for example, during the debate on paying common jurors
outlined in section G of this chapter.

D. Provincial issues

As a representative of Otago, Prendergast was closely connected with the gold rush
of the 1860s. On 7 August 1865, James Crowe Richmond moved the second reading
of the Goldfields Acts Amendment Bill. During the discussion in the Legislative
Council, Prendergast supplied legal advice.[45] His three years of experience as an
Otago lawyer had provided Prendergast with a comprehensive knowledge of
mining law. The main focus of the debate was land use and ownership, a critical
issue during nineteenth-century New Zealand history.

An interesting debate took place in the Legislative Council on 10 October 1865,
only six days before the collapse of the Weld Ministry. John Hall of Canterbury,
who in later times would work with Prendergast to destroy Parihaka, introduced a
motion to increase the customs revenue of Canterbury, without the same provision
for any of the other provinces.[46] Several of the Councillors, including Prendergast,
spoke against Hall's motion, arguing that its provincial bias would undermine
'equality' between the different provinces. The provincial debate was still very much
at the centre of New Zealand political discussion in 1865 and 'pork-barrel' politics
were common. Prendergast often sided with the majority view in the Council,
which did no harm to his support network and future career opportunities. If he
did disagree with an influential figure, such as John Hall, he always used moderate
and non-confrontational language, unlike many of his political peers.

One of the most controversial political issues of the mid-1860s was the location
of the nation's capital. In 1864, it was decided that Wellington should be the seat

of government and the transfer of power from Auckland to Wellington was made official in 1865. In 1866, the Wellington members of the Legislative Council spoke in support of retaining their home as the permanent capital. Prendergast, who would soon shift his geographic allegiance from Dunedin to Wellington, supported them. Dr Menzies stated the case for Wellington:

> He could not see, geographically speaking, that any advantage could arise if the next session of the Assembly were held in any other part of the colony. Wellington, being central, possessed many advantages over any of the other cities, and its communication with other places was more regular and frequent.[47]

Colonel Peacocke of Auckland disagreed with Menzies, demonstrating the Auckland–Wellington rivalry which has permeated New Zealand's history ever since 1840. Peacocke's argument was rebutted by Mantell, another Wellingtonian. Prendergast stated that the matter was one for the Governor alone, but "proceeded to speak of the expense and inconvenience that would be felt by a removal of the Legislature".[48] Wellington's political dominance was becoming difficult to challenge and the Council supported the Wellingtonians (who comprised six members out of a total of 35). This debate demonstrated the continuing tension over movement towards centralisation, supported by Prendergast and his Premier, Stafford. Prendergast would live to see Wellington grow from a small village to a thriving city. In 1864, Wellington had a population of 4741. When Prendergast retired in 1899 it had nearly reached 50,000, and by the time he died in 1921, the city had 100,000 citizens.[49]

E. Parliamentary dissolution

On 25 and 26 October 1865, the Legislative Council faced the issue of parliamentary dissolution. On 16 October, Weld's Ministry had fallen. It was replaced by a Ministry led by Stafford. Weld's supporters were outraged and prepared to make Stafford's position as difficult as possible. A rumour circulated that Stafford had secretly met with Governor Grey and obtained a promise that Parliament would be dissolved even if the Parliament refused supplies to Stafford. Stafford desired a dissolution to allow him to seek an election to secure his position. The Legislative Council, led by Tancred, moved the adoption of an address to the Governor seeking clarification on the controversy.[50] Prendergast was unsure about the course of action proposed by the Council. The evidence was insufficient and lacked credibility:

> [H]e had already expressed his opinion that this taking notice of an unknown document was a highly improper course to take . . . His Excellency himself was perfectly aware whether or not he had made this promise to Mr. Stafford. If this statement affected any place it affected the other branch of the Legislature[.][51]

In this case, Prendergast spoke out unsuccessfully against the majority of the Council and supported Stafford in his actions. Stafford had only six days earlier promoted Prendergast to the position of Attorney-General. Prendergast's reasoning was that the Council's actions were effectively ultra vires. Unlike Stafford, Frederick Weld was widely considered a man of honour and integrity and his fall from power caused great consternation in Parliament. Although Prendergast was appointed during Weld's premiership, he owed his position to Sewell's influence. Stafford was treated with suspicion by many of his parliamentary colleagues and was often the subject of controversy. The Weldites were convinced that Stafford:

> had done a deal with Grey. The two Machiavellis had outwitted the virtuous men . . . The Legislative Council, restrained in tone but committed in its corporate hostility to Stafford, asked Grey, firmly but politely, for a reconciliation between Stafford's denial that he had asked for a dissolution and Pharazyn's statement [to the contrary]. Grey replied that it was up to the Government to make whatever statement it thought fit.[52]

F. Legislation

Prendergast's central role in the Council during his two years of service was to introduce and give advice upon new legislation. During the first session of the fourth Parliament (30 June–8 October 1866), in Prendergast's second and last year as a colonial politician, he was appointed to the Select Committee for Standing Orders, along with leading councillors such as Alfred Domett.[53] Within the first month of the 1866 session, he had introduced the Legislative Council Limitation Bill and amended the Offences Against the Person Bill.[54] The Legislative Council Bill limited the number of councillors and could have been proposed to retain the select and elite nature of the Upper House, while the Offences Against the Person Bill was to become the first of a range of criminal statutes introduced as Bills while Prendergast was political Attorney-General.

Prendergast's most important contribution to New Zealand statute law was his introduction, improvement and codification of criminal law. The criminal statutes introduced as Bills under his supervision included the Accessories Act 1867, the Affirmation in Lieu of Oaths in Criminal Proceedings Act 1866, the Coinage Offences Act 1867, the Criminal Law Procedure Act 1866, the Forgery Act 1867, the Indictable Offences Trials Act 1866, the Indictable Offences Repeal Act 1867, the Introduction of Convicts Prevention Act 1867, the Larceny Act 1867, the Malicious Injury to Property Act 1867, the Neglected and Criminal Children Act 1867, the Offences Against the Person Act 1867 and the Vagrancy Act 1866.

G. Jurors

Certain legal issues that dominated discussion in nineteenth-century New Zealand have remained contentious issues to this day. An apposite example is the payment of jurors. In 1866, common jurymen (as opposed to special jurors) received no compensation for their services and, as Colonel Peacocke explained:

He had been induced to bring the matter forward from personal observation of the hardships which poor men and their families were subjected to through being compelled to attend the Supreme Court at the sacrifice of their time, which was their daily bread.[55]

Peacocke cited Victoria as a colonial example where this issue had been addressed. Robert Stokes countered the Victorian example with a more binding precedent, that of English law:

> Certainly common jurymen were not paid in England; and, as the New Zealand Legislature took the laws of that country for their model, they should be cautious, particularly when they were told on every hand that peculiar economy was required. It appeared to him that citizens owed to their country a duty which they were bound to discharge.[56]

The opportunity cost for common jurors was much higher in 1866 than the present day, for employers would not continue paying wages to workers while they were absent on jury duty (many, if not most, New Zealand employers now continue paying wages). Prendergast showed interest in the plight of the common juryman: "For his own part, he did not see why special jurors should be paid a guinea a day while common jurymen received nothing."[57]

H. The legal profession

Prendergast also looked out for the interests of the legal profession, both advocates and adjudicators, while Attorney-General. In a Council debate on 15 August 1866, Prendergast disagreed with John Acland's motion to have Private Bills first brought before the Supreme Court and then to the Legislature. Colonel Whitmore asked the Attorney-General for advice and Prendergast stated that he:

> was not in favour of this course. The Council should consider the matter thoroughly before they referred to the Judges a work which had generally been performed by the Legislature . . . there was no power in the Council to insist upon an answer from the Judges, but he could not conceive that any of the Judges would refuse to give their opinion when asked.[58]

One of Prendergast's most important pieces of legislation was the Law Practitioners Amendment Act. Section 3 of the Act, passed on 8 October 1866, ensured that:

> No person who has or shall have been convicted in any part of the British dominions of forgery or perjury or subornation of perjury shall be enrolled or admitted to practice or shall practice as a Barrister or Solicitor in New Zealand.[59]

The regulation of the legal profession was vital to protect the public and the integrity of the profession. Forgery in particular undermines the public's trust in a lawyer to act with complete honesty when performing the key role of drafting documents. In a Council debate on 7 September 1866, Prendergast successfully argued that the words "or any felony" should be left out of clause 3 of the Bill. By rejecting a wider net, Prendergast was able to regulate the profession while reducing parliamentary control over admission of lawyers in New Zealand.

Prendergast's approach in the Legislative Council was pragmatic, formal and logical. His arguments, like his judgments, reflected a commitment to justice and law rather than to mercy and emotion. In the debate over the Crown Lands Sales Extortion Prevention Bill, Prendergast took a typically hard-line attitude: "[H]e thought the person paying the money ought to be equally liable with the extortioner. The object of the Legislature was not in this matter to protect individuals, but to prevent frauds on the revenue."[60] Prendergast showed little patience with colleagues who did not devote themselves entirely to their public duties. On 20 September 1866, Prendergast successfully argued against a leave of absence for George Lee on the basis that there were already 15 members of the 35-strong Council absent.[61] It is clear that Prendergast believed the role of the Legislative Council was of great importance in the New Zealand constitutional framework.

The key issues of the late 1860s were argued in the Legislative Council, and by studying the New Zealand Parliamentary Debates the diverse range of views held by councillors can be seen. When the Legislative Council was abolished in 1950 it was a shadow of its former self, but during the 1860s it was an integral part of the colonial constitutional structure. While the Legislative Councillors were an elite group of men, they echoed the concerns of important sectors of colonial New Zealand, for example, farming and business interests.

Prendergast played many roles as political Attorney-General, including being a member of the executive, councillor, legal advisor and leader of the legal profession. During Council debates (such as the debate on regulating the legal profession) Prendergast was sometimes forced to play several roles simultaneously. His efforts in the Legislative Council most certainly contributed to his successful career as Attorney-General, and later, Chief Justice.

3. Prendergast's role as Attorney-General during the New Zealand Wars

Prendergast's judicial decisions relating to Maori did not exist in a vacuum but rather should be seen in the context of earlier cultural encounters. To gain a greater insight into how and why Prendergast adjudicated as he did, it is necessary to understand his experiences in the New Zealand Wars. This period had a profound influence on Prendergast's racial attitudes. While Prendergast is known primarily for his judicial role, it was not on the bench that he developed his views on Maori society. Prendergast played a leading role in the latter stages of the Wars as Attorney-General. Despite only arriving in Dunedin in 1862 and Wellington in

1865, Prendergast was prominent in some of the most iconic conflicts of the Wars, including the campaigns against Riwha Titokowaru and Te Kooti Arikirangi Te Turuki, and the invasion of Parihaka. The military conflicts that tore apart the fabric of colonial New Zealand influenced the racial attitudes of the man who, as much as any other, would ensure the dominance of British law over Maori.

This section primarily focuses on Prendergast's defining experiences in the New Zealand Wars: his legal opinions as Attorney-General relating to the latter stages of the New Zealand Wars (1865–1870) and his prosecutions as Attorney-General in 1869.

In 1865 Prendergast was a recent immigrant and a newly appointed Attorney-General with virtually no experience of indigenous cultures. His racial views were common amongst the settler community. While Prendergast's views appear extreme to present day New Zealanders, he was not as openly prejudiced as, for example, John Bryce. Nevertheless, Prendergast's actions, language and legal judgments clearly support the assertion that he believed Maori to be greatly inferior to Europeans. This viewpoint was not restricted to Maori in arms against the Crown but to all Maori. For example, in *Rira Peti v Ngaraihi Te Paku* (1888),[62] Prendergast refused to acknowledge the legitimacy of Maori customary law relating to marriage. In *Broughton v Donnelly* (1888),[63] Prendergast's Supreme Court decision relating to a Maori will will be reviewed by the Court of Appeal. Prendergast had ruled that Maori witnesses did not have the same credibility as other witnesses and were inherently unreliable. It was not that many of his fellow settlers failed to see his racial attitudes, but rather, that they agreed with them. The key difference was that Prendergast was in a privileged position to implement his views. While many settlers may have had similar ideas about Maori, only the most powerful were in a position to enforce these ideas.

By 1862, Prendergast had an impressive number of different life experiences, but even though he had spent a brief time in Australia, he had never had to deal directly with other races or different cultures. While Prendergast's actions and decisions as a powerful New Zealand legal figure reflect his upbringing, education and life in England, he did not arrive in New Zealand with a clear racial philosophy. Prendergast was a pragmatist and there is little direct mention of philosophical or political influences in his private and public papers.

Background alone does not adequately explain how Prendergast developed his views on Maori issues. It is also inadequate to argue that his actions as a legal officer were merely a reflection of his professional role, that is, he was obliged to consistently make extreme decisions harmful to Maori society because he was the Government's Attorney-General. New Zealand's history includes many colonial figures who held powerful roles yet showed empathy towards Maori.

This section is not a wide-ranging study of racial thought in New Zealand and the British Empire during the nineteenth century. This topic has been the focus of many in-depth studies.[64] For the purposes of this section it is accepted that Prendergast must have been influenced by existing societal views on race, as were all New Zealand settlers to differing extents. As stated above, Prendergast's personal and official papers provide no evidence of his racial views before 1865. Even after 1865 Prendergast's racial views are to be found in official documents rather than in his personal records. These racial views are pragmatic and make little reference to theory.[65] Therefore any intellectual contextualisation of Prendergast's racial views must proceed by surveying dominant racial theories, such as the stadial theory, and attempting to find indirect evidence of the theories in Prendergast's official pronouncements and actions. This is a lengthy undertaking and a task for another work.

A. Legal opinions relating to the New Zealand Wars

The Waikato War between Imperial Britain and Kingite Maori ended in 1864. The conflict then transformed from open warfare to guerilla warfare. The period from 1864 to 1872 saw a number of Maori campaigns launched against settler dominance and land confiscations. The most well-known campaigns were those of Te Kooti (1868–1872) on the East Coast of the North Island and Titokowaru (1868–1869) on the West Coast of the North Island.[66] As Attorney-General, Prendergast became embroiled in the conflict as the settler government repeatedly sought his opinion on legal matters.

There is a difference between Prendergast's outlook at the beginning, and then after, the bitter struggle of the late 1860s, suggesting that the conflict was a key factor in affecting his racial attitudes. As discussed above, in his first recorded speech as a Legislative Councillor on 1 August 1865, Prendergast argued in favour of Maori parliamentary representation on the basis that Maori were British subjects and were the largest landholders in New Zealand.[67] This view seems at odds with his later opinions on Maori issues.

In December 1865, Prendergast also provided a balanced legal opinion on the courts-martial of Maori charged with the murders of Carl Volkner and James Falloon in the Bay of Plenty. The courts-martial found the accused guilty, but Prendergast argued that subjecting ordinary subjects to martial law breached both the Petition of Right 1627 and the Magna Carta 1297.[68] Given the heated debate in Britain during the 1860s over the use of martial law in the colonies, Prendergast's opinion appears as an inspiring assertion of the rule of law.[69] He also questioned the quality of the evidence which led to the convictions.[70] The convictions were quashed and new trials arranged in the Auckland Supreme Court, which took place in 1866.[71] Despite the high-profile nature of the trials, Prendergast did not prosecute on behalf of the Crown.[72] This approach can be compared to subsequent events in late 1871. Prendergast did not miss his opportunity in the spotlight five years later when he successfully prosecuted Kereopa Te Rau for the murder of

Volkner. Despite the case being primarily based on the evidence of unconvincing witnesses, Prendergast gained a guilty verdict from the jury in Napier and Johnston J sentenced Kereopa to death.[73] Kereopa was hanged in January 1872.

Prendergast's role in this trial has recently been analysed by Peter Wells in *Journey to a Hanging*.[74] As with Maurice Shadbolt's *Season of the Jew*, Prendergast is portrayed as a two-dimensional villain. Wells is unimpressed with Prendergast's legal skills and professionalism. He is particularly interested in the political aspects of the trial and brushes over Prendergast's legal obligations as Attorney-General, that is, to represent the Crown and prosecute on its behalf. Wells' view of Prendergast is encapsulated in the following quotation:

> So it is clear from this that Prendergast saw it as a show trial right from the get-go, as a piece of public theatre, which delivered a controlled political message. Kereopa Te Rau was to be found guilty before he even stepped into the dock. The question was how best to deliver a guilty verdict?[75]

From 1866 to 1870 Prendergast was involved in some of the most oppressive legal measures against Maori in New Zealand's history. In February 1869, at the height of Titokowaru's War, the British Secretary for the Colonies, Earl Granville, implied that Maori in arms should be treated as a "foreign enemy" with whom the "usual laws of war" should be observed.[76] New Zealand's Premier and Colonial Secretary, Edward Stafford, asked Prendergast for legal clarification.[77] This was a vital issue, as rebellious subjects could potentially be treated without regard to the laws of war, thus validating some of the more extreme government actions during this stage of the New Zealand Wars.

The opinion given by Prendergast on 30 June 1869 regarding the "legal status of Maori now in arms" stands as the most extreme statement on Maori affairs ever offered by Prendergast. His language is unforgiving and confrontational. Firstly, Prendergast confirmed that Maori were British subjects. He then separated the question to specifically explore whether the Government was obligated to observe the usual laws of war in respect to Maori rebels. Regardless of whether Maori were classified as foreign or British subjects, they had forfeited any right to protection under these laws because "the revolt has been carried out in defiance of all the laws of nature, and there can be no doubt that all who have taken part in it have forfeited all claim for mercy".[78] As Maori were not abiding by the laws of war there was no obligation on the colonial government to do so. The rules of war between civilised nations did not apply to war with the Maori.

In his September 1870 opinion, Prendergast argued that the Maori were "rebels in arms, and that such rebellion was not of such an extent or character as to make it expedient or proper to treat the rebels otherwise than as persons guilty of a breach of the municipal law".[79] The distinction is effectively between a 'war' and a 'rebellion' and also between a 'major rebellion' and a 'minor rebellion'. In a 'minor rebellion' the usages of war can be ignored, especially if the rebels are of a 'savage' nature. In true lawyer fashion, Prendergast supplied a number of arguments to support his general proposition, which was that the Government could act in the way it had chosen.

Prendergast's inability to recognise Maori rebels as in any way 'civilised' is consistent with the decision in *Wi Parata*; his view that the Maori in question were British subjects in rebellion against their Queen, rather than members of a foreign state, is not.[80] In *Wi Parata*, Prendergast and Richmond argued that transactions between Maori and the Crown were acts of state, yet in 1869 Prendergast argued that war between Maori and the Crown was a 'rebellion'.[81] The common law rule is that no act of state can be made against the Crown's own subjects and therefore if Crown-Maori land transactions are acts of state, logically Maori must be something other than Crown subjects. In both cases, Prendergast's interpretation of Crown-Maori relations conveniently favoured the Crown.

The 1869 correspondence between London and Wellington had been sparked by the extreme, and possibly illegal, measures adopted by the colonial government in its war with Titokowaru. Reflecting the desperation of the colonial establishment, Governor George Bowen, following the advice of Defence Minister Theodore Haultain, controversially placed a bounty on the Maori leader in 1868, to be paid on his capture, dead or alive.[82] The price was 1000 pounds.[83] Titokowaru supposedly responded by placing a price on the head of the Governor: two shillings and sixpence.[84] A five pound reward was offered for the capture of live prisoners. In his February 1869 dispatch, Earl Granville pointed out that the placing of these rewards was legally dubious.[85]

In the concluding paragraph of his June 1869 opinion, Prendergast justified this extreme measure and provided a clear statement of his pragmatic political philosophy: "The object of the Government is self-preservation. The peaceful citizens must be protected at all costs." Prendergast ended by quoting Vattel's *The Law of Nations*:[86]

> When we are at war with a savage nation, who observe no rules, and never give quarter, we may punish them in the persons of any of their people whom we take (these belonging to the number of the guilty), and endeavour, by this rigorous proceeding, to force them to respect the laws of humanity.[87]

This is akin to the concept of 'total war'.[88] With Prendergast, the ends justified the means and provided legality to otherwise illegal actions. Prendergast provided no context for the Vattel quotation, despite the fact that it was written 111 years before Prendergast's opinion and in a treatise on international law. This is representative of Prendergast's cursory approach to legal theory and intellectual contextualisation.

In reaching his conclusion, Prendergast refused to acknowledge any possible grievance motivating Maori actions. He ignored Maori claims for land retention and rangatiratanga, stating:

> The Maoris now in arms have put forward no grievance for which they seek redress. Their object, so far as it can be collected from their acts, is murder, cannibalism, and rapine. They form themselves into bands, and roam the country seeking prey.[89]

Is this merely an example of the Government's Law Officer mechanically fulfilling his duty? It is important to note both the conclusion and the language used in this quotation. As in *Wi Parata*, Prendergast could have reached a conclusion which supported the settler establishment without using emotive and damning language. Yet from the late 1860s onwards Prendergast chose to clothe his legal opinions in a discourse which consistently dismissed Maori perspectives. Prendergast demonstrated a complete inability to recognise and appreciate valid Maori concerns, for example, the struggle to retain land.

Granville was not to be assuaged by Bowen, Stafford and Prendergast. In his November 1869 dispatch,[90] he queried the right for any citizen to kill Titokowaru in accordance with colonial edict, especially since the New Zealand Government had refused to pronounce martial law.[91] In his long-delayed September 1870 opinion on the extreme measures carried out by colonial forces, Prendergast argued that "The justification of the proceedings was based on the universal and supreme law of necessity and preservation of the state."[92]

He then proceeded to use English law against the English:

> The law of England on the subject is as follows:- 'If a person having actually committed a felony will not suffer himself to be arrested . . . so that he cannot possibly be apprehended alive by those who pursue him . . . he may be lawfully slain'.[93]

Prendergast added that it is the duty of every man to prevent the escape of a felon and, if the felon is killed while fleeing, this will be justifiable homicide. He also added that the Government's motives were righteous and denied that they "were inciting on any of the people subject to its rule to an indulgence in an appetite for blood or needless cruelty".[94] Prendergast relied principally upon legal textbooks rather than specific statutes or cases. In response to Granville's request for a statutory justification, Prendergast rather cheekily gave him the English Laws Act 1858 which confirmed the reception of English law in New Zealand.

The controversy over the reward for Titokowaru spilled over from the executive to the legislature on 16 June 1869 when the House of Representatives argued the issue. Robert Creighton MP, also a leading newspaper editor, moved a motion requesting more information relating to the reward and clearly disagreed with the Government's ruthless approach, despite qualifying his position by stating he "was not a Maori worshipper, and never had been".[95] Speaker after speaker condemned

Creighton's position with arguments that can be summarised with the words of Henry Harrison: "when such ogres, such obscene beasts of prey as Titokowaru and Te Kooti appeared, he thought the Government was imperatively called upon to adopt such a course of action, and that the less said about it the better".[96] Creighton's motion was negatived. Prendergast also received strong support from non-official quarters, such as the *Evening Post*:

> Mr Prendergast's opinion, borne out by Vattel and other great authorities on the unwritten, yet well-defined, laws of nations, gives a most triumphant answer to Earl Granville's cavilling hints about the injustice and inhumanity of offering rewards for Titoko Waru [sic], Te Kooti, and others, and the unfair means we have adopted in carrying on war with the pets of Exeter Hall. Different from legal opinions in general, it is enveloped in no cloud of mystery, but is so clear and distinct that he who runs may read. We would recommend its careful perusal to those among ourselves who have hankerings after wishing the belligerent rights of nations to be conferred upon the "noble savage" who has so long been a stumbling block in the path of our advancement.[97]

This is the context in which Prendergast was making decisions. He was never in any danger of reproach from the majority of his political peers; the humanitarian concerns of the Colonial Office in London were not shared by the ruling colonial elite in New Zealand facing the prospect of continuing warfare. Atrocities on both sides reflected an increasingly bitter conflict. Ironically, by the time Prendergast penned his September 1870 opinion the guerilla campaign of Titokowaru was over and Te Kooti's resistance was waning.

In 1896, Dom Felice Vaggioli, using a quote from G. W. Rusden's controversial 1883 *History of New Zealand*, described, in his extreme way, Prendergast's reputation amongst Maori and their Pakeha supporters:

> He [Prendergast] was a bitter enemy of the Maori. 'His contemptuous scorn for the treaty of Waitangi and for the rights of Maori, who were British subjects, was clearly demonstrated by him when Government compensation for Maori heads was discussed.' He had the gall to write that the Maori had no right to be treated humanely. And this man was the colony's chief judge! Justice had fallen into such disreputable hands![98]

In analysing Prendergast's wartime opinions, David Williams has argued, "I do not think that these wartime opinions can be used as evidence that Prendergast himself had a distinctive, clearly formed and well-known personal view on Maori issues generally."[99] This statement supports the argument that Prendergast did not enter the Wars with clearly enunciated racial views. Rather the Wars helped to fix his views on Maori so that by the late 1870s he did have more "distinctive, clearly formed and well-known personal views". Williams also argues that, "The opinions show Prendergast as an officer of the Crown willing to find, as was his duty, legal arguments to support the position adopted by the colonial government he served."[100] Prendergast was asked by the Government to provide advice as to the legality of the actions and he did indeed have a duty to do this. It does not necessarily follow that Prendergast had a duty to blindly support the Government's actions, especially if he found them to be extreme or illegal. Prendergast not only delivered advice to support his Government, he delivered advice which legitimated all government violence towards Maori, no matter how extreme. The extent to which this advice reflected Prendergast's personal views, or rather the legal precedents he found, is debatable, but what is certain is that Prendergast, as Attorney-General, signed his name to these legal opinions.

Prendergast demonstrated a binary response to the New Zealand Wars. He used his powers both to crush Maori resistance and to protect colonial leaders. Throughout his career as Attorney-General and Chief Justice, Prendergast showed a willingness to side with the ruling elite, especially the conservative elements of the elite. In 1868, Prendergast provided a legal opinion on the question of indemnity for officials who committed crimes, including those committed in the course of suppressing rebellion. As in 1866, Prendergast sought to protect military commanders and his fellow political leaders:

> I am of opinion that if the Colonial Legislature, by Act, authorizes the Governor or any officer or other person to adopt any measures for suppression of rebellion or other disturbances, no Court of Law in Great Britain could adjudge any act done under such authority to be a crime. The Legislature of New Zealand may also, after unauthorized and illegal acts have been done in suppression of rebellion, by Act, indemnify or pardon the person so acting on account of and for such acts, and I am of opinion that such an Act, if not disallowed by the Queen, would be pleadable in all Courts in England, and be a discharge there as well as here.[101]

In authorising retrospective legislation to indemnify criminal acts, Prendergast was once again justifying extreme measures that potentially undermined the rule of law in New Zealand. Despite his outlook as a loyal imperialist, Prendergast was ready to prioritise the colonial reality over London's sensibilities. While Prendergast may have used extreme measures, Acts of indemnity were passed in other colonies. In fact, the ability of colonial officials to suspend due process during internal conflicts became a *cause célèbre* debate in Britain during the late 1860s after Governor Eyre's brutal repression of the 1865 Jamaican Rebellion.[102] In waging war during the late 1860s, the colonial government looked to James Prendergast to legally bless its more dubious actions.[103] This pattern climaxed in the section 20 'indemnity clause' of the Disturbed Districts Act 1869.

Prendergast's legal opinions earned him a reputation as an unforgiving enemy of Maori in arms against the Government. There is no evidence that Prendergast was ever well disposed towards Maori, but this section shows a progression from more moderate views and actions in 1865 to more hard-line views and actions during the late 1860s and 1870s. Prendergast had experienced a baptism by fire in his role as wartime Attorney-General. Most of his contact with Maori from 1865 to the early 1870s was in the context of a bloody colonial war.

B. *The 1869 treason trials*

During the latter stages of the New Zealand Wars the colonial government also looked to Prendergast to provide symbolic vengeance by prosecuting scapegoats. Due to the failure to capture Te Kooti and Tikokowaru, the Government had to make do with punishing lesser protagonists. In September and October 1869, the Government prosecuted 83 Maori prisoners in the Wellington Supreme Court for treason.[104] These prisoners had been captured during the campaigns against Titokowaru and Te Kooti. Presiding was Justice Alexander Johnston, with Attorney-General Prendergast and Wellington Crown Solicitor Charles Izard representing the Crown as prosecutors. William Allan was appointed by the Crown to defend the prisoners.

By 1869 Prendergast was well-established in Wellington as Attorney-General, and this vast trial was the most high-profile court appearance of his career as an advocate. All except three of the Maori prisoners were tried under the recently passed Disturbed Districts Act 1869. The Act was only imposed for a short period, but its sweeping disregard for due process reflected the bitter state of New Zealand race relations during the late 1860s.[105] It would be difficult to imagine a clearer example of emotive law-drafting than that found in the preamble:

> Whereas certain aboriginal Natives subjects of Her Majesty within the Colony of New Zealand have for a long time been and are now in open rebellion and engaged in levying war against the Queen many of whom have been guilty of outrages and atrocities such as murder rape torturing of prisoners and cannibalism. And whereas in the course of such rebellion large tracts of settled country have been devastated whole families have been massacred in cold blood and much property has been destroyed whereby the Colony has become impoverished its people disheartened and its resources exhausted in the attempt to suppress rebellion. And whereas it is expedient to amend and adapt the ordinary course of law for the purpose of promptly bringing to punishment persons engaged in such rebellion.

The section 20 indemnity clause virtually gave the colonial forces discretion to act in any way necessary: "No act matter or thing done in any such proclaimed district as aforesaid in pursuance or execution of any power or authority hereby conferred shall be questioned in any Court having jurisdiction civil or criminal except as herein mentioned."

Prendergast, as non-political Attorney-General, played the leading role in drafting this statute. In support of the argument that Prendergast's views towards Maori were becoming increasingly extreme, he was ordered by Premier Fox to revise his original bill to make it "less violent and repulsive to the constitutional rights".[106] The Act allowed the Attorney-General special powers, including the power to dispense with the grand jury process. The Supreme Court was effectively reconstituted as a quasi-military tribunal with the ability to override due process, for example, the suspension of habeas corpus for six months after detention in custody.[107] When Walter Mantell discovered that the prisoners were possibly being detained without warrants he threatened to apply for habeas corpus. The threat was a hollow one, as Colonial Secretary Gisborne pointed out: "[he] hoped the honourable member would not lose his money on such an object, as the Disturbed Districts Bill, which had passed the Assembly, would legalize the trial of the prisoners".[108] Prendergast's statute effectively allowed the Government to obtain convictions without being restricted by due process.

There is nothing to indicate that Prendergast took extreme measures *during* the actual trials.[109] However, this was a set-piece forum to demonstrate government power. As Attorney-General, Prendergast orchestrated the set-piece on behalf of the Government. In seeking the death penalty in respect of three of the accused,[110] Prendergast's trial strategy could be considered ruthless and arbitrary, but the Crown was open from the beginning about its intention only to seek the death penalty in respect of aggravated treason and rebellion, for example, the perpetration of the Matawhero massacre.[111] As with the *Wi Parata* decision and the invasion of Parihaka, the 1869 trials have become iconic symbols of colonial oppression. This is principally due to the conviction and execution of Hamiora Pere, one of Te Kooti's warriors.

Pere was possibly forced to fight for Te Kooti after being captured. He was later captured again after the bloody siege of Ngatapa in 1868, this time by colonial troops. As an example to other Maori rebels, Pere was charged with, and convicted of, high treason and levying war against the Queen.[112] It is arguable that Pere was not guilty beyond reasonable doubt, or at least, did not deserve the death sentence. This argument is based on the evidence produced by Prendergast being circumstantial, Pere's possible inability to comprehend the crime of treason and the possibility that he may have acted under duress. His trial features prominently in the 2004 Turanganui a Kiwa (Gisborne) Waitangi Tribunal Report.[113] The Tribunal presents a convincing argument that ultimately agrees with the treason conviction but not the sentence.[114]

Through historical fiction, leading New Zealand novelists Maurice Shadbolt and Witi Ihimaera have helped to return Hamiora Pere to New Zealand public consciousness.[115] The final section of Shadbolt's *Season of the Jew* focuses on Pere's trial. In the novel, Pere's defence lawyer describes Prendergast in less than flattering terms: "His [Fox's] Attorney-General, a devious monster named Prendergast, is taking the case. Prendergast will make the trial his next step up the ladder to the post of Chief Justice. He knows what Fox needs."[116] During the trial, Prendergast emerges as a cold, formal, but not especially malicious figure: "his youthful face suggested disdain for the business on hand, and his voice professional impatience".[117] Prendergast, the Machiavellian lawyer, is apparent in Shadbolt's description: "It seemed Prendergast was not one to rely on the letter of the law to win a conviction . . . . never at a loss in milking the last drop of prejudice."[118] Prendergast was of course successful in his prosecution but is given a reprieve by Shadbolt in the final stages of the trial, as Johnston takes the mantle of villain: "Prendergast, with compassion apparent for the first time, permitted Fairweather to leave the witness stand . . . . Prendergast, as if fatigued by truths too familiar, made a passionless summary of the crown case."[119]

Commentators have raised questions relating to the integrity of the 1869 trials and, in particular, the trial and execution of Pere,[120] but it is important to see the trials in the context of the period. Five of the prisoners were accused of direct participation in the Matawhero massacre which occurred just outside Gisborne on 10 November 1868. Te Kooti's forces murdered 60 inhabitants, including men, women and children, both Maori and Pakeha. While Te Kooti's violence may have been in response to his unjust imprisonment on the Chatham Islands, it is impossible to justify the brutality of this raid on a civilian population.[121] The 1869 trials were partly an attempt by the Government to seek justice for those who died at Matawhero. This attempt failed primarily due to the inability to bring the key perpetrators, and in particular Te Kooti, before the court.

The prisoner Wi Tamararo was convicted of murdering Pera Kararehe at Matawhero,[122] but he committed suicide in prison before he could be executed, thereby robbing the Government of a powerful symbolic execution. Hamiora Pere was used instead, despite being convicted on less convincing evidence than Tamararo.[123] All the prisoners tried were found guilty, but Pere was the only prisoner executed. Whether justified or not, the executive and judiciary were open about the exemplary nature of the sentence, as seen in Johnston J's letter to Governor Bowen: "I am glad to know that Mr. [Donald] McLean thinks that one execution will be as useful as more would have been, by way of example and caution."[124] The Government's attempt to provide justice created a perception of further injustice. Prendergast played a pivotal role in the 1869 trials. The high drama of the event allowed him to directly participate in a life-and-death battle between Maori and the Crown, albeit of a legal nature. It also cemented his reputation as the 'wartime' Attorney-General.

The actions of Titokowaru and Te Kooti created palpable fear and rage in the settler community, while government campaigns and confiscations devastated Maori society. The 1869 trials serve as the most high-profile example of Prendergast's work as wartime Attorney-General. The trials also symbolise the fraught nature of the cultural encounter between Prendergast and Maori in arms against the Crown. It must be noted that Prendergast's views and actions related in this section did not specifically relate to those Maori who fought for the Crown.

Prendergast is the most infamous judge in New Zealand's history exclusively due to his legal actions relating to Maori. Without the contextual understanding provided in this book, Prendergast becomes a 'cardboard cut-out' villain whose racial attitudes exist because of this villainy. This is an inadequate approach to history. Giselle Byrnes summarises this approach in relation to Waitangi Tribunal historiography:

> the European historical characters who appear in these narratives are typecast largely as one-dimensional individuals . . . . this includes the inversion of colonist personas, where they are transformed from heroes to villains; the vague and rather thin descriptions of Crown officials; the negation of difference within the European settler community, and the assumption that all settlers thought and therefore acted in the same manner; the polarisation of Maori and European world views and habits of thought as mutually exclusive; and finally, the passing of moral judgments and the creation of 'good' and 'bad' characters.[125]

Prendergast played an important role in the New Zealand Wars as Attorney-General. His actions were not token, but rather instrumental in executing and intensifying the Wars. The colonial establishment requested his support as Attorney-General and he provided it wholeheartedly. In both actions and words, Prendergast supplied the Government with legal ammunition to wage war on Maori. An analysis of Prendergast's actions and words shows that at times he went above and beyond what could be expected of a colonial official in terms of treatment of indigenous peoples. The defence that Prendergast was 'only following orders' is a weak one. Prendergast's attitude toward Maori became more extreme as the conflict developed.

As in the *Wi Parata* decision, Prendergast was continually open to legal interpretations favouring colonial power during the New Zealand Wars, for example, in his justification of bounties. These opinions clashed with the more liberal-minded views of the Colonial Office but were largely popular with New Zealand's leaders, and most of its Pakeha population.

4. Advisor to the Government

As Attorney-General from 1865 to 1875, Prendergast fulfilled a variety of roles: legal expert in the Legislative Council for two years, legal advisor to the Government, legal advocate for the Government in the higher courts, President of the Law Society and chief drafter of legislation. As legal advisor, Prendergast's opinion was often sought on matters of national importance. This chapter has already closely analysed Prendergast's opinions relating to the New Zealand Wars but it is important to look at other areas to provide a balanced assessment.

With Prendergast's appointment as non-political Attorney-General in 1867, his role of providing opinions to the Government increased. From 1867 to 1875, successive governments consulted Prendergast on issues ranging from conduct during the New Zealand Wars to guano-collecting on the Bounty Islands. Matters of confusion between the New Zealand Government and Imperial Britain were often passed to Prendergast for his opinion. During 1867, clashes appeared between Imperial legislation and the New Zealand Land Registry Act 1860.[126] The legal obstacles were preventing the introduction of the 1860 Act and Prendergast studiously analysed the situation, eventually recommending that the Imperial Parliament legislate to remove conflicting law.

Another issue facing Stafford's Government in 1867 was the administration of Vice-Admiralty Courts for the colony. Prendergast argued strongly for the reform of this jurisdiction to make it more efficient and practical. The reasoning of the Attorney-General was clear:

> I think that the step that should be taken is to bring to the attention of the Secretary of the Colonies the Resolution of the House, and the necessity there is for the establishment of a Vice-Admiralty Court in various parts of the Colony, arising from the great distances of the several ports from each other, and the unfrequent communication between the various parts of the Colony.[127]

Prendergast's opinion highlighted the limited communication networks that existed in New Zealand during the 1860s. During the 1870s, the Vogel Government would invest heavily in creating a communications and transportation infrastructure. Due to the structure of the New Zealand court system during the 1860s, Prendergast suggested that the simplest remedy was to make each Supreme Court judge (Auckland, Wellington, Nelson, Christchurch and Dunedin) also a judge of the Vice-Admiralty Court for his province. Before 1867, only Chief Justice Arney, presiding in Auckland, was a Vice-Admiralty judge. As New Zealand was a maritime colony with poor connections between major cities, one judge sitting in the north of the North Island could not effectively serve the rest of the colony on matters of maritime law. Prendergast was supported by the judges of the Supreme Court.

Land was at the centre of many, if not most, of the political controversies from 1865 to 1875. Available lands in New Zealand were contested by various power groups, including the Crown, Maori, the provinces, individual developers and overseas interests. A Select Committee investigating disputed land in Dunedin, 'the Princes St Reserves', called on Attorney-General Prendergast for advice. The issues included the validity of Crown grants, the separation of powers between central government and the provinces, and Maori land rights.[128] Prendergast also represented the Crown in court in *R v Macandrew* (1869).[129] As Williams explains:

> Those critical of Prendergast as Chief Justice should note that in 1869 as Attorney-General he was both defending the government's policies on war bounties for 'rebels' and also was the prosecutor on the record for this case

supporting Ngai Tahu's rights to the Princes Street reserves. Lawyers argue the cases that their clients require them to argue.[130]

Prendergast was unsuccessful in annulling the Crown grant so that the reserves could be created for Ngai Tahu. The court's staunch refusal not to look behind a Crown grant was echoed eight years later in Prendergast and Richmond's *Wi Parata* judgment. Prendergast's legal legacy is primarily in the area of land ownership, around which issues of sovereignty and individual rights revolve.

Constitutional issues also occupied the time and attention of Attorney-General Prendergast. Only two years after Prendergast had been appointed to the Legislative Council, he was asked to provide his opinion on a number of controversial appointments.[131] The powers and jurisdiction of the Governor formed another constitutional issue which arose during the late 1860s, and in 1874 Prendergast advised the Government to delay the beginning of the parliamentary session due to a constitutional irregularity.

The period from 1865 to 1875 was a pivotal ten years in the development of the New Zealand legal system. With the advent of responsible government in 1856, New Zealand politicians sought to create a new society through legislation. After emerging victorious from the New Zealand Wars, the colonial government began the creation of a 'Better Britain'[132] in earnest. Prendergast was at the forefront of this movement. A large amount of legislation was passed during his Attorney-Generalship and older legislation was rationalised and sometimes discarded. In 1871, Prendergast analysed a host of ordinances made by the provincial governments and found many of their sections *ultra vires*, for example section 16 of Wellington's Fencing Act 1867 and section 37 of Auckland's Highways Act 1867.[133] Prendergast provided several important opinions relating to the validity of Provincial Council ordinances. As in all federalised systems, difficult questions arose over the relationships between provincial and national legislation. Prendergast developed a systematic and methodical process for ascertaining the validity of provincial law.

During 1871, Prendergast delivered an opinion concerning a libel case taken by the Fox Government against George B. Barton, lawyer and editor of the *Otago Daily Times*. George B. Barton was known as 'long Barton', as opposed to Prendergast's nemesis, George E. Barton, who was referred to as 'little Barton'.[134] The Bartons, though not related, shared similar causes and both were outspoken public figures. In this case:

> Barton alleged that there had been manipulation by the Government of the telegraph service, which resulted in messages intended for the *Otago Daily Times* being withheld and supplied first to other sources which were more pro-Government in outlook. There were protracted hearings and, with politics involved, tense feelings developed. Later the argument on behalf of the New Zealand Government, in justification of the conduct of its Ministers, was dealt with in a memorandum from the then Attorney-General, Sir James Prendergast.[135]

In the memorandum, Prendergast explained how he had advised the Governor to pardon a Charles Muston, whose evidence proved Barton to be the author of the defamatory words.

Questions arose during the trial as to whether the Governor had the ability to grant a pardon before a conviction was obtained, with Prendergast again providing an opinion which pleased the Government:

> There can be no doubt that it is necessary that the Governor of a Colony, such as any situated at so great a distance from England as is New Zealand, should have the power to promise free pardons, and to fulfil his promise; and that any limitation upon this power, such as it is contended is contained in the Commission, would be found to create grave difficulties in the administration of the Government and of justice.[136]

In 1871, the prosecution abandoned the case, handing a victory to Barton. As editor of the *New Zealand Jurist* during the 1870s, Barton was an opponent of several of Prendergast's more controversial actions.

Prendergast was involved in the development of the New Zealand university system from its earliest beginnings. From 1884 to 1903, Prendergast served on the New Zealand University Senate.[137] In November 1871, Prendergast supplied an opinion supporting the right of the University of Otago to confer degrees under the Otago University Ordinance 1869.[138] This issue resulted from the establishment of the University of New Zealand in 1870. In his opinion on Otago University degrees, Prendergast sought a balance between the two competing powers: "I think that the Ordinance is not *ultra vires*, and that degrees may be conferred under it, but such degrees will be recognized and give rank and precedence only within the Province."

Not all of Prendergast's legal opinions were officially published. Much personal correspondence passed between Prendergast and the Premier and Governor regarding important matters of state. For example, on 19 August 1868, Governor Bowen reported to Prendergast that his views on the re-swearing of the Executive on the arrival of a new Governor had been supported by Law Officers in London. Bowen invited Prendergast to meet with him personally to discuss the issue further.[139] In another example, on 15 June 1869, Prendergast reluctantly provided a non-professional legal opinion for Walter Buller.[140]

During his first two years as Attorney-General, Prendergast was placed in the difficult position of being the Attorney-General based in Wellington and also acting as Crown Solicitor for Otago and senior partner of a Dunedin law firm. Prendergast's correspondence during 1865–66 demonstrates the logistical difficulties and conflicts of interest he faced.[141] During 1866, Prendergast was involved in the trial of the infamous Burgess Gang (Robert Hart prosecuted for the Crown in Nelson). Interestingly, Michael Prendergast had earlier defended

Thomas Kelly and Richard Burgess in Dunedin in May 1862 on the charge of shooting with intent. Michael's defence was unsuccessful and somewhat erratic.[142] Over a period of several years the gang had committed a series of grisly crimes, including the infamous Maungatapu murders of 1866. The first 'Maungatapu Murders' trial resulted in the execution of Burgess, Kelly and Phil Levy, while the second trial acquitted James Wilson of wrongdoing, followed by Wilson's counsel unsuccessfully attempting to lay the charge of murder on Joseph Sullivan. As the key Crown witness, Sullivan (one of the gang members), needed protection before, during and after the second trial, and much of Prendergast's correspondence is from Dunedin regarding a case being heard in Nelson and Wellington.[143]

In November 1866, Prendergast authorised the removal of Sullivan from Nelson gaol to Hokitika for the second trial. The decision was difficult to enforce, as Sullivan was possibly the most hated man in the colony at this point. Sullivan's movements were to be kept secret but:

> Despite this, word leaked out, and when the steamer carrying the informer was seen off Hokitika in December, a large crowd was awaiting developments. All available police marched to the wharf, surrounded by a mob calling for Sullivan to be lynched. When the passengers began disembarking, there was no sign of him amongst the waiting police. He had been brought ashore in a whaleboat while the vessel was still outside the bar and was already in the Revell Street Gaol.[144]

Hokitika was part of Westland, the final province to be created before the end of the provincial system in 1875. It became an independent county on 1 January 1868 and a province on 1 December 1873.[145] As a developing region, it needed a court system to administer justice. Prendergast was involved in the appointing of a District Court judge in Westland during 1870 and the establishment of rules and regulations for the Court.[146] The telegraph provided an effective form of communication between Wellington and Hokitika during this period.

The final years of Prendergast's time as Attorney-General were dominated by the bitter and protracted dispute over the abolition of the provinces. Throughout the period 1865 to 1875, tension had been evident between provincialists, led by Grey and Fox, and centralists, led by Stafford. In 1872, Colonial Treasurer Julius Vogel requested an opinion from Prendergast over responsibility for toll collection at the Wanganui Bridge. Prendergast's opinion reflects an attempt to address the concerns of both province and central government:

> the Colonial Treasurer [Vogel] cannot now insist upon receiving the tolls or appointing collectors. Nevertheless, the Colonial Government cannot, by anything that has taken place, be deemed to have assented to the Province denuding itself of those revenues which are derivable from the tolls.[147]

The argument over the provinces, originally established by George Grey under the Constitution Act 1852, reached a climax during 1874–5. In the high-profile

Court of Appeal case *Attorney-General v Bunny*, the Wellington Provincial Council represented by William Travers faced Attorney-General Prendergast representing the Vogel Government. The Bridges, Roads, and other Works Appropriation Act 1874, passed by the Wellington Provincial Council, was disallowed by the Governor. The Bench of the Court of Appeal hearing the case consisted of Arney CJ, Johnston J, Gresson J and Richmond J. A year later, with the retirement of Arney, these judges would be under the leadership of Prendergast. William Fitzherbert, the ultra-provincialist superintendent of the Wellington Province, and his treasurer, Henry Bunny, challenged the ability of the Government to intervene in provincial law-making.[148] Prendergast was successful. A year later the provinces were abolished under the Abolition of Provinces Act 1875. Ironically, the 1875 Act was passed by Vogel's Government. Vogel had originally been a staunch defender of the provincial system.

Prendergast supported Vogel's move to abolish the provincial system. In one of his final acts as Attorney-General, he based his opinion on the Act of the Imperial Parliament (31 and 32 Vict, or 1868/9), which had the long title, "An Act to declare the Powers of the General Assembly to abolish any Province, or to withdraw from any such Province any part of the Territory thereof".[149] With the backing of Imperial Britain and the Vogel Government, the provinces were swept aside despite a desperate effort by George Grey to rally support for their continued existence. In this matter of grave political importance, Prendergast looked towards English legal experts to support his finding:

> though I see no room for doubt or question, I think that it would be well that the Secretary of State should be asked to take the opinion of the Law Officers in England; and if any doubt whatever is entertained by them, that a Bill should at once be passed for removing the doubt.[150]

Prendergast's views on the provinces debate aroused the anger of George Grey. While Chief Justice in August 1875, Prendergast defended himself against charges from Grey that he had later expressed a differing opinion about the power to abolish the provinces. Speaking in Parliament, Grey claimed that Prendergast had later given a differing opinion supposedly supporting the provinces, but Prendergast flatly denied this in a letter dated 2 August 1875. Prendergast's relationship with the 'Liberal' leaders, Grey and Stout, was often strained. With such an influential position, Prendergast was always bound to cause offence to some parties. The role of Attorney-General required opinions on extremely controversial issues and the overseeing of drafting of pivotal legislation. Much of the key legislation during the period 1865–1875 would be interpreted by Prendergast as Chief Justice, centring an extraordinary amount of legal power in one man. While Prendergast was often soft-spoken and retiring, his power was real and his influence growing all the time.

5. The Government's advocate

As Attorney-General, Prendergast also represented the Government in the Supreme Court and Court of Appeal (though primarily in the Court of Appeal). A detailed description of Prendergast's advocacy in the 1869–70 New Zealand Wars cases has already been provided. Prendergast was also involved in a number of other important cases from 1865 to 1875. Many of these were reported in the Court of Appeal Reports, edited by Johnston J. Johnston was the resident Wellington Supreme Court judge during this period. Given the lack of formal law reporting during this period, the other key source is contemporary newspapers, in particular, the *Evening Post*.[151] Johnston's reports focus on those cases providing important legal precedents, whereas the newspaper's focus is on cases of public interest.

After his advocacy experience in London and Dunedin, Prendergast was a seasoned lawyer and proved an effective barrister. In his court appearances as Attorney-General, Prendergast worked with leading lawyers such as William Travers and argued against high-profile advocates such as Robert Stout and Frederick Chapman. The Court of Appeal Bench at this time included Johnston and Richmond JJ, both of whom would later serve under Prendergast as Chief Justice.

A survey of *Evening Post* court reports during this period provides a rough idea of Prendergast's court workload in Wellington. The survey is limited due to the fact that while most criminal cases in the superior courts were reported in the newspaper, only some civil cases (the most common type of case) were reported. Prendergast appears in 64 case reports from the Wellington Supreme Court (43 civil/21 criminal) and 42 from the Court of Appeal, which sat in Wellington (34 civil/8 criminal). Prendergast's court workload was not evenly balanced throughout the period. For example, nearly half of Prendergast's Supreme Court appearances relate to the 1869–70 New Zealand Wars cases. With the exception of these atypical two years, and for some reason 1874, Prendergast averaged only a few reported court appearances in a calendar year. In 1865 and 1866, Prendergast's advocacy was primarily in Dunedin as Crown Solicitor (55 cases in 1866).[152] He also represented the Crown in a small number of cases outside Wellington, most famously in the 1868 trial of William Larkin and John Manning in Hokitika.

Analysing Prendergast the judge using primary sources is much easier than analysing Prendergast the litigator. Johnston's reports and the newspaper articles provide summaries and some excerpts from Prendergast in court but these provide limited insights into Prendergast's legal contributions. Prendergast the lawyer is arguing on behalf of his client rather than taking an objective legal position. By definition, an advocate is not providing a personal view, but presenting the position of the client in the best possible light. Prendergast was involved in a number of high-profile cases, for example, *Attorney-General v Bunny*,[153] which focused on the division of power between central and provincial governments; *In re "The Lundon and Whitaker Claims Act 1871"*[154] which focused on Maori land issues and the schemes of Frederick Whitaker; and the mid-1869 Native Land Court hearing regarding the sale of Maori land in the Rangitikei-Manawatu region (the area in which Prendergast would soon make major private land purchases). Prendergast also provided legal opinions on these issues in his role as advisor to the Crown.

With the exception of the New Zealand Wars trials, Prendergast's most famous court appearance as Attorney-General was in the *cause célèbre* trial of newspaper editor John Manning and Irish Catholic priest William Larkin in May 1868. Both men were outspoken Irish nationalists and supporters of home rule. The trial took place during sectarian tension on the West Coast, in particular, the so-called Battle of Addison's Flat in April 1868, a clash between Irish loyalists and nationalists. Manning had fought with the Eureka Stockade defenders and was one of the accused in the subsequent trials, which had featured Michael Prendergast as an advocate.

The controversy featured two trials. The first trial concerned charges of inciting rioting and forcible entry. Manning and Larkin, along with the five other accused men, took part in a mock funeral in support of Irish nationalists recently executed in Britain, the 'Manchester Martyrs'. During the protest the marchers tore up a cemetery gate in order to plant a Celtic cross and lay an empty coffin in the Hokitika cemetery. Unfortunately for the protesters, this show of solidarity coincided with the assassination attempt upon the Duke of Edinburgh in Sydney by an Irish nationalist.

In an added touch of glamour, Irish miners funded Australia's top criminal barrister and former Victorian Attorney-General, Robert Ireland, to represent the defendants. The aptly named Australian was treated as a celebrity upon his arrival on the West Coast. Prendergast, the safe but predictable special pleader, squared off against a true legal legend and top criminal defence lawyer, in the rowdy, bustling gold town of Hokitika.

Both cases were heard in the Supreme Court before Richmond J. The defendants pleaded not guilty in the first trial but all were found guilty. Prendergast held his own in the first trial, delivering a strong opening statement and careful examination-in-chief and cross-examination. He provided a balanced summary of the charges but showed little empathy with Irish nationalism, accurately describing the 'Manchester Martyrs' as "men who by the law of the land have been condemned and executed as murderers".[155] Prendergast grappled with the relationship between unlawful assembly and sedition. The language used by Prendergast in this trial cannot be termed 'anti-Catholic' despite the sectarian tension surrounding the trial. When Ireland challenged Prendergast on a seemingly dismissive reference to Catholicism, Prendergast told the court that:

When I spoke, your Honour, of a mock funeral, I meant no disrespect to the members of the Catholic Church, I was merely stating what one of the witnesses had stated who, probably, as a Protestant not used to Catholic ceremonies, would feel somewhat surprised that a funeral ceremony should take place and no corpses be present.[156]

The second trial was for seditious libel on the part of Manning and Larkin. This resulted from a war of words between their pro-Catholic newspaper, *New Zealand Celt*, and the anti-Irish Home Rule newspaper, the *West Coast Times*. Manning and Larkin decided to enter a plea of guilty and were each sentenced to a month's imprisonment.[157] Overall, the sentences for all defendants on all counts were lenient. In judging and prosecuting this trial, Richmond J and Attorney-General Prendergast showed professionalism and tolerance. The situation was a potential powder-keg in 1860s colonial New Zealand. The fact that it never exploded is partly due to these two men.[158]

In high-profile trials such as this, Prendergast cemented his place as one of New Zealand's leading lawyers. The commentary on his court performances is generally positive. Prendergast approached court work in a methodical, focused way while also managing to inject the occasional quip and political or societal reference.

6. Drafting legislation

One of Prendergast's most important legal legacies is the body of legislation introduced from 1865 to 1875. Prendergast played an integral role in the formulation of many of the 926 Acts introduced during this ten-year period. To gain an understanding of Prendergast's role in developing statute law, key statutes must be analysed. From this analysis, the legal historian can view Prendergast's style, substance and reliance on other jurisdictions. While every statute was important enough to be passed by the New Zealand Parliament, the Offences against the Person Act 1867 is of more general and lasting importance than, for example, the Wairarapa Racecourse Exchange Act 1867. It must also be pointed out that Prendergast was aided in the formulation of legislation by fellow politicians, his staff in the Attorney-General's Department, officials in the Judicial Branch of the Colonial Office, and other leading figures. The key figure in the physical drafting was actually the Assistant Law Officer, who worked directly under Prendergast. The Attorney-General was ultimately responsible for advising the Government as to the drafting of all Bills, whether or not they were specifically drawn up by the Attorney-General and his staff.

Legislation from the 1860s and 1870s has similarities and differences to the legislation of the present day. Much of the legislation is brief and written in semi-archaic English, for example: "Subject and in addition to the conditions hereinbefore contained every such lease shall contain such covenants stipulations and conditions as the Court shall decree expedient with reference to the special circumstances of the demise".[159] There is also a heavy reliance on English legislation and sometimes wholesale adoption of specific English statutes.

The legislation from 1865 to 1875 covers a range of areas, though there is a clear emphasis on land law and introducing a criminal code. Both these areas were of particular interest to Prendergast. Certain statutes deal with issues that are non-existent or of little relevance to present-day society, for example, the Railway Offences Act 1865. Some statutes are still very relevant, for example, the Debtors and Creditors Act 1865. According to the Parliamentary Counsel Office's website,[160] only one national statute from the period is still in force,[161] along with 19 local Acts (although this could be through a lack of updating). Despite this confusion, many of Prendergast's Acts have been used as the basis for more recent pieces of legislation.

Commentators on Prendergast's statutes focus on his criminal legislation and dense prose. Prendergast's colleague, William Gisborne, described the statutes as "shocking examples of the old style of Acts of Parliament in the time of the Georges, when 'words, words, words', paraphrase and parenthesis created a block worse than any caused by carts, cabs, and 'buses in these days in the City".[162] As Colonial Secretary from 1869 to 1872, Gisborne worked closely with Prendergast during this period. Scholefield cites Prendergast's impressive achievements in "consolidating the criminal law of the Colony", and notes that he "succeeded in getting passed by Parliament no less than 94 acts with this object".[163] Prendergast had no practical experience in legal drafting when he became Attorney-General in 1865, but he did have recent experience of English legal developments, and he therefore relied heavily on Imperial legislation. Prendergast had a moderate amount of success in modifying English law to fit the New Zealand environment, but in certain areas, such as law relating to Maori, Prendergast failed to modify 'foreign' law to take into account the presence of Maori society.

The growing importance of legislation has been a theme throughout New Zealand legal history. Following the shift in focus of English law from case law to statute, New Zealand has become one of the most heavily legislated nations in the world. The speed and flexibility of statute law was of great assistance in the task of quickly creating a settler society in New Zealand. Case law takes many years to develop and New Zealand judges tended to rely heavily on English common law until relatively recent times. In creating the unique New Zealand legal system, the statute has been the most effective tool and therefore New Zealand governments have always wielded a huge amount of power.

When analysing the importance of statutes from well over a century ago, the historian tends to focus on statutes which have continued to have influence in hindsight. For example, during Prendergast's time as Attorney-General, landmark statutes were passed, such as the Maori Representation Act 1867 (which created the four Maori seats), the Land Transfer Act 1870 (which introduced the Torrens system of land registration), the New Zealand Law Society's Act 1869 (which created the Law Society), and the Offences Against the Person Act 1867 (which helped form the basis of the Crimes Act 1961). Unlike the present day, legal expertise was a relatively rare commodity in mid-nineteenth-century colonial New Zealand. Prendergast, though aided by competent colleagues, demonstrated strong legal leadership in his legislative actions.

While serving in the Legislative Council, Prendergast initiated and introduced 30 public bills. This was an impressive achievement but these efforts formed only a minority of the 176 public bills introduced during 1865 and 1866.[164] It is unclear how many bills Prendergast drafted of the 146 which he did not introduce. This task would have been shared with the Assistant Law Officer. Officially, the Attorney-General was responsible for the drafting of legislation:

> the work of drafting legislation was first carried out by the Attorney-General and his officers. In 1873 a Crown Law Office was set up, and four years later the first Law Draftsman was appointed as a member of this Office.[165]

The structure of this area of government was erratic and confused from 1865 to 1872. When Prendergast became Attorney-General in October 1865, John Fountain was the Assistant Law Officer. Although under the Attorney-General's Department, Fountain also answered to the Colonial Secretary through his role as bureaucratic head of the Judicial Branch of the Colonial Secretary's Department. In 1867 one of Wellington's leading lawyers, Robert Hart, took over as Assistant Law Officer. Despite performing well in the role, Hart could not accept the restrictions placed on his private legal work and resigned within a year.[166] William Pharazyn, a Wellington lawyer from the influential Pharazyn family,[167] replaced Hart and continued to work for Prendergast until his premature death in 1872, aged only 30. During his final two years Pharazyn's health hampered his ability to carry out the demanding job. In fact, it was reported that the job itself had led to the health problems,[168] though a diagnosis of tuberculosis is more accurate.[169] In 1871, Pharazyn resigned the full-time position but "continued, however, to do some work for the Attorney-General".[170] Prendergast's long-time professional friend and ally William Travers helped out on an ad hoc basis. When Travers was questioned as to the nature of his agreement with Prendergast, he stated that "from personal friendship for Mr Prendergast, [he] offered his own services, as far as he could give them".[171]

In 1872, major structural changes were put in place. The Crown Law Office was created, with the Attorney-General as its head. Walter Reid took the position of Assistant Law Officer. The Judicial Branch was transformed into the Department of Justice, the forerunner of today's Ministry of Justice. The Crown Law Office was responsible for drafting legislation. When Prendergast left for the bench in

1875, the Attorney-General position once more became political and Reid was appointed non-political Solicitor-General and head of the Crown Law Office (as is the case today).[172] Reid continued in this role until 1900. The nature of Prendergast and Reid's working relationship was described as follows:

> That our statute law then requires careful revision and consolidation is admitted on all hands, and, as our legislators are not of course possessed of the requisite legal knowledge to undertake the task themselves, it behoves them to employ men by training and experience fitted to do it for them. Mr Reid has been a practising New Zealand solicitor, and his experience as such and as a clerk previous to admission, well fitted him for the post he held, whilst Mr Prendergast's extensive practice as counsel and solicitor enabled him to turn Mr Reid's knowledge to the best advantage, and the two formed an extremely valuable combination.[173]

Prendergast and Reid were assisted by a small number of clerks including Hudson Williamson and Alexander Gray, both of whom would become leading New Zealand lawyers.[174] Reid and Prendergast would work successfully together again on the 1882 court reforms.

After being made non-political Attorney-General in March 1867, Prendergast would have been able to devote more time to the drafting process. He did not individually compose every statute from 1865 to 1875, but he would have had an integral role in the formation of the legislation. Therefore, the body of legislation passed from 1865 to 1875 can be referred to as 'Prendergast's statutes'.

Prendergast's involvement in creating statute law began in 1865. In the *Journal of the Legislative Council* 1865, Prendergast is credited with initiating the following public bills: Sale and Lease of Settled Estates, Bank Shareholders Liability (lapsed), District Courts Act Amendment, Sale of Poisons Regulation (lapsed), Commencement of Acts, Otago Provincial Public Offices Site, Printing and Publishing Regulation (lapsed), Fisheries Protection (lapsed), Legislative Council Quorum, and Grants and Leases Validation (lapsed).[175]

Important Acts passed in 1865 included the Debtors and Creditors Act, the Law Practitioners Amendment Act, the Native Lands Act (which set up the Native Land Court and discussed Crown grants) and the New Zealand Settlements Amendment and Continuance Act. One which had a direct impact on Prendergast was the Wellington Supreme Court House Site Act 1865. Under this Act, the Government acquired land from the Presbyterian Church to use as a site for the new court in which Prendergast would act as an advocate and adjudicator.

During 1866, Prendergast was political Attorney-General for the whole parliamentary period, and he made his presence felt with a raft of legislation. The following public bills were initiated by Prendergast in 1866: Partnership Law Amendment, Resident Magistrates (lapsed), District Courts Jurisdiction Extension, Criminal Law Procedure, Appeals from Justice (lapsed), Justices of the

Peace, Offences Against the Person, Summary Procedure on Bills Amendment, Supreme Court Practice and Procedure Amendment, Sale of Poisons, Aliens, Law Practitioners Amendment, Innkeepers Liability, Justices of the Peace Acts Repeal, Intestate Estates Amendment, Affirmation in lieu of Oaths in Criminal Proceedings, Lunatics, Justices Protection, New Zealand Post Office Amendment (No. 2), and Wellington Hospital Reserve (lapsed).[176]

Legislation of particular importance in 1866 included the Law Practitioners Amendment Act, the Criminal Law Procedure Act, the Justices of the Peace Act and the Offences against the Person Act. One of Prendergast's main tasks was to regulate the criminal law of New Zealand. Criminal law in the colony before the Criminal Code Act 1893 has been described in the following way:

> Even so the criminal law, both substantive and procedural, was often obscure and needlessly complex. The New Zealand Parliament paid little attention to the criminal law for many years, and what little was done was normally only by way of adoption of changes made in England. Thus the Justices of the Peace Act 1858 adopted the English reforms of 1848 and in 1867 a number of statutes were passed to adopt the English reforms of 1861.[177]

This statement is accurate when applied to the period before 1866, but unfair if applied to the period following Prendergast's appointment as Attorney-General. Prendergast introduced a range of relatively accessible criminal statutes from 1866 onwards, including the Criminal Law Procedure Act 1866, which amended "the law of evidence and practice on Criminal Trials and for facilitating the despatch of business before Grand Juries".[178] This statute regulated evidential procedure in criminal trials, including summing up and examination of witnesses. The Justices of the Peace Act outlined the jurisdiction of Justices in a detailed fashion. Justices of the Peace were given an impressive degree of power to hear cases of assault, larceny and indictable offences. With a court system limited in judges and funding, Justices of the Peace played an integral role in the legal system of the nineteenth century. The Offences Against the Person Act focused upon the unlawful administration of poison but also touched upon attempted murder. Several of the most high-profile criminal trials during Prendergast's career, including the Jarvey trial, featured unlawful use of poison.

The most productive year for Prendergast as a legal draftsman was 1867. During this year, Prendergast was relieved of his duties as a politician and could concentrate more fully on his role overseeing and actively engaging in the drafting process. In 1861, criminal law reform had taken in place in England. Six years later, Prendergast introduced these reforms to New Zealand.[179] The most important criminal statutes were the Accessories Act, the Coinage Offences Act, the Forgery Act, the Indictable Offences Repeal Act, the Larceny Act, the Malicious Injury to Property Act and the Offences Against the Person Act. Another major statute introduced during 1867 was the Bankruptcy Act. The year 1867 has been used as an example of New Zealand's heavy reliance on English law:

> In 1867 amidst statutes which drew on Australian precedents [the Neglected and Criminal Children Act and the Introduction of Convicts Prevention Act] there were nine statutes which reproduced English enactments, seven transcribing recent English reforms of the criminal law, and the Old Metal and Marine Stores Dealers Act 1867 and the Bankruptcy Act 1867. That may have been an exceptional year, but only in that it showed in exaggerated form a common pattern.[180]

The important criminal law statutes of 1867 begin by stating, "whereas it is expedient to consolidate and amend the Statute Law relating to . . . ". The Larceny Act 1867 is representative of the criminal statutes in its description of the crime, outline of punishments and detailed referencing to different situations of larceny. Some sections remain apposite today, for example section 54, which deals with "Entering a dwelling house in the night with intent to commit any felony", while some are indicative of the time, such as section 17: "Killing hares or rabbits in a warren in the night-time". The Forgery Act 1867 provides examples of the continuing influence of British society on colonial New Zealand. Section 6 outlines the crime of "Forging an East India bond", while section 16 describes the penalties for "Engraving or having any plate &c. for making notes of Bank of England or Ireland or other banks or having such plate &c. or uttering or having paper upon which a blank bank note &c. shall be printed".

The Offences Against the Person Act 1867 was more comprehensive than its 1866 predecessor, covering homicide, attempted murder, assault, rape, child-stealing, bigamy, attempts to procure abortion, and unnatural offences (sodomy, bestiality). While Prendergast's statutes were described as "legal labyrinths",[181] section 1 of the Act is very clear: "Whosoever shall be convicted of murder shall suffer death as a felon." The morality of the Victorian era is evident in most of the sections, particularly section 58: "Whosoever shall be convicted of the abominable crime of buggery . . . . shall be liable at the discretion of the Court to be kept in penal servitude for life or for any term not less than ten years." Victorian standards were also applied in the Divorce and Matrimonial Causes Act 1867, in which a husband could seek a divorce if his wife had committed adultery, but a wife must prove adultery coupled with an aggravating circumstances such as bigamy to obtain a dissolution (ss 17–18). A husband could also claim damages from an adulterer as one could seek damages for harm to property, but his wife could not (ss 31–34).

Several important non-criminal statutes were also passed in 1867. The voluminous Bankruptcy Act was a vital piece of legislation in a growing colony which experienced boom and bust periods in rapid succession. The Armed Constabulary Act 1867 marked the beginnings of a state-run police force, taking responsibility for law enforcement away from the provinces. The attempts of the

State to regulate Maori society also increased during 1867, with the Native Schools Act which provided funds for Maori Schools, the Confiscated Lands Act which created the power to set aside reserves for Maori, and the Maori Representation Act which created the four Maori seats in Parliament.

The year 1868 did not include the amount of landmark legislation that had appeared in 1867, but a number of important statutes were prepared by Prendergast and his staff. The Immigration Act 1868 marked the beginning of mass immigration to New Zealand. Under the Act, Provincial Councils were authorised to make permanent appropriations for promoting immigration. The policies of Julius Vogel during the early 1870s would see a flood of immigrants enter New Zealand to aid in the building of the colony's infrastructure. Not surprisingly, one of Prendergast's speciality areas was legislation directly relating to the administration of law. During 1868, the Juries Act, the Treason-Felony Act and the Supreme Court Practice and Procedure Amendment Act were passed. In 1869 the Disturbed Districts Act and the New Zealand Law Society's Act were passed.

An impressive range of statutes were produced in 1870, including the landmark Land Transfer Act, which introduced the Torrens system of registration of title to land. This system had originally been introduced in South Australia in 1858 by Robert Richard Torrens and had proved a marked improvement on earlier systems.[182] The Torrens system continues to be used (in a modified form) today and is the basis of New Zealand's land law. Another major piece of legislation introduced in 1870 was the Immigration and Public Works Act. This comprehensive statute enabled the construction of roads, railways and waterworks and encouraged wide-scale immigration. The statute attempted to define the differing powers of central government and the provinces. The Immigration and Public Works Loan Act authorised Vogel and his allies to raise millions of pounds to finance public works schemes.

In the area of criminal law, 1870 saw the introduction of the Punishment of High Treason Act. In a 'humanitarian' move, the penalty for high treason was made less barbaric. The original punishment of being hung, drawn and quartered was modified (despite having long fallen out of use in practice). No longer would the felon be:

> drawn on a hurdle to the place of execution and be there hanged by the neck until such person should be dead and that afterwards the head should be severed from the body of such person and the body divided into four quarters should be disposed of as His Majesty and his successors should think fit.[183]

Instead, the guilty party would "be taken to the place of execution and be there hanged by the neck until such person be dead"(s 3).

The grand schemes of Julius Vogel continued to dominate legislation during the early 1870s, for example, with more statutes in 1871 and 1872.[184] Prendergast continued to oversee criminal legislation such as the brief Criminal Law Amendment Act 1872 and the Assaults on Constables Act 1873, but the pace of legislative reform had slowed from the heady days of the late 1860s. An example of key social legislation introduced during Prendergast's term as Attorney-General is the Employment of Females Act 1873. The Act regulated the female workplace, restricting working hours to eight a day, providing set holidays and ensuring proper workplace ventilation. Inspectors were appointed under the Act to enforce its provisions.

Prendergast took a keen interest in the development of the New Zealand university system. As well as providing legal opinions, Prendergast oversaw the establishing statutes. The New Zealand University Act 1874 repealed the earlier 1870 Act and regulated the administration of the university colleges. The Act regulated the powerful University Senate, a panel of leaders which would include Prendergast only ten years later.

Perhaps the most controversial Act passed during 1865–1875 was the Abolition of the Provinces Act 1875. As previously mentioned, Prendergast played an important role leading up to this constitutional change, but because he took the role of Chief Justice in early 1875, Walter Reid was primarily responsible for managing the drafting of the Act.

7. The personal affairs of Prendergast while Attorney-General

With the establishment of a permanent, non-political Attorney-Generalship in 1867, Prendergast left Dunedin and focused all his attentions on Wellington. During the period 1865 to 1867, he had been torn between his practice in Otago and his government position in Wellington. With limited transport available, this situation was difficult and untenable in the long term. While Dunedin remained the focus of the New Zealand legal profession during the 1860s and early 1870s, moving to Wellington introduced Prendergast to the most powerful politicians in the colony. Not only did he mix with the Wellington-based political elite, but also all the politicians who journeyed from their home provinces to meet in the capital city during the parliamentary session. Letters from the period include a dinner invitation from Donald McLean to James and Mary Prendergast in August 1868.[185]

Prendergast bought land on Bolton Street and began to build a house, using his comfortable salary and probably savings from five years of successful practice in Dunedin. The impressive house, with a panoramic view of the Wellington harbour, took some time to build, and much interest was displayed in its construction. In 1869, Prendergast's uncle, Thomas Jeffrey, mentions the building in a letter from Britain: "Your house when built will I hope be all that you and Mrs Prendergast can desire."[186] Prendergast would remain in the Bolton Street address until his death in 1921.

Prendergast's main concern from 1865 to 1875 was his flourishing professional career. His workload was immense, as evidenced by the different roles discussed in this chapter. During this period he must have effectively become a workaholic. Outside involvements were limited, though family matters did demand his attention. The career and life of James' brother, Michael, disintegrated during the 1860s, placing James in the difficult position of having to support his brother and his brother's son. This sad tale is told primarily by inward letters to Prendergast from his English relations. Prendergast's outward letters are lost. A letter dated 17 February 1866, from Thomas Jeffrey, mentions Michael's problems: "I hope that what Michael has suffered will be one means of inducing him to alter his conduct for the future and that he will not disgrace himself and the Attorney General."[187] During the mid-1860s, Michael had become an alcoholic. At this time his wife died and by 1867 James and Mary Prendergast were caring for their young nephew, Michael junior. In 1875, Uncle James and Aunty Mary gave Michael junior the opportunity to travel to London for schooling. The Mannings looked after him, even taking him on a tour of Prendergast family sites.[188] As noted in Chapter 3, Michael senior returned to Victoria by the late 1860s and was committed to a lunatic asylum in 1870 after being found near death in the Australian outback.

Philip's continued mental illness also weighed on the mind of Prendergast during his time as Attorney-General. The Prendergast family letters kept James continually updated as to Philip's treatment in cousin Henry Manning's lunatic asylum. The accounts describe Philip as seriously ill but in fair physical health.

During the late 1860s, the extended Prendergast family in London was in crisis over family money and looked to James for assistance: "We all agree in what you say about carefully avoiding any family feud and above all law proceedings. We all wish very much that you were in England."[189] Prendergast's colonial success had made him the most respected figure in his wider family and his relations' letters become more and more reverential over time. The letters tell of social and political events in Britain and also reflect a curious, if somewhat vague, approach to New Zealand affairs. For example, in a letter from Thomas Jeffrey to Prendergast in 1869, Jeffrey places the New Zealand Wars in Wellington.[190]

Letters from the Mannings to Prendergast during the early 1870s indicate Prendergast's ultimate aim of a position on the bench.[191] Charles Manning junior attempted to use Prendergast's new-found power and influence to further his own stifled career: "I thought perhaps that you as Attorney General might be able to give a hand to a relative and create a necessity for a suitable post for him. Others in high office do, why shouldn't you?"[192] Nepotism was a factor in Victorian politics and law, with Prendergast later providing work for his nephews, Michael, Henry Hall and Charles Prendergast Knight. Manning junior's letters to Prendergast often provide insights into the relationship between the New Zealand and British legal systems, for example:

> I heard your promotion in a letter from home last week and write a line to congratulate you. The only thing against it is that it will probably interfere with your coming over. Perhaps you can imitate the example of the Law Officers in this Country [Ireland] who the moment they are raised to the Bench take their Law Libraries and go to reside miles away in the Country. They sit in Court of course occasionally but as a rule if you want to find an Irish Common Law Judge you must look for him at the Athendum Club Pall Mall or . . . at his Country seat in Ireland.[193]

Manning's rather cynical view of Irish judges would be almost the opposite of Prendergast's experience as Chief Justice of New Zealand from 1875 to 1899.

8. Prendergast as Attorney-General

James Prendergast achieved success as Attorney-General. This success enabled him to take the position of Chief Justice in 1875. Through legal talent, good connections and sheer hard work, he rose to the pinnacle of the New Zealand legal profession. The non-political nature of the Attorney-Generalship from 1867 to 1875 suited Prendergast's strengths as a legal administrator. While his performance as a Legislative Councillor (1865–7) was sound, his main achievement in this role was providing helpful legal advice, rather than political leadership. Prendergast knew the importance of good connections, but did not owe his rise to power to any one man. Sewell, Stafford and Vogel all supported him at key moments in his career. Essentially, it was Prendergast's skills and the support of the governing elite that guaranteed his success. While he did speak out on unpopular issues, for example, Stafford's accommodation in 1869, his support was often with the powerful majority. With the exception of Maori issues, Prendergast was a patient and reasoned Councillor and Attorney-General.

The amount of work Prendergast achieved over his ten years as Attorney-General was impressive. Prendergast's output included two years as an active Legislative Councillor, an integral role in the creation of hundreds of statutes, regular advocacy work in important cases, and a host of legal opinions. His workload was reduced somewhat by his strong reliance on English precedent, especially in the drafting of legislation. However, under enormous pressure to reform New Zealand law in readiness for large-scale national development, Prendergast sometimes adopted English law without effectively modifying it to the New Zealand colonial environment.

In 1872 the *Evening Post* described Prendergast in the following terms: "The present Attorney-General may not be perfect – no man is – and he has no doubt committed blunders at various times; but on the whole it would be difficult to replace him with a better man."[194] As Attorney-General, Prendergast had finally found an arena in which his talents could flourish. As a top legal administrator, Prendergast's diligence and patience were well rewarded, and by 1875, he had cemented his place amongst the New Zealand elite. While his brothers had both met with disaster and disappointment, James Prendergast had become a sterling example of colonial success. The stage was now set for his most important historical role, as Chief Justice of New Zealand.

6

CHIEF JUSTICE PRENDERGAST
1875–1899

While James Prendergast made a lasting impact as a lawyer and Attorney-General, it was his career as Chief Justice which provides his primary historical legacy. Prendergast's 24 years as Chief Justice (April 1875 to May 1899) stands as the second longest Chief Justiceship after Robert Stout's tenure of 27 years. As Chief Justice, Prendergast became the head of the New Zealand judiciary. An analysis of Prendergast's role as Chief Justice requires knowledge of his fellow judges, in particular, Prendergast CJ's fellow Wellington Supreme Court judge, Richmond J. As the Supreme Court judges also acted as Court of Appeal judges during the late nineteenth century, Prendergast CJ also played an integral role as head of the Court of Appeal.

A judicial biography requires a close analysis of the body of legally important judgments delivered by the individual under scrutiny. Prendergast CJ personally delivered approximately 600 judgments which were recorded in law reports. These reported cases provide the legal historian with insights into his judicial ability, jurisprudential background and intellectual framework. The New Zealand Law Reports and their predecessors provide descriptions of key legal decisions. Prendergast CJ sometimes sat with Richmond J on the Supreme Court Bench in Wellington[1] and on the Court of Appeal Bench without actually personally delivering the judgment. Many of Prendergast's decisions were reported in newspapers such as the *Evening Post*. The criterion for inclusion in a newspaper was public interest rather than legal precedent. Some of the 600 law report judgments also feature in the *Evening Post*, but many do not. Hundreds of unreported judgments can be found in newspapers. The advent of the National Library's digitisation project Papers Past has radically improved the accessibility of these newspaper court reports. A few notable unreported judgments will be discussed in this section and a statistical overview provided to show Prendergast's court workload during the period. However, the case analysis focus will be on Prendergast's legal legacy and thus his judgments which were considered important enough for inclusion in the law reports.

It is important to note that decisions which were considered pivotal during the late nineteenth century do not necessarily leave a legal legacy. By analysing more recent law reports, Prendergast CJ's judgments which have been utilised during the twentieth and twenty-first centuries can be discovered. This is his true legacy. Prendergast CJ's key areas of judicial expertise and prominence included land law, criminal law and law relating to Maori. Prendergast CJ's decisions regarding Maori land have become his most obvious legal legacy. Also of historical interest are Prendergast CJ's judgments in *cause célèbre* cases such as the Minnie Dean trial and the controversial case concerning the appointment of Edwards J.

It is only recently that Prendergast has become a well-known Chief Justice in New Zealand historiography. Before 1975, he had received little historical recognition and would have been placed alongside low-profile Chief Justices such as George Arney, rather than high-profile ones such as William Martin and Robert Stout. Prendergast CJ's decisions on Maori land became increasingly topical as the twentieth century drew to a close, and his name is now arguably as recognisable to readers of history as William Martin. Unlike Martin CJ, Prendergast CJ's recognition has been largely negative, and commentators have largely ignored his judicial work outside law relating to Maori. Prendergast CJ has become a two-dimensional judge. A third dimension is needed, if Prendergast CJ is to be properly understood and critically analysed.

1. The nature of the position of Chief Justice

As Chief Justice, Prendergast was the most important legal figure in New Zealand. As head of the Supreme Court and the Court of Appeal, the Chief Justice wielded an impressive amount of power in the colony's legal system. But although he was the most powerful judge, several of the judges working under his leadership arguably had greater public profiles. Alexander Johnston, a Scottish lawyer trained in London, became a Supreme Court puisne judge in 1858 and continued until his death in 1888. During the period 1875 to 1888, Johnston J was second-ranking judge after Prendergast CJ and served as acting Chief Justice in both 1867 and 1884.[2] Johnston J sat in Wellington until Prendergast's elevation to Chief Justice in 1875, and Prendergast appeared before him when acting as Attorney-General in the Supreme Court. Scholefield describes Johnston J as "A man of great culture and high attainments", and notes "he had a dry humour, was socially popular and interested in social movements, and was a lover of music in all forms, and of art".[3]

Relations between Prendergast CJ and Johnston J seemed cordial, though Johnston J was unimpressed with his removal to Christchurch to make way for the new Chief Justice in 1875:

> the sum mentioned in your letter [is] quite inadequate to compensate me for the loss and charges I shall be put to by my removal . . . . It is important that I should know the final decision of the Government on the subject as soon as possible; inasmuch as I shall have but a brief period for making the necessary

preparations for breaking up my home, disposing of my property, and making fresh arrangements for my family.[4]

Prendergast CJ's nephew, Henry Hall, blatantly criticised Johnston J in a private letter to his uncle on 28 May 1884: "The general opinion is that Johnston acting C.J. has been most unbearable in his bearing on the Bench this Court of Appeal."[5] It is unlikely that Hall, who had great respect for his uncle, would have criticised Johnston J in this fashion if Johnston J had been a close associate of Prendergast CJ.

Prendergast CJ's strongest ally on the Supreme Court Bench was Christopher William Richmond. Their role in the *Wi Parata* decision is discussed in Chapter 8. The primary reason for the closeness of their relationship was that both sat in Wellington. In such a situation, mutual admiration will build a strong friendship, but mutual dislike would be disastrous. As mentioned in Chapter 2, Richmond J's background was very similar to Prendergast CJ's and the two men formed a supportive working partnership that lasted for two decades. Initially, Richmond J served in Dunedin and Prendergast conducted many cases before him during the period 1862 to 1867. Richmond J moved to Wellington in 1873 and remained there until his death in 1895. Richmond J's death was a blow for Prendergast CJ,[6] but as Richmond J had suffered from ill-health for many years, it was not unexpected. Richmond was a regular visitor to Prendergast's Bolton Street mansion and even composed landscapes from its hilltop vantage. The two men were often present together at social functions and in all the archival material which mentions their professional and personal relationship, there is not one indication of tension or conflict. They were certainly close friends, and it is quite probable that Prendergast considered Richmond his best friend.

Three new Supreme Court judges were appointed in the judicial reshuffle of 1875: Prendergast, Joshua Williams and Thomas Gillies.[7] Gillies, originally from Scotland, was the first New Zealand judge to have qualified for admission to the bar by New Zealand examination.[8] Like Richmond, Gillies arrived in New Zealand during the early 1850s and had firmly established himself by the time he became a judge. Prendergast arrived approximately ten years later than Gillies, but was favoured over him for Chief Justice when the two men were appointed in 1875. Gillies was a practising lawyer in Dunedin during the 1860s and would have known Prendergast during that time. While serving as Attorney-General in 1862, Gillies was embroiled in the New Zealand Wars and struggled to pursue his political career in Wellington while conducting a practice in Dunedin. These problems were shared by Prendergast. Like Johnston J and Richmond J, Gillies J never had the opportunity to enjoy retirement. After serving 14 years on the Auckland Bench, Gillies J died in 1889. He was considered an able judge with a liberal bent. During the controversial trials of Parihaka's leaders, Gillies J was uncomfortable with the treatment of the Maori defendants. While Prendergast CJ,

Johnston J and Richmond J all shared hard-line views on Maori affairs, Gillies J could be considered more racially tolerant.[9]

The year 1875 was a watershed one for New Zealand judicial history. A new generation of judges replaced three retiring judges who had been involved in setting up the New Zealand legal system during its formative years (1840s–1860s). Three of the five Supreme Court judges retired in 1875: Arney CJ (Auckland), Gresson J (Christchurch) and Chapman J (Dunedin). Prendergast CJ took Arney's position of Chief Justice while Gillies J received Arney CJ's seat on the Auckland Bench. Johnston J was shifted to Christchurch to replace Gresson J and make way for Prendergast CJ, while Williams J became the new judge for Dunedin.[10]

Joshua Williams was the most popular and widely respected New Zealand judge during the nineteenth century. While William Martin and Henry Chapman may have been his intellectual equals, Williams J was venerated by the New Zealand legal profession, especially in his later years. Williams arrived in New Zealand in 1861 and spent most of his practising years in Christchurch, before being elevated to the bench in 1875. The *New Zealand Mail* claimed that Prendergast was responsible for Williams' rise: "Mr Justice Williams was raised to the bench and assigned to that district. The new judge had previously been Registrar-General of Lands, and he was discovered, as the saying goes, by the Chief Justice when the latter was Attorney-General."[11] As with Johnston J and Gillies J, Williams J would have come into contact with Prendergast CJ primarily during Court of Appeal sittings in Wellington.

It seems Prendergast CJ and Williams J had a healthy working relationship. Some members of the profession felt that Williams J should have succeeded Prendergast CJ in 1899, as Williams J was the senior puisne judge,[12] but instead the lawyer and politician Robert Stout was chosen over Williams J, in the same way Attorney-General Prendergast was chosen over senior puisne judges in 1875. At the unveiling of Prendergast CJ's portrait in October 1899, Williams J spoke highly of his former leader:

> I have had the honour and happiness of having been associated with Sir James Prendergast for all but a quarter of a century. During the whole of that time he worked with the utmost harmony and friendship, not only with myself but with every other Judge with whom he was associated. It is, indeed, difficult to imagine a more loyal or unselfish colleague . . . . I can only say that it affords me infinite pleasure to be able to look upon the counterfeit presentment of my old colleague, and, I hope I may say, my old friend.[13]

While Johnston, Richmond, Gillies and Williams JJ were the longest serving judges during Prendergast's chief justiceship, four other permanent judges also adjudicated under Prendergast's leadership: Buckley, Conolly, Denniston and Edwards JJ. Patrick Buckley was a judge for only a matter of months preceding his death. Edward Conolly replaced Gillies J in Auckland in 1889, though he also travelled on circuit to New Plymouth and Gisborne.[14] Appointed in his late sixties, Conolly J was four years older than Prendergast but came to the bench 14 years later. John Denniston replaced Johnston J in Christchurch in 1889. Denniston had been a young man in Dunedin during the 1860s and was eventually admitted to the bar in 1874.[15] Therefore Denniston, Richmond, Gillies and Edwards JJ were all in Dunedin during the period 1862–1865, the time during which Prendergast established himself as a legal figure in New Zealand.

The most controversial judge to serve with Prendergast CJ was Worley Bassett Edwards. In 1890, Edwards J was appointed as the sixth member of the Supreme Court Bench. Provision was only available for five members, and thus began the long-running saga to prevent Edwards taking his position on the bench. The case *Buckley v Edwards* and the Edwards J affair will be discussed later in this chapter. Prendergast CJ had opposed the appointment, but with Richmond J's death in 1895, and the death of his replacement (and Edwards' nemesis) Patrick Buckley less than a year later, Prendergast found himself sharing the Wellington Bench with Edwards J in 1896. Edwards J was the first judge to have his complete education in New Zealand. While an intelligent man, he was, "Naturally arrogant and vindictive", and "his behaviour may also have owed something to a feeling that fate had sentenced him to life in a coarse-grained colony".[16] He also harboured great bitterness over his initial rejection as a judge during the early 1890s. One would imagine that sharing a bench with Edwards J would not be a pleasant experience, and perhaps this contributed to Prendergast's decision to retire three years later, shortly after his wife's death.

Prendergast's success as Chief Justice of New Zealand must be placed in the context of New Zealand judicial history since 1841, when William Martin was appointed first Chief Justice of New Zealand. From 1841 to 2014, there have been only 12 Chief Justices. From 1841 to 1926, there were only four. Martin CJ had a well-earned reputation as a liberal and a humanitarian. He also "closely identified himself with the missionary and evangelical aspirations of the Anglican church in the south Pacific",[17] and was a strong advocate for Maori and the Treaty of Waitangi. George Arney replaced Martin CJ in 1857 and served as Chief Justice until 1875. Prendergast's predecessor was quietly successful, working to establish the New Zealand legal system, and in particular, helping to fuse the common law and equity. In one of his few outspoken moments, Arney CJ called for social justice for Maori during the Taranaki War of 1860.[18] Prendergast appeared before Arney a number of times as counsel, when addressing the Court of Appeal.

When Prendergast CJ retired in 1899, he was the longest serving Chief Justice in New Zealand's brief settler history. This achievement was bested by Robert Stout, who acted as Chief Justice from 1899 to 1926. While Stout CJ was a successful judicial administrator, he was ultimately less successful as a judge than one would have expected from one of the colony's leading legal figures. Stout CJ's judgments, "were seldom the product of prolonged deliberation, often being written in haste and lacking literary quality. One in three cases taken on appeal from his decisions was successful."[19] Unlike Prendergast, Stout was a liberal, both in politics and in his interpretation of the law. Therefore, of the first four Chief Justices, Prendergast CJ appears the most conservative; personally, politically and judicially.

Prendergast had demonstrated a desire to join the Supreme Court Bench since his arrival in Wellington. He had been promised, by Fox's Ministry, the next vacant seat on the Bench of the Supreme Court, but Fox had refused to guarantee the Chief Justiceship to Prendergast if it should fall vacant and also refused to bind any other Ministry in any way. Fox's Ministry fell in 1873, to be replaced by Vogel's. Two years later, in a letter to the Colonial Secretary dated 20 February 1875, George Arney announced his retirement, noting "I think I understood you on recent occasions to say that arrangements were already in contemplation of the Government for the appointment of my successor."[20] Prendergast was appointed Chief Justice on 1 April, five weeks after Arney's retirement announcement and three months before the fall of the Vogel Government in July 1875.

Julius Vogel had been one of Prendergast's first contacts in Dunedin and was aware of Prendergast's credentials. He was not obligated to give Prendergast the Chief Justiceship, but of the other eventual appointees to the Supreme Court Bench in that year, Williams lacked Prendergast's experience and Gillies was an outspoken opponent of Vogel's policies.[21] Tradition held that puisne judges should not be elevated to the Chief Justiceship, restricting the chances of Richmond J and Johnston J. Prendergast was therefore the clear choice. Daniel Pollen, Colonial Secretary, informed Prendergast of his elevation officially on 1 April 1875:

> I have the honour to inform you that His Excellency the Governor in Council has been pleased to appoint you to be Chief Justice of the Supreme Court of New Zealand, and to assign to you the Judicial District of Wellington . . . . Your salary will be at a rate of 1,700 pounds a year.[22]

Prendergast CJ appointed his nephew, Henry Hall, as his marshal and secretary. While Hall proved an able administrator, this appointment was also indicative of nineteenth-century nepotism.

The appointment of a Chief Justice has a sizeable component of chance involved. When a Chief Justice resigns, the best possible candidate at that time must be appointed. Many of the most suitable people may already have taken puisne judgeships, lack the necessary experience or refuse to leave lucrative practices. While he was leader of the profession from 1875 to 1899, Prendergast CJ's ability as a judge was inferior to others such as Williams and Richmond JJ.

As Chief Justice, Prendergast CJ was based in the capital city of Wellington, but the Wellington District during Prendergast's reign included Blenheim, Hokitika, Napier, Nelson, Wanganui and Gisborne, requiring a great deal of travel and time away from home. Though Richmond J shared the Wellington District with Prendergast CJ, of the two men, Prendergast CJ was more robust and was often away on circuit. Therefore, Prendergast CJ played an important role in the legal history of the several New Zealand centres.

As well as the judicial duties of a Supreme Court judge, the Chief Justice must fulfil the role of leader of the bench and chief judicial administrator. This is a weighty task, involving:

> the allocation of duties to the members of the judiciary; it includes dealing with the government of the day as spokesman for the judiciary; it covers acting as administrator of the government in the absence of the Governor-General; above all it means being regarded by people generally as the embodiment of the law.[23]

Prendergast CJ's speciality was the administration of the law and he proved himself an effective Chief Justice in this respect. By acting as Attorney-General and Chief Justice, Prendergast served at different times as leader of both the legal profession and the judiciary. His successor, Robert Stout, would also fulfil both these roles, though in a more high-profile fashion.

Through the period 1875 to 1899, Prendergast CJ issued judgments while dealing with the day-to-day administration of the New Zealand legal system. An analysis of the Department of Justice Indexes during this period reveals the variety of issues that Prendergast CJ faced. These issues included formulating rules for various courts, providing opinions on controversial prison sentences, setting bar examinations, assigning judicial districts, appointing secretaries, purchasing new technologies (including telephones and typewriters) and making decisions regarding expenses.[24]

Prendergast CJ was a strict manager of finances and was wary of expensive new developments, especially during the Long Depression of the 1880s:

> When the judges of the Supreme Court were consulted in 1885 as to the employment of shorthand writers in that court, Sir James Prendergast gave it as his opinion that note-taking by stenographers could not in this colony supersede the taking of notes by judges and counsel respectively, but would be an assistance to the bench and Bar. "The whole question", he added, "is one of expense".[25]

2. Case Analysis

As Chief Justice, James Prendergast delivered numerous legal judgments. The most important judgments are those which have remained as useful precedents or landmark cases up to the present day. This is the judicial legacy of Prendergast CJ. The controversial *Wi Parata* case is one such example, though its authority diminished from the 1980s onwards. Several other Prendergast judgments, such as *Merrie v McKay* and *Doyle v Edwards*, have been referred to a number of times in reported cases since 1945. While Prendergast CJ is not considered a great jurist compared to figures such as Joshua Williams, John Salmond and Robin Cooke, his decisions form an important part of New Zealand's legal history.

Several commentators have referred to Prendergast CJ's ability as a judicial decision-maker, not always favourably. William Gisborne, who worked closely with Prendergast as Colonial Secretary (1869–1872) and as a fellow Royal Commissioner in 1881, described the Chief Justice's approach to the law: "Sir James was slow, but he was sure and safe. He was careful, cautious, and he always looked before he leaped."[26] On his death, Charles Skerrett stated that:

> Although he may not have possessed the brilliance of some of his colleagues, yet for sound law, for shrewd judgment of human nature and character, for painstaking unravelling of difficult problems of law or fact he was the compeer of any of his colleagues.[27]

Francis Bell provided a complimentary account of Prendergast's judicial qualities, as he:

> remembered his always seeming to regard the argument of counsel as being offered for his assistance and he always offered what help he could. When he tried a case alone he gave an early indication of the difficulties before him; but where there was a jury it was almost a complaint against him that his attitude throughout the case and in summing up was colourless, and the jury was left to try the case.[28]

A social commentator in 1907 described Prendergast: "As a judge, like Lord Eldon, he doubted to the last minute, but his 'reserved judgments' were hard to upset in the Appeal Courts."[29] The same newspaper also stated that "reversals of his judgments were practically nil".[30] These comments are not accurate, as Prendergast CJ had a sizeable number of his Supreme Court decisions overturned on appeal, and his record was similar to that of Chief Justice Stout, who had one in three of his decisions taken on appeal overturned.[31] In a newspaper report from 1899, further criticisms of Prendergast CJ were mentioned, including his lack of assistance to juries, indulgence to barristers and yielding of precedence to his brethren.[32]

Later summations of his performance as Chief Justice have also been both positive and negative:

> There have been better Chief Justices than Sir James Prendergast . . . . Scorning any attempt at well-rounded periods, or even figures of speech for display, he went straight to the point, frequently to the degree of bluntness. His vigorous personality was reflected in many uncompromising judgments and opinions which, whether right or wrong, were always interesting. It was said of him that on the principle that thirsty men want beer, not explanations, he was concerned primarily with reaching a decision, and only secondarily with the mechanics

of elaborating it. But at the same time he was slow, safe, careful, and cautious, despite surprising slips and misunderstandings.[33]

Similar comments were made in *Portrait of a Profession*:

> His personal qualities of caution, thoroughness, and care enabled him to fulfill all his forensic duties . . . in a sage and forthright manner . . . and also with industry, but perhaps without noticeable distinction. His qualities are typified by his reputation as a particularly sound real-property lawyer. So by a fortuitous confluence of events the New Zealand judicial system, after its initial inception and period of initial growth, had as its head a man whose personal characteristics enabled him to impart the stability and confidence required during a period of consolidation.[34]

Therefore, opinion on Prendergast CJ as a judge was mixed, with praise for his reliability, diligence and leadership, and criticism for his lack of brilliance and bluntness of approach. There are obvious differences of opinion amongst commentators and the only way to obtain an accurate view of Prendergast CJ's judgments is to analyse them. As Robert Stout said about Prendergast, "I do not need to speak of his fame as a judge. The reports show his ability and his work."[35]

Many of Prendergast CJ's judgments have been referred to in recent New Zealand legal history. These judgments can be utilised to support a number of observations regarding Prendergast CJ's judicial approach. The decisions delivered by Prendergast alone in the Supreme Court allow the historian to see clearly his legal reasoning at work. When Prendergast CJ delivered judgments with Richmond J or on the Court of Appeal, one must be aware that Prendergast CJ was not acting alone and, while the judgment may be his, he could be heavily influenced by his brother judges.[36]

During the course of his judicial career, Prendergast CJ made hundreds of decisions that have been recorded in various law reports. Some of these decisions have created important precedents still utilised today, and some attracted much public interest when they were decided in the late nineteenth century. The bulk of Prendergast CJ's reported judgments were neither influential precedent nor controversial. Many of these decisions were simply the application of legislation to a specific fact situation or the clarification of an important common law precedent. Amongst these cases are particular decisions which serve to highlight interesting aspects about Prendergast CJ as a judge. The scope of this analysis does not allow for a discussion of each decision by Prendergast CJ, nor would such a comprehensive survey be particularly useful. In analysing Prendergast CJ's approach as a judge, a select number of his judgments can be used as historical evidence. Most of the judgments chosen have had some influence in New Zealand legal history, while several serve primarily to demonstrate aspects of Prendergast CJ's adjudication style.

Prendergast CJ's judgments are not as poorly written as Gisborne would have us believe. While Prendergast CJ was not an inspired writer, judicial reports are written to elucidate on points of fact and law, not to be read for their literary quality. One difference that the modern lawyer notices when reading the judgments of the nineteenth century is their brevity. Few of Prendergast CJ's judgments took more than four to five pages, as compared to the lengthy and involved judgments often delivered in modern courts. When analysing Prendergast CJ's judgments which continue to be used as legal precedents, special attention will be given to those used most often. These are Prendergast CJ's most successful judgments, his common law legacy, and they continue to have resonance in today's legal environment.

The judgments of Prendergast CJ can be found in a variety of historical sources. Law reporting in New Zealand between 1875 and 1899 was a developing area. For the first eight years of Prendergast's Chief Justiceship (1875–1882), there was no standard series of law reports in which to find his decisions. The *New Zealand Jurist Reports* (Old Series Vol II and New Series Vols I–IV) provide a number of decisions made by the Chief Justice. Complementing these early reports are Johnston J's *Court of Appeal Reports* (Vols I–II) and *Ollivier, Bell and Fitzgerald's Reports* (1878–1880). In 1881 and 1882, no official law reports existed, though cases from these years can be found in the New Zealand Law Reports.[37] Therefore, for this period, it is difficult to gain a comprehensive picture of Prendergast CJ's important decisions. The New Zealand Law Reports were first produced in 1883, a landmark year for New Zealand legal history. These reports continue to the present day and provide a goldmine of information for the legal historian.

A. Ability as a judge

i. Comprehensive treatment of legal issues

As a judge, Prendergast CJ displayed an impressive ability to treat legal issues in a comprehensive fashion, although he was not always consistent in this regard, and at times provided brief, vague judgments on important areas of law. An example of Prendergast CJ's comprehensive treatment of legal issues is *R v Potter* (1887) 6 NZLR 92. This decision was later referred to in the Court of Appeal decisions *R v Te Kira* [1993] 3 NZLR 257 and *R v Rogers* [2006] 2 NZLR 156. The *Potter* decision related to the obtaining of evidence by a police officer. Prendergast CJ held that, "Although it is the duty of a constable when arresting a prisoner, not to ask questions, yet, if he does so without using any threat or promise the answers in reply are evidence."[38] Prendergast CJ had delivered his original decision in the Christchurch Supreme Court and also delivered the judgment of the Court of Appeal on 29 November 1887. The Court of Appeal decision unanimously upheld Prendergast CJ's earlier judgment. In this case, Prendergast CJ supported controversial actions by the police, but expressed his discomfort at doing so:

As to the other point raised, that of improper questioning, no doubt there were questions asked. If it were necessary to express an opinion I should express disapproval of what was done; it was too much like trying to convict the prisoner out of his own mouth. But there is not sufficient authority for saying that if questions are put by an arresting constable, the answers given by the prisoner are not evidence.[39]

In *Te Kira*, Richardson J noted the complexity of Prendergast CJ's decision:

Indeed over 100 years ago this Court in *R v Potter* (1887) 6 NZLR 92, 96 held that it was the duty of the arresting constable not to ask questions . . . . But, in delivering the judgment of this Court in *Potter*, Prendergast CJ went on to note that if no threat or promise was used the evidence of answers to police questions could not be rejected. That ambivalence is also reflected in the Judges' Rules 1912.[40]

Richardson J therefore correctly views Prendergast CJ's decision as a complex and pivotal statement on the law regarding arrest. More recently, Baragwanath J reflects this view in *R v Pennell* [2003] 1 NZLR 289 at 300 and in the *Rogers* decision: "The tension between the competing public interests of the ability of the police to investigate and prove offending and those of a prisoner has long been an area of uncertainty."[41]

In the case of *Nankivell v O'Donovan* (1893) 13 NZLR 60, Prendergast CJ also provided a comprehensive approach to adjudication. In *Nankivell*, Prendergast CJ was faced with a breach of the Licensing Act 1881. The case was on appeal from the Resident Magistrates Court in Wellington. Appearing for the appellant was Charles Skerrett, the future Chief Justice. Skerrett was unsuccessful in his attempt to overturn the decision of the magistrate, with Prendergast CJ affirming the conviction. The facts of the case involved a publican who was charged with illegally selling beer on a Sunday to a customer who was not a *bone fide* traveller or lodger. In his judgment, Prendergast made an important ruling on admission of evidence:

In substance, the question is whether the sufficiency of the evidence adduced in support of an issue is a question of law. Certainly it is not: it is a question of law whether any evidence has been adduced upon which a Magistrate's finding could be based, but it is not a question of law that, such evidence as adduced being all one way, and tending to prove a fact, the Magistrate was bound to accept it as sufficient.[42]

In *Nankivell*, Prendergast CJ wrestled with the intricacies of evidential procedure. His reasoning was referred to and discussed by Fisher J in *Auckland City Council v Wotherspoon* [1990] 1 NZLR 76, 88.[43]

Prendergast CJ was most impressive in the area of land law, especially law relating to the Land Transfer System. His expertise in land law extended beyond the Land

Transfer Act and encompassed areas such as Maori land law and mining law. As a Dunedin barrister during the 1860s, Prendergast had ample opportunity to work in the area of mining law. In the case of *McKenzie v Couston* (1898) 17 NZLR 228, the Court of Appeal dismissed an appeal from a decision of acting Supreme Court judge, Pennefather J. In his judgment, Prendergast CJ stated that a perpetual lease should not be included in the definition of Crown land under the Mining Act 1891. Though both counsel had "elaborately examined the course of legislation in the various Goldfields Acts, Mining Acts, and Land Acts",[44] Prendergast CJ ignored most of this discussion to focus on the central issue in question.

Prendergast CJ was an efficient judge who was able to distil the key legal issue from the range of issues presented to him by counsel. At times his efficiency is almost brutal, but with only five Supreme Court judges in a colony of nearly one million people, a need for efficiency is understandable. In *McKenzie*, Prendergast opened his judgment by stating, "We think, notwithstanding the very full examination of the Land Acts and Mining Acts which has been made by the learned counsel on both sides, that we can dispose of this case satisfactorily without any elaborate purview of legislation."[45] Prendergast CJ's decision was used by Moller J in *Echolands Farms Ltd v Powell* [1976] 1 NZLR 750.

Several of Prendergast CJ's decisions were comprehensive enough to withstand scrutiny under appeal and remain as binding precedent to the present day. Business in colonial New Zealand was enterprising and risky. The commercial cases dealing with large corporations which dominate modern law reports were not as prevalent during Prendergast CJ's term as Chief Justice. But as business in any era requires legal support, Prendergast CJ heard many commercial cases, including the Supreme Court case of *The Picturesque Atlas Publishing Company (Limited) v Harbottle* (1891) 10 NZLR 348. Prendergast CJ's decision in the Supreme Court was appealed, but upheld in a Court of Appeal consisting of Denniston, Williams and Conolly JJ. In this case, the vendor had been extremely tardy in the delivery to the purchaser of *The Picturesque Atlas of Australasia* in 42 parts. Instead of delivering in instalments, the vendor eventually delivered the entire atlas on one specific date. The purchaser refused to complete the contract, and was supported by Prendergast CJ, who stated that:

> I also think that it appears sufficiently clear from the contract that the subject-matter about which the parties were agreeing was a book to be delivered in parts and at intervals, and not to be delivered at once and as a complete book. It is to be assumed that the delivery in parts and at intervals was essential, and that the plaintiff is seeking to compel the buyer to accept an essentially different thing from that bargained for.[46]

This was the portion of the judgment appealed and upheld by the Court of Appeal and also used as an authority in Eichelbaum J's exhaustive judgment in

Innes v Ewing [1989] 1 NZLR 598, 625. Prendergast CJ also held that the Foreign Companies Act 1884 did not render it illegal for a foreign company to carry out business in New Zealand without an attorney present in the colony.[47]

Prendergast CJ's comprehensive knowledge of New Zealand legislation was appreciated by his brother judges. In *Reid v Official Assignee of McCallum* (1886) 5 NZLR 68, 82, Johnston J stated, "I entirely concur with His Honor the Chief Justice both in the conclusion at which he has arrived, and also as regards the valuable practical exposition which he has given of the enactments affecting the case."

Prendergast CJ's initial decisions were usually sound, largely as a result of his cautious and attentive approach to decision-making. It must be remembered that a sizeable number of the decisions that were appealed from the Wellington Supreme Court were made by both Prendergast CJ and Richmond J. In *Young v Hill, Ford and Newton* (1883) 2 NZLR 62, the Court of Appeal upheld a Prendergast CJ decision, with Richmond J stating:

> His Honor the Chief Justice, who heard this case, also came to the same conclusion. After a very attentive perusal of the evidence, and the careful addresses of counsel, we are all of opinion that the conclusions of the jury and His Honor the Chief Justice are justified by the evidence.[48]

Respect from fellow judges is also evident in *Hadfield v Armstrong* (1894) 12 NZLR 476, in which Denniston J refers at length to Prendergast CJ's decision in *Re Roche* (1888) 7 NZLR 206. As a judge, Prendergast CJ had the ability to effectively canvass relevant legal precedent and deliver comprehensive and efficient judgments, though this did not always lead him to the same conclusions as his brother judges.

The case of *Re Cairns; Ex parte New Zealand Land Mortgage Company (Limited)* (1888) 7 NZLR 42, further demonstrates Prendergast's comprehensive treatment of legal issues. This case related to a bankruptcy action (bankruptcy cases formed a large part of Prendergast's judicial workload, especially during the economic downturn of the 1880s).[49] The Court of Appeal, led by Prendergast CJ's judgment, held that, "The secured creditor of a bankrupt who realises his security after the bankruptcy, is not entitled to prove under the bankruptcy for the difference between the price he sold at, and the total amount of his debt."[50] The relevant legislation was the Bankruptcy Act 1883, which was used by Prendergast CJ in his judgment. Prendergast CJ's judgment was used as precedent in *Re H. (A Bankrupt)* [1968] NZLR 231. This case was an appeal from the 1967 Supreme Court decision in which Prendergast CJ's *Re McGregor* precedent was utilised. McCarthy J held that *Cairns* was "a judgment which has stood and has controlled our practice for almost 80 years and from which we should not depart".[51] Prendergast CJ's decisions in the area of bankruptcy law have continued to stand as precedent throughout the twentieth century. Ratios such as that of *Re Cairns* demonstrate Prendergast CJ's enduring legacy in New Zealand common law.

ii. Interpreting his own legislation/using past experience

One of Prendergast CJ's defining qualities as a judge was his ability to utilise past experience to aid in deciding cases. Prendergast CJ was in a particularly strong position to interpret key New Zealand statutes because as Attorney-General he had been responsible for overseeing the drafting of many of them. One of Prendergast CJ's lasting contributions as a judge was his landmark rulings in the area of real property. Land is a central theme running through New Zealand's history. It is a central concern of both Maori and Pakeha and was a principal cause of the New Zealand Wars. Therefore, any ratio decisions in the area of land law were to have a great effect on New Zealand society. As Attorney-General, Prendergast had been partly responsible for introducing the South Australian Land Transfer System (the Torrens system) into the New Zealand legal system. As Chief Justice, Prendergast was partly responsible for interpreting his own statute.

In two modern High Court cases regarding the Land Transfer System and Maori land, Prendergast CJ's legacy has been apparent. In 1976, Beattie J heard the case of *Chan v Lower Hutt City Corporation* [1976] 2 NZLR 75, while in 1987, McGechan J heard *Housing Corporation of New Zealand v Maori Trustee* [1988] 2 NZLR 662. Both cases mentioned the 1888 Supreme Court decision *Paraone v Matthews* (1888) 6 NZLR 744. In this case, Prendergast CJ attempted to reconcile the Native Land Acts of 1867 and 1873 with the Land Transfer Act 1885, the descendant of Prendergast CJ's original statute. Prendergast CJ heard the case in Gisborne, but reserved it for argument in Wellington. The three defendants, Matthews, Russell and Murdoch, believed they had obtained the land of the plaintiffs with the assistance of the District Land Registrar and their solicitors. Prendergast CJ ruled that the Registrar had been wrong to attempt to transfer the land to the defendants as this transfer conflicted with the Native Land Act 1873. The Native Land Act stated that a conveyance cannot be made before subdivision, which is what the defendants attempted to do. As Prendergast CJ clearly stated, "The conveyance is not a transfer within the meaning of the Land Transfer Act."[52] The Maori owners of the lands won this case due to Prendergast CJ's decision.

In the 1976 *Chan* case, only a fleeting reference is made to Prendergast CJ's decision, but in the 1987 *Housing Corporation* case, *Paraone* received more detailed attention. McGechan J referred to Prendergast CJ's decision as being an important interpretation of the 1885 Act, "a case in which a purchaser presented a void transfer, signed correct, and obtained registration. This in itself, with no element of fraud, was regarded as the carrying out of a 'wrongful' act."[53] McGechan J attempted to place the 1885 Act in context, referring to the uncertain nature of land ownership and the need for a rigid system of land registration. Parihaka is used as an example to highlight this uncertainty. Prendergast CJ had been involved in creating the tension over land which the Land Transfer Act sought to successfully manage.

Prendergast CJ dealt with a similar case in 1892: *Re Stewart & Co., Ex parte Piripi Te Maari (No.2)* (1892) 11 NZLR 745. The Land Transfer Act 1885 was analysed alongside the Native Land Act 1873, to decide whether an unregistered transferee could successfully remove a caveat on a summary application. The applicant, Piripi te Maari, was unsuccessful in removing the caveat and was described by Prendergast CJ as "a mere tool of Paraone and the Native lessors".[54] After refusing to remove the caveat, Prendergast CJ stated (semble) that "Oral contracts by Natives relating to land may still be enforceable, if there has been part-performance, notwithstanding the provisions of section 83 of the 'The Native Land Act, 1873.'"[55] Prendergast CJ's decision was used to aid Perry J in the 1971 case *Scott v Broadlands Finance Limited* [1972] NZLR 268.

In 1890, Prendergast CJ was called upon once more to clarify the Land Transfer System in *Re Mrs. Jackson's Claim* (1890) 10 NZLR 148. Jackson's representative did not conduct a thorough search of the register, failing to make an inquiry into whether any instrument had been received for registration but not yet entered upon the register. Such an instrument had been received and not registered, but Jackson only discovered this after parting with her purchasing money. Prendergast CJ took a hard-line approach and showed no mercy for what he considered an omission on the part of Jackson and her representative.[56] The complexities of the Land Transfer System were for those working with it to discover for themselves. In *Bradley v Attorney-General* [1978] 1 NZLR 36, O'Regan J referred to Prendergast CJ's decision and expressed dissatisfaction at the modern-day workings of the Land Transfer System:

> The decision [Jackson's] has stood for more than three-quarters of a century and been accepted by the courts, the textbook authors and the profession over those long years . . . . "the necessities of the office" have of recent time assumed proportions beyond the possible contemplation of the Chief Justice and, indeed, such as might well have Torrens himself turn in his grave with despair at the cavalier attitudes of those entrusted with the administration of his enlightened system.[57]

As one of the architects of New Zealand's Land Transfer System, Prendergast CJ was in a commanding position to interpret the system when it came before the New Zealand courts.

Prendergast CJ's decision in *Merrie v McKay* (1897) 16 NZLR 124, has been referred to in seven twentieth and twenty-first century New Zealand cases. Only *Wi Parata* (1877) and *Doyle v Edwards* (1898) can claim similar importance in modern times. All three cases deal with land law. *Merrie v McKay* is a relatively brief judgment dealing with fraud under the Land Transfer Act 1885. Prendergast CJ ruled on the issue of whether fraud may be committed after registration has taken place. In an oft quoted passage, Prendergast CJ stated:

If the defendant acquired the title intending to carry out the agreement with the plaintiff, there was no fraud then; the fraud is in now repudiating the agreement, and in endeavouring to make use of the position he has obtained to deprive the plaintiff of his rights, under the agreement. If the defendant acquired his registered title with a view to depriving the plaintiff of those rights, then the fraud was in acquiring the registered title. Whichever view is accepted, he must be held to hold the land subject to the plaintiff's rights under the agreement, and must perform the contract entered into by the plaintiff's vendor.[58]

A host of later decisions have followed Prendergast CJ's ratio, including Salmond J's decision in *Wellington City Corporation v Public Trustee* [1921] NZLR 423, the Court of Appeal decision in *Waimiha Sawmilling Co Ltd v Waione Timber Co Ltd* [1926] AC 101; NZPCC 267, Cooke J in *Harris v Fitzmaurice* [1956] NZLR 975, Woodhouse J in *McCrae v Wheeler* [1969] NZLR 333, Turner P's dissenting judgment in *Sutton v O'Kane* [1973] 2 NZLR 304 (CA), McMullin J in *Bunt v Hallinan* [1985] 1 NZLR 450 (CA) and Venning J in *Instant Funding Limited v Greenwich Property Holdings Limited* (2007).[59] Analysis of these cases clearly proves that Prendergast CJ's legacy has been prominent in the New Zealand legal system throughout the twentieth century and beyond. In his rulings on the Land Transfer System, Prendergast CJ demonstrated a depth of experience and a resourceful approach to decision-making.

Prendergast had the rather unique opportunity as Chief Justice of interpreting his own legislation, created under his watch as Attorney-General. A leading barrister admitted to the bench would normally not have this experience, though some other exceptions exist, most notably John Salmond. Prendergast demonstrated a willingness to explore different approaches to statutory interpretation. In the Court of Appeal decision *Wilson and King v Brightling* (1885) 4 NZLR 4, 8, Prendergast CJ provided a liberal interpretation of the Land Transfer Act 1870:

The clause, no doubt, if read literally, does involve some little difficulty, or at least a great incongruity . . . . What the Legislature probably intended was that the clause should be read as if the words "as lessee" at the end of the section had not been introduced . . . . the clause does not read very clearly.

The *Wilson* decision was praised by Tipping J in *Corunna Bay Holdings Ltd v Robert Gracie Dean Ltd* [2002] 2 NZLR 186 (CA) at 190: "We see no reason to question the interpretation of what is now s97 which this Court took over 100 years ago." *Wilson* is also one of three Prendergast decisions included in the New Zealand Law Reports Leading Cases series, the other two being *Wi Parata* (1877) and *Re Aldridge* (1893).[60]

As a Supreme Court judge, Prendergast CJ adjudicated in a variety of different legal areas. In 1891, Prendergast CJ gave judgment in the case of *Re Campbell's Application* (1891) 10 NZLR 197. This case focused on the Patents, Designs, and

Trademarks Act 1889. While Attorney-General, Prendergast also fulfilled the role of Patent Officer and was therefore well-versed in patent law. Colonial New Zealand demanded new and ingenious devices for solving practical problems in the areas of farming, fishing and mining. In *Re Campbell's*, an application for a patent by Campbell, an Otago miner, had been challenged by another inventor who charged Campbell with infringing his patent. Prendergast CJ decided that the patent ought to be granted, supporting the decision of the Registrar. In his judgment, Prendergast CJ displayed an impressive understanding of basic engineering, proving that his knowledge extended beyond the law:

> The object of both schemes is to add to the force of hydraulic pressure acting on loose material mixed with water in an uptake pipe by combining air with the water and material . . . . [but] . . . . The opponent in this case does not satisfy me that in this case there is not in Campbell's machine a different mechanical contrivance from that of Robertson's, though the principle applied is the same.[61]

Prendergast CJ's judgment also explored the nature of the Registrar's function. This section of the judgment was of great use to Davison CJ in *Beecham Group Ltd v Bristol-Myers Company (No 2)* [1979] 2 NZLR 629, 633. Prendergast CJ's experience as Patent Officer provided the background experience to successfully create a lasting, binding precedent.

One of Prendergast CJ's most enduring legacies is his judgments concerning the nature of Crown grants. The *Wi Parata* case is the most famous example. Another important decision was *Rangimoeke v Strachan* (1895) 14 NZLR 477. This decision, made 18 years after *Wi Parata*, held that Crown grants must be treated with greater reverence than other land ownership methods, and gave judgment to Rangimoeke. Prendergast CJ's support of a Crown grant under challenge was reminiscent of the *Wi Parata* decision, though this time the judgment favoured the Maori plaintiff.[62] Prendergast CJ was able to use his experience in the area of Crown grants to aid his adjudication in *Rangimoeke*. In making his decisions, Prendergast CJ was ready to draw back into his past for knowledge and inspiration.

iii. Ability to successfully deal with high-profile cases
Another successful trait of Prendergast CJ's adjucation was his ability to deal successfully with controversial, high-profile cases. *The Wellington City Election Petition* (1897) 15 NZLR 454 is a case which was high-profile when delivered and remains an important legal precedent today. The case was tried before Prendergast CJ and Conolly J in the Election Court, Wellington, during February 1897. It deals with the petition of Arthur Richmond Atkinson, nephew of Sir Harry Atkinson and of William Richmond. Atkinson challenged the election of his rival George Fisher as the Member of Parliament for the City of Wellington seat. Atkinson had been narrowly defeated and demanded a recount. Atkinson employed Martin Chapman as his lawyer, while Skerrett represented the respondent.

Atkinson argued against the validity of the election on a number of grounds. Firstly, he argued that the votes were incorrectly counted. Prendergast CJ allowed a recount to proceed, citing some of the problems with election procedures: "Incompetent persons may be appointed to the positions of Deputy Returning Officers. Everything is hurried through on the night of the polling-day for the purpose of satisfying the eagerness of the public."[63] The recount confirmed the original result. Atkinson also charged that his opposition had sought to influence the election by providing entertainment on a day other than the polling day, providing taxi cabs to promote the election of Liberal candidates and allowing offensive crowds to dissuade conservative voters from casting their ballot. All these charges were rejected by Prendergast CJ, who held that, even if true, they were not grounds for voiding the election. Atkinson's petition was dismissed with costs and Prendergast CJ, despite his personal sympathies with conservative politicians, confirmed the victory of Seddon's Liberal Party in the City of Wellington electorate.

In his decision, Prendergast CJ made a number of interesting comments about late-1890s New Zealand society. The 1896 Liberal election victory was the second election in which women could vote. Atkinson had accused 'The Women's Social and Political League' of providing afternoon tea the day before the election to sway voters towards Liberal candidates. While Prendergast CJ agreed that this action was intended to sway voters, he could not connect these actions with Fisher.[64] Atkinson also complained that certain conservative women voters were prevented from voting by offensive behaviour at the polling booths. While Prendergast CJ was brought up as a patriarchal English gentleman, he was not convinced of the frailty of women, stating, "I have no doubt that if these ladies really wanted to vote, they could have done so; if not there, elsewhere."[65] *The Wellington City Election* case clearly shows the development of the two-party New Zealand electoral system, a different system to the one Prendergast had worked with during most of his career. Prendergast CJ's decision analysed several areas of election law and was referred to in Cooke J's judgment in *Re Wellington Central Election Petition, Shand v Comber* [1973] 2 NZLR 470, 475 and *Re Te-Au-O-Tonga Election Petition* [1979] 1 NZLR S26, heard in the High Court of the Cook Islands.

Though Prendergast CJ was close to the Richmond-Atkinson clan, this did not prevent him from ruling against Atkinson in this important case. In studying legal history, it is tempting to look for realpolitik and Machiavellian influences in the decisions of judges, especially in controversial cases such as *The Wellington City Election* and *Wi Parata*. In a series of high-profile cases, Prendergast CJ demonstrated an ability to rise above partisan alliances and make decisions based on specific fact situations.

During his 24 years on the bench, Prendergast CJ heard a number of celebrated cases. This book analyses the seminal *Wi Parata* decision (Chapter 8) and the controversial case of *The Attorney-General v Mr Justice Edwards* (this chapter). Other high-profile decisions delivered by Prendergast CJ included *R v Woodgate* (1876), *R v Tuhiata* (1880), *R v Veitch* (1883), *R v Chemis* (1889) and *R v Dean* (1895). These five cases concerned charges of murder. This selection of cases provides insights into Prendergast CJ's handling of controversial decisions.

In only his second year as a Supreme Court judge, Prendergast CJ tried the murder case of *R v Woodgate*. William Woodgate lived with his niece, Susan, in a remote area of the Marlborough Sounds. Susan had become pregnant with her uncle's child and immediately after it was born, Woodgate murdered the child. No body was found. The case hinged on whether or not the child had been born alive or dead and whether the evidence of Susan Woodgate without proper corroboration was enough to win a conviction. Prendergast CJ allowed the evidence to proceed to the jury on the charge of wilful murder, though he wisely reserved the question of evidence for the Court of Appeal.[66] Woodgate was found guilty and the case was taken to the Court of Appeal in January 1877 to be heard by Johnston J and Prendergast CJ. Prendergast CJ was sitting in judgment on his own case, a rather odd situation that occurred in the Court of Appeal on many occasions. Johnston supported Prendergast CJ's decision and William Woodgate was hanged; Prendergast CJ's first judicial death sentence. In his criminal judgments, as in his opinions as Attorney-General, Prendergast CJ showed little tolerance for criminals. His judicial conclusions in high-profile murder trials were not noticeably influenced by media coverage or public debate.

In December 1880, after a jury trial in the Wellington Supreme Court, Prendergast sentenced Tuhiata to death for the murder of Mary Dobie. The murder of a young white woman by a Maori man was always going to attract headlines in colonial New Zealand. According to Treadwell:

> The Chief Justice summed up strongly against the prisoner . . . . the fact that he had acted under the stimulus of intoxicants did not exonerate the prisoner. The prisoner's statement showed that there had been no provocation. He asked the jury to weigh the evidence with care. It was really very simple.[67]

In 1883, Prendergast CJ was faced with the unusual case of *R v Veitch*. Phoebe Veitch had been charged with murdering her four-year-old child by drowning it in the Wanganui River.[68] The Crown Prosecutor called Veitch's seven-year-old son as a witness, and Prendergast CJ "questioned the boy as to his comprehension of an oath, but the answers not being altogether satisfactory, His Honor ruled that he was too young to be examined".[69] Veitch claimed in her defence that the father of the child was responsible for the drowning. The police were unable to find the supposed father, a problem referred to by Prendergast CJ during his two hours of summing-up. The jury concluded that Veitch was guilty but recommended mercy. At this point it was brought to the court's attention that the prisoner was probably pregnant. Prendergast CJ ruled that in order to confirm the pregnancy, a jury of matrons must be called. This unusual step demonstrated the Victorian morality present in late nineteenth-century New Zealand. It was not considered appropriate for men to judge a female matter of such a personal nature.

The criterion for selection as a 'matron' was to be a lady "of whom any town has the right to be proud".[70] The matrons examined Veitch with the aid of a doctor and concluded that she was pregnant. Prendergast CJ stayed the sentence of death and forwarded the original jury's recommendation of mercy to the Government. Veitch escaped execution. Prendergast CJ was criticised for his handling of the case in the *Wanganui Herald*:

> Juries of Matrons, we think, ought to have become an institution that was. There is no necessity to bring respectable modest women from their home to perform such irksome and unpleasant duties. Two professional men could give the information required.[71]

During the same criminal sittings, Prendergast CJ was also criticised for his ignorance in respect of Maori juries. The *Herald* finished its tirade against the Court by providing its own rationale for the actions of Pheobe Veitch, stating that she:

> was fertile soil for criminal results . . . . For it was a kind of insanity, led up to by a life of abandoned profligacy, that a mother, otherwise kind to her child, should deliberately drown it in order to get rid of it.[72]

As with many of the cases tried before Prendergast CJ, *R v Veitch* has much resonance in New Zealand society today. While certain elements of the media disagreed with Prendergast CJ's approach, he again showed a determined ability to remain constant to his view of the case, rather than be swayed by outside influences.

This can also be seen in the *cause célèbre* case of the Italian immigrant Louis Chemis. Chemis had been charged with the murder of Thomas Hawkins. The Crown alleged that Chemis had shot Hawkins twice in the Ngaio Gorge and then finished him off with a stiletto knife. The motive was revenge, relating to a property dispute. The Crown produced limited evidence, and it was suspected that the most convincing evidence had resulted from police corruption or error, in a similar fashion to the infamous cartridge case in the 1970s Arthur Allan Thomas investigation. There was public shock when the jury found Chemis guilty on 15 July 1889: "The Chief Justice was deeply affected, to such an extent, indeed, that he passed sentence incompletely, and the prisoner had to be brought back for the formula to be gone through again."[73] Prendergast sentenced Chemis to death, but the sentence was commuted to life imprisonment due to the controversy. Thus began the long public struggle to free Chemis.

Prendergast retained a staunch position, unaffected by the public and media storm:

I am not aware of any reason why the sentence of death should not be carried into execution. The verdict was, in my opinion, justified by the evidence. This statement is not intended to convey any conclusion of my own on the evidence as to the prisoner's guilt.[74]

Chemis' counsel unsuccessfully petitioned the Court of Appeal for a new trial, but in 1897 the Government bowed to public and political pressure and recommended the release of Chemis. A year later, Chemis walked to Evans Bay, placed a stick of dynamite in his mouth and lit the fuse.[75]

The most high-profile murder case in nineteenth-century New Zealand history was *R v Dean*. Minnie Dean is possibly New Zealand's most famous murderer – the only woman to be hanged in New Zealand history. As with many other memorable New Zealand events in the second half of the nineteenth century, Prendergast CJ was involved in this murder case. Dean has received relatively favourable treatment by scholars in recent times,[76] but during her trial in 1895, she was a hated figure. Dean was accused of "the murder of an infant received by her upon a pretence of adoption, in consideration of a small sum paid to her for its support. Death was alleged to have been caused by the administration of laudanum."[77] The bodies of two infants and the skeleton of another were found buried in her garden, and Dean was sentenced to death by Williams J in Invercargill in June 1895. Questions had arisen during the trial regarding the admission of contentious evidence, including evidence relating to the act of poisoning, the unidentified skeleton, and four undiscovered infants that Dean had also received. Dean's lawyer, Alfred Hanlon, could not be present at the Appeal hearing.[78] The Court of Appeal delivered a strong judgment in favour of Williams J's decision, with Prendergast CJ refusing to allow leave to appeal to the Privy Council.

In his reasoning Prendergast CJ stated that:

the admission of evidence was not contrary to any principle, and is in accordance with what has been decided in reported cases to be permissible. The decision in *Makin's case* is so exactly in point, and, being a judgment of the Privy Council, is of such high authority, that I think it unnecessary to refer to others.[79]

The decision was unanimous (Williams, Denniston, Conolly, Richmond JJ). Richmond J was unable to prepare a judgment due to poor health, so Prendergast CJ spoke on his behalf. The Court of Appeal hearing took place on 27 and 29 July 1895. Richmond J died on 3 August. Richmond had been a legal colleague of Prendergast's for 33 years, including 20 as a judge. Only Michael Prendergast QC had comparable personal and professional influence upon James Prendergast for a similar length of time.

As Chief Justice, Prendergast was faced with several cases involving high-profile political figures, including William Larnach,[80] Edwards J,[81] Francis Bell,[82] and Arthur Richmond Atkinson.[83] In *Re The Puhatikotiko No. 1 Block* (1893) 12 NZLR

131, Prendergast CJ even had to deal with a judgment delivered by his old nemesis, George E. Barton, now a judge of the Native Land Court. To his professional credit, Prendergast CJ displayed impartiality during all these trials, even though he worked with these political figures in the administration of government – a difficult personal challenge. Despite being faced with controversial situations, Prendergast CJ received consistent support from the political establishment and his brother judges.

Many controversial case reports were not covered in the New Zealand Law Reports, but instead were detailed in contemporary newspapers. For example, in 1897, the *Thames Advertiser* discussed a Prendergast CJ decision relating to compensation to miners after the Brunner mine disaster.[84] Newspaper reports were seldom neutral, and in this particular case, the *Thames Advertiser* clearly sided with the Miners' Union. Denniston J provided a decision which effectively reduced the amount of compensation due to the miners, but this was contradicted by a later Prendergast CJ decision:

> The question seems to have hung over until another action came before the Chief Justice a week or two ago, and Sir James Prendergast, so far as we understand the Press Association wire, took a diametrically opposite view, for he seems to have said in effect that the plaintiff having benefited by the [public] fund was no grounds for mitigation of the amount claimed as damages. The point is most important, and will have to go before the Court of Appeal.[85]

Though Prendergast CJ had conservative leanings, in a controversial case such as this, his decision supporting the miners reflects an unbiased and impartial approach to adjudication.

iv. Dissenting judgments on the Court of Appeal Bench

In analysing judicial decision-making, it is important for the legal historian to take special note of dissenting judgments. In these judgments, the adjudicator is forced to clearly outline their ideas and philosophy to justify taking a different position to the other Appeal Court judges. In his 24-year career as Chief Justice, Prendergast CJ rarely delivered dissenting judgments on the Court of Appeal. Statistical analysis of the Law Reports reveals that Prendergast dissented in 16 out of 321 cases (5 per cent). This could have been due to a number of reasons. Through strong leadership Prendergast CJ could have convinced his brother judges to follow his judicial lead, or the Appeal Court judges may have often been of a similar outlook. While Prendergast CJ was a strong administrative leader, critics charged that he often yielded precedence to his brother judges in the Appeal Court.[86] Finally, the rarity of Prendergast CJ's dissenting judgments could be due to his innate conservatism and unwillingness to allow dissension to undermine the clarity and security of the law. Prendergast CJ was committed to delivering justice and if the need arose would speak out with a dissenting voice, but if any opportunity could be found to reconcile his view with the other Appeal Court judges, Prendergast CJ would take that opportunity.

Prendergast CJ's judicial decisions were not always in line with his brother judges. In the Court of Appeal decision *Fanzelow v Kerr* (1896) 14 NZLR 660, Prendergast CJ dissented from the majority judgment of Williams, Denniston and Conolly JJ. The case was one of malicious prosecution and Prendergast believed this charge against the defendant was adequately supported by evidence. In stating his judgment, Prendergast CJ did not hide his doubts and his unease at taking a dissenting viewpoint:

> I take a different view, though I am bound to admit that the question is a doubtful one, not only because it appears to myself upon the case to be a doubtful one, but also because the other members of the Court take a different view of it from that which I take.[87]

Split decisions in the Court of Appeal can cause problems for modern courts, as demonstrated in Richardson J's judgment in *Commercial Union Assurance Co of NZ Ltd v Lamont* [1989] 3 NZLR 187, 194–5 (CA). In this case, Richardson J compared the majority judgments in *Fanzelow* with Prendergast CJ's minority judgment, finding the majority decision more convincing. In taking a different viewpoint from the other Court of Appeal judges, Prendergast CJ demonstrated an independent streak and a willingness to support his own judgment even if it could lead to dissension.

Prendergast CJ's most famous dissenting judgment was in the high-profile case of *The Attorney-General v Mr Justice Edwards* (1891) 9 NZLR 321. The facts of this case will be dealt with later in this chapter, but the decision delivered by Prendergast CJ reveals a judge ready to take a courageous stand, even in the glare of the public spotlight. While essentially cautious, in certain circumstances, Prendergast could be outspoken and controversial. Prendergast CJ's decision was exhaustive and thorough. In his conclusion, Prendergast clearly stated his case against appointing Edwards as a Supreme Court judge:

> As I think there was no authority in law to make the appointment, the judgment of this Court ought to be for cancelling the letters patent; but, the opinion of the majority of the Court being otherwise, the judgment will, of course, be for the defendant.[88]

Conolly J also provided a dissenting judgment in the case and Prendergast CJ's decision was eventually vindicated by the Privy Council. While rare, Prendergast CJ's dissenting judgments provide vital insights into his approach to decision-making.

B. *Conservatism*

i. *Reliance on English precedent*

James Prendergast was a conservative Chief Justice. In his reliance on English precedent and cautious, suspicious approach to change, Prendergast CJ displayed a reverence for tradition and past experience. Though land and criminal law were the two most notable areas of Prendergast CJ's legal legacy, he also delivered important judgments in solicitor and client relations, torts, bankruptcy, patents, commercial, family, liquor licensing and election law. For example, in the year of the *Wi Parata* decision, the Court of Appeal heard the case of *Barton v Allan* (1878) 3 NZ Jur NS 46. In this case, the solicitor G. B. Barton (not Prendergast's nemesis) effectively sought to charge his client on two separate occasions for one whole piece of work. Prendergast CJ delivered the judgment of the Court supporting the Supreme Court decision of Williams J. As Attorney-General, Prendergast had paid particular attention to the ethical actions of solicitors, and in this case the client claimed victory. Prendergast's ratio was quoted at length by Eichelbaum J in the case of *Parsons v Young Swan Morison McKay* [1986] 2 NZLR 204:

> it must be assumed that the employment by the defendant of the plaintiff was that ordinarily existing between solicitor and client . . . . It must be assumed therefore that the work was done under an entire contract; therefore the plaintiff could not maintain an action for any part of the work done until the whole contract was performed, and all work done under the contract formed one indivisible cause of action.[89]

Prendergast CJ's decision was strongly supported with relevant English case law. In the early years of his Chief Justiceship, Prendergast was able to depend upon English precedent to support his decisions.

The importance of English legal precedent also featured in the case of *Tarry v The Taranaki County Council* (1894) 12 NZLR 467. In this case, the Magistrate Court's decision in favour of the Council was upheld in the Court of Appeal. The decision was a divisive one, with Richmond J and Prendergast CJ agreeing with the overall judgment, but taking issue with the criticism of an important precedent by Williams and Denniston JJ. The *Tarry* case provides the historian with insights into the nature of New Zealand's infrastructure during the late nineteenth century. Tarry sustained injuries to himself and his coach through the neglect of the Taranaki Council in not repairing a hole in a road. The Court of Appeal decided that the Council could not be held liable for mere nonfeasance.[90] Denniston and Williams JJ attempted to reconcile decisions of the Privy Council and House of Lords but were unable to do so, leading them to criticise the Privy Council judgment in *The Borough of Bathurst v Macpherson* 4 App. Cas. 256.

Richmond J's judgment also canvassed the relevant case law, but stated that the cases could be reconciled. Richmond J continued to argue:

> If, however, there is any real conflict between the decision of the Privy Council
> in the *Bathurst* case and the decision of the House of Lords in *Cowley v The
> Newmarket Local Board*, and of the Privy Council again in the *Pictou* case, I do
> not think it is for us to intervene.[91]

Prendergast CJ followed Richmond J's argument, conservatively stating, "I
entertain the same hesitancy as Mr Justice Richmond in criticizing the judgment
in the *Bathurst* case. We are taking a new departure, and it behoves us to move
somewhat carefully."[92] Richmond J and Prendergast CJ were unwilling to criticise
the higher English courts. When the New Zealand Court of Appeal angrily
confronted the Privy Council in 1903, the conservative influence of Richmond J
and Prendergast CJ was gone from the bench, but Williams and Denniston JJ were
present. In the case of *Hocking v Attorney-General* [1963] NZLR 513, North J shared
the doubts of Williams and Denniston JJ, reflecting an age in which there was a less
reluctant approach to criticising English decisions.[93]

As Attorney-General, Prendergast relied heavily on English statute law in
formulating his legislation. As Chief Justice, Prendergast again turned to English
legislation when supporting his judgments. In the case *Bell v Finn* (1896) 14 NZLR
447, Prendergast CJ interpreted the Arbitration Act 1890, in a dispute over counsel's
fees. Prendergast CJ opened his judgment by stating:

> The case of *Longman v East*, on which the application was principally based,
> turned wholly on the Judicature Act. Since then the English Arbitration Act has
> introduced a substantial difference; and our Act is a close copy of the English
> Arbitration Act. Under the Judicature Act the whole cause could not be referred,
> but only particular facts; and that makes all the difference.[94]

Part of the problem in the *Bell* case was the dual nature of many New Zealand
lawyers, who acted as both barristers and solicitors. In *Bell*, "The statement of
defence disputed the right of the firm of solicitors who were also counsel to sue
for counsel's fees payable to members of their own firm."[95] The New Zealand
legal system attempted to simplify the English tradition of keeping barristers and
solicitors separate. In doing so, new problems arose, as in the *Bell* case, and also,
Robinson and Morgan-Coakle v Behan [1964] NZLR 650, in which the *Bell* case is
applied to modern legal practice.

Prendergast CJ's reliance on English common law was shared by many of his
contemporaries.[96] In *Wotherspon v Dobson* [1893] 11 NZLR 283, 287, Prendergast
CJ noted, "we ought generally in such a case [concerning damages] to follow the
English practice, because it is probable that good sense will be found in it". He did
not rely on English law exclusively; he also made reference to the law existing in
the Australian colonies, especially Victoria and South Australia. Prendergast CJ
had personal experience in the Victorian colony and had relied upon the Torrens
system of land registration invented in South Australia. Occasionally, Prendergast
CJ referred to United States law, for example, in the *Wi Parata* decision.

In some areas of New Zealand's legal system, the English influence was fading. For example Prendergast CJ's legal speciality was in the area of pleading, but this area of the law was removed on the instructions of recommendation 14 of the 1881 Royal Commission on Common Law Procedure: "That in all cases there be no formal pleadings, save particulars of claim and statement of defence." The convoluted English approach to special pleading had already largely been removed from New Zealand by William Martin's 1844 Supreme Court Rules.[97] In cases from 1875 to 1881, Prendergast CJ's comprehensive knowledge of special pleading is evident. Trained in the English legal system, Prendergast utilised this background when adjudicating as Chief Justice.

ii. Support of the establishment
While Prendergast CJ was by all accounts an impartial judge, it must be noted that many of his decisions were in favour of established and powerful institutions such as the Crown, local government and high-ranking professionals. Fairly or unfairly, he was not known as a judge for the underdog.

Prendergast CJ played a role in the celebrated poisoning case *R v Hall* during 1886 and 1887. Thomas Hall had been convicted of attempting to poison his wife in 1886 and the following year was found guilty in the Supreme Court of murdering his father-in-law by poisoning. In the second trial, Williams J had sentenced Hall to death. This verdict was quashed on a technicality by the Court of Appeal, headed by Prendergast CJ.[98] Prendergast concurred with the judgment delivered by Johnston J but left Wellington before it was written, leaving a note that "he must not be taken as assenting to every expression of opinion which may occur in the written judgment about to be pronounced".[99] The evidence used to convict Hall in the second trial was the unsuccessful attempt on his wife's life. The Court of Appeal ruled that this was insufficient evidence.

Hall was the nephew of Sir John Hall, the prominent Premier, who had been closely involved with Prendergast CJ during the invasion of Parihaka in 1881. The Court of Appeal judgment caused an angry outburst from the public and press, who accused the Court of ruling in favour of Hall because of his family connections.[100] Johnston J was directly in the firing line, partly due to Prendergast's absence. The Court of Appeal was vigorously criticised for its decision by the New South Wales Court of Appeal when it later heard a similar case, *R v Makin*. It has been argued that a different set of rules was applied by Prendergast CJ and the Court of Appeal to Thomas Hall in 1887 than to Minnie Dean in 1895.[101]

iii. Literal approach to statutory interpretation
New Zealand law has been dominated by legislation, therefore making judicial statutory interpretation of great importance. Prendergast CJ was often faced with the task of interpreting recent New Zealand legislation. He did allow for liberal interpretation of statutes at times, referring to the 'spirit' of the legislation. But

usually Prendergast took a conservative, literal approach, as in *Re A Lease, Whakarare to Williams* (1894) 12 NZLR 494, 495: "The safe construction of any legislative Act is to take the literal words of the Act, unless you can see a clear meaning to the contrary appearing from the provisions of the Act itself." Sometimes, Prendergast CJ also discussed recent New Zealand case law, though this body of law was still in its early stages. Relying on New Zealand common law became somewhat easier during the final stages of Prendergast's Chief Justiceship, with the continued success of the New Zealand Law Reports.

As Chief Justice, Prendergast was called upon to interpret legislation relating to local government matters. Two important decisions in this area included *Nelson City Corporation v Nelson College* (1896) 14 NZLR 507 and *Jenkins v The Mayor, Councillors, and Citizens of the City of Wellington* (1896) 15 NZLR 118. While the *Nelson City Corporation* case, dealing with rateable property and water supply, was briefly referred to in the 1966 decision *Auckland City v Auckland Metropolitan Fire Board* [1967] NZLR 615, 622, it is Prendergast CJ's decision in *Jenkins* which has left a more noticeable legacy. In *Jenkins*, a claim had been made for compensation when a public drain was constructed under private land. Prendergast CJ applied a narrow approach to statutory interpretation:

> I think that the proper reading of this section is to connect the word "suffering" with the preceding word "person", and not with the word "land"; though in the present case, as the damage alleged to have been suffered is to land, it is not necessary to do more than decide that, at any rate all cases of damage by reason of land being "injuriously affected" would be within the provision.[102]

Edwards J, in an *obiter* decision, disagreed with Prendergast CJ's approach, but did not receive the support of his fellow judges.

While Prendergast CJ preferred a literal approach to statutory interpretation, he demonstrated a certain amount of flexibility. In the Supreme Court case of *Arihi Te Nahu v Locke* (1887) 5 NZLR 408, Prendergast CJ made an interesting judgment regarding costs and taxation between solicitor and client. The case, which dealt with land law, was tried in Napier by Prendergast CJ, but the Chief Justice did not properly settle the question of costs. Later in Gisborne the plaintiffs managed to elicit extremely high solicitor's costs out of the estate in question. Prendergast CJ set aside this unfair situation and in his judgment essentially looked to what was fair in that specific fact situation:

> It is to be hoped, however, that when the decree comes to be settled, it may be found possible to fix by consent or otherwise, a gross sum for the costs, for this is more in accordance with the spirit, if not the requirements of the Judicature Act and the scale thereby fixed.[103]

In this decision, Prendergast CJ proved that he could move beyond the black letter of the law and look to the general purpose of a statute.

iv. Caution

Prendergast CJ's approach to adjudication included a mixture of pragmatism, efficiency and caution. In delivering his judgments, Prendergast CJ sometimes used cautious language, indicating doubt on his part. For example, in the case *R v Vowles* (1885) 3 NZLR 111, concerning embezzlement by a government officer, Prendergast CJ concluded that:

> I *think* that the facts might have been more precise. . . . This fund is *in a sense* public money, and in a sense also trust money, but it is only in a sense . . . . I *think* the regulations may be good . . . . I therefore *think* we may look upon him as a person employed in the public service under Her Majesty, and that the conviction therefore *ought* to be affirmed.[italics added][104]

In *Piripi Te Maari v Stewart* (1892) 11 NZLR 205, Prendergast CJ's caution and uncertainty aided in having his decision overturned in the Court of Appeal. In giving judgment, Richmond J stated:

> In the judgment appealed from, His Honour the Chief Justice said he was very doubtful as to the interpretation of the statute which he adopted. We should have taken time to consider our judgment if the Chief Justice had expressed anything like a positive opinion contrary to that which we have arrived at.[105]

While often careful and cautious, Prendergast also assertively maintained discipline in his court. In *Hawera County Council v Standard Insurance Company* (1889) 7 NZLR 268, 270, Prendergast stated, "I think it is important that parties should not be able to play fast and loose in any Court". As a Chief Justice, Prendergast brought discipline to the courtroom.

C. Weaknesses as a judge

i. Brief treatment of important legal issues

While Prendergast CJ was widely respected by his peers, there were notable deficiencies in his approach to adjudication. The Supreme Court case of *Doyle v Edwards* (1898) 16 NZLR 572 has been referred to numerous times in recent legal decisions. Prendergast CJ's decision affirmed the ability of Crown land to be free from restrictive by-laws. In a very brief judgment, Prendergast CJ once more upheld the power of Crown land. The judgment does not seek to explore relevant authorities but is basically Prendergast CJ's opinion on the Municipal Corporations Act 1886. Though it could seem that Prendergast CJ was remiss in providing so brief a decision on an important matter of law, it must be remembered that judgments were noticeably shorter in the nineteenth century and Prendergast CJ was clearly certain of his decision. The Chief Justice stated:

> I think it is plain what construction must be given to the words of section 3 of "The Municipal Corporations Act, 1886." It is plain there is a property in the

land and building vested in the Crown. It is true, that there is a property in the
lessee; but, inasmuch as serious liabilities would be imposed on the Crown if its
land, though under lease, were subject to all building by-laws, and to the various
provisions of the Municipal Corporations Act relating to nuisances, &c., I think
section 3 does exempt land belonging to and vested in the Crown, although a
leasehold interest is created, and that it cannot be said that this builder was liable
to get a permit. To hold so would be to affect the land.[106]

The Court of Appeal in 1964 followed Prendergast CJ's decision, but only after
expressing dissatisfaction with its formulation. In *Lower Hutt City v Attorney-General*
[1965] NZLR 65, Turner J described his opinion of Prendergast CJ's judgment:

> Prendergast C.J. did not take time to consider his judgment, which occupies
> only twenty lines in the report. The judgment contains no reasoning supporting
> its conclusion, nor does it cite any authority . . . . [but] . . . . *Doyle v Edwards* is
> by virtue of its age a compelling authority.[107]

Wilson J, in *Victory Park Board v Christchurch City* [1965] NZLR 741, avoided
Turner J's predicament by simply distinguishing *Doyle* and *Lower Hutt City*.[108] In
more recent times, Cooke J applied the *Doyle* ratio in *Wellington City Council v
Victoria University of Wellington* [1975] 2 NZLR 301, while Prichard J found the
decision unhelpful in *Retaruke Timber Co Ltd v Rodney County Council* [1984] 2
NZLR 129. Like *Wi Parata*, the *Doyle* decision has been utilised by some judges
and ignored by others; either way, Prendergast CJ's brief and insufficient reasoning
has created problems for later judges.

Prendergast CJ was a tireless worker and a model of judicial endurance. His
ability to carry out both the decision-making and administrative functions of
Chief Justice for 24 years is a testimony to this fact. Prendergast CJ's efficiency
occasionally appeared excessive, as in *Light v Milton* (1883) 2 NZLR 214: "It is
not necessary to consider our judgment. I think we may decide the question by
looking at the Act generally." Prendergast CJ's decisions actually improved as his
judicial career progressed, and most of his landmark judgments were made in the
final years of his career. Approximately a quarter of Prendergast CJ's judgments
reported in the Law Reports appear in the final four years of his career.

In *Olsen v Bailey* (1888) 6 NZLR 713, Prendergast CJ adjudicated in the area
of trespass by cattle. The case was heard in Gisborne in 1888, when Prendergast
CJ was aged 62 years. Arduous journeys, such as from Wellington to Gisborne,
were an integral part of a Supreme Court judge's work, and must be taken into
account when analysing their contributions. Prendergast CJ was especially
dedicated to circuit work throughout his long judicial career, suggesting that he
had an impressive physical constitution. In *Olsen*, Prendergast gave judgment to
the defendant despite his sheep trespassing on Olsen's land. Olsen was held to
be to blame for the poor upkeep of his fence.[109] The decision was another basic

application of legislation to a specific fact situation and no case law is mentioned in Prendergast CJ's brief decision. A lack of attention to relevant common law precedent is apparent in a number of Prendergast CJ's important judgments.

In the long-running saga of *Russell v The Minister of Lands* (1898) 17 NZLR 241 and 780, the second reported case (*No.2* – May 1899), which was presented before a full Supreme Court, is an apposite example of a complex real property case. The case was appealed from a decision by Edwards J in the Compensation Court and upheld by Prendergast CJ, Denniston, Conolly and Edwards JJ in the Supreme Court. The case dealt with the acquisition of land by the Crown for public purposes and relevant compensation. The case had also been heard by Prendergast CJ in the Supreme Court in October 1898. In the final 1899 decision, Prendergast CJ delivered the leading judgment confirming the ability of the Compensation Court to award extra compensation, "No doubt the compensation for compulsorily taking ought to be included in the amount to be awarded for compensation."[110] When the *Russell* case was mentioned in *Coomber v Birkenhead Borough Council* [1980] 2 NZLR 681, Speight J and R. J. MacLachlan Esq. bypassed Prendergast CJ's judgment, as it "was upheld with brief reasons and the ratio can be best followed from the observations of Edwards J in the Compensation Court".[111] Thus, *Russell* is another example of modern judicial criticism of Prendergast CJ's brief treatment of legal issues in his decisions.

ii. Vague judgments

Prendergast CJ was a master of brief judgments. In the Court of Appeal decision *Blaymires v Ewing* (1890) 9 NZLR 567, Prendergast CJ delivered one of his most vague decisions. The case was on appeal from a decision by Richmond J in the Supreme Court, arguing that Richmond J had acted on an incorrect principle when awarding costs. Prendergast CJ defended Richmond J's decision, stating: "The spirit of our rules is to give the Judge a discretion as to costs . . . . If there is anything at all in the nature of a hard-and-fast rule, it is that a successful party is to have his costs."[112] Prendergast CJ did not provide any legal evidence to support his reasoning.

Prendergast CJ's decision in *Re Rickman, Ex parte The Bank of New Zealand* (1890) 8 NZLR 381 is another example of vague adjudication. In the case *Rural Banking and Finance Corporation of New Zealand Ltd v Official Assignee* [1991] 2 NZLR 351, Fisher J dismissed Prendergast CJ's decision as it "contained no reasons other than the bald comment with respect to mortgaged land that 'it cannot, to my mind, be said that this is land subject to onerous covenants.'"[113] The *Re Rickman* case concerned that power of the Official Assignee under the Bankruptcy Act 1883 in regard to mortgages on land. Prendergast CJ referred to the relevant practice in England, but then stated that this was irrelevant to the present New Zealand case. Prendergast CJ relied heavily on English law and often seemed frustrated that he could not use it more readily in New Zealand courts.

Another weakness apparent in Prendergast CJ's judgments relates to his writing style. In *Low v Hutchinson* (1893) 13 NZLR 55, Prendergast CJ adjudicated on the Licensing Act 1881. In this case, there had been a temporary transfer of a publican's license. During the temporary transfer, the original licensee was convicted of an offence committed before the transfer was granted. Prendergast CJ held that the conviction could not be recorded upon the license as it was currently vested in the temporary transferee. In the judgment, Prendergast CJ's ratio contains a clear example of his complex syntax:

> It is in my opinion quite clear that, when, in consequence of a change of tenancy of the premises in respect of which a publican's license is granted, the licensee procures a temporary transfer of his license to be made to the new tenant and indorsed on the license, such temporary transfer is, pending the application for an ordinary transfer at the then ensuing quarterly licensing meeting, for all purposes a transfer of the license.[114]

This judgment was discussed at length in the decision of Richmond J in *Johns v Westland District Licensing Committee* [1961] NZLR 35. While the *Low* ratio has been influential, it is not an accessible precedent due to its awkward, dense construction.

iii. Weak judgments/overturned decisions

The sizeable number of decisions made by Prendergast CJ in the Supreme Court and later overturned in the Court of Appeal suggests a number of unconvincing judgments on the part of the Chief Justice. Despite Prendergast CJ's command of bankruptcy law, in 1896, three years before his retirement, his Supreme Court decision *Re Reimer, Ex parte The Official Assignee* (1896) 15 NZLR 198 was overturned by the Court of Appeal. The Court of Appeal consisted of Denniston, Conolly and Edwards JJ. Richmond J had died the previous year, leaving Prendergast CJ without his most loyal legal supporter. Prendergast CJ's judgment in the Supreme Court is confusing and contradictory. The case dealt with a debtor who had sold his business to his creditor with a term of the sale being that the creditor should be entitled to set off the indebtedness against the price payable for the business. In the case of *Re Proudfoot, A Bankrupt, Ex parte Ballins Breweries (New Zealand) Limited* [1961] NZLR 268, Prendergast CJ's decision caused problems for the Court of Appeal. In his judgment, Cleary J stated that:

> Sir James Prendergast C.J. made somewhat inconsistent findings. He found that the substantial object of the transaction on the part of the creditor was to acquire the hotelkeeper's business . . . . He also found, however, that so far as the arrangement for set-off was concerned, it was stipulated for by the creditor with the object of getting a preference and the bankrupt's agreement thereto constituted a preference, and he ordered the creditor to make a refund to the Official Assignee. In the Court of Appeal, this order was set aside.[115]

In the preceding Supreme Court decision of Hutchinson J,[116] the judge spent a sizeable portion of his decision coping with Prendergast CJ's awkward reasoning. The maxim 'hard cases make bad law' has some resonance in Prendergast CJ's *Reimer* decision.

iv. Difficulties in dealing with Maori issues

It has been argued in this book that Prendergast CJ's judicial legacy is primarily in the areas of land law, criminal law and the law relating to Maori. Earlier in this section, Prendergast CJ's influence on land and criminal law was mentioned, and in Chapter 8, Prendergast CJ's impact on Maori land and the Treaty of Waitangi is analysed in depth. But within Prendergast CJ's corpus of cases are a number of decisions relating to Maori but not directly concerned with land or sovereignty. For example, in the Supreme Court case of *Rira Peti v Ngaraihi Te Paku* (1888) 7 NZLR 235, Prendergast CJ discussed the law relating to Maori and matrimony. The decision in *Rira Peti* bears all the trademarks of a Prendergast CJ judgment: it is relatively brief, deals with a moderate range of common law and statute, is influenced by English precedent and shows little regard for non-English perspectives. The case facts concern a will, but the ratio of *Rira Peti* in relation to Maori customary law was that "Marriage between persons of the native race is governed by the common law of England . . . and must, therefore, be solemnized before a minister of some Christian denomination."[117]

Prendergast CJ refused to accept the validity of Maori 'usages' although he did state: "The natives are British subjects, their relations to each other are governed by the laws of the land, and not by their usages, unless, and only so far as these laws have provided for the recognition of their usages."[118] This statement is interesting, given the dismissal of statutory references to Maori custom in the *Wi Parata* decision. The *Rira Peti* decision has been described as "ludicrous", due to Prendergast CJ's proposition that tribal marriages had been subject to the common law since 1840.[119] Seuffert argues that Prendergast's judgment "ignores 20 years of British policy in New Zealand, and the legislative context and intent of the section exempting Maori marriages from the successive Marriage Acts".[120] Seuffert concludes that: "In 1888 Chief Justice Prendergast was to ignore the early history of the colony, violently erasing Maori law and custom with respect to marriage, unequivocally excluding it from the boundaries of jurisdiction, and from the nation."[121]

The case of *Broughton v Donnelly*, relating to a Maori will, was mentioned in one of Prendergast CJ's obituaries. The *Dominion* incorrectly stated that Prendergast CJ's decision in this high-profile case "was not upheld by the Appeal Court, but the Privy Council took the same view as he had".[122] In fact, the Privy Council affirmed the Court of Appeal decision. In *Broughton*, Prendergast CJ held that the will in question was valid and that Maori witnesses must be accorded differing treatment to European witnesses:

It is impossible for native witnesses to give reliable evidence when a question depends upon the time when an alleged fact occurred, or upon the lapse of time . . . . it is not possible to apply the same tests of their credibility as in the case of other witnesses.[123]

The Court of Appeal, in a judgment delivered by Richmond J, disagreed with Prendergast CJ's approach. Therefore, in this particular case relating to Maori, the *Wi Parata* decision-makers disagreed. Prendergast's decisions in the area of Maori affairs strongly reflect racial attitudes of the era and seem paternalistic from a modern perspective.

D. Decisions reflecting the colonial environment

The cases heard by Prendergast CJ from 1875 to 1899 reflected the colonial environment from which they arose. New Zealand during the late nineteenth century was a rapidly growing agricultural community, focused on land. In this community, actions in tort often related to farming practice. While a case such as *Webber v Finnimore* (1880) 1 OB&F (SC) 150, dealing with the shooting of a dog for chasing sheep, may seem of minor importance today, in 1880 it was of major importance. Livestock and land were the keys to prosperity, and sheep and cattle must be protected at all costs. The Injuries by Dogs Act, passed in 1865 when Prendergast CJ first entered the Legislative Council, governed this area of the law. In *Webber*, Prendergast CJ stated that the right to destroy a dog found in the Act was only "at the time when the dog was at large among sheep" and did not extend to hours afterwards. With a 17-line application of the statute to the facts, Prendergast CJ set a precedent which would still be used 78 years later, in the case of *Payze v Everitt* [1959] NZLR 423, 425. The plaintiff, Webber, had appealed from the decision of a Resident Magistrate, and Prendergast CJ allowed the appeal. Prendergast CJ seemed far more ready to overturn appeals from the Magistrates' Courts than those from the Supreme Court.

The fledgling New Zealand economy during the late nineteenth century was often unstable and moved in cycles of boom and bust. A severe depression during the 1880s saw many would-be businessmen face bankruptcy and financial ruin. With a salary fixed by statute, James Prendergast flourished financially throughout the depression, but many of those who appeared in court before him were not so fortunate. In the case of *Re McGregor; Ex parte McGregor* (1888) 7 NZLR 241, Prendergast CJ was faced with a legal question relating to the Bankruptcy Act 1885. In this case, Prendergast CJ ruled against the creditor, stating, "Creditors who, knowing that a dividend has been declared, and is about to be paid, delay claiming by sending in their proof, do so at the risk of losing payment of the dividend."[124] The case was heard at Wanganui, the scene of several important decisions by Prendergast CJ. During Prendergast's time as Chief Justice, Wanganui played a more prominent role in New Zealand affairs than it does today.

One of the staples of New Zealand colonial life was alcohol. In a social culture dominated by males, beer and spirits were consumed in large quantities. The licensing of alcohol was a complex legal issue, especially due to the fact that the liquor industry was a powerful voice in political life. Several prominent nineteenth-century politicians took very public stands on the alcohol issue. Richard Seddon, who was a publican before becoming Premier, was a strong supporter of the alcohol industry, while Premier William Fox was a vocal supporter of complete prohibition. No mention is made in Prendergast's personal archival material regarding alcohol. It is likely that Prendergast supported moderation in this area, as in most other areas of life. The alcoholism of his father and two brothers may have influenced his views. Prendergast CJ made several influential judgments in the area of liquor licensing. Though they provide some insights into Prendergast's views on the topic, the legal historian must be wary of assuming judicial decisions in some way reflect personal viewpoints. While no judge is totally objective and free from personal bias, the role of the judge is to apply the law to the facts, not to make personal value judgments about the issues involved. Prendergast CJ took his role as a judge very seriously and respected the impartiality of the position.

In *Jull v Treanor* (1896) 14 NZLR 513, Prendergast CJ found himself faced with a case dealing with the Licensing Act 1881, with arguments provided by Skerrett and Gully, the same lawyers who appeared in *Nankivell* (1893). This *déjà vu* case was on appeal from the Magistrates' Court, where a licensee was convicted of selling liquor during closing hours, vicariously through the actions of a staff member. Prendergast CJ quashed the conviction because the staff member was not authorised to sell liquor. While stating his reasons, Prendergast CJ argued that, "The penalty is on the person who sells. No doubt the licensee is liable if he himself sells, or if any person sells who is his agent in the sale."[125] This ratio was used by North P and Turner J in *Gifford v Police* [1965] NZLR 484, 488, 495. In the *Jull* judgment, Prendergast CJ did not hesitate to openly criticise the decision of the Woodville Magistrate, describing it as "an erroneous view of the law".[126] Prendergast CJ was understandably more reluctant to use this language when dealing with cases on appeal from the Supreme Court.

In an era which included corporal and capital punishment, Prendergast demonstrated some progressive thinking. Nine-year-old John Thomas Reid had committed a string of minor offences by the time he appeared before Prendergast CJ in 1876 for stealing clothing at the Thorndon Baths. As he was a repeat offender, Prendergast had no choice under law but to commit him to prison briefly and order a flogging. In passing judgment, Prendergast argued that: "The only way to reach cases of this sort is, clearly, to establish a reformatory, where young offenders may be taught some useful trade, and by means of which the evil that is in them may be somewhat eradicated." Prendergast was not particularly concerned about the flogging but saw the incarceration as inappropriate and futile. The speech was a clear signal to lawmakers to examine and reform youth sentencing.[127]

Prendergast CJ's decisions reflected the colonial environment in which they were created. The legal historian must attempt to view judicial decisions on subjects such as farming, bankruptcy, liquor and criminal sentencing in the context in which they were made. An analysis of Prendergast CJ's decisions sheds light on the nature of late nineteenth-century New Zealand society.

E. Summary

From this summary of Prendergast CJ's legacy in case law, it becomes clear that his most important decisions, with the exception of *Wi Parata*, were made in the final years of his Chief Justiceship. Of Prendergast's 46 cases referred to in reported cases since 1959, 18 were in the final four years of his judicial career, or 39 per cent of the cases in 17 per cent of his career. This could well be a reflection of his maturity as a judge, the large number of cases he heard during this period, or perhaps the greater precedential strength of more recent decisions. Two of Prendergast CJ's most important decisions, *Merrie v McKay* (1897) and *Doyle v Edwards* (1898), were delivered in his final two years as a judge. His least convincing landmark decision, *Wi Parata*, was made only two years into his judicial career. Interestingly, the decisions of Prendergast CJ's final years were made without the influence of Richmond J, who died in 1895.

A common, though approximate, indication of a judge's success is the number of cases upheld in a higher court. A number of Prendergast CJ's decisions in the Wellington Supreme Court were appealed to the Court of Appeal, and a few appealed beyond to the Privy Council. The clear majority of appeals against Prendergast CJ were unsuccessful but in terms of the New Zealand Law Reports, approximately 30 per cent of appeals from Prendergast CJ's Supreme Court decisions resulted in the Court of Appeal overturning the judgment. This is a similar figure to Robert Stout's 33 per cent. It is possible that these reversals were reported due to their controversial nature, but regardless of this, Prendergast CJ had approximately 13 decisions overruled in the New Zealand Law Reports. While this is not an alarming number, it casts doubt upon the claim that Prendergast CJ's decisions were very seldom overturned.[128]

Prendergast CJ often took an active approach to adjudication. During the arguments of counsel, Prendergast CJ was always ready to interrupt if necessary to provide his views on a statute, case or line of reasoning. As Supreme Court Judge in Wellington, Prendergast CJ was fortunate to have the services of a highly competent bar, including advocates such as Martin and Frederick Chapman, Francis Bell, Hugh Gully, William Travers, Charles Izard, Charles Skerrett and Robert Stout. As a lawyer in Dunedin, Prendergast had been part of the strongest bar in New Zealand and as a judge in Wellington, he adjudicated before what had replaced Dunedin as the strongest bar in New Zealand.

The Court of Appeal Bench from 1875 to 1899 was made up of a variety of different personalities and perspectives. Prendergast CJ and Richmond J were conservative judges and close associates. Williams, Johnston, Denniston and Conolly JJ tended to avoid activist judgments, though could be outspoken on occasion. Gillies and Edwards JJ were the most likely members of the Court to support judicial activism and deliver controversial judgments. While there was natural disagreement in the Court of Appeal, in the Wellington Supreme Court Prendergast CJ and Richmond J almost always supported each other's judgments. Disagreement in the one Supreme Court with two judges would have undermined that court, when all other Supreme Courts had solo judges delivering unanimous judgments. A split decision in the Supreme Court would also require a case to proceed to the Court of Appeal to be heard again.

From 1875 to 1895, Richmond J and Prendergast CJ shared the bench of the Supreme Court in Wellington. The volume of cases in the Wellington Supreme Court steadily increased as this period progressed, culminating in Prendergast's busiest year, 1895. In this year, Richmond J died, leaving Prendergast CJ as the sole Supreme Court judge in Wellington. The number of judgments delivered by Prendergast CJ in the Court of Appeal and Supreme Court and reported in the New Zealand Law Reports averages approximately 27 per year. In 1895, the number of cases is 51.[129]

Prendergast CJ's decisions attest to strengths and weaknesses in his adjudicative approach. Prendergast CJ was able to marshal past experiences and legal training to deliver many comprehensive and influential decisions. His professional approach allowed him to securely deal with high-profile cases and interpret his own legislation. He showed a strong reliance on English precedent and preferred a literal approach to statutory interpretation. As Chief Justice, Prendergast had limitations, including a tendency to deliver brief, vague decisions, and a rather dismissive and paternalistic attitude towards Maori affairs. In summary, Prendergast CJ was a solid judicial decision-maker, but not an inspired one.

3. Jurisprudential influences in decisions

The issues facing Prendergast were essentially practical in nature, but the approach he took was influenced by his intellectual and theoretical background. Prendergast CJ was not a legal philosopher, but he was so well-versed in the law that he would consciously and subconsciously deal with the great jurisprudential issues of the era. Prendergast CJ's judgments do not include many references to sources of a jurisprudential nature. Even legal textbooks received little mention in his decisions as Chief Justice. Most of his decisions rely on statute and case law, though some

are essentially common sense applied to a specific fact situation. Prendergast was
an intelligent man with a degree from one of the world's leading universities, but
his reading was mainly confined to the law. In looking for the intellectual context
of Prendergast CJ's decisions, it must be remembered that Prendergast CJ was a
practical judge, rather than an intellectual one. Unlike Henry Chapman, Joshua
Williams and John Salmond, Prendergast CJ did not usually canvass large amounts
of relevant literary material in reaching his legal conclusions.

While Prendergast CJ's decisions did not usually utilise jurisprudential texts to
any great extent, there are exceptions. In *R v Bern* (1895), Prendergast CJ made
reference to Joseph Chitty's *Criminal Law*. Joseph Chitty was the patriarch of the
famous Chitty legal dynasty and father of Prendergast's English mentor, Thomas
Chitty. In *Rangimoeke v Strachan* (1895), Prendergast CJ considered the real property
text *Sugden on Powers* (8th edition). In one of his earliest landmark decisions, *Barton
v Allan* (1878), he referred to *Bigelow on Estoppel* and *Taylor on Evidence*. In the *Wi
Parata* decision, also made in 1877, Prendergast CJ (probably led by Richmond J)
also canvassed a large range of legal sources, possibly reflecting the desire of a new
judge for intellectual credibility. While Prendergast CJ's references to texts were
limited, it must be remembered that it is primarily the duty of counsel to provide
the court with legal evidence. The judge utilises this evidence in the course of
reaching a judgment.

The legacy of Prendergast CJ's decisions is their practical effects on New
Zealand society, for example, the effect of *Wi Parata* on the retention of Maori
land. With the exception of Treaty law and native title, Prendergast CJ did not
greatly shape legal theory in New Zealand. The jurisprudence existing in New
Zealand during the late nineteenth century was primarily imported from England.
It must also be noted that Prendergast CJ was a busy judge, and brief judgments
dealing solely with the facts and law in question made for a more efficient court.
The number of reported judgments made by Prendergast CJ during his time on the
bench is impressive, though the quality of decision-making varies.

Prendergast CJ's jurisprudential outlook can be further explored by analysing
his role in the formulation of the 'Examinations for Barristers and Solicitors'
in 1875.[130] As Chief Justice, Prendergast was nominally responsible for setting
the examination papers for prospective barristers. It is unclear to what degree
Prendergast CJ was personally responsible for the formulation of the examinations,
but they bear his name. Prendergast CJ's examinations are clearly modelled on
English ones. The subjects that candidates were expected to study for the general
knowledge examination included Latin (Cicero, Livy, Virgil's *Aeneid*), Greek
(Homer's *Iliad*, Sophocles' *Antigone*, Herodotus), and Law (Property, Common
Law, Torts, Crimes, Equity, Pleading, Evidence and 'A knowledge of the leading
decisions in the Court of Appeal in New Zealand').[131] While these subjects are
based on an English model, the inclusion of the study of New Zealand Court

of Appeal decisions suggests a very gradual movement towards a distinct New Zealand legal identity.

Candidates were also expected to study international law (*jus gentium*) and constitutional law, including Broom, Blackstone, and Hallam. Also included in the curriculum was the study of Euclid and Algebra. Euclid was Prendergast's speciality subject at Cambridge University. History was another important subject examined. Conventional texts were set, such as Alison's *History of Europe* and Hallam's *Constitutional History*. No mention was made of New Zealand history or society. For those barristers wary of Greek, this requirement could be replaced with the more 'modern' languages of French and German. Lastly, prospective barristers were expected to be competent in English, both etymology and composition. Candidates sat both a written and an oral examination, the oral examination being conducted by a judge of the Supreme Court. Henry Robert Richmond (William's younger brother) described Prendergast's approach as examiner as "severe and technical".[132]

The examination for solicitors was based on the barristers' examination, but less demanding. The solicitors' examination included works such as Joshua Williams on the law of real property and personal property, possibly the most relevant book set in both examinations.[133] The examinations clearly demonstrate the European, and in particular English, focus of legal study in nineteenth-century New Zealand. While an attempt was made to test knowledge beyond the law, Maori culture was ignored, while the law relating to women was only briefly touched upon, under the heading of 'Rights and Liabilities of Married Women'.

While the Chief Justice's examination papers cannot be taken to completely reflect Prendergast's viewpoints, they provide insights into his conservative, English-based intellectual framework. The most obvious influence on Prendergast CJ's jurisprudence is classical positivism, such as seen in the works of John Austin. Austin's command concept of law, separation of law and morality, and theories on sovereignty are reflected in the career and decisions of Prendergast CJ.[134]

Prendergast CJ was a product of Victorian England. In his work *The Victorian Frame of Mind 1830–1870*, Walter E. Houghton describes the fundamental beliefs of the Victorians.[135] Houghton argues that the Victorians had a range of values and beliefs in common, for example, a reverence for science and business, a fear of revolution, a rigid puritanical belief system, a strong work ethic and a hypocritical moral outlook. Of course, all these were challenged during the Victorian era, but many of these Victorian traits can be found in Prendergast's personality, which was essentially conservative. Prendergast was a tireless worker and a supporter of business interests, and he had the ability to act with integrity while also being responsible for seemingly crafty actions. Though Prendergast spent only 33 years of his life in Victorian England, he spent 59 years in Victorian New Zealand. Prendergast was a Victorian gentleman, with a passion for the more practical pursuits of law, farming and business.

4. Prendergast as Judicial Administrator

While Prendergast CJ was not inclined towards legal theory, he was an able administrator of the justice system. As well as hearing cases in the Wellington Supreme Court and the Court of Appeal, Prendergast CJ also devoted himself to the administration of colonial justice. Many of the administrative and bureaucratic decisions made by Prendergast as Chief Justice are somewhat mundane, but some provide fascinating insights into the development of the New Zealand legal system. Prendergast came to the job of Chief Justice with a large amount of experience in legal administration. Not only had he acted as Attorney-General for ten years, he had also held the posts of Provincial Solicitor and Crown Solicitor in Dunedin and clerical appointments in Victoria, Australia. Prendergast CJ was a well-organised and efficient administrator and provided strong leadership in this area.

As Chief Justice, Prendergast was involved in the management of the New Zealand judiciary, including Supreme Court and District Court Judges, Resident Magistrates and Justices of the Peace. Prendergast was required to administer the oaths of office to new judges and oversee their work. Appointments such as Registrars of the Court were also under Prendergast CJ's administrative jurisdiction.[136] Prendergast CJ's views were often passed onto the Governor to receive rubber-stamping. The Chief Justice was aided in his work by a personal secretary. Prendergast CJ allowed nepotism to influence several of his choices. His first secretary was Henry Hall, his nephew. Hall was followed in 1882 by an Atkinson (not Richmond's nephew), with Michael Prendergast acting as temporary secretary in the interim.[137] In November 1884, Alexander Hadfield, son of the Bishop of Wellington, was appointed Chief Justice's secretary. This strengthened Prendergast's links to the Anglican Church. Finally in 1889, Charles Prendergast Knight, another nephew, took the role of aiding Prendergast CJ.[138]

As an administrator, Prendergast CJ was also faced with mundane issues relevant to any large organisation or institution. For example, in June 1877, Prendergast dealt with the question of whether it was necessary for judges to obtain receipts when travelling on government railways. Other similar issues included furniture orders, accommodation matters and the installation of new communication technology such as the typewriter and telephone.[139] Thus was the nature of the Chief Justiceship: one day, dealing with office equipment; the next, death sentences.

Administrative issues could also be quite fascinating and have long-lasting implications. For example, Prendergast CJ was involved in the organisation of a new Court House in 1877. The conditions in the original Court House had become unsuitable for the large amount of legal business being conducted. In July 1877, the Grand Jurors of Wellington made a formal complaint to Prendergast CJ about "the very insufficient and miserable nature of the accommodation provided for the Courts of Justice in this City and the urgent necessity which exists for an improvement therein".[140] Moves were already afoot to build the new Court House and Henry Hall had organised a meeting between Prendergast CJ and Richmond J and the Colonial Architect's Office.[141] The new Supreme Court opened for business in 1881.

The contentious issue of Grand Juries was addressed by Prendergast in his first year as Chief Justice. In his first appearance as judge in Marlborough, the Grand Jury at Picton provided him with the following petition:

> it is their humble opinion that the time has now arrived when Grand Juries could very well be abolished, and the duties performed by such Juries, could with great relief, to those liable to serve on such juries, and also with great advantage to the administration of Justice, be transferred to an Officer, legally qualified, to be appointed by the Government for that purpose.[142]

Prendergast CJ conveyed the presentment to the Colonial Secretary for consideration. With the New Zealand legal system undergoing rapid change, new issues were constantly arising. Most issues were related to the implementation of the English legal system in a new and challenging environment.

Prendergast CJ was involved in the day-to-day workings of the legal system. Issues relating to specific prisoners, for example, petitions for the remission of sentences, were brought before the Chief Justice. On 21 June 1875, Prendergast CJ supplied an opinion on Prisoner Tsong Tsi to the Colonial Secretary. Prendergast wrote that "the prisoner was convicted in due course of law, and that I am aware of no reason for the remission or commendation of the sentence passed upon him".[143] Prendergast CJ gave a similar opinion in the matter of Prisoner Buchanan on 28 June 1877.[144] Evidential issues were also brought before Prendergast CJ. In *R v Woodgate*, Prendergast CJ was not only judge but reported on the evidence in the case in his capacity as administrator as well.[145]

5. Coping with controversy: Edwards J and Frederick Moss

Prendergast CJ's first appearance as a judge was at Dunedin in April 1875, thirteen years after he had first begun practice there as a lawyer. He dismissed the official welcome that had been arranged for him, apparently eager to press on with the business at hand:

> A large number of the members of the Bar were present in court when his Honour took his seat on the bench. It had been their intention to present him with an address, but he previously expressed a wish that this should not be done.[146]

Prendergast CJ worked late into the night to complete cases, and his debut was a success, although he did not entirely escape criticism: "A light sentence for infanticide led to considerable condemnatory comment of a vigorous kind, but generally, so it is recorded, the new Chief Justice 'created a very favourable impression.'"[147]

During his time as Chief Justice, Prendergast CJ heard a myriad of cases. Of the cases heard, few were reported. Of the cases reported, few were high-profile or controversial. Despite this, part of Prendergast CJ's legal legacy is his role in controversial legal actions. Two of the most prominent controversies he dealt with were the cases of Edwards J and Frederick Moss.

A. The Edwards J affair

During the 1890s Prendergast CJ became a key player in a nation-wide legal controversy involving Worley Bassett Edwards, who has been described as "undoubtedly the most controversial man to have sat on the Bench of the Supreme Court of New Zealand".[148] In 1889, Edwards was appointed as the sixth judge on the Supreme Court Bench. Problems arose when the Ballance Government came to power in 1891, and the Attorney-General, Patrick Buckley, claimed that as there was no fiscal or constitutional provision for a sixth judge, Edwards J's appointment was null and void.[149] Edwards J was unwilling to relinquish his newly found judicial position, and he fought a long and bitter rearguard action to maintain the judgeship. A frank and difficult man with an impressive grasp of the law, he provided the Government with a strong opponent. The fight to dislodge Edwards J from the bench continued for several years and drew all the Supreme Court judges into the fray.

From the beginning, Prendergast CJ was unhappy with the sixth appointment. In 1889 and 1890 he voiced his doubts as to whether the Government could appoint a fifth puisne judge, but after discovering that several other Supreme Court judges had been appointed before vacancies had appeared, he withdrew his opposition. Prendergast CJ admitted his doubts to Sir Harry Atkinson,[150] who was Premier at the time, and to his brother judges. His views remained consistent throughout the controversy and were eventually vindicated by the Privy Council. The judicial leadership shown by Prendergast CJ during the drawn-out proceedings was level-headed and impressive. When comparing the Edwards J affair with the Barton affair, the biographer can see the maturing of Prendergast from a proud and hard-line Chief Justice into a calmer and wiser authority figure.

A key issue worrying Prendergast CJ was whether he would be compromised as a judge by administering the oath as Chief Justice. Prendergast CJ remembered well the Parihaka aftermath (outlined in Chapter 9) and was wary of being publicly compromised again. In a letter to Denniston J, Prendergast CJ revealed his tense state of mind:

> What appears to me a serious question has arisen . . . . I have suggested that I, at any rate, ought not to be asked to administer the oaths till after Parliament has met; but I may be pressed to administer the oath at once.[151]

Richmond J offered his support to Prendergast CJ in a telegram dated 12 March 1890: "If the Chief Justice continues to entertain doubt as to the legality of the appointment, he should certainly not be asked to swear in Mr. Edwards."[152] The other Supreme Court judges – Denniston, Williams and Conolly JJ – also offered helpful advice and support.

But the Government was not to be hampered by judicial doubt. In a letter to Atkinson, Frederick Whitaker stated that, "If the Chief Justice has scruples about the administering of the oath, the only alternative I see is the substitution of some one else to do so."[153] After reconciling himself to Edwards J's appointment, Prendergast CJ requested his services as soon as possible to relieve the heavy burden of cases hampering the Supreme Court.[154] Prendergast CJ was a judge of integrity, but he was above all a pragmatist.

With the election of the first Liberal Government in January 1891, Edwards J found himself under attack. Ballance and his Attorney-General Buckley attempted to prevent Edwards J from adjudicating. Prendergast CJ found himself in the unenviable position of having to appease the executive branch of government and support his brother judge. Throughout his career as Chief Justice, Prendergast had been associated with the conservative section of New Zealand politics, including the Richmond-Atkinson clan and John Bryce. It is unlikely that Prendergast was pleased with the election of the Ballance Liberal Government. It is also unlikely that Prendergast CJ gladly accepted continuing interference with the judicial branch of government. In a brief exchange of letters between Prendergast CJ and Ballance in February 1891, there was a dispute over whether Edwards J could be appointed Deputy Judge of the Vice-Admiralty Court, with Prendergast CJ supporting Edwards J.[155] A meeting was arranged between Buckley and Prendergast CJ to discuss the Edwards J issue. In this meeting, Prendergast CJ referred Buckley to the earlier correspondence in which he doubted the ability of Edwards J to take his position as the sixth Supreme Court judge.[156]

When asked to prevent Edwards J sitting at the Napier court, Prendergast CJ stepped back from the conflict:

> As Mr. Edwards has not informed me that he does not intend to sit at Napier, I can only repeat what I stated in my former letter to you, that I do not see what steps I can take in the matter of the sittings appointed to be held at Napier.[157]

Prendergast CJ once again organised the judges of the Supreme Court to provide opinions for the Government, but his own opinion was noticeably absent:

> For myself, though I still entertain the doubts I have always felt on the subject, I have not been able at this time to find sufficient leisure to write on the subject, but propose to do so as soon as possible.[158]

Prendergast CJ displayed a cautious approach to controversy, perhaps remembering the Barton affair (see Chapter 7) and the dangers of impulsive words and actions.

The uncompromising attitudes shown by the Government and Edwards J forced the matter into the Court of Appeal. The case of *The Attorney-General v Mr Justice Edwards* (1891) 9 NZLR 321 was heard in May 1891. Robert Stout represented the Government, while Martin Chapman and Theophilus Cooper represented Edwards J. The decision was split, with the majority of Richmond, Williams and Denniston JJ ruling for Edwards J, and Prendergast CJ and Conolly J dissenting. The matter had already harmed the prestige of the Court, showing it to be either in conflict with, or under the power of, central government. The Court of Appeal decision further undermined the Court, as the split decision failed to deliver a conclusive answer. Prendergast CJ's judgment was lengthy and involved, highlighting the importance of a strong and independent judiciary supported by legislation supplying salaries and job security.

Undeterred, the Government pressed onwards to the Privy Council; meanwhile Edwards J received support from the New Zealand Bar, worried about the impact of the dispute on the prestige and authority of the Supreme Court.[159] Prendergast maintained his opinions throughout the controversy, but also acted practically when necessary and attempted to carry out his duty to the Government and his fellow judges. Despite his defeat in the Court of Appeal, Prendergast CJ immediately began organising work for Edwards J in the following weeks.[160]

Prendergast CJ's verdict was vindicated by the Privy Council several months later, in 1892. Edwards returned to practice and was legally appointed to the Supreme Court Bench in 1896. It is unclear whether he harboured any resentment against Prendergast CJ for adjudicating against him in the 1891 case.

One interesting result of the Edwards J affair was the important Court of Appeal decision *Re Aldridge* (1893) 15 NZLR 361 (CA). A man tried and sentenced by Edwards J in 1890 challenged his conviction on the basis that Edwards J was not a valid judge. Prendergast and the court denied the appeal.

B. The Moss affair

Prendergast CJ's adjudicative skills were called upon in a somewhat different capacity in 1897. Trouble had erupted in the Cook Islands between its inhabitants and the British Resident, Frederick Moss. Moss had been a high-profile figure in New Zealand politics during the late nineteenth century and had been appointed to the post in Rarotonga as a man of high standing. As an MP he had spoken out in support of Barton during the 1870s feud (see Chapter 7). Moss was not popular amongst the inhabitants of the Cook Islands, particularly the European settlers. Prendergast left New Zealand in December 1897 aboard the HMS *Torch*, aged 71 years. The fact that Prendergast could successfully undertake such a strenuous voyage and mission at this advanced age is testimony to his impressive health and longevity. Prendergast's personal secretary and nephew, Charles Prendergast Knight, travelled with him to aid in conducting the inquiry. Prendergast was not empowered by Governor Ranfurly to compel the attendance of witnesses or to take sworn evidence.[161] Rarotonga in 1897 was a New Zealand protectorate[162] and Ranfurly felt obliged to intervene in its troubled domestic affairs.

The report provided to Ranfurly was comprehensive and dense. Prendergast's instructions were to conduct a fact-finding inquiry into the state of the Cook Islands constitution and society in general. Prendergast's experience in dealing with the rights of indigenous peoples made him especially suitable from Ranfurly's perspective. Twenty years after *Wi Parata*, Prendergast took his hard-line approach to race relations beyond New Zealand shores. On his arrival Prendergast was treated with due ceremony and his inquiry was welcomed by many who were relieved to find that matters had been taken out of the hands of Moss.[163] The charges against Moss were not criminal:

> It will be seen that in no case is a charge of corrupt, fraudulent, or dishonest conduct made; the most that can be inferred is a charge of erroneous policy, mistake, want of judgment, overbearing conduct, and wilful disregard of the opinions of others.[164]

While Prendergast found that Moss had overstepped his jurisdiction in certain matters, he found most of the charges made against the British Resident frivolous and unsupported by evidence.

Mentions of 'savages' and 'barbarians' are noticeably absent from Prendergast's report, although Prendergast does use the term "partially-civilised people" and believes the effectiveness of native judges is limited.[165] From Prendergast's perspective, and reflecting stadial theory, either the Cook Islanders must have reached a higher state of civilisation than Maori in 1877, or Prendergast's views on indigenous people were becoming more tolerant. Ultimately, Prendergast supported Moss and dismissed the charges against him. Prendergast blamed much of the disruption on Moss' European enemies and credited Moss with attempting to aid the indigenous Cook Islanders. But it was clear to Prendergast that Moss' position was no longer tenable and Moss was recalled.[166] Prendergast concluded his report with a prediction: "it is only a question of time, and that ere long it will be found inevitable to give up the Protectorate, or modify the position of the British Resident, or to annex these islands to the British Crown".[167] His prediction soon came to pass: in 1901, New Zealand's boundaries were extended to include and annex the Cook Islands, and in 1965 the Cook Islands became a self-governing state in association with New Zealand.[168]

6. The Royal Commission of 1881

While Chief Justice, Prendergast was involved in the Royal Commission that altered the nature of common law procedure in New Zealand. As Chairman of the Commission, Prendergast CJ presided over a pivotal event in New Zealand's legal history. The recommendations of the Commission heavily influenced the practice and administration of law in New Zealand. While source material detailing the findings of the Commission is comprehensive, material detailing Prendergast CJ's specific role in the investigation is limited.

The Commission of Inquiry was established by Governor Hercules Robinson on 7 July 1880.[169] The Commission featured the elite of the New Zealand legal system in 1880, including the five Supreme Court judges (Prendergast CJ, Gillies, Richmond, Johnston and Williams JJ), the Solicitor-General Walter Reid, the Attorney-General Frederick Whitaker, and leading barristers such as Edward Conolly and Robert Stout. Others on the Commission included two District Court judges, a Resident Magistrate and three Justices of the Peace, including William Gisborne. Martin Chapman, whose father Henry had been pivotal in earlier legal changes, was appointed secretary. The 19 members provided one of the most impressive gatherings of legal minds in New Zealand during the nineteenth century. The Commission had specifically been charged with:

> inquiring into the constitution, practice, and procedure of the several Courts of judicature in our said colony, that is to say, – (1.) The Supreme Court, including the Court of Appeal; (2.) The District Courts; (3.) Resident Magistrates' Courts; (4.) Courts of Petty Sessions of the Peace; (5.) Courts held before Justices of the Peace.[170]

The chief achievement of the Commission was to adapt common law procedure to better suit the New Zealand colonial environment. Public criticism of court delays and expense had led to the Commission and after the Commission's deliberations, Parliament passed the Supreme Court Act 1882, the Court of Appeal Act 1882 and the Law Amendment Act 1882.[171] Meetings were held in the main centres of New Zealand in 1880 to gather suggestions from the wider legal profession. The Commission's first formal meeting was on 23 November 1880. After seven sittings, a number of important resolutions were made.[172] Many suggestions were made to the Commission by District Law Societies and leading lawyers including Travers, Ollivier and Stout (who was also on the Commission). Some of these suggestions were adopted, but many were not, for example, the suggestion of A. E. T. Devore, "That the sittings of the Court of Appeal should be held consecutively in the various centres of population – ie, Dunedin, Christchurch, Wellington, and Auckland".

It is not the purpose of this section to provide a detailed account of the Commission's findings. Prendergast CJ was only one member of 19, and, though

Chairman, he was not necessarily the leading intellectual figure on the Commission. Prendergast CJ did provide strong leadership and a patient and professional attitude, and, as Chairman, he presided over pivotal and long-lasting changes to the New Zealand legal system, most of which were clearly improvements. The main achievements of the Commission were to abolish the District Courts in their present state, abolish special pleading and special forms of action (Prendergast's speciality), and simplify legal procedure. Where Law and Equity conflicted, Equity would prevail and all proceedings in the Supreme Court were to be made uniform. The system of awarding costs in cases was reformed and simplified. Many of the changes reflected changes that had recently occurred in English law.

Ultimately, the Commissioners, with the exception of Gillies J, predicted that their changes would generally reduce expense to suitors and improve the efficiency of the court system. In a memorandum with Johnston and Richmond JJ, Prendergast CJ added a note of caution:

> there are new methods proposed to be introduced in some of which we are not confident. Seeing, however, that the recommendations were adopted by the great majority of the Commissioners after ample discussion, we are not prepared to refuse to recommend that a trial should be given to the new proposals.[173]

Prendergast CJ was a conservative reformer, and while he played his part on the Commission, changes such as the abolition of special pleading, must have seemed to draw the curtain on the old era of legal practice of which he had been a part.

7. The personal affairs of Prendergast while Chief Justice

James Prendergast's personal life between 1875 and 1899 was relatively settled. With his brothers both in psychiatric institutions abroad, Prendergast had little contact with his personal past. The ongoing support of his wife, Mary, was a key factor in Prendergast's longevity and success as a judge. Quietly supportive, Mary Prendergast was the most important person in the later life of James Prendergast. For a quarter of a century, Mary assisted James in hosting functions and attending official occasions. These functions ranged from welcoming Governors to hosting an elaborate children's fancy dress ball. Husband and wife shared some interests, in particular, gardening and music. Despite his commitment to his wife, Prendergast was first and foremost a man dedicated to his career in the law.

Several nephews of James Prendergast played a role in his career as Chief Justice. Henry Hall, the son of Mary's brother, became Prendergast's secretary on his appointment as Chief Justice in 1875. Hall was an able secretary and his letters to Prendergast during the mid-1880s provide insights into their relationship. In 1888, Charles Prendergast Knight, the son of Mary's sister, also fulfilled the role of secretary to the Chief Justice. Knight enjoyed social life and was probably less diligent than Hall, but Prendergast was fond of them both. Knight's diaries during the 1890s contain interesting anecdotes about his uncle and the cases that occupied the time of the Chief Justice. Michael Prendergast junior also acted as Prendergast's secretary, but only for a brief time, and he did not perform particularly well in the role. Michael found greater satisfaction managing his uncle's large farms in the Manawatu.

James made two visits to England while Chief Justice, in 1884 and 1893. These opportunities allowed him to reacquaint himself with his English relatives, some of whom went to great lengths to keep in regular correspondence with Prendergast, often to obtain financial assistance. Prendergast seems to have borne these requests with a patient sense of familial duty.

Prendergast enjoyed a vigorous and fast-paced lifestyle. During his time as Chief Justice, he travelled extensively, especially throughout the southern North Island. His endurance, especially during the late 1890s, when he was in his seventies, was a testimony to his active and healthy lifestyle. Prendergast was a survivor, physically, professionally and emotionally. A tireless worker, he was happiest when dealing with the law. It was said of Prendergast that he found a law report more entertaining than any other form of literature.[174] The Chief Justice had a sense of humour, albeit not a particularly impressive one:

> Even stolid Chief Justice Sir James Prendergast can't resist the temptation to indulge in the usual weak judicial joke. A bank manager at Napier, who wanted to escape jury service, told the Bench that the doctor advised him not to sit in draughts. And His Honor's little quip was this:– 'It is certainly not pleasant to sit in a draught, but I have no objection to bank drafts.'[175]

During the final decade of his long public career, Prendergast had become a Wellington fixture. The diaries of Charles Prendergast Knight refer to Prendergast's day-to-day activities, such as strolls along the Wellington harbour with Knight, attendance at official functions, picnics, tennis parties, opera concerts, games of draughts and reading.[176] While acting as Administrator, Prendergast was required to perform the public and social functions of the Governor. This involved a seemingly endless series of balls, dinners, opening nights and patronage. Prendergast held numerous non-legal roles, including President of the Festival Choral Society and the Lex Cricket Club; Vice-President of the Rifle Association; Chairman of the Horticultural Society; Patron of the Wellington Poultry, Pigeon, Canary and Dog Show Society; Trustee for the Home for Friendless Women; and Committee Member for Queen Victoria's Jubilee Celebration.

Of particular importance to Prendergast was his role as President of the Wellington Boys' Institute during the 1890s. This organisation was "concerned to catch boys who are in need of wholesome, healthy recreation and companionship that will make them more robust in both mind and body".[177] As noted earlier in this chapter, Prendergast had advocated sentencing reform for youth offenders. The Boys' Institute could potentially prevent disadvantaged youth from becoming young offenders.

While not obviously devout, Prendergast was a loyal member of the Anglican Church. He served on Anglican committees and donated large sums of money, for example, 100 pounds to the Wellington Cathedral Fund in 1896.[178] Despite his strong connections to the Anglican Church, Prendergast seemed to embrace ecumenism. When laying the foundation stone of St John's Presbyterian Church in 1885, Prendergast "referred to the friendly feeling which existed among the various churches, and said he had never, during his twenty years' residence in Wellington, observed the slightest symptom of discord".[179]

In 1884, Prendergast took extended leave with his wife, but was kept up-to-date with New Zealand developments through his secretary, Hall. The letters written by Hall provide insights into Prendergast's political and moral views. In a letter dated 1 March 1884, Hall states that all Prendergast's mortgagors were keeping up with payments, except the Anglican Church. Hall wrote, "It would give me much pleasure to make them pay this, in order to make the Church practise what it preaches – payment of debts: but your instructions were not to press the matter."[180] Despite this leniency, Prendergast's finances continued to flourish during the severe economic depression of the 1880s. In his letters, Hall describes the difficulties many lawyers were facing finding work. Hall also describes the political situation, openly stating his support of the 'conservatives': "Atkinson in obtaining an unconditional dissolution certainly seems to have outwitted the Rads."[181] While this does not prove Prendergast's political leanings, it is unlikely Hall would speak so candidly against his uncle's views.

During Prendergast's absence a rumour had arisen that the Chief Justice was to resign due to ill health and would not return to New Zealand. Hall quickly quashed the rumour and wrote to Prendergast that "Stout is quite ready to assume that your health will not permit of your retaining the Chief Justiceship long, and I fancy he got the above rumour published."[182] Prendergast was actually in poor health at this time and sought medical assistance in England. His personal letters suggest he was seriously considering leaving New Zealand during the mid-1880s. His cousin Charles Manning provided advice in early 1886: "In your letter of the 6 June 1885 you wound up by saying you could not determine whether you would prefer remaining in New Z. or coming home. I myself should not hesitate. I should come home."[183] Prendergast's uncertainty had gone by the end of the decade and in his later trips he was always ready to return to his adopted home of New Zealand.

On his return voyage to New Zealand in late 1884, Prendergast stopped at Melbourne to visit his brother Michael in a private retreat.[184] Prendergast had taken responsibility for organising Michael's affairs and overseeing his treatment.[185] On his return, Prendergast set to work consolidating his position as Chief Justice. While Prendergast may have been a conservative in politics, he was also a judge, and therefore he attempted to remain politically neutral. In the later stages of his career, Prendergast was closely associated with many of the prominent figures in New Zealand colonial history, including Richmond J, Harry Atkinson and successive Governors. While his relationship with Stout, Grey and other liberals may have been very formal, the historian must be careful not to read too much into brief comments. By all accounts, Prendergast had effective working relationships with most members of the New Zealand legal and political elite.

8. Prendergast as Chief Justice

Despite a number of challenging situations and professional setbacks, James Prendergast was a successful Chief Justice. His ability as leader of the bench and chief judicial administrator outshone his ability as a judge, though many of his judgments retain their influence in the modern legal system. Prendergast CJ delivered approximately 600 reported judgments in a variety of legal areas. To remember him for one decision, namely that of *Wi Parata* (1877), is to distort his judicial impact. In the context of Prendergast CJ's corpus of cases, *Wi Parata* is one of his weaker decisions, delivered at the beginning of his career. Prendergast CJ was *prima inter pares* on the Supreme Court Bench of New Zealand. Surrounded by intelligent and competent judges, 'Prendergast's Bench' was one of the strongest in New Zealand legal history. As a judge, Prendergast CJ worked in the shadow of some of his more talented peers, namely, Johnston, Williams and Richmond JJ. While he was able to work successfully with all his judicial colleagues, Prendergast CJ's relationships with his brother judges ranged from a close friendship with Richmond J to a very formal relationship with Edwards J.

In his appointment as Chief Justice, Prendergast benefited from good timing, a high profile in the Wellington legal environment, and strong political connections. The length of Prendergast CJ's career is testimony to his endurance and fortitude. Commentators have described the defining qualities of Prendergast CJ's adjudication as being caution and safety. These qualities are evident in the published Law Reports, but Prendergast CJ's approach to adjudication was far more complex. His judicial style included both impressive strengths and worrying weaknesses. While he had the ability to deliver comprehensive judgments on key legal issues, Prendergast CJ could also deliver brief, vague judgments based on little legal precedent. Prendergast CJ's strengths were in land law and criminal law and he tended to adjudicate most effectively in these areas. He was also experienced enough to handle controversial cases with poise and impartiality. Despite assertive decisions such as *Wi Parata*, Prendergast CJ was essentially a passive judge who preferred to interpret and apply law rather than make it.

Prendergast adopted a literal interpretation of legislation in line with standard nineteenth-century judicial thought. While at times he looked to the 'spirit' of a statute, Prendergast was a conservative judge who believed his job was to apply the law as it was written. For ten years as Attorney-General, Prendergast had been in charge of drafting legislation. As Chief Justice, Prendergast had the opportunity of interpreting that legislation. This domination in the executive, legislative and judicial branches of government is impressive but somewhat unnerving. It could be argued that Prendergast faced a conflict of interests; Robert Stout found himself in a somewhat similar position on becoming Chief Justice in 1899. Prendergast CJ wisely drew upon his legal and political background to inform him when making decisions.

Prendergast CJ combined efficiency with caution in his adjudication. In a busy court system, he could move cases through with speed but he was also careful in his setting of precedents, avoiding maverick, assertive decisions if possible. He was adept at interpreting important statutes relating to real property, and in particular, the Land Transfer System. Three decisions made by Prendergast in the area of land law remain highly influential in the modern courts: *Wi Parata* (1877), *Merrie v McKay* (1897) and *Doyle v Edwards* (1898).

The cases heard by Prendergast CJ between 1875 and 1899 reflected the developing colonial environment from which they came. Issues relating to farming, finance and liquor were often placed before him. In his rulings on these 'colonial' issues, Prendergast CJ relied heavily on English precedent. This was partly due to his English heritage and sympathies, but also due to the relatively undeveloped state of New Zealand common law. As his judicial career progressed, Prendergast CJ used more New Zealand precedent in his decisions, but he always remained an 'English' judge working in a colonial environment.

Prendergast CJ's judgments improved as his career progressed. From unconvincingly argued cases such as *Wi Parata* (1877) to succinct and intelligent decisions such as *Merrie v McKay* (1897), Prendergast CJ developed his judicial abilities throughout his time on the bench.

As Chief Justice, Prendergast had little time for a personal life. He remained a man dedicated to his career and the law. For 24 years, Prendergast CJ was at the pinnacle of the New Zealand legal system. By 1899, he had become a New Zealand institution and had influenced several generations of prominent legal figures, including William Richmond, Joshua Williams, Robert Stout, the Chapman brothers, Charles Skerrett and Michael Myers, to name but a few. In 1899, Prendergast CJ was at the height of his judicial prowess, having recently delivered some of his most influential judgments. But in March 1899, Mary Prendergast died. Two months later, Chief Justice Sir James Prendergast resigned his office, expressly forbidding any kind of farewell,[186] and became just another Wellington citizen.

7

THE BARTON AFFAIR, 1876–1878

When looking at the Wellington Supreme Court Bench in the late 1870s, legal historians invariably focus on the landmark case of *Wi Parata v Bishop of Wellington* (1877). Prendergast and Richmond handed down the decision in *Wi Parata*. George E. Barton represented Wi Parata while William Travers represented the Bishop of Wellington. Yet it was not this case that dominated headlines during the period. It was another, featuring a remarkably similar cast.

On 30 January 1878, *Gillon v MacDonald* was heard before the Wellington Supreme Court.[1] The case concerned a commercial partnership issue but should be considered a leading case due to Barton being held in contempt of court and imprisoned for one month by the Chief Justice. This incident was the climax of many months of feuding between the two Wellington judges and Barton. The feud was primarily between Barton and Prendergast up until the final months when Barton focused more on attacking Richmond.

The unprecedented nature of Barton's punishment made *Gillon* the *cause célèbre* of the year and split the New Zealand legal profession. The feuding did not end with Barton's imprisonment but instead became more intense and bizarre as the year continued. The matter finally dissipated at the end of 1878, though not before it had destroyed the careers of Barton and his client Gillon, and seriously undermined the early years of Prendergast's Chief Justiceship. It is also arguable that the feud had some effect on the 'other' leading case of this period, namely, *Wi Parata*.

There are many ways in which the legal historian can approach the *Gillon* case and the Wellington Supreme Court feud. This chapter investigates what these events can tell us about the nature of the New Zealand legal profession during the late 1870s. This multifarious story touches on the relationship between bench and bar, the relationship between fellow lawyers, the operation of the 'separation of powers' doctrine in colonial New Zealand, contempt of court and the removal of judges.

1. The *Gillon* saga

A. The events leading up to *Gillon*

In the late 1870s, the New Zealand legal profession included many men who had previously sought their fortunes in other colonial contexts. The Englishman Prendergast and the Irishman George E. Barton had 'history'. Two previous gold rushes had brought the men together, first in Victoria and then in Otago. After leaving legal practice in Dublin for the Victorian goldfields during the 1850s, Barton was a political associate of Michael Prendergast. There is no direct evidence that James Prendergast knew Barton in Victoria but given that both men were working in the same geographical area, and the strong relationship between Michael Prendergast and Barton, it is highly likely that James had some acquaintance with Barton at that time.

During the early 1860s, James Prendergast, Michael Prendergast and Barton migrated separately to Dunedin as news spread of a major gold rush. They were part of a third wave of colonists following gold, the first wave being in California, the second in Victoria, and the third in Otago. When the gold rush began to subside, many in Dunedin's legal profession moved north to the newly established capital of Wellington; Barton, Prendergast and Christopher William Richmond among them. Barton's personal relationship with Richmond before 1876 is unclear. A professional relationship definitely existed. Richmond spent the first five years of his judicial career in Dunedin, beginning in 1862, the year Barton commenced practice in the same city, so for five years Barton would have advocated in the court over which Richmond presided.

Prendergast and Barton had worked together in the Dunedin Supreme Court, including in the 1864 defamation case involving Julius Vogel.[2] While in Dunedin, Prendergast and Barton appeared in other cases together and also appeared against each other. By all accounts, the two men were on civil terms up until their third meeting in Wellington during the late 1870s.[3] In 1876 Barton used the phrase "former friendship" in relation to Prendergast. Barton also stated: "Although I cannot forget that I am addressing a gentleman who for years practised with me at the Dunedin Bar, and who until I came to reside permanently in Wellington was on terms of friendship with me, yet I will study to remember that I am addressing the Chief Justice of New Zealand."[4] Richmond also appears to have been on civil terms with Barton before 1876.

However, it is worth noting that George E. Barton was an Irish Protestant, and Prendergast's early personal correspondence reveals anti-Irish sentiment. Much of the sentiment is second-hand and appears in letters from his brothers to his father, Michael Prendergast QC.[5] Philip and Michael junior were scathing about the Irish Protestants in power in Victoria during the 1850s, and blamed them for James' failure to establish himself there. This prejudice could have some bearing on the *Gillon* saga, although the link is tenuous.

The Wellington legal profession which Barton joined in the late 1870s was thriving. Government and commercial interests provided a plentiful supply of work for the small group of lawyers working in New Zealand's new capital city. The Wellington legal profession consisted of long-established lawyers whose Wellington careers had preceded the relocation of the capital, and more recent arrivals, such as Barton.

The 15 August 1877 address made by 14 leading Wellington barristers in support of Prendergast and Richmond reads as a *Who's Who* of the Wellington legal fraternity. The lawyers in attendance were Chapman, Edwards, FitzGerald, Fitzherbert, Allan, Izard, Lewis, Moorhouse, Ollivier, Quick, Travers, Hart, Brandon and Brandon junior.[6] These men were at the centre of the Wellington legal profession and had little time for those like Barton who sought to challenge the establishment. Martin Chapman was a founder of Chapman Tripp; Worley Bassett Edwards became a controversial Supreme Court judge; William FitzGerald (along with Martin Chapman) was the *New Zealand Jurist*'s court reporter for Wellington; Charles Izard established the firm that would become Bell Gully; Brandon senior, Moorhouse and Travers were all members of the House of Representatives, which would debate Barton's petitions; and Brandon senior and Prendergast's former colleague, Robert Hart, were responsible for establishing Wellington's earliest law firms in the 1840s.[7] Other leading Wellington lawyers at the time who were not present on 15 August included Francis Bell, Hugh Gully and Walter Buller. Interestingly, Fitzherbert was Barton's partner at the time in the firm of Barton and Fitzherbert.

The profession was small but impressive. The public and private relationships between practitioners were complex and sometimes compromising. For example in the *Gillon* feud, William Travers appeared for the defendant in court, publicly supported the judges at the 15 August meeting and spoke on their behalf in parliamentary debates. Like the Supreme Court judges, Travers found himself in constant conflict with Barton from 1876 to 1878.

Barton left New Zealand under a cloud of controversy in the 1870s, only to return to practice in Wellington a few years later in 1876.[8] The controversy apparently concerned an action for slander against Barton for accusing another lawyer of stealing a document. Barton was found liable and immediately left New Zealand.[9] When Barton arrived in Wellington in 1876 it was very clear to him that his former colleague Prendergast had far outstripped him in terms of career success.[10] During *Re GE Barton* (1876), Barton stated: "whatever my fate is likely to be, no word shall escape my lips unworthy of my standing at this bar; my age, which exceeds your Honour's; my seniority at the bar – of 27 years – which also exceeds your Honour's." Both men were of similar age and backgrounds, yet by 1875 Barton had failed to receive the recognition that a man of his experience might have expected, especially in a small legal community such as that of colonial New Zealand. In Robert Stout's eulogy to Prendergast in 1921, he describes Barton as "a brilliant advocate" when referring to the 'golden age' of the New Zealand legal profession in Dunedin during the 1860s and early 1870s.[11]

Barton had a very hot temper and throughout his career was in a state of almost constant feuding with a myriad of different individuals. His confrontational personality, possibly augmented by jealously, resulted in a stand-off with Prendergast very soon after Barton began appearing before the judge in the Wellington Supreme Court. In October 1876 Barton took offence at Prendergast's remarks during the trial of Te Puni.[12] According to Barton, Prendergast and Richmond had been disrespectful towards him and the comments in this case were the final straw. Barton penned a letter to the Colonial Secretary requesting an inquiry into the judges' behaviour.[13] He also informed Prendergast of this course of action via a letter. By writing the letters, Barton had made conflict inevitable. Bench and bar would clash and Prendergast's rash response confirmed this. Prendergast held Barton in contempt of court for sending him the letter, the first of three times Prendergast charged Barton with this serious, strict liability offence.

In the subsequent hearing, *Re GE Barton*, Barton argued as to why the contempt charge was unjustified.[14] Barton's demeanour was almost humble as he outlined why he had sent the letter and how he had not meant any offence by it. While this may have appeared disingenuous given the gravity of Barton's allegations, Prendergast retracted his decision and the first contempt ruling was discharged.[15]

The Colonial Secretary did not act on Barton's request for an inquiry. Despite the apparent truce in *Re GE Barton*, the feud between bench and bar intensified during 1877. In case after case, Barton found reasons to be aggrieved at the treatment he received from Prendergast and Richmond.[16] In August 1877, Barton once again attempted to take official action against the judges. Breaking ranks with the profession, he directly petitioned the House of Representatives, asking for an inquiry into the judges' behaviour.[17] Under the New Zealand constitution, past and present, only the House of Representatives can remove judges of the higher courts.[18] Barton accused the judges of treating him in a disrespectful manner, undermining his reputation, showing bias towards his clients and directly insulting him.

It is at this point in the story that a harmful split in the Wellington legal profession becomes evident. Legal news in August 1877 was dominated by the scandal of Barton's attack on the judges,[19] yet these very judges were also hearing a case involving a parcel of Ngati Toa land. This case was *Wi Parata v Bishop of Wellington*. It says much about the priorities of the colonial legal establishment that the fates of the native title doctrine and the Treaty of Waitangi were put on hold so that leaders of the Wellington Bar could read out a statement in the Supreme Court supporting Prendergast and Richmond.[20] Barton claimed that the statement reflected "the cringing servility of the Wellington local bar".[21] Given that Barton was representing the plaintiff in the case before the court, we can only guess at the reaction of Wi Parata, rangatira of Ngati Toa. With so much at stake for Maori, the lawyer charged with defending Maori interests was in effect publicly branded a pariah by the overwhelming majority of his local colleagues. While so much space was devoted to the reporting of the bench and bar feud, the result in *Wi Parata* is relegated to a tiny paragraph near the end of the October 1877 *Jurist* edition.[22] In twenty-first-century New Zealand, every law student studies *Wi Parata* while very few will have heard of George E. Barton.

In late August, Prendergast, the head of the judiciary, took the assertive step of personally defending himself in a letter to the executive regarding Barton's petition to the legislature.[23] In a recent case with some strong parallels, the New Zealand Supreme Court judge Bill Wilson, unlike Prendergast, defended himself through his lawyer in line with the convention that a judge will not publicly comment on a case, even one in which he or she is involved.[24] In his letter, Prendergast dismissed the need for an inquiry on the basis that the allegations were untrue and even if they were true they would not constitute grounds for removal. Prendergast's arguments to the Colonial Secretary were taken up by Parliament in its debate on the issue with Attorney-General Frederick Whitaker supporting the Chief Justice.[25] Swayed by its legal advisor, Parliament received, read and discharged the petition.[26] During the parliamentary debates, Travers effectively advocated for the judges.[27] Given his role in the Wellington Bar's statement of support and his professional rivalry with Barton, it is not surprising that Travers was challenged in the House on the grounds of partiality.[28] Despite his vehement defence, Travers' awkward position once again demonstrates that clear role boundaries did not exist in the 1870s New Zealand legal profession.

B. Gillon v MacDonald *and Prendergast's contempt ruling*

It is important to note that by this point Barton seemed absolutely committed to his cause of bringing about the dismissal of the Wellington Supreme Court Bench. By January 1878 the relationship between Barton and the judges had broken down and was threatening to undermine the integrity and credibility of both the Wellington Supreme Court and the New Zealand Court of Appeal, which sat in Wellington and was staffed by the New Zealand Supreme Court justices. *Gillon v MacDonald* is one of New Zealand legal history's leading cases, but unlike most other leading cases this is not due to its specific legal content. The events that occur in *Gillon* are of most importance to the extent that they directly relate to the feud in question.

Gillon, a high-profile journalist and managing partner of the *Evening Argus* newspaper, was dismissed as editor of this periodical in 1877.[29] One of the partnership agreement terms was that Gillon had the right to act as editor. Gillon brought an action to the Wellington Supreme Court stating that his partners were in breach of that agreement and asserting his right to act as editor. Barton acted for the plaintiff and William Travers and Frank Morton Ollivier for the defence. In the first hearing, in October 1877, Gillon's case was put to a jury which failed to agree on a verdict and was subsequently discharged.[30]

The matter was heard again on 16 January 1878.[31] In the second hearing, the jury reached a verdict and found for Gillon. Gillon was still a partner and could continue to act as editor. This was a major victory for Barton and shows his ability as an advocate in a jury trial. While Barton's opinion of himself as the foremost barrister in New Zealand is open to debate, he was an articulate, forceful and fearless courtroom lawyer. From the *North Otago Times* report, the victory seems a clear one and the fact that it ultimately became a hollow victory is in part due to the actions of Prendergast and Richmond.

On 19 January, Gillon, flush with victory, proceeded to the *Evening Argus* premises to exercise his rights. Ultimately Gillon wanted the business wound up and to receive his share of the wealth. Gillon's partners refused to acknowledge his partnership rights, and one of them, Kent, refused to allow Gillon to view the accounts. The result was a physical confrontation which led to Gillon being bodily removed from the offices.[32] While not quite the 'Wild West', colonial Wellington had a rough and ready way in which to resolve disputes. Immediately following this fracas, Barton lodged a motion in the Supreme Court for an injunction to prevent the other partners from obstructing Gillon in exercising his rights as managing partner and editor of the *Argus*.

At a hearing on 30 January, this motion was denied by Prendergast and Richmond on two grounds.[33] Firstly, Gillon acted improperly in not waiting for the court to grant relief in the form of a decree. Secondly, one of the *Argus* partners (Saunders) was not named in the proceedings. It is easy to empathise with Barton. The first ground seems to undermine the jury's clear declaration in favour of Gillon. The second appears contrary to a fact supposedly established in the first hearing. Counsel for the defence, William Travers, is reported as admitting that Saunders was no longer a partner and that the jury did not need to make a finding on this issue. This became a contested issue as Richmond later claimed that Travers never made this admission.[34]

Barton was aghast at this turn of events which, in his mind at least, confirmed that the judges were carrying out a personal vendetta against him and his clients. He also lashed out at Ollivier and Travers, accusing them of "rascality".[35] Prendergast and Richmond denied Gillon's application with costs. Barton refused to accept the judgment and continued to interrupt the judges, stating that the court was mistaken and that he must be able to speak for his client. At this point, Prendergast finally lost his temper. The *New Zealand Jurist* captures the moment:

> [Prendergast:] Mr Barton, I have many times requested you to keep your seat and not to interrupt the proceedings of the Court, – notwithstanding such reiterated orders and rules you have continued interrupting the proceedings, and I therefore declare that unless you see fit to apologize to this Court and express regret for such transgressions, you will be adjudged guilty of contempt of court.
>
> Mr. Barton replied that he had not the shadow of a doubt that the statement made that Gillon had no right to go on to the premises among his partners was utterly contrary to law. It was so monstrous that he could not help speaking on the subject as he did.

> The Chief Justice: You are again interrupting the Court while it is delivering
> its judgment. I was very desirous indeed that you should have regretted your
> conduct.
> Mr. Barton: This mode of procedure must end, it is perfectly clear. It must be
> stopped in some way. I know what the Court means, and I hope it knows what
> I mean.
> The Chief Justice: The Court adjudges you guilty of contempt of court, and
> commits you to the public prison in Wellington for one month.[36]

Prendergast had broken with usual judicial practice and imprisoned an advocate
for contempt in face of the court, a strict liability criminal offence. Barton knew
what to expect and almost dared Prendergast to take this extreme measure. It
is important to note that in the Court of Appeal hearing of *Spence v Pearson*,
immediately preceding *Gillon v MacDonald*, Barton accused the judges of partiality
and was found in contempt of court and fined 50 pounds.[37] Both Prendergast
and Richmond briefly retired to agree upon this course of action. The case
concerned the ability of Barton's client to appeal to the Privy Council and provides
important context for what occurred soon after in *Gillon*. The charge and fine
were subsequently dismissed when it became apparent that the Court of Appeal
was sitting illegally.[38] The court then 'transformed' into the Supreme Court to
hear *Gillon*. Therefore, in the course of 1876 to 1878, Barton was charged with
contempt three times but only the *Gillon* charge was not revoked.

Was Prendergast's decision to imprison Barton inconsistent with English and
colonial practice? As mentioned earlier, an historical examination of contempt
is not the aim of this case study, but some interesting debates on this matter can
be found in the *New Zealand Jurist* following the ruling.[39] The *Jurist* notes that
similarly extreme rulings relating to contempt were more common in small
colonial courts, such as in Sierra Leone and Hong Kong, than in English courts.
Many of the cases cited resulted in the order for contempt being reversed or in a
fine rather than imprisonment.[40] The closest case on the facts to be found by the
Jurist is from the Supreme Court of Sierra Leone, in which a lawyer was struck
off for disrespectful demeanour in Court, leading the *Jurist* commentator to note:
"It is a painful reflection that we should be under the necessity of going to Sierra
Leone – a colony of negroes and 'mean whites' – in order to find a parallel for the
proceedings of our own Court."[41]

New Zealand judges during the period in question were generally reluctant to
find counsel in contempt of court. Discussions of contempt frequently appear in
the *Jurist* from 1876 to 1878, yet few New Zealand examples are provided. One
example occurred in *Barry v Gladstone Gold-Mining Company* (1878).[42] The case
was heard in the Warden's Court at Macetown. The defendant's counsel, Finn,
was held in contempt for interrupting proceedings and contradicting the judge.
In a similar fashion to Barton, Finn challenged Warden Stratford to hold him

in contempt, which the warden duly did. The bailiff arrested Finn but Stratford immediately allowed him the opportunity to apologise. Finn apologised and the contempt ruling was discharged. This case occurred in a relatively lowly setting but could lend weight to the argument that Prendergast should have offered Barton another opportunity to apologise after passing the sentence of imprisonment.

A recurring theme is that Prendergast's ruling was in stark contrast to the more liberal approach displayed by English judges.[43] A particularly controversial issue in the New Zealand context was whether a judge could disbar counsel for contempt. In *Re GE Barton* (1876) Prendergast stated:[44]

> For myself, I hope the authorities are as I believe them to be – I believe that they ought to be if they are not – that the deprivation of the power to act in a professional capacity with regard to barristers and solicitors, should be appropriate punishment for contempt, and not imprisonment or fine.

On 30 January 1878 Prendergast chose a fine and then imprisonment as the appropriate punishments. It is the decision to imprison Barton that ultimately made *Gillon* the *cause célèbre* of this period.

Barton's prison sentence appears unprecedented,[45] and raises questions about Prendergast's state of mind when making the ruling. It is probable that Prendergast lost his temper. If he had taken time to reflect he may have imposed a fine, as he had attempted to do in *Spence v Pearson*. This would have been more in line with the decision in *Re Pollard*, in which the Chief Justice of Hong Kong faced a similar situation.[46] It can also be argued that Prendergast's decision risked undermining the right of counsel to defend clients to the best of their ability. If faced with imprisonment for mounting a vociferous defence, counsel may think twice before speaking up. By all accounts, the events in *Gillon* created a precedent in the British Empire, though probably an unfortunate one. It should be noted that Prendergast's brother judge Richmond supported his decision in the hearing itself and during the events that followed.

In assessing whether Prendergast overreacted in his ruling, it is useful to briefly note the law relating to contempt in the face of the court for advocates. This area of law has remained largely consistent and textbooks from past and present provide a useful guide.[47] In criminal contempt proceedings the judge is able to proceed upon his own motion.[48] This allows the judge to decide upon guilt and sentencing. These wide-ranging powers granted to judges are justified due to the threat contempt poses to the administration of justice, but judges should only ever use these powers sparingly.[49] It is debatable whether Barton's actions constituted a clear threat to the administration of justice, but, if seen in the context of the previous clashes between bench and bar, they could well have posed a threat to the effective operation of the Wellington Supreme Court.

As pointed out at length in the *Jurist*, advocates should always be allowed great latitude to proffer arguments in support of clients and correct the court if the advocate believes an error has been made.[50] In support of Barton's specific allegations of 30 January, it is established law that it is "proper for counsel to raise the matter of bias or lack of impartiality where there are reasonable grounds for doing so even if the judge is not in fact biased".[51] Given the many defeats that Barton experienced before Prendergast and Richmond, he obviously believed "reasonable grounds" existed for claiming personal bias towards him and his clients.

In terms of the specific 30 January *Gillon* hearing, Prendergast possibly did overreact, but when considering the wider context and past history between bench and bar, his actions can be justified. What is very clear is that Prendergast acted within his powers as a Supreme Court judge. While his decision to imprison Barton appears inconsistent with other jurisdictions, it was still legal. On 12 and 30 September and 1 October 1878 the House of Representatives debated this issue, amongst others, in relation to the Judicial Commission Bill. MPs used case precedents and even legal textbooks to support their arguments. The two most convincing speeches were given by Attorney-General Robert Stout and former Attorney-General Frederick Whitaker.[52] These two speeches provide a good summary of the law as it stood at 1878. Stout was adamant that "There can be no doubt as to the power of the Judges in England to commit persons for contempt. The Supreme Court of New Zealand has all the power possessed by the superior Courts in England . . ."[53] He cited textbooks by William Blackstone and Thomas Starkie,[54] and a number of cases,[55] to support his claims. Despite Stout's belief that Barton's punishment was too severe, he voted against the Bill on the basis that the law was clear and that the judges had not committed misconduct that should lead to removal. Whitaker echoed Stout's view that the law was clear and quoted from Chief Justice Cockburn's decision in *ex parte Goliffe* (1872):

> It is very true that it is laid down by high authorities, and it is according to the reason of the thing, that every Court of record has power to fine and imprison for contempt committed in the face of the Court, while the Court is sitting in the administration of justice. Such a power is obviously necessary for the administration of public justice, which may be interrupted or obstructed unless there is a power to summarily repress such outrages.[56]

Several of the Bill's supporters went to great lengths to prove that Barton's committal was unique and excessive, while the Bill's opponents provided several examples in rebuttal.[57] On the issue of whether Prendergast possessed the power to commit, the Bill's opponents emphatically won the argument.

Unsurprisingly, Barton appealed the contempt ruling and in *Re George Elliot Barton* on 29 March 1878, Richmond ruled that Prendergast indeed possessed the power to commit a barrister instantly to prison for contempt of court.[58] This was well-established law. Barton should have known this and focused solely on whether the particular circumstances justified the ruling rather than whether the ruling was within the judge's powers or whether the correct process was followed by the judges. Despite this, justice should not only be done but also be seen to be done. Having Richmond decide upon Prendergast's ruling is a clear conflict of interests, given that Barton had been officially complaining about the behaviour of both judges. Despite there being only two judges in Wellington, this matter could have probably waited for the arrival of another Supreme Court judge, which would have occurred at the next sitting of the full Court of Appeal.

Barton received support for his cause from the Dunedin and Christchurch Bars and a meeting of Wellington citizens.[59] In written statements these groups supported the possibility of an inquiry, placing Prendergast and Richmond in an embarrassing position. It is telling that no resolution was passed by the Wellington Bar. Prendergast, though originally a Dunedin barrister, had focused his energies on Wellington for over a decade since moving permanently to the capital city in 1867.

In the *New Zealand Jurist* (February 1878), the editor George B. Barton, an ally of George E. Barton, attacked Prendergast.[60] While he did not speak for the New Zealand legal profession, his journal was circulated throughout the colony. It is important to note that much of the reporting of the feud is to be found in G. B. Barton's publication, which raised questions of bias against the judges:

> Whatever there may be to regret in Mr. Barton's demeanour in this case, it must be admitted that there is still more to be regretted in the action of the Bench . . . no one who will read the [*Gillon*] report can fail to be struck with the utter want of proportion between the offence and the punishment; nor can anyone fail to see that such a mistake is fatal to the reputation of a Judge.[61]

While serving his prison term, Barton stood for, and won, the election for Wellington Central.[62] The campaign was organised by his son, L'Estrange Barton, and Gillon loyally spoke on his behalf at rallies.[63] Barton supported George Grey's 'liberal party' placing him politically in opposition to Prendergast and Richmond, who personally leaned towards 'conservatives' such as Harry Atkinson. Ironically, Barton replaced William Travers, who had chosen not to stand again for the high-profile electorate. This vote of confidence in George Barton can be seen as a popular vindication of the outspoken lawyer and a rejection of Prendergast's contempt ruling. To his dismay, Barton did not receive the same vindication from New Zealand's power brokers, most of whom supported the judges.

Gillon v MacDonald did not end with Barton's imprisonment. More hearings ensued, all of which confirmed Barton's failure to obtain a suitable remedy for his client. Upon Barton's release, he made an application to hold Gillon's partners in contempt of court for selling the *Argus* and Gillon's shares in the *Argus* while the matter was before the court.[64] At the hearing on 12 April 1878, Richmond noted that the defendants' actions were improper but, unlike the third hearing, the bench refused to rule contempt of court as no court order had been breached.[65] Barton then proceeded to argue that the suit's subject matter had now disappeared and therefore the court should provide a remedy for Gillon. Upon this matter Richmond reserved judgment.

In the 12 April hearing, Barton gamely attempted to gain a reversal of the judges' 30 January refusal to grant an injunction.[66] Barton had never accepted the court's decision and importantly it was the 30 January hearing during which he was adjudged in contempt of court. This unrepentant attitude did not impress Richmond, who rejected Barton's motion and pointed out that an injunction would be irrelevant now that the property in dispute had been sold. The 4 June hearing is formally reported in the *Jurist* and concerns Barton's notice of motion for decree.[67] The notice was to be heard on 25 May and while the defendant's counsel Ollivier was present, Barton was not. The matter was postponed until 4 June, when once again, Barton was absent. Prendergast struck the case off the list due to Barton's failure to support the motion, though he refused Ollivier's request to have the matter absolutely dismissed. Prendergast then awarded costs to Ollivier for his two appearances in court to defend the motion.

In a final hearing on 21 August, Richmond belatedly delivered judgment for the plaintiff on the motion for decree and also declared the partnership dissolved from the commencement of the suit.[68] Richmond added the caveat that if Saunders was found to be a partner then Gillon would need to undertake a new action. By this time, Gillon had been declared bankrupt and his shares in the *Argus* had been sold.[69] Richmond suggested that the matter of the accounts be decided in chambers if the parties could not agree but at this stage the matter had, to a large extent, become redundant. Despite this final judgment, events had overtaken the court's ruling and Gillon had failed in his battle with his partners. Barton used the outcome to strengthen his appeal to the Colonial Secretary later that year:[70]

> Judge Richmond's misconduct in corruptly sheltering Gillon's opponents and refusing protection to Gillon, while those opponents were 'spiriting away' the whole property of the subject-matter of the litigation, thus converting that litigation into a 'hollow mockery,' and the decree, when he afterwards made it, into a 'Dead Sea apple.'

C. The events following Gillon

The *Gillon* case dragged on throughout 1878 and provided a legal forum for a feud which was also being played out in a political forum, namely, the New Zealand Parliament. On his release from prison, Barton once more petitioned the

Government for an inquiry into the behaviour of Prendergast and Richmond. In the first instance, Barton approached a minister in the presiding Grey Government, John Ballance. Ballance correctly noted that it is the legislature's role to ultimately decide on whether a judge should be removed from office,[71] though Barton was also correct in stating that the executive should play a role in initiating this process. In any event, Barton was now part of the legislature and could affect proceedings from within the House of Representatives. Following the defeat of the Judicial Commission Bill, Barton launched tirades against Prendergast and Richmond under the shield of parliamentary privilege.[72] Richmond was even forced to submit a letter to the House of Representatives pointing out inaccuracies in Barton's claims.[73] While the feud began with a focus on Prendergast's actions, it ended with Richmond taking the lead in the struggle against Barton. This is due to Richmond taking the leading judicial role in the post-January 1878 *Gillon* hearings and also Richmond's October 1878 letter defending himself against Barton's accusations.

The contestability of early law reports, and in particular the *New Zealand Jurist*, is illustrated by the letter submitted by Richmond on 3 October 1878 to the House of Representatives outlining misstatements of fact in Barton's allegations.[74] Richmond also questioned the trustworthiness of the *Jurist* reporting of the *Gillon* proceedings. Part of this complaint is based on the claim that the *Jurist* largely follows the trial report appearing in the *New Zealand Times* newspaper. That a law report would rely on a newspaper is of credit to the newspaper but raises questions about the credibility of the law report. As Richmond argues in his letter:[75]

> It does not appear to have occurred to any one who relied upon the report in the *Jurist* to inquire into the origin of that report. I declare it to be quite untrustworthy, so far as it is original. I have reason to believe that it was not furnished to the *Jurist* by either of the barristers who are announced as the reporters for this district. The report in the *New Zealand Times* of 31st January is a fair report so far as it goes; but it fails, as almost any report must do, to convey an adequate idea of the scene in Court. It also fails, or rather it does not attempt, to show the nature of the questions before the Court. Without some apprehension of these questions it is not possible for any one to understand how thoroughly without ground of complaint Mr. Barton has been.

The limitations of law reporting are made clear in Richmond's letter but, more importantly, the credibility of the *New Zealand Jurist* is attacked. To state that the *Gillon* report is "untrustworthy" calls into question the general quality of reporting in the *Jurist*. To what extent could lawyers and judges rely on its accuracy when researching and applying relevant case law? Richmond also insinuated that Barton used his close relationship with the *Jurist* editor to influence the wording of the report.[76] Barton countered Richmond's claims in Parliament, stating that the *Jurist* report was fair and accurate.[77]

In August 1878, Cecil Albert De Lautour MP introduced the Judicial Commission Bill into Parliament.[78] The Bill aimed to set up a commission of inquiry to investigate Barton's imprisonment for contempt, the power of judges to rule in this way and the role of Parliament in controlling judicial misbehaviour.[79] The judicial prerogative relating to contempt has been enshrined in English common law for several centuries. As mentioned earlier, leading MPs with legal backgrounds, including Robert Stout and Frederick Whitaker, made this point in the ensuing parliamentary debate.[80] It is unlikely that any investigation following from De Lautour's Bill would have advocated overturning the law, however, Parliament could still potentially find Prendergast's ruling unjust in the specific circumstances. MP for Parnell, Frederick Moss, who served on the Otago Provincial Council during Prendergast and Barton's time in Dunedin, spoke in support of Barton, arguing that Prendergast's response was an overreaction.[81] As with its previous debate on this matter, Parliament voted down the Bill and declined to initiate Barton's much anticipated inquiry.

The debates relating to the Judicial Commission Bill can be found in the New Zealand Parliamentary Debates; they provide fascinating insights into different aspects of the feud and touch upon many of the constitutional issues raised in this book. To a large extent the MPs reflected the arguments and legal precedents found in the *Jurist* and newspaper reports,[82] rather than furnishing new evidence to support their arguments. The partisan nature of the House is also revealed through the debates. After Barton's stinging parliamentary attack upon the judges on 18 October 1878, other MPs lined up to reply either in support of Barton or to show their disgust at the vicious attack.[83]

Consistent with his behaviour throughout this saga, Barton refused to let the matter rest after the defeat in the House of Representatives. With the legislature route blocked he again targeted the executive in the form of Colonial Secretary Whitmore.[84] Whitmore rejected Barton's claims as lacking specificity and asked for clarification.[85] Barton's clarifications, which do seem to answer Whitmore's queries, were also rejected as lacking specificity.[86] It seems Whitmore was set on denying Barton his inquiry. Barton made the fair assertion that Whitmore had effectively ignored his charges and then, true to form, rashly accused him of allowing Richmond to ghost-write his previous reply despite it being signed by Whitmore.[87] This was one step too far. The New Zealand Government, in the form of one of its most powerful ministers, made it very clear to Barton that the matter was now at its natural conclusion.[88] At this point Barton finally accepted defeat and made no more attempts to force an inquiry.

It is unclear to what extent Prendergast and Richmond had personal support amongst the Grey Ministry. Whitmore was a Prendergast ally from the 1860s and Richmond was a highly respected former government minister, but Barton claimed Grey and Stout were in support of his claims.[89] This seems unlikely given

that the Government refused to assist Barton in his attempts to initiate an inquiry.
It should be noted that the Grey Ministry did not make any concerted efforts to
defend the judges though, possibly due to respect for the separation of powers
rather than any antipathy towards Prendergast and Richmond. Given the outcome
of the saga, Barton was most probably seen as a thorn in the side of the Grey
Ministry rather than an asset to be supported.

Barton lost his parliamentary seat in 1879 and left New Zealand soon after,
his legal and political careers in ruins and ostracised from the establishment. His
brief return as a Native Land Court judge in 1888 lasted only two years before he
resigned following a bitter feud with a fellow judge. He then left New Zealand
permanently and died in Paris in 1903.[90]

2. Insights into the nature of the New Zealand legal profession

Gillon provides excellent insights into the nature of the New Zealand legal
profession. Few other cases in New Zealand's legal history so vividly reveal the
tension between bench and bar. Parallels can be drawn to modern times, most
obviously in the recent inquiry into the actions of Supreme Court Justice Bill
Wilson in deciding a 2007 Court of Appeal case that involved a lawyer with
whom Wilson had a close business relationship.[91] While the Wilson case captured
headlines, the vitriol and scandal associated with the *Gillon* saga renders the
coverage of the modern example tame in comparison.

Much has been made of the homogenous and tight-knit New Zealand legal
fraternity of the past. It is often concluded that this led to an 'old boys' network' in
which male lawyers closed ranks to protect the interests of the profession against
outsiders. A ready example is the shameful way in which New Zealand's first
female lawyer, Ethel Benjamin, was ostracised by the Otago legal profession after
her admission in 1897.[92] A small group with shared histories also has the potential
to act in the opposite fashion. Closely linked careers and a limited amount of
suitable applicants for top positions can easily lead to the rivalry and internecine
warfare that occurred in the Wellington feud. The Wellington legal profession
of the late 1870s was tiny and insular, and to have three of its leading lights in
constant battle would have affected every practitioner in some way. Professional
and personal links affected the nature and outcome of the feud.

The New Zealand legal profession could not close ranks in this instance as
the dispute was very much within its ranks. Barton and Travers were the most
experienced lawyers at the Wellington Bar.[93] In early 1877, Barton argued for a
system of seniority to be implemented in New Zealand but was rebuffed. However,
it was agreed that either Barton or Travers would rank first at the New Zealand
Bar if a system was put in place. In terms of experience, they were the peers of
Richmond and Prendergast, and if the judicial selection process had turned out

differently it could just as easily have been Prendergast appearing before Barton in the Wellington Supreme Court.

Ultimately, enough of the profession, including lawyers in Parliament, sided with the judges to protect them against Barton's campaign for dismissal. The rank and file of the profession split, but the legal power brokers were clearly aware of the potential for disaster if Barton was successful in launching an official inquiry. Prendergast and Richmond may have expected more vocal support from the establishment but they received enough tacit support to remain in office. Post–1878 their careers flourished, while Barton's disintegrated. Barton's failure demonstrates the challenges involved in directly confronting established power. This is a constant throughout history and Barton's inflammatory approach backfired as he eventually alienated most of his powerful supporters.

The reputation of the New Zealand legal profession was undermined significantly by the *Gillon* saga. The competence of two leading judges, including the Chief Justice, was questioned by lawyers, politicians and the media.[94] Leading figures at the Wellington Bar accused each other of deception and the career of an outstanding courtroom advocate was irredeemably damaged. The unfortunate affair also illustrates the chaos that can be caused by a renegade, populist barrister. That the situation should have been allowed to progress so far is a poor reflection on Prendergast's leadership skills in his early years as Chief Justice. This damage to Prendergast's reputation could have been one of Barton's key aims. A call for judicial dismissal is among the most controversial actions that can be taken, especially within the legal profession, as it goes to the heart of the relationship between bench and bar. Trust and mutual respect from both parties is vital to the effective functioning of the courts and to the successful implementation of the rule of law. Judges rely on advocates to act as responsible officers of the court, while advocates rely on judges to adjudicate in an impartial fashion.

This example also raises interesting issues relating to the separation of powers. Barton would argue that the legislature twice abrogated its role in failing to launch an inquiry. In rebuttal it could be argued that if there ever was a legislature to unseat the reactionaries Richmond and Prendergast, it was the liberal-led legislature of the late 1870s, and by choosing not to, it clearly indicated that no inquiry was necessary. The legislature chose not to act and the executive rightly refused to usurp the legislature's power.

Intriguingly, this feud could also have affected New Zealand's most infamous legal decision. After analysing the *Gillon* feud one is forced to read the *Wi Parata* judgment in a different light and pay closer attention to its main actors. If there is even a sliver of truth in Barton's accusation that Prendergast and Richmond showed bias towards his clients on account of the feud, then the dismissive treatment of Wi Parata's claim could have partly resulted from the feud.[95]

The controversy surrounding the Wellington Supreme Court from 1876 to

1878 reaches its climax in the case of *Gillon v MacDonald*. *Gillon* is the vehicle for a feud that split the New Zealand legal profession and undermined the authority of the Wellington-based judiciary. While not important for its specific subject matter, *Gillon* contains one of the most startling episodes of contempt of court by a barrister in New Zealand's legal history. The bitter feud between bench and bar developed and transformed over several months as the case proceeded, having a ripple effect. Firstly, it affected the parties involved in the *Gillon* case, including the plaintiff, the lawyers and the judges. It also affected Barton's clients, including possibly Wi Parata in his bid to gain judicial recognition of native title. The three branches of government were all dragged into the conflict, though the legislature and executive avoided launching an inquiry into the matter, despite Barton's best efforts.

Driven by resentment and personal animosity, the rivalries in the fledgling New Zealand legal profession are laid bare in this case. Both parties in the feud must share some blame for the damage wrought, but Barton's bloody-mindedness was at the heart of events. Time after time, Barton refused to compromise in any way and demonstrated an Ahab-like monomania in attempting to remove the judges from the bench. Prendergast's decision to imprison Barton was possibly rash and definitely backfired, yet it should be remembered that the Chief Justice was attempting to use the tools at his disposal to protect the authority of the Supreme Court, an authority that Barton failed to respect. This fact was quietly accepted by most other power brokers of the time, including Crown ministers. To see this as merely a closing of ranks by the elite fails to acknowledge Barton's leading position at the New Zealand Bar and the support he received from powerful sources. The end result was defeat for both Barton and his client Gillon.

The *Gillon* saga is an unflattering portrayal of the New Zealand legal profession and unfortunately serves to confirm some of the prejudiced insults levelled at colonial courts by the English legal establishment. Frederick Moss stated that "this case has lowered our Supreme Court in the eyes of thousands of people in the colony".[96] There were no winners in the *Gillon* saga and the biggest casualty was the reputation of the New Zealand legal profession.

8

THE TREATY IS A SIMPLE NULLITY
Prendergast and *Wi Parata v The Bishop of Wellington*

In recent decades, New Zealand as a nation has increasingly focused on Maori and Pakeha relations. Dominating the debate has been the Treaty of Waitangi. This debate has taken many forms: political argument, academic analysis and legal reasoning. The Treaty debate has also transformed a late nineteenth-century New Zealand Supreme Court case into the most notorious judicial decision in New Zealand history. In 1877 Chief Justice James Prendergast declared in the case *Wi Parata v The Bishop of Wellington*[1] that the Treaty of Waitangi was "a simple nullity". This decision heavily influenced New Zealand law until directly challenged during the mid-1980s. While Prendergast's career included many important achievements, it is his decision in the *Wi Parata* case for which he is best remembered.

1. Background to the *Wi Parata* fact situation

The facts of the *Wi Parata* case stretched back almost three decades to a period of increasing European dominance in New Zealand. In 1848, the Ngati Toa tribe in the south-west of the North Island reached an agreement with the Anglican Bishop of New Zealand to place a parcel of land in Porirua aside for educational purposes. This land was held under native or aboriginal title. In 1850, Governor George Grey issued a Crown grant to the Bishop.[2] During the intervening 27 years, no school had been established and Maori numbers in the area had substantially diminished. Wiremu Parata, a Maori member of Parliament and a Ngati Toa chief, decided to take the case to the Supreme Court in an attempt to recover the entrusted land for his tribe.[3] Parata had become prominent in the support of Maori land cases and was aware of the importance that would be attached to this particular case.

The facts behind the 1877 decision were not unique and therefore served as a test case for similar situations in the colony. A Royal Commission in 1869 had shown that many similar trusts around the colony had also failed to achieve their purpose. As Frederika Hackshaw has argued: "The political implications of that claim are self-evident: a favourable decision for the plaintiff would open the floodgates to native demands for the return of every similarly situated trust property."[4] The case demonstrated that the issue of land ownership had the potential to unravel the delicate fabric of Pakeha society. Parata petitioned the Court for the return of the land to its original Maori owners on the basis that the expected school had not been built.[5] The judges who were assigned the task of hearing Wi Parata's case were therefore adjudicating on a controversial issue, namely, the struggle for control of land between Maori and Pakeha.

2. Other key players in the *Wi Parata* decision

Prendergast's present historical reputation rests on his decision in *Wi Parata v The Bishop of Wellington*. Until the publication of David Williams' 2011 book *A Simple Nullity: The Wi Parata case in New Zealand law and history*, only a few legal commentators (including myself), when discussing the case, emphasised that the decision was a co-operative effort made by two judges.[6] Both James Prendergast and William Richmond were responsible for Supreme Court decisions in the Wellington judicial region from 1875. The blame for the controversial and bloody Taranaki War (1860-61), which left a legacy of misunderstanding and distrust between Maori and Pakeha, has been partly attributed to Richmond by some commentators.[7] Richmond was also no stranger to difficult decisions regarding Maori land rights. During his time as Minister of Native Affairs (1858-60), he demonstrated a hard-line, unsympathetic attitude towards Maori.[8] The *Wi Parata* decision was formulated near the beginning of Prendergast's tenure as Chief Justice and at the beginning of his professional relationship with Richmond. Williams argues that Richmond was primarily responsible for the *Wi Parata* decision. While hearing the case, Richmond made brief notes in his judicial notebook whereas Prendergast did not. Richmond led the questioning of counsel during the trial and also annotated a published copy of the decision found in the Crown Law Office library. Beyond this it is impossible to say which judge was most responsible for the decision. As Williams points out: "Without private access to confidential memoranda and conversations in the chambers of judges and their clerks, one can seldom prove conclusively who wrote what in the joint judgments of judges in a common law system."[9]

Williams' claim that Prendergast only delivered the judgment because he was the senior judge is not supported by the New Zealand Law Reports. From 1875 to 1895, Richmond delivered several judgments on behalf of the combined court. Williams also claims that some of the statements in the judgment seem to reflect Richmond's view of Maori society and land ownership. As can be seen in Chapters 5 and 6, Prendergast's views on these topics were very similar to Richmond's. As Attorney-General, Prendergast dealt with Maori issues for ten years. He was well aware of key international law texts such as Vattel's *The Law of Nations*, especially given that his mentor's father (Joseph Chitty) had provided an English translation in 1834.

Taking all of these factors together, it is likely that Richmond took a lead in formulating the decision, but there is not enough firm evidence to prove that it was 'Richmond's decision'. Instead it must be seen as a co-operative effort. In 1877 Prendergast and Richmond were still fine-tuning their judicial relationship, but they had already adjudicated together for two years and they had known each other well for 15 years. Regardless of this debate, Prendergast officially delivered the judgment and therefore it is still primarily ascribed to him. However, for the purposes of this chapter, the decision will be referred to as being made by 'Prendergast and Richmond', or 'the judges' or 'the court'.

Indeed, the *Wi Parata* decision featured a kaleidoscope of prominent New Zealand public figures. Wiremu Parata was a Ngati Toa leader and spokesman who had also served in Parliament during the 1870s. A vocal supporter of Maori issues, "[h]e expressed the view that the law-makers were making decisions affecting Maori without understanding them".[10] On his departure from Parliament, Parata championed Maori land cases, most famously the 1877 landmark case regarding the Ngati Toa land in Porirua. In the *Wi Parata* case, Parata was representing the Ngati Toa tribe: "Quære, whether a Maori chief can sue on behalf of his tribe . . . . Prayer:—1. That the lands may be declared to be part of the native lands lawfully reserved for the use and benefit of the Ngatitoa tribe."[11] Parata's commitment to Maori justice was further demonstrated by his support of Te Whiti at Parihaka. Parata was present at Parihaka in 1881 when the Taranaki village was invaded following Prendergast's proclamation.[12]

The legal advocates involved in the *Wi Parata* decision were all leading figures at the Wellington Bar: Barton from the firm Barton and Fitzherbert (plaintiff); Travers from the firm Travers, Ollivier and Co. (defendant, Bishop of Wellington); and Charles Izard (defendant, Attorney-General). During 1877, the year in which the *Wi Parata* case was heard, Travers was the member of the House of Representatives for Wellington City.[13] Therefore, Travers was a member of the Government attempting to acquire more Maori land, while acting as an advocate in a decision which enabled the acquisition of Maori land.

In 1870, Prendergast and Travers worked together on the first New Zealand Law Society Council,[14] and, as mentioned previously, Travers assisted Prendergast as acting Assistant Law Officer during the early 1870s. When James Prendergast was formally congratulated for his time as Administrator during and after the tenure of Governor Gordon, a group of private citizens was there to pay respects, including Travers. Prendergast and Travers were friends, and a degree of respect existed in their relationship which was clearly absent in the case of Barton and Prendergast.

Izard was another established Wellington practitioner. An English lawyer with a specialist knowledge of equity, he had been a leading figure at the Wellington Bar since its earliest days. He was also partly responsible for the creation of today's large law firm, Bell Gully, which he helped create alongside Sir Francis Bell.[15] Izard was a political conservative and supporter of Harry Atkinson.[16]

The offending Crown grant which effectively provided the basis for the *Wi Parata* case, and the following Privy Council cases *Nireaha Tamaki v Baker* (1900–01)[17] and *Wallis v Solicitor-General* (1902–03),[18] was given by Governor George Grey to Bishop George Augustus Selwyn. Grey's relationship with Maori ranged from meticulously recording their oral history to invading their tribal lands during the Waikato War. Selwyn, a key missionary figure in New Zealand history, was committed to the welfare and conversion of Maori but found himself torn between Government and Maori during the New Zealand Wars.[19] Selwyn was the Bishop of Wellington in 1850, when the grant was made, but in 1877 the Bishop was the high-profile and widely respected Octavius Hadfield. While Hadfield was an outspoken supporter of Maori in the Porirua-Otaki region, the Anglican church found itself directly in conflict with Ngati Toa in the *Wi Parata* case.

Analysis of the main players in the *Wi Parata* affair aids in viewing the case in context. The dry manner in which many decisions were written and recorded during Prendergast's era masks the personalities and rivalries of those involved in creating the decision. While the legal system strives for objectivity, the system is composed of individuals, with individual personalities and backgrounds. These factors may affect a legal decision to varying extents, but even if their influence is limited they provide context for what appears in the law reports. The antagonistic behaviour of Barton towards Prendergast and Richmond throughout 1877, and the intense frustration that the new Chief Justice experienced in response, is not evident in a reading of the official law reports. The individuals prominent in the *Wi Parata* decision were also representatives of larger groups in colonial New Zealand society. Prendergast and Richmond represented the legal system of New Zealand, Parata and Barton represented the Ngati Toa tribe, Travers spoke on behalf of the Anglican Church, and Izard was the advocate for the New Zealand Government. These large and powerful forces in New Zealand colonial society met in the Wellington Supreme Court in 1877.

3. The judgment

The judgment in *Wi Parata v The Bishop of Wellington* was far from just a simple one-line quotation. The judgment of Prendergast and Richmond was complex and discussed a variety of related issues. The ruling stated that unless native customary title was supported by a Crown grant it could not be accepted or enforced by the Courts. The imposition of British legal theories upon Maori land-ownership would result in the loss of much Maori land and give the impression that 'English law' was a tool to aid in dispossession. The Crown grant made to the Bishop was unable to be annulled by the Court, and the existence of this grant implied that the Crown had used its sovereign powers to extinguish any existing native title. When the Crown acquired the North Island of New Zealand by occupation and the South Island by discovery, it also acquired the exclusive right of extinguishing native title. By effectively deeming the South Island *terra nullius*, the Maori iwi Ngai Tahu, who were living in the South Island at the time of European arrival, became a casualty of a broad and sweeping system of extinguishment. The Crown's right to extinguish native title was accompanied by a treaty-like duty to protect Maori against infringement of their right of occupancy. Land transactions with Maori were a matter for the Crown only, and the Court had no jurisdiction to diminish the Crown powers.[20]

Instead of only discussing the nature of Crown grants and native title, however, Prendergast and Richmond ventured beyond the scope of the mere facts of the case to pass judgment on the Treaty of Waitangi. They used the *Wi Parata* decision as an effective vehicle for enshrining Eurocentric, imperialist views into law. To justify the opinion that New Zealand was acquired by occupation and discovery, vital to the overall reasoning, Prendergast and Richmond had somehow to dispose of the Treaty. The method used became the most notorious example of legal reasoning in New Zealand history. The judgment stated that:

> So far indeed as that instrument [The Treaty] purported to cede the sovereignty – a matter which we are not here directly concerned – it must be regarded as a simple nullity. No body politic existed capable of making cession of sovereignty, nor could the thing itself exist.[21]

In the court's view, New Zealand was peopled only by "primitive barbarians" and "savages" who had no sovereignty to cede, nor any existing body of customary law that could be legally recognised. This primitive race was to be quickly subdued as New Zealand was transformed into a 'Better Britain'.[22] After giving a landmark judgment on the most controversial aspect of New Zealand history, Prendergast and Richmond returned to the specific facts. They applied the doctrine of *cy-près*[23] and decided that if *cy-près* was not possible, the land would revert not to the surviving donors, but to the Crown.[24]

While Prendergast and Richmond adjudicated upon several issues relating to Maori land, the *Wi Parata* decision is remembered for three words: "a simple nullity". If these three words were preceded by "The Treaty of Waitangi is . . .", all three articles of the Treaty, according to the judges, would be null and void. But the judgment did not state this. Instead it related 'nullity' to the ceding of sovereignty. Both the Maori and English versions of the Treaty discuss more than sovereignty. Other issues include possession of Maori land, forests, fisheries and other taonga,[25] the Crown's preemptive right of purchase, and the imparting of the rights and privileges of British subjects to Maori.[26] A similar line of argument has been presented before by E. J. Haughey and forces one to examine the exact language in the judgment in more detail.[27] While there seems little doubt that the judges were seeking to sidestep the Treaty, they did not necessarily condemn it entirely. In the judgment, Prendergast and Richmond made an attempt to widely canvass existing law, both statute and common. The effect of the judgment was to minimise the role of the Treaty and emphasise that the Treaty in itself had no binding force.

In the course of their *Wi Parata* judgment, Prendergast and Richmond referred to previous landmark cases dealing with native title and the Treaty of Waitangi. They provided a confusing reference to the 1847 New Zealand Supreme Court case of *R v Symonds* (1847),[28] stating that "Our view of this subject [indigenous peoples' rights] is in accordance with previous decisions of this Court."[29] Prendergast and Richmond then discussed the *Symonds* case as an apposite example, implying concurrence with its findings. Later in the judgment, though, the judges took issue with specific arguments made by Chapman J in deciding the *Symonds* case.[30] The judges agreed with Chapman J's argument that the Treaty had affirmed rights already vested in the Crown, but Peter Spiller argues that they:

> rejected Chapman J.'s statement that the American courts would allow a grant of land to be impeached by a native Indian, on the basis that the Indian title had not been extinguished. The [Prendergast] court said that this was not a legitimate inference from the Commentaries of Kent.[31]

Prendergast and Richmond found both helpful and unhelpful statements in Chapman J's landmark decision. It is clear that the judges did not agree with Chapman J's views on native title and customary law. In the *Wi Parata* decision, Prendergast and Richmond stated: "On the foundation of this colony, the aborigines were found without any kind of civil government, or any settled system of law . . . . The Maori tribes were incapable of performing the duties, and therefore of assuming the rights, of a civilised community."[32] The judges did not accept that Maori customary law could exist. According to the court, references to customary law found in section 3 of the Native Rights Act 1865 were inapplicable: "The Act speaks further on of the 'Ancient Custom and Usage of the Maori people', as if some body of customary law did in reality exist. But a phrase in a statute cannot call what is non-existent into being."[33]

Customary law can be differentiated from aboriginal or native title. Customary law is a uniquely Maori construction while native title is a legal doctrine imported from Europe. Customary law refers to the system of rules and social regulations in existence in Maori society up to the assertion of British sovereignty in 1840. Prendergast and Richmond could give limited recognition to native title, while dismissing the existence of any Maori customary law.

Prendergast's views on Maori customary law can be linked to his positivist approach. As Maori law did not strictly follow John Austin's requirements of being "commands issued by a sovereign backed by sanctions", it could not be properly classed as law. This approach was roundly criticised by the Privy Council in the 1900-1901 *Nireaha Tamaki v Baker* decision.[34]

This raises the possibility that Prendergast and Richmond manipulated relevant precedent to reach a judgment favourable to contemporary colonial land policy. Analysis of the *Wi Parata* judgment could lead to a number of conclusions. The judges may have purposely engineered a line of legal reasoning to aid in the alienation of Maori land, or given a sincere but mistaken judgment in an effort to clarify a complex area of law. Alternatively, Prendergast and Richmond may have provided an accurate decision in accordance with convincing precedent, demonstrating wise and logical legal reasoning. Between the polarities of an ethnocentric conspiracy and a triumph of justice is where the answer lies. Williams argues that Prendergast and Richmond "'cobbled together' a series of arguments in their judgment that would enable them to arrive at the conclusion they felt bound to come to".[35]

When analysing the *Wi Parata* case it is necessary to separate the various issues raised by Prendergast and Richmond and explore each in turn, and then work out how they relate to one another. First, the ratio of the decision deals with the nature of native title and its relationship to a Crown grant. When discussing a Crown grant, the ability of the Courts to question an Act of State is analysed. Secondly, the obiter dictum of the case deals with the Treaty of Waitangi and whether that document was an act of cession or a "simple nullity". Thirdly, Prendergast and Richmond's decision must be seen in the context of contemporary international law: was it representative or not?

In *Wi Parata*, the Chief Justice discussed a number of cases which have become high-profile in today's indigenous people's rights debate, including *Johnson v McIntosh* (1823),[36] *Cherokee Nation v The State of Georgia* (1831)[37] and *R v Symonds*.[38] Also discussed are important New Zealand statutes such as the Land Claims Ordinance 1841, the English Laws Act 1858 and the Native Rights Act 1865.

On the issue of native title and its relationship to a Crown grant (ratio), the judges stated, "the right of extinguishing native title being exclusively in the Crown . . . . further, we are of opinion that the Court has no jurisdiction to avoid a Crown grant".[39] Therefore, Prendergast and Richmond used the term native title, but argued that the Crown had complete authority to extinguish this title by issuing a Crown grant and the Court could do nothing to prevent this. Crown sovereignty was supreme and "in the case of primitive barbarians, the supreme executive Government must acquit itself as best it may, of its obligation to respect native proprietary rights, and of necessity must be the sole arbiter of its own justice".[40] Transactions with the Maori "for the cession of their title to the Crown were thus to be regarded as acts of State, and therefore are not examinable by any Court".[41] Though referring to native title, Prendergast and Richmond were not convinced that it was a particularly relevant concept in this case as "there existed amongst the natives no regular system of territorial rights nor any definite ideas of property in land".[42]

On the issue of the nature of the Treaty of Waitangi (obiter), Prendergast and Richmond argued that the Treaty was not one of cession: "No body politic existed capable of making cession of sovereignty."[43] Cession of sovereignty can only be made by a body that has sovereignty and the judges decided that 'savages' did not have this vital power. Therefore the Treaty, as a legal instrument ceding sovereignty, was a nullity.

On the question of procedure, Prendergast and Richmond decided that "a Crown grant cannot be avoided for a matter not appearing upon the face of the grant".[44] The doctrine of *cy-près* was to be applied, meaning that the funds would be applied as near as possible to the application specified by the donor, that is, the building of a school. This decision would cause ongoing legal actions in the Courts. Also, the Court decided that the Crown was the legal donor of the land, not Ngati Toa, and if necessary the land would revert to the Crown.

Therefore, the land originally belonging to Ngati Toa, and then given to the Bishop of Wellington by a Crown grant, remained with the Bishop. The Crown grant was valid and native title could not undermine this fact and the Court could not question a Crown grant. Wi Parata's case failed due to a host of legal reasons offered by Prendergast and Richmond. The reasoning, though elucidated at length in the judgment, was in 1987 described by Paul McHugh as completely incorrect: "There were no portions of the judgment in which important errors of detail or interpretation did not occur."[45] However, the decision has also been described by Auckland practitioner, Guy Chapman, as having, "stood the test of time. In its clarity of exposition, and basic soundness of judgment, it is fitting testimony to the quality of that most learned Chief Justice's judicial work."[46]

Since 2011, the authoritative account of the case can be found in Williams' *A Simple Nullity*. Williams' conclusions are nuanced. In terms of correct legal decision-making as at 1877, Williams agrees with some parts of the judgment but disagrees with others. He argues that Prendergast and Richmond were upholding established law in refusing to question the Crown grant. In contravention of the 2003 *Ngati Apa* decision, Williams argues that the modern view of native title entering the New Zealand legal system through the adoption of common law in 1840 is a recent invention, and therefore Prendergast and Richmond did not ignore the obvious in 1877. Williams and I have both noted that in many ways the Treaty of Waitangi was, and still is, a nullity. This is primarily due to the fact that it cannot be enforced in courts until specifically incorporated into domestic legislation. Williams places the judges' language in context, arguing that it must be seen as reflective of prevailing nineteenth-century colonial views. As with many modern commentators, Williams disagrees with Prendergast and Richmond's claim that Maori had no customary law. Williams goes so far as to argue the judges wilfully abrogated their judicial duty by refusing to recognise clear statutory provisions in the Native Rights Act 1865. Ultimately Williams concludes that, while he welcomes the rise of native title rights in recent decades, the *Wi Parata* case and its judges have been unfairly demonised.

Williams' thesis is convincing. At some points he overstates the evidence for Richmond's leading role but in general he treats the decision as a joint one. His description of Prendergast is very brief and underestimates Prendergast's intellectual ability, but Williams is correct in stating that Richmond possessed the more impressive legal mind. Williams rightly challenges the practice of judging the judges from a modern perspective:

> From this contemporary point of view, the Prendergast remarks are useful only in order to show how crass, offensive and incorrect were the opinions of nineteenth-century settler colonial judges . . . . Distancing modern law from the colonial past, we seem to want to reject 'a simple nullity' as often and as vehemently as possible.[47]

With experts in disagreement over the judgment, it remains the most controversial legal decision in New Zealand history.

It is not the aim of this chapter to investigate in depth the domestic and international law relating to native title. This work has been extensively carried out by others. In a New Zealand context, scholars such as David Williams,[48] Paul McHugh,[49] Richard Boast and Mark Hickford[50] have provided exhaustive coverage of the doctrine's history. There appear to be two schools of thought on the matter, one supporting the doctrine of native title in a New Zealand context, as outlined by the New Zealand Court of Appeal in 2003, and one effectively dismissing the doctrine, exemplified by Prendergast, Richmond, and the New Zealand legal establishment up until the 1980s. In judicial decision-making it is possible to have a range of different precedents to follow, allowing a judge great flexibility. Prendergast and Richmond used this flexibility in the law to decide *Wi Parata*. In adhering to the concept of Crown sovereignty, Prendergast and Richmond were following a long line of established jurisprudential thinking, from Hobbes to Austin. In this respect, they were judges of their time. If Prendergast and Richmond had ignored the ultimate power of a Crown grant, they would have been taking a liberal course in direct collision with New Zealand settler society. They were not the men to do this.

Prendergast and Richmond's comments relating to the Treaty were extreme but were also *obiter dicta*, and therefore not technically a precedent. While always a key concern for Maori, the Treaty has only recently been recognised by wider New Zealand society as a vital constitutional document. For all the attacks made on the *Wi Parata* view, the Treaty of Waitangi is not in itself legally enforceable, although its principles have often been incorporated into New Zealand law by individual statutes. Prendergast and Richmond's language regarding Maori society was unforgiving, but their desire to avoid allowing the Treaty to have a true part in the New Zealand legal system remains to this day. If one agrees with modern 'orthodox' thought that the Treaty was one of cession, then Prendergast's view that it was 'a simple nullity' is not correct, but in terms of its legal power, the Treaty remains limited. The Treaty does not, in the positivistic sense, have intrinsic legality. The legal recognition of the principles of the Treaty is a far different matter from the legal recognition of the Treaty itself.

4. The influence of the decision

When the *Wi Parata* decision is described as the most notorious in New Zealand's history, this is with reference to the legal legacy of the case rather than just specific ethnocentric statements. Prendergast and Richmond's 1877 decision in the Supreme Court created a precedent that resulted in the alienation of large amounts of Maori land. Effectively, any Maori land not bolstered by a Crown grant could not be claimed using the doctrine of native title. Throughout the twentieth century, examples can be provided demonstrating the legacy of the *Wi Parata* decision. In 1909, the *Wi Parata* reasoning was incorporated into statute form with the passing of section 84 of the Native Land Act 1909 and later the Maori Affairs Act 1953.[51] The judgment was relied upon to defeat Maori claims in several important twentieth-century cases, for example, *Re the Bed of the Wanganui River* [1962][52] and *Re Ninety-Mile Beach* [1963].[53] The legal boundaries established by Prendergast and Richmond were maintained and strengthened by many lawmakers who followed them.

The triumph of the *Wi Parata* line of reasoning was not without legal dispute, as demonstrated by the controversial Privy Council decisions in *Nireaha Tamaki v Baker* and *Wallis v Solicitor-General*. Analysis of these Privy Council decisions helps to place the reasoning of the New Zealand judiciary in a Commonwealth context. The Privy Council stated that it was "rather late in the day" to argue before a New Zealand court that there was no customary Maori law which the courts could recognise, as had happened in *Wi Parata*.[54] While the Privy Council harshly criticised the actions of the New Zealand Supreme Court in a general manner, it stated that *Wi Parata* had been correctly decided on its own facts. Lord Davey of the Privy Council said:

> In the case of *Wi Parata v The Bishop of Wellington* . . . the decision was that the Court has no jurisdiction by *scire facias* or other proceeding to annul a Crown grant for matter not appearing on the face of it, and it was held that the issue

of a Crown grant implies a declaration by the Crown that the Native title has been extinguished. If so, it is all the more important that Natives should be able to protect their rights (whatever they are) before the land is sold and granted to a purchaser. But the dicta in the case go beyond what was necessary for the decision. Their Lordships have already commented on the limited construction and effect attributed to s. 3 of the Native Rights Act, 1865, by the Chief Justice in that case. As applied to the case then before the Court however, their Lordships see no reason to doubt the correctness of the conclusion arrived at by the learned Judges.[55]

It was not until the mid–1980s that *Wi Parata* would be challenged directly. It could be argued that by this time the damage had been done.

Damage was done not only to Maori society but also to the relationship between the Judicial Committee of the Privy Council and the New Zealand Court of Appeal. The *Wi Parata* case formed the basis of the *Solicitor-General v Bishop of Wellington* (1901)[56] case in the Court of Appeal and then the *Wallis v Solicitor-General* case in the Privy Council. The Privy Council severely criticised the conduct of the Court of Appeal. In an adjourned sitting of the Court of Appeal in Wellington on 25 April 1903, the Bench and the Bar of New Zealand defended themselves against the attack from London. On a day that would in future times represent the New Zealand legal profession's 'coming of age', colonial lawyers and judges asserted their independence and *raison d'être*.

Chief Justice Stout led the protest by defending the decisions of Prendergast, the Supreme Court and the Court of Appeal: "I feel the aspersions under the circumstances in which they have been made are a greater reflection on the Privy Council than on the Appeal Court of New Zealand."[57] Stout had not been part of the controversial Court of Appeal decision. He and Edwards J had made the earlier Supreme Court decision which was successfully appealed. In fact, Stout was congratulated by the Privy Council for his decision.

Williams J was more obviously indignant than Stout, being one of the Court of Appeal judges responsible for the decision in question:

If the Court had displayed subserviency or want of independence of the Executive it would have been loudly condemned by a unanimous public opinion. No suggestion of the kind has ever been made here. It has been reserved for four strangers sitting 14,000 miles away to make it . . . . Whether, however, they [decisions] should be reviewed by the Judicial Committee, as at present constituted is a question worthy of consideration. That Court, by its imputations in the present case, by the ignorance it has shown in this and other cases of our history, of our legislation, and of our practice, and by its long-delayed judgments, has displayed every characteristic of an alien tribunal.[58]

Williams defended the decision of his former leader, Prendergast.

After a further indignant speech by Edwards J, Prendergast's associate, Travers, rose and stated that while he had not consulted his fellow lawyers, the bar was in complete support of the bench. As Travers spoke, the lawyers surrounding him rose to their feet and remained standing in a show of solidarity. This was Travers' final action as leader of the Wellington Bar. He was killed the following day in a railway accident.

When attacked by the powerful Privy Council, the legal establishment of New Zealand closed ranks to protect its own, and to protect Prendergast and Richmond's decision. Even Prendergast's rivals, Stout and Edwards, spoke openly in support of colonial independence and judicial loyalty.

In the case *Hohepa Wi Neera v Bishop of Wellington* (1902),[59] Stout followed the decision in *Wi Parata*. There was widespread support for Prendergast and Richmond's views from the New Zealand judiciary for over a hundred years. Even New Zealand's greatest jurist, Sir John Salmond, supported the *Wi Parata* doctrine when he created section 84 of the Native Land Act 1909.[60] The *Wi Parata* decision's legacy was diminished somewhat by the *Hoani Te Heuheu Tukino v Aotea District Maori Land Board* [1941] decision,[61] which recognised the Treaty in international law as one of cession and not a simple nullity. But the decision supported Prendergast and Richmond's claim that the Treaty could have no domestic legal effect unless incorporated into statute. The judicial support for *Wi Parata* fell away only during the mid-1980s, a time of radical governmental change and judicial activism.

In 1986 Williamson J recognised Maori customary fishing rights and native title in *Te Weehi v Regional Fisheries Officer* [1986].[62] This decision, according to some commentators, successfully challenged *Wi Parata*.[63] McHugh heralded Williamson J's decision as the end of Prendergast's legacy: "The common law doctrine of aboriginal title has returned to New Zealand at the cost to the personal reputation of the primary adjudicator against it, Chief Justice Prendergast."[64]

While the *Te Weehi* case challenged Prendergast and Richmond's views on native title, the landmark case *NZ Maori Council v Attorney-General* [1987][65] addressed another controversial issue raised by *Wi Parata*: the validity of the Treaty of Waitangi. This case concerned the effects of section 9 of the State-Owned Enterprises Act 1986, which declared that Government actions must accord with the principles of the Treaty. In interpreting what these principles were, the President of the Court of Appeal, Cooke P, stated that "those principles require the Pakeha and Maori Treaty partners to act towards each other reasonably and with the utmost good faith".[66] The *Wi Parata* decision in relation to the Treaty was briefly discussed and criticised in the *NZ Maori Council* case. Bisson J stated that: "With the advent of legislation invoking recognition of the principles of the Treaty no longer is it to be regarded as a 'simple nullity' (as in *Wi Parata v Bishop of Wellington*)."[67] Although the Court of Appeal has stressed that the Treaty does not have legal force except where incorporated by statute, the negative attitude taken by modern legal leaders towards Prendergast and Richmond's decision stands in contrast to the support the decision received at the time it was made and in the following 100 years.

Six years after the *Te Weehi* decision had given recognition to the doctrine of native title, the High Court of Australia heard the landmark case *Mabo v Queensland (No 2)* (1992).[68] In this case, native title was discussed and recognised and the doctrine of *terra nullius*, the concept that Australia was not inhabited when discovered by Europeans, was cast aside. The idea of *terra nullius* is similar to the statement in *Wi Parata* that the South Island of New Zealand was acquired by 'discovery'.

The *Wi Parata* decision has been analysed and discussed at length in the reports of the Waitangi Tribunal. In the Orakei Claim report, the approach of Prendergast and Richmond was compared with that of Chapman J: "In *Wi Parata* the Court no longer spoke of 'aboriginal natives' or 'Maori New Zealanders' as Chapman J had done thirty years before, but of 'savages' and 'primitive barbarians'."[69] This observation highlighted a generational change with regards to Maori issues between the 1840s and 1870s. 'Liberal' judges such as Henry Chapman and William Martin had dominated the bench in the two decades after the signing of the Treaty. 'Conservative' judges such as James Prendergast and William Richmond dominated the bench after the New Zealand Wars of the 1860s.

The Orakei report claimed that the Privy Council contradicted the *Wi Parata* view in *Nireaha Tamaki* and *Wallis* but "Thereafter, and although the decisions of the Privy Council were meant to be binding, the New Zealand Courts pursued the *Wi Parata* view."[70] As mentioned earlier, while the Privy Council did criticise the *Wi Parata* decision, they also stated in *Nireaha* that Richmond and Prendergast had decided *Wi Parata* correctly on the facts.[71]

In the Kaituna River Claim, the Tribunal report relied heavily on the work of McHugh and his argument that Prendergast's decision "was wrong being based on a concept of international law and not on the established principles of colonial law".[72] The Ngai Tahu Sea Fisheries Report also referred to *Wi Parata* and discussed at length the conflict between the New Zealand Court of Appeal and the Privy Council during the early years of the twentieth century.[73]

Overall, the Waitangi Tribunal has taken an unfavourable view of *Wi Parata*, in line with the new 'orthodox' view prevalent in Treaty jurisprudence, which is discussed in the next section. As mentioned in the Rangiteaorere Land Claim, the Tribunal reports cannot overturn legal precedent, nor are their recommendations binding on the New Zealand Government.[74] Nevertheless, the opinion of the Tribunal and its researchers has much influence, and the Tribunal reports have further served to undermine Prendergast's judicial reputation. The literature on the Treaty of Waitangi that has appeared over the past 25 years is vast and diverse. Numerous commentators – legal, academic, political and otherwise – have provided their viewpoints. Most recently, native title has been at the centre of the national debate following from the foreshore and seabed case decided by the Court of Appeal in June 2003. *Wi Parata* was referred to in the judgment of Elias CJ and subsequently dismissed:

> I am of the view that the approach taken by Turner J in the Supreme Court and by the Court of Appeal in *In Re the Ninety-Mile Beach* can be explained only on the basis that they were applying the approach taken in *Wi Parata v Bishop of Wellington*. On that approach Maori property had no existence in law until converted into land held in fee of the Crown. Until then it was assumed to be Crown property . . . . For the reasons already given, such view is contrary to the common law and to successive statutory provisions recognising Maori customary property.[75]

More recently, *Wi Parata* has been cited unfavourably in *Takamore v Clarke* [2012] 1 NZLR 573 (CA) and *R v Mason* [2012] 2 NZLR 695 (HC). There is clearly no place for *Wi Parata* in twenty-first-century New Zealand law.

In Treaty jurisprudence, recent commentators have found it necessary to analyse the *Wi Parata* decision, either briefly or in depth. The result of this analysis has been a largely negative view of the decision. Therefore, the *Wi Parata* decision is arguably the most notorious in New Zealand's history, though this notoriety is a recent development. The lack of recognition given to the Treaty before 1975 is the principal reason for the relatively recent revisionist attention given to the judgment by academics.

5. Academic opinion on the role of Prendergast

Recent academic opinion on the *Wi Parata* case has been divided. This division has not been balanced, with most commentators condemning the decision as incorrect at best and manipulative ethnocentrism at worst. The critics of Prendergast and Richmond's decision are vocal and numerous. Williams' *A Simple Nullity* comprehensively outlines the debate from both sides. This section will look at academic opinion, which has specifically (and inaccurately) focused on Prendergast as the sole author of the decision. In this way, the sources of his present-day notoriety can be discovered.

In his early groundbreaking research into the common law concept of native title, Paul McHugh dismissed *Wi Parata* as an example of misguided judicial activism. McHugh argued that, far from following established law, Prendergast propagated the view of a small, unrepresentative group of English writers.[76] By disregarding the doctrine of native title, the Chief Justice steered New Zealand law off course for over a century. McHugh's research is of a jurisprudential nature and does not include comprehensive discussion about Prendergast himself. That said, Prendergast remains a key figure in McHugh's work.[77] More recently, McHugh has argued that native title as common law, in the sense that we understand it today, is actually a modern construction.[78] In 2004, McHugh wrote:

> Despite the ill-will that its principles generated, the judgment in *Wi Parata* reflected the received position in New Zealand and other British colonies of

the same period. It prevented Maori recourse to the courts to vindicate the aboriginal property rights guaranteed under the Treaty of Waitangi, leaving that role to the Crown as their legal protector.[79]

Therefore, Prendergast and Richmond did not have a clear common law concept upholding native title which they could follow.

In his analysis of the *Wi Parata* decision, Boast refutes several of Prendergast and Richmond's claims:

> Prendergast CJ famously denied that Maori had any 'settled system of law'. This remark is not only untrue but is inconsistent with contemporary statutory directions to the Native Land Court in the Native Lands Acts that determinations of Maori title to land were to be made according to "Maori custom."[80]

The most controversial use of Prendergast's judicial legacy has been by Stuart C Scott and Walter Christie. Scott's *The Travesty of Waitangi*, released in 1993, captured headlines, became a bestseller and gained a reputation for being an anti-Treaty handbook. Scott used Prendergast's judgment to support his claim that the Treaty of Waitangi is not a valid document and should be ignored. Little legal argument is used by Scott, and Prendergast's usefulness is primarily in his "simple nullity" quotation.[81] Scott's arguments are one-sided and poorly supported by primary evidence. While many commentators have accused Prendergast of building up legal boundaries, Scott defends the Chief Justice.

Christie places a picture of Prendergast on the dust cover of his book, *New Zealand Education and Treatyism* (1999), the only other time Prendergast has appeared on the cover of a book. After presenting a brief and selective factual background, Christie states that the *Wi Parata* decision was completely correct:

> In short, modern treatyism teaches that Prendergast and Richmond were wrong, when their fellows at the time and over the following years saw them as certainly right, as did every contemporary government. A variety of ways including ridicule, have been used in modern times to discredit the Prendergast-Richmond 'simple nullity' dictum, yet it remains, as it must always remain, a tough if not impossible nut to crack.[82]

Like Scott, Christie does not argue his case in depth, but rather uses *Wi Parata* as a quotation to support their overall argument relating to the Treaty's influence in present-day New Zealand.

Scott and Christie's work is not convincing when compared with the other writers mentioned, but the popularity of *The Travesty of Waitangi* highlights the support for Prendergast's viewpoint in large sectors of the New Zealand community. The work of the Waitangi Tribunal in investigating Maori land claims relating to the Treaty of Waitangi has been extremely controversial and demonstrates the very real tensions still existing in New Zealand between Maori and Pakeha. The protests and disruptions surrounding Waitangi Day are further evidence of distinct differences in opinion over the nature of the Treaty. The issues surrounding the Treaty that Prendergast was faced with in 1877 are as important today as they were when *Wi Parata* was decided.

So Prendergast is still used by both sides in the debate over the validity of the Treaty of Waitangi. Pro-treaty writers condemn Prendergast as an ethnocentric imperialist, but usually in a few brief sentences. Anti-treaty writers see in Prendergast a credible champion for their views.

Radical scholarship on the Treaty of Waitangi has not been kind to Prendergast. 'Radical' in this context refers to writers who express views challenging established, mainstream ideas. Prendergast's views on the Treaty and native title are seen as blatant support of the settler establishment. Writers such as Jonathan Lamb argue that Prendergast is just one oppressor in a long line:

> there has been a Machiavellian theme, neatly summarised by Prendergast, which has justified the seizure of land by any finesse, deceit or force as requisite to a sound economy and stable polity. Its effect has been to privilege a land-owning elite that has consistently disguised its self-interest as bluff pragmatism and common sense.[83]

Scholars such as Ranginui Walker[84] refer negatively to Prendergast, but not directly in relation to his *Wi Parata* decision. In an increasingly polarised debate, Prendergast is cast by pro-Treaty writers as a villain, while Chief Justice William Martin, for example, is cast as a hero. There are obvious historical problems with this polarised view: as this book reveals, the situation is more grey than black and white.

In his role as Chief Justice, James Prendergast was the acknowledged leader of the New Zealand judiciary. Prendergast's views on Maori land differed somewhat from those of New Zealand's first Supreme Court judges, Chief Justice William Martin and Henry Chapman, but, as Williams has argued, there are strong similarities as well. The forthright dismissal of the validity of native title in *Wi Parata* diverged from the more nuanced views of Martin and Chapman. But it does not follow that Prendergast and Richmond were poor representatives of judicial attitudes during the mid to late nineteenth century. Martin in particular was criticised during his career for favourable views towards Maori and may provide a better example of uncommon judicial attitudes than Prendergast and Richmond.[85] The *Wi Parata* judgment stood virtually unchallenged by New Zealand judges until 1986. In comparison, Martin and Chapman's decision in the *Symonds* case lasted only 30 years before being superseded by Prendergast's judgment in 1877, demonstrating institutional and societal support for the *Wi Parata* decision.

In *Wi Parata*, Prendergast and Richmond described Maori as "primitive barbarians" and "savages". The inability to appreciate cultural difference due to ethnocentric biases was a common trait among those in positions of power in New Zealand during the late nineteenth century. Even leaders such as George Grey, steeped in knowledge of Maori society, took a paternalistic attitude towards Maori people.[86] The few powerful, later nineteenth-century figures who fought for Maori rights, including William Martin and Governor Arthur Gordon, were often unpopular amongst other colonists. Gordon's outspoken support of Maori welfare helped to sour relations between himself and the settler government. Placed in historical context, Prendergast and Richmond's views on Maori culture were not unique and show them to be men of their time. These views did not prevent Prendergast and Richmond from being widely admired by their peers and colleagues: in fact, quite the opposite.

Prendergast was praised by leading contemporary figures for his judicial integrity and dedicated leadership of the bench.[87] His loyalty to the British Empire and the New Zealand colonial government made him a highly respected and celebrated figure during the late nineteenth century. Prendergast now features in New Zealand historiography only to be criticised for the *Wi Parata* judgment and his support of the infamous Parihaka invasion;[88] Michael King's best-selling general history of New Zealand made reference to Prendergast only in relation to his description of the Treaty as a "simple nullity".[89] But at the time that these events occurred, many of Prendergast's European peers approved of his actions. Prendergast has been judged differently by different generations; the Chief Justice has been transformed from a hero to a villain. Prendergast lacked the humanitarianism of Martin and outspoken reputation of Gordon, but his present role as ruthless imperialist is undeserved.

In analysing the role of Prendergast in the *Wi Parata* legacy, the historian must be wary of judging the past by the values of the present. The subjugation of the Maori race and the destruction of their culture was not the aim of James Prendergast. Instead, during his career in New Zealand, Prendergast hoped to help lay the foundations for a thriving colonial society, where Maori could play a limited and supporting role. These foundations required the successful consolidation of British power. To a modern audience, this seems blatantly paternalistic, but it is far from genocidal.

While Prendergast and Richmond's views of native title, Crown sovereignty and the legal status of the Treaty have been challenged over recent decades, the Treaty of Waitangi remains essentially an important constitutional document outside of the New Zealand law. The debate over its validity has become fierce and divisive, both in circles of power and wider New Zealand society. Instead of a legal ratio and accompanying dicta, the case has become a political weapon to be used at will by different factions in the Treaty debate. James Prendergast, the historical figure, has been lost in the chaotic war of words.

To dismiss the *Wi Parata* decision as completely incompetent and false is to dismiss 100 years of historical support for Prendergast and Richmond's viewpoint. Although it was perhaps legally dubious, the decision was a reflection of political thought and settler desires. There is enough strength in the decision for it to retain substantial support from different sectors of the debate, but its power has been effectively reduced by decisions in the modern New Zealand courts. The *Wi Parata* decision is in danger of becoming a simplified quotation, taken out of context as an example of the worst kind of racism.

An appreciation of the personal and professional relationships of the key figures in the *Wi Parata* decision is vital in understanding the decision. The judicial relationship between the new Chief Justice Prendergast and his older and more experienced colleague Richmond is fascinating and important. The effects of Prendergast and Richmond's feud with Barton, and Prendergast's ties with Travers, on the decision must be considered. New Zealand politics in the nineteenth century was made up of a small number of men who worked and often socialised together. In 1870s New Zealand settler society, political-legal figures such as George Barton and Wi Parata were 'outsiders' while James Prendergast, William Richmond, and William Travers were definitely 'insiders'.

Chief Justice Sir James Prendergast does not deserve his role as the arch-villain of New Zealand legal history. Not only has the *Wi Parata* decision been regularly treated in a superficial way, but it is highly likely that Prendergast only played a supporting role to Richmond's main part. Williams notes that Prendergast's 'simple nullity' statement

> will be mentioned many more times yet during the course of future debates. It is too convenient a stick with which to beat the judges of the past for its constant repetition to cease suddenly as a result of the publication of one book.[90]

There are now two books for critics to contend with, but Waitangi Day 2014 suggests that Williams is correct. Mana Party leader and prominent Maori activist Hone Harawira utilised Prendergast in a *New Zealand Herald* opinion piece, comparing the 'simple nullity' quotation to the Government's 'full and final' Treaty settlement policy.[91] His words echo the 2006 speech of Maori Party leader Tariana Turia, which appeared to lay all blame for Maori grievances upon Prendergast's shoulders:

> For the infamous judgment of Chief Justice Prendergast declared that Maori were a primitive tribal society, that New Zealand was an 'uninhabited territory' and that the Treaty of Waitangi was no more than a 'simple nullity' – having no legal effect. And with those words, a precedent was established from which future claims would be based on the Treaty of Waitangi. Maori custom had been ignored, our existence, our indigeneity denied, our rights of aboriginal title overturned.[92]

Thus the title of this book: *Prendergast: Legal Villain?*

9

PRENDERGAST AS 'ACTING GOVERNOR' 1875–1899

While Chief Justice, Prendergast also took the roles of Administrator of New Zealand and Deputy-Governor in the absence of a permanent Governor. During these times, Prendergast was, by the nature of the position, closely linked to both Governors and politicians. Prendergast's relationships with these pivotal figures provide the historian with an insight into the political history of New Zealand during the late nineteenth century. While Prendergast worked closely with leaders such as Governor Jervois and John Bryce, he found himself in confrontation with key figures such as Governor Gordon and the Maori leader Te Whiti o Rongomai. Prendergast's time in Government House also had a social and ceremonial aspect to it, which provides insights into Prendergast's personality.

During Prendergast's time as Administrator in late 1881, he played an instrumental and controversial role in the invasion of the Maori settlement of Parihaka. Aside from Prendergast's decision in *Wi Parata*, this is the historical action for which he is now most remembered. The role of Prendergast in the Parihaka controversy needs to be re-examined and subjected to in-depth analysis. A close look at Prendergast's achievements while Administrator of New Zealand can aid the historian in assessing the extent of Prendergast's success while in this position. Like many other aspects of his career, Prendergast's role as Administrator received much praise during his lifetime, but has recently received much criticism. This period of Prendergast's career is pivotal to exploring his views on race relations, and deciding whether these views had altered since his time as Attorney-General.

1. The Dormant Commission

As Chief Justice, Prendergast held the Dormant Commission, empowering him to "execute during Our pleasure all things that belong to the Office of Governor and Commander-in-Chief, according to the tenor of these Our Letters Patent, and according to Our Instructions as aforesaid, and the Laws of the Colony." This would occur "In the event of the death, incapacity, or removal of the Governor, or of his departure from the Colony."[1] Although Prendergast was praised for his ability to juggle two official posts, "besides performing his own judicial duties, [he] efficiently manages, when occasion requires, to fill up these Gubernatorial gaps", doubts were raised about the nature of the Dormant Commission:

there is much to be said against a system which is frequently, or for a long period of time, imposing on a Chief Justice of a Colony the additional duties of administering its Government. It would be preferable that the Chief Justice should temporarily relinquish his judicial office while he was Administrator. Or, better still, that no ordinary intervals between two Governorships should take place, leaving only provision to be made for those created extraordinarily by death or unavoidable causes.[2]

The suggested solution of temporarily relinquishing judicial office while Administrator would have created more problems than it solved. An Acting Chief Justice would have had to be appointed, acting as leader of the bench. Johnston J, as the most long-serving puisne judge, took this role in 1884 during Prendergast's extended trip to Britain, but it was not a particularly satisfactory arrangement and effectively created a hierarchy amongst the puisne judges.

While the presumption was that the Chief Justice would assume the role of Administrator, controversy occurred in 1907 when Governor Plunket appointed Prendergast to act as Deputy-Governor while Plunket was visiting several Pacific islands. Here the confusing distinction between Administrator and Deputy-Governor was again raised. The Colonial Under-Secretary, Hugh Pollen, was of the opinion that the Letter Patents required an Administrator (in New Zealand, the Chief Justice) to be appointed "in the event of the death, incapacity, or removal of the Governor, or his departure from the colony - when, that is to say, he is leaving permanently".[3] Pollen argued that if the Governor had merely left for a short period and would return:

In such a case the Letters Patent provide that the Governor may appoint some person . . . to be his deputy during his temporary absence . . . . there is no reason, so far as constitutional procedure is concerned, why any person other than the Administrator should not be appointed Deputy-Governor. There is no novelty about it.[4]

Pollen cited an example when Prendergast was appointed Deputy-Governor in 1900, while Robert Stout was Chief Justice and Administrator. In this case, Governor Ranfurly was temporarily absent attending an official function in Australia.[5] The offices of Administrator and Deputy-Governor were different, as set out in the Letters Patent. In his comprehensive work on the New Zealand governors, Gavin McLean states: "Deputies covered absences of four weeks or less (extendable to six weeks) and administrators longer periods, so in practice the former covered short vice-regal trips to Australia or the Pacific Islands and the latter served between vice-regal terms."[6] This definition is generally in line with the various Letters Patent.

Governor Ranfurly raised the issue of the Dormant Commission in a letter dated 7 July 1899 to Joseph Chamberlain, Secretary of State for the Colonies. Ranfurly, a supporter of Prendergast, hoped to clarify the position of Deputy-

Governor in New Zealand and appoint Prendergast. As with the Plunket incident of 1907, the evidence suggests that both Ranfurly and Plunket held Prendergast in high regard, considering him for Deputy-Governor despite Robert Stout being the obvious first choice. In his letter to Chamberlain, Ranfurly states:

> The Dormant Commission will now place His Honour Sir Robert Stout K.C.M.G. as Administrator during the absence of a Governor, as there is no Deputy Governor in the Colony, under other circumstances I should have recommended Sir James's appointment as Deputy Governor, but I understand that Sir Robert Stout has been led to expect that the Dormant Commission would still remain in force, he is further in every way suited to act as Administrator.[7]

Prendergast's success as Administrator can be clearly seen when comparing him to Stout. In 1903, after only four years as Chief Justice, Stout clashed with the Government over an issue of precedence, which in turn was related to the bitter rivalry between Stout and Premier Richard Seddon. As McLean explains, "Two days later, metaphorically (and farcically) wearing his chief justice's wig, Stout wrote to himself as deputy governor outlining his complaints and asking himself to forward the memorandum to the Colonial Office."[8] This rather arrogant approach contrasts markedly to Prendergast's more diplomatic actions (with the exception of 1881): "the dispute strained the smooth workings of government and Stout's behaviour as administrator meant that for the next twenty years governments were reluctant to leave him in even temporary change of Government House".[9]

The most historically relevant debate over the roles of Administrator and Deputy-Governor occurred during the Governorship of Arthur Gordon. In a series of letters to Prendergast during the middle of 1881, Gordon expressed confusion over the two roles:

> I am not as yet, quite certain whether, for the first month of my absence, my locum tenens should be "Deputy" or "Administrator". I myself think the latter; for, although I may return within the month allowed by the Royal Instructions, it is more probable that I shall not do so.[10]

After seeking advice from the ministers of the Hall Government, Gordon concluded in a later letter, "The ministers have determined that you are to be Administrator and not Deputy, and they are, I think, quite right, though the decision will cost me in all probability a good deal of money."[11]

2. Summary of the Administrator periods

Prendergast served as Administrator for the Colony of New Zealand on seven different occasions. The majority of these occasions were the periods of time between the departure of one Governor and the arrival of the next Governor. When the Marquis of Normanby retired as Governor on 21 February 1879, Prendergast acted as Administrator until the arrival of Sir Hercules George Robert Robinson in March of that year. Normanby's term had included a number of constitutional clashes with his ministers,[12] and Robinson was welcomed by many New Zealand political leaders as a positive change, but his term was to be brief, falling short of two years.

When Robinson left New Zealand on 9 September 1880, Prendergast took office until 29 November 1880, when Sir Arthur Hamilton Gordon arrived. Gordon had an even more acrimonious relationship with his ministers than Normanby had experienced and he "was probably more out of step with his government here than any governor before or since".[13] The most controversial period as Administrator was during Gordon's absence in Fiji from 13 September to 20 October 1881. This was the only time Prendergast would act as Administrator during the term of a Governor.

When Gordon left New Zealand in controversial fashion in June 1882, Prendergast again took the role of Administrator until Gordon's replacement, Lieutentant-General Sir William Francis Drummond Jervois, took up his post in Wellington during January 1883. Jervois had a successful and lengthy term as Governor, which ended on 22 March 1889. Prendergast became Administrator until the Earl of Onslow became the next Governor in May 1889. Like Normanby and Gordon before him, Onslow found himself embroiled in constitutional controversy, in particular, with John Ballance.[14] Between 25 February and 6 June 1892, Prendergast took over from the departing Onslow and waited for his replacement, the Earl of Glasgow. Prendergast's final time as Administrator came in February 1897 with the departure of Glasgow, who had relinquished the Governorship "on the grounds that the remuneration left him unable to uphold the dignity of the office".[15] Glasgow was replaced by the Earl of Ranfurly in August 1897. Ranfurly also had major difficulties with the low level of remuneration.[16]

Historical sources, mainly primary, reveal the nature of Prendergast's relationships with these different governors. As Administrator and Chief Justice, Prendergast often came into contact with the Governor, both professionally and socially. Prendergast had a cordial relationship with Jervois, Onslow, Glasgow and Ranfurly but had a serious break with Gordon. Insufficient evidence remains to comment on Prendergast's relationship with Normanby and Robinson. The first Administrator period that has sufficient evidence to analyse is during the governorship of Gordon in 1881. This eventful period will be dealt with in relation to Prendergast's role in the invasion of Parihaka.

The period between the governorships of Gordon and Jervois was interesting from a historical point of view, as it was the interregnum between possibly the most unpopular Governor in New Zealand history and one of the most popular. Many colonists were glad to see Gordon depart and were thankful to Prendergast for his support of the Hall Government, which had often clashed with Gordon. In a ceremony in January 1883, members of the Wellington City Council, leading citizens and a selection of Cabinet ministers gathered to thank Prendergast for his half-year contribution as Administrator. Notable among the Cabinet ministers were Frederick Whitaker and John Bryce, conservative politicians with reputations for being 'anti-Maori.' The prepared address was read:

> We, the Mayor, Councillors, and Citizens of Wellington, desire, on the occasion of your resigning the reins of Government into the hands of his Excellency Sir William Jervois to convey to your Excellency our deep sense of appreciation of the manner in which you have fulfilled the high and important duties of Administrator of the Government. The expressions of the people at all public assemblies, held during your term of office, prove clearly that you are held in the respect and esteem of all classes of the community, not only in your official capacity, but as the dispenser of a warm-hearted and genial hospitality.[17]

Prendergast's nephew by marriage, Charles Prendergast Knight, kept a detailed diary of his life during the 1890s. As secretary to Prendergast, he made many references relating to his uncle's career and social life. On 15 February 1892, nine days before Lord Onslow's departure as Governor, Knight met Onslow at Government House for instructions: "I was ushered into the presence chamber and Lord Onslow took me into the Secretary's room and showed me the way that dispatches were filed." Later that day Knight returned to Government House to attend Lady Onslow's final levee.[18]

As Administrator, Prendergast was present at official farewells and greetings: "Uncle [Prendergast] and I went down to the Railway station to see Governor and the Countess of Onslow off a large crowd was present. I stood and looked on musing at the title-loving crowd that gaped around."[19] The Administrator was expected to fulfil a variety of roles, both political and social, including meeting with the Executive Council and hosting social functions. For example, on 13 May 1892, Prendergast was the guest of honour at a Royal Command performance evening,[20] while on 24 May 1892, he hosted a levee at Government House and a ball in honour of the 73rd birthday of Queen Victoria.[21] Notable power-brokers present at the levee included Richmond J, Premier John Ballance, Richard Seddon, William Pember Reeves, Jock McKenzie and Harry Atkinson.

The Government House ball, held on a Wellington autumn evening, was described by a newspaper commentator in idyllic terms:

> It was lovely night, calm, cloudless, and starlit, while the nipping air outside gave an added zest to dancing . . . . The guests as they arrived were received by Sir James and Lady Prendergast . . . . Soon after 9 o'clock the ball was opened by Sir James Prendergast, who danced with Mrs Buckley; the other couples in the set being the Hon W. P. Reeves and Lady Hector, the Hon R. Seddon and Mrs Godfrey Knight, Sir James Hector and Miss Hilda Williams.[22]

Whether the Government was liberal or conservative, James Prendergast was secure in his place amongst the power elite of late nineteenth-century New Zealand society.

Prendergast's relationship with most of the Governors from 1875 onwards was cordial and one of mutual respect. For example, on 19 July 1892, Lady Glasgow rang to tell the Prendergasts that she would pay a visit, eventually staying "over the conventional 10 minutes".[23] On 8 August 1892, Prendergast was walking from Bolton Street to Brooklyn, when he met Governor Glasgow and engaged in a friendly chat.[24] On Prendergast's retirement as Chief Justice in 1899, Lord Ranfurly wrote to the British Secretary of State for the Colonies suggesting that Prendergast be awarded the KCMG:

> I think if any recognition is made of his services that the permission to bear the title of Honourable will be considered by him, under the circumstances, as hardly adequate for his long public career . . . . I venture to suggest for your consideration the advisability of making Sir James Prendergast K.C.M.G., in addition to the title of Honourable.[25]

The happy relationship Prendergast enjoyed with popular Governors such as Glasgow and Ranfurly was not present with Arthur Gordon. Their formal relationship would deteriorate into mutual dislike on Gordon's return from Fiji.

One of Prendergast's roles as Administrator was to exercise the prerogative of mercy. An interesting and awkward situation arose in 1883 when Prendergast was under pressure to release George Longhurst, whom he had earlier tried and sentenced as Chief Justice in 1880. The controversial Longhurst case had featured two juries arriving at completely opposite conclusions. The first jury had found Longhurst guilty of assaulting a seven-year-old girl while the second jury found that he had been falsely accused. As the *Evening Post* pointed out, Prendergast would "practically be reviewing his own action as judge".[26] Ultimately, Longhurst was not pardoned, but that decision was made by Jervois, not Prendergast. However, Prendergast did commute the death sentence for 'the Taranaki murderer', Antonio Schnell, in 1882 on the basis of insanity. [27]

3. Prendergast and the invasion of Parihaka

There is no consensus amongst historians as to the end date of the New Zealand Wars. Possibilities include Te Kooti's retreat to the King Country in 1872, the invasion of Parihaka in 1881 or the arrest of Rua Kenana at Maungapohatu in 1916. In many ways, 1881 is the most convincing option.[28] Parihaka featured several key figures from the 1860s conflict, including Prendergast, Bryce and Titokowaru. The invasion of Parihaka, practically and symbolically, serves as the most blatantly oppressive and inexcusable use of colonial force during the Wars.

Despite moving from the executive branch of government to the judicial branch in 1875, Prendergast was to continue to play a key role in the final acts of the New Zealand Wars. Throughout the late 1870s the peaceful Maori village of Parihaka became increasingly prominent as a symbol of passive resistance. Led by Te Whiti o Rongomai and Tohu Kakahi, Maori protested against government measures to take land in Taranaki. These protests took the form of erecting fences and ploughing disputed property, all to disrupt government encroachment on traditional Maori lands. The Government began arresting protesters and by September 1880 had imprisoned 216 without trial.[29] Tension reached a climax in late 1881 as the Government finally decided to invade the peaceful township.

Governor Arthur Gordon openly supported Parihaka and the relationship between the Governor and his ministers was strained and unhappy. The Government's desire to take assertive action against Te Whiti was being partly restrained by Gordon. Aside from his constitutional powers as Governor, Gordon was also in a position to make negative reports to London and could potentially damage the reputation of the New Zealand Government in Britain. However, in an unforced error and perhaps naive misjudgment, Gordon left New Zealand to visit Fiji, in his capacity as High Commissioner for the Western Pacific, from 13 September to 20 October 1881, leaving Prendergast as Administrator.[30] With Gordon powerless to harness government action, the way was now clear to move on Parihaka.

Specific dates and details are pivotal in assessing Prendergast's culpability in the Parihaka invasion. In a letter dated 23 June 1881, Gordon informed Prendergast of his decision to travel to Fiji: "I intend to go to Fiji, for the sittings of the Lands Appeals Court, and, possibly, to visit some other parts of the Western Pacific. During my absence, the administration of the Government will, of course, devolve upon you."[31] Gordon was unsure as to the length of time he would be absent from New Zealand: "although I _may_ return within the month allowed the Royal Instructions, it is more probable that I shall not do so".[32] Gordon intended to keep in touch with New Zealand developments through his trusted private secretary, Mr Murray. In another letter to Prendergast dated 8 September 1881, Gordon stated his wish "that you will continue to employ my private Secretary, Mr Murray, who is fully _au courant_ of the business of my office and who in Mr G's absence acts as Clerk of the Executive Council".[33] On the day of his departure, 13 September, Gordon penned a final preparatory note to Prendergast:

> I believe it is usual for the Governor after the session to make a sort of review of it to the Secretary of State. If you have no objection I should prefer to do this myself after my return and it will I think come perhaps more fitly from the permanent Governor than from an acting one.[34]

These actions were an attempt by Gordon to retain some control while absent. By asking Prendergast to retain Murray, Gordon could keep up-to-date with all developments in New Zealand and by retaining his duty to provide a report to London, Gordon could continue to influence the reputation of the New Zealand Government abroad. While there is no specific evidence to suggest that Gordon did not trust Prendergast, Gordon attempted to ensure that Prendergast would not have complete freedom of action while the Governor was absent. On 16 September, the day before Te Whiti delivered a supposedly 'war-like' speech at Parihaka, Prendergast sent a brief note to Gordon informing him that the situation in New Zealand was calm. In a letter from Gordon in Fiji to Prendergast in Wellington, dated 7 October 1881, Gordon expressed dismay at the Parihaka situation:

> The news [from Murray] brought by the "Southern Cross" is so alarming, and so at variance with what I was led to expect when leaving New Zealand, that I have made up my mind to return immediately. We shall probably reach Wellington about the same time that the "Southern Cross" reaches Auckland; but in case we may meet with any unexpected hindrance, and her mails reach you first, I write a line to announce my return to you. I trust I may be in time to anticipate any hasty or inevitable proceedings in a warlike direction.[35]

The *Southern Cross* did not reach New Zealand before Gordon returned, so Prendergast was unaware of this letter when the Parihaka proclamation was made on 19 October.[36]

While Gordon was in Fiji, the New Zealand Government began to take decisive action against Te Whiti and Parihaka. Only hours before Gordon's return to Wellington late on the evening of 19 October, John Bryce, the most avid supporter of an invasion of Parihaka, was reinstated as Native Minister. Bryce was sworn in by Prendergast, and a proclamation was prepared by Prendergast and the ministers, in particular Hall and Whitaker.[37] The proclamation gave Te Whiti a chilling ultimatum:

> Te Whiti and his adherents must now accept the proposals of the Government, or all that they might now have under these proposals will be beyond their reach. In the Parihaka Block, 25,000 acres on the Mountain side of the road are, as recommended by the Commissioners, offered as an ample provision for the Parihaka people, besides other reserves on the seaward side of the road. About the latter, the Government has said that it was willing to consider the wishes the Natives might lay before it. The Government now states plainly that these offers will, after fourteen days, be withdrawn, unless, within that time, Te Whiti and his adherents signify their acceptance of them, and their willingness to submit to the law of the Queen and to bring their claims before the Commission. If they do so, the recommendations of the Commissioners, and the promises made, will be liberally interpreted and fulfilled.[38]

If the Government's offer was not accepted, the proclamation promised that drastic action would follow:

> The Queen and the law must be supreme at Parihaka as well as elsewhere. Te Whiti and his people are now called upon to accept the proposals made to them, which would give large and ample reserves to the people. If they do not do this, they alone will be responsible for the passing away from them for ever of the lands which are still proffered by the Government, and for the great evil which must fall on them.[39]

The proclamation was given under the hand of Prendergast as Administrator of the Government. Premier John Hall briefed Prendergast in a memorandum before the signing.[40] Hall's memo highlights a certain amount of pressure applied on Prendergast by leading government ministers, but there is no indication that Prendergast was unhappy with this pressure.

The question facing historians of Parihaka is whether or not Gordon's ministers took advantage of his absence to take aggressive action against Te Whiti, or whether they were just responding to an apparent 'hardening' in Te Whiti's attitude. Did Prendergast take an assertive role in the issuing of the proclamation, or was he just acquiescing to his minister's demands? Gordon had been alerted by Murray of the changing situation in New Zealand and, as mentioned earlier, rushed back as quickly as possible. He was furious at the proclamation and at Prendergast; he questioned "the legality of the proclamation, which he regarded as 'injudicious', 'disputable' and 'inequitable', but gained no support from the Colonial Office".[41] At an Executive Council meeting called soon after Gordon's return, Prendergast was called for a private interview with the Governor. Prendergast emerged "ashen and fuming".[42] A rather distant relationship between the Governor and his Administrator had transformed into mutual dislike and resentment. Gordon's rage was in vain. Te Whiti did not answer the proclamation and, on 5 November 1881, 1589 troops marched on Parihaka, led by Bryce. Te Whiti and other leaders were arrested and the village was largely destroyed.[43] Bryce and his men had been met with passive resistance, after Te Whiti instructed his followers not to use violence.

During the invasion and occupation of Parihaka during early November 1881, many of the pivotal figures in Prendergast's Wellington career were present. Several Maori leaders who had crossed paths with Prendergast on other occasions were at the township. On 9 November, Bryce arrested Titokowaru,[44] who had acted as one of the leaders of the Parihaka community after retiring from warfare. Also on 9 November, Wiremu Parata, the Maori MP and plaintiff in the landmark legal decision, left Parihaka with several of his supporters.[45] Bryce had ordered Parihaka to be evacuated after the 5 November invasion. Prendergast also had a number of friends, and even a relative, present at the invasion. Bryce was associated with Prendergast during the early 1880s,[46] and Michael Prendergast, James' nephew, was a part of the invasion force.[47] Prendergast was most definitely a friend of the invaders and a foe of the invaded.

One of only five pictures of Prendergast that remain (excepting group photos). This photograph was taken in approximately 1880. Ref: 1/2-079213-F. Alexander Turnbull Library, Wellington, New Zealand. http://natlib.govt.nz/records/23175340

Caroline Prendergast, mother of James Prendergast. Painted by Caroline's brother, the prominent portrait artist George Dawe R.A. Hall Collection. Photographed by Pete Nikolaison.

Right: Michael Prendergast QC, James Prendergast's father. Pencil portrait by Thomas Wright, associate of George Dawe R.A. Hall Collection. Photographed by Pete Nikolaison.

Below: London's Central Criminal Court, the 'Old Bailey', one of the many professional locations in which Michael Prendergast QC worked. James may have appeared here as a barrister. *Illustrated London News*, 4 March 1843. Kent State University Libraries. Special Collections and Archives.

The goldrush to the Ballarat goldfields during the mid-1850s, which included the Prendergast brothers. Painting by Samuel Thomas Gill (1872). Courtesy of the National Library of Australia.

Dunedin in 1868. Prendergast was a leading figure of this boomtown from 1862 to 1867. Ref: 0518_01_010A. Hocken Collections, University of Otago Library, Dunedin, New Zealand.

Lambton Quay, Wellington, in 1873, showing, from left, the Athenaeum, St Andrew's Church and the Supreme Courthouse. Prendergast appeared in this court as Attorney-General and during his early years as Chief Justice. Ref: 1/4-010013-F. Alexander Turnbull Library, Wellington, New Zealand. http://natlib.govt.nz/records/23213072

The next Wellington Supreme Court, built in 1881 and Prendergast's professional residence from 1881 to 1899. Ref: 1/2-011634-G. Alexander Turnbull Library, Wellington, New Zealand. http://natlib.govt.nz/records/22775418

Left: George E. Barton, the gifted but erratic barrister, and Prendergast's arch-nemesis. Reproduced with the permission of the Victorian Parliamentary Library, Australia.

Below: Prendergast's mansion on Bolton Street, built during the late 1860s, was one of the most prominent landmarks in Wellington. Prendergast lived in the house for over 50 years. Ref: NegE748/37. Hocken Collections, University of Otago Library, Dunedin, New Zealand.

Right: Christopher William Richmond in 1888, Prendergast's good friend and closest colleague. Ref: 1/1-013502-G. Alexander Turnbull Library, Wellington, New Zealand. http://natlib.govt.nz/records/22719131

Below: Richmond was a regular visitor at Prendergast's Bolton Street mansion. During one visit in 1879, he sketched this picture of Thorndon. Ref: E-284-040. Alexander Turnbull Library, Wellington, New Zealand. http://natlib.govt.nz/records/23131426

Sir James Prendergast's house - Bolton St. Wellington - Soo House - Scott Bandalus, about 1879   C.W.R.

Wiremu Parata, Ngati Toa leader and the plaintiff in Prendergast's most infamous case. Ref: PA2-2577. Alexander Turnbull Library, Wellington, New Zealand. http://natlib. govt.nz/records/23013231

Parihaka

The iconic settlement of Parihaka at the time of the November 1881 invasion for which Prendergast was partly responsible. Ref: PA1-q-183-18. Alexander Turnbull Library, Wellington, New Zealand. http://natlib.govt.nz/records/23014599

Government House, Prendergast's residence during the many times when he acted as Administrator for the colony. Ref: 1/2-140327-G. Alexander Turnbull Library, Wellington, New Zealand. http://natlib.govt.nz/records/23013231

Left: Cartoon of Prendergast during his retirement in 1907, from the *Free Lance*, a publication covering Wellington's social scene. *New Zealand Free Lance*, Vol. VII, 30 March 1907. Courtesy of Papers Past, National Library of New Zealand.

Below: Prendergast (seated, far left) was the New Zealand delegate to the Imperial Court of Appeal Conference in London. *Illustrated London News*, 20 July 1901. Hocken Collection, University of Otago Library, Dunedin, New Zealand.

Mr. W. B. Moram, K.C.,
South Africa.

Sir John Edge,
India.

Sir W. J. Smith,
British Guiana.

Mr. Justice Hodges,
Victoria.

Hon. Sir. J. Prendergast,
New Zealand.

Hon. David Mills,
Canada.

Hon. J. Rose-Innes, K.C.,
South Africa.

Mr. Justice Emerson,
Newfoundland.

THE COLONIAL DELEGATES TO THE IMPERIAL COURT OF APPEAL CONFERENCE.

PHOTOGRAPH BY ELLIOTT AND FRY.

The Court of Appeal in 1903, featuring some of Prendergast's former colleagues and his replacement (left to right): Cooper, Conolly, Williams JJ, Stout CJ, Denniston, Edwards JJ. Ref: 2075_01_001A.jpg. Hocken Collection, University of Otago Library, Dunedin, New Zealand.

The author visited Prendergast's gravesite in 1998 and found it completely overgrown and unrecognisable. This is perhaps symbolic of Prendergast's fall from leading colonial figure to legal villain. Morris Collection.

James Nairn's portrait of Prendergast which hangs in the Wellington High Court, unveiled in 1899.
Courtesy of the Wellington High Court.

In the aftermath of the Parihaka invasion, Gordon launched a series of attacks on the men he felt were responsible. In 1883, Gordon having returned to England, the 'Blue Book' containing his public and private despatches while Governor of New Zealand was presented to the British Parliament. Along with his own damning comments about the New Zealand Government, Gordon had also included a range of clippings from the liberal New Zealand newspaper, the *Lyttelton Times*.[48] Prendergast was accused by Gordon of being aware of the Governor's imminent return from Fiji in October 1881. In a letter to the new Governor Jervois, dated 27 January 1883, Prendergast defended his actions as Administrator. Prendergast focused on a despatch sent by Gordon to the Secretary of State dated 22 October 1881.[49] Gordon argues that immediately after he departed for Fiji on 13 September 1881, the Government prepared to step up the pressure on Parihaka.[50] On 4 October, Gordon learned of these developments through Murray, his private secretary, and by reading New Zealand newspapers.

Gordon believed he had not been kept properly informed by his ministers and administrator. In a separate memorandum, Frederick Whitaker argued that "it would have been irregular and improper for them [the ministry] to communicate with Sir Arthur Gordon as Governor during his absence and the existence of an Administrator".[51] Prendergast believed that Murray, having access to all relevant governmental information, would keep Gordon informed,[52] and in fact Murray did keep Gordon informed to the best of his ability.[53] Prendergast stated that "It has always been and still is my opinion that a Governor absent under such circumstances as Sir Arthur Gordon was, ought to be kept generally informed of any matter of extraordinary importance occurring in his absence."[54] Prendergast also argued, consistent with Gordon's earlier letters to Prendergast, that the duration of Gordon's absence was uncertain.[55]

Therefore, assuming that Gordon was fully informed of important developments in New Zealand, why did Prendergast sign the drastic proclamation on 19 October, without waiting for any communication from Gordon on the Parihaka issue? Did Prendergast and the Ministry know of Gordon's imminent arrival in Wellington and hastily move before Gordon could intervene? If so, this would probably rank as Prendergast's most dubious and underhand action in his long career as a public official. The options open to Prendergast were either to make the proclamation or refuse and wait for communications from Gordon. If Prendergast had refused to make the proclamation, he would have alienated many of his powerful friends. It is also possible that if Gordon was Governor at the time, he would have had little choice but to make the proclamation or resign, for the power of the Governor was in reality primarily dependent on the support of his ministers. This was the period in New Zealand's history when the role of Governor was transforming from leading colonial powerbroker to symbolic constitutional head of government. The transition was not a smooth one and Gordon was just one example of a Governor who desired more practical power than he appeared to possess. The Administrator is effectively the Governor's substitute, so in 1881 the powers of the Administrator directly mirrored those of the Governor.

Gordon, in a memorandum to his ministers written on the day following his return to Wellington from Fiji, stated that "his own return within twenty-four hours [of the Proclamation] was known to be at least probable, if not well nigh certain".[56] Prendergast argues that though Murray communicated to him on 19 October that Gordon could well have decided to return to New Zealand after hearing about the escalation in tensions on the West Coast:

> Mr Murray's utterances did not convey to my mind that he had received any communication from Sir Arthur Gordon or that he knew anything more about Sir Arthur Gordon's probable movements than I or the general public knew. Mr. Murray was present at the time when the Proclamation was signed and said not one word to me about the matter of Sir Arthur Gordon's return.[57]

Gordon had managed to place a message on a ship bound for Sydney, which could then be telegraphed to New Zealand. This message reached New Zealand on 15 or 16 October and stated that Gordon's return to New Zealand was imminent. Prendergast states that Murray did not pass this information onto him: "for some reason which I am not able to discover, the fact of such communication having been received was intentionally suppressed, and not made known to me".[58] Prendergast was apparently furious at Gordon and had:

> expressed to him my astonishment at his entertaining such a belief of my conduct, and at his communicating his intended return to others and not to me, and that I had shown to him very warm indignation that he, by refraining to inform me of his intended return had placed me in a position inevitably to be suspected of availing myself of his absence to complete an important act of State.[59]

In Hazel Riseborough's scathing criticism of the New Zealand Government's action during late 1881 it is stated that, although ministers had not been officially told, and denied knowing at all, that Gordon's arrival was imminent, "There is little doubt that they knew what they had not been officially told, and their actions between 17 and 19 October confirm what they tried to deny . . . . The ministers' memories a year or two later were as convenient as their consciences at the time."[60]

Prendergast's role in the Parihaka invasion has been examined by a number of historians and most importantly, by Gordon himself after the incident. Prendergast has been damned as a conspirator and a racist. The Catholic priest and polemicist Dom Felice Vaggioli in 1896 described Prendergast's role:

> Judge Prendergast, a bitter enemy of the Maori, was acting as acting-governor. The government used him to carry out an unwarranted attack on Parihaka . . . . For his part in the illegal action, Prendergast was knighted by the British government on 30 October.[61]

Vaggioli, along with Riseborough,[62] incorrectly links Prendergast's knighthood with the Parihaka invasion. It was a matter of course for Chief Justices of the colonies to be knighted, and in a letter dated 23 May 1881, months before the Parihaka invasion, Gordon wrote to Prendergast, "the Queen has been pleased to give directions for conferring on you the honour of knighthood. I beg to offer you my best congratulations."[63]

More recently, the Waitangi Tribunal's Taranaki Report – Kaupapa Tuatahi criticised Prendergast:

> The then chief justice, whose descriptions of Maori as 'savages' and 'barbarians' informs his disposition, became administrator of the Government in the Governor's absence . . . . The proclamation of the chief justice, as administrator of the Government, berated the people [of Parihaka] for making themselves poor by their useless expenditure on feasts; for neglecting the cultivation of their own land (though one could not tell whether they legally owned one acre); for listening to the sound of Te Whiti's voice, which had unsettled their minds; for assuming a 'threatening attitude'; and the like.[64]

Riseborough describes Prendergast as "the pliant chief justice",[65] and criticises Prendergast's failure to keep Gordon properly informed of the developments in New Zealand during his absence.[66] In describing Prendergast's role in the issuing of the proclamation, Dick Scott calls Prendergast "a ruthless Attorney-General of the war days",[67] while Ranginui Walker says the Executive Council was called together "while the anti-Maori Justice James Prendergast was still Acting Governor".[68] In an earlier work, Gordon's biographer, James Chapman, similarly condemns Prendergast's actions.[69]

Not all accounts of Prendergast's role during October 1881 are negative. William Hunter in 1959 defended Prendergast's actions:

> in 1881, it fell to his lot to sanction in the Executive Council military operations against the Maoris in Taranaki who, under the leadership of Te Whiti, a 'prophet' of a kind not unknown to the native race, were defying surveyors of land acting under instructions from the Government. Prendergast has been criticised for so doing but without justification. Ministers and people feared that the actions of the Maoris were the prelude to another outbreak of Hau Hauism and its deplorable attacks on settlers and that it must be put down with a strong hand.[70]

Two years later, in 1961, D. K. Fieldhouse published a closely argued article essentially absolving Hall, Prendergast and the administration from blame: "the course of events demonstrates that the essential policy of the ministry was pacific; and that the final use of force resulted, not from deferred decisions, but from radically altered circumstances".[71] Fieldhouse also argues that the belief the administration hurried through the proclamation on 19 October due to Gordon's return is an "historical myth".[72] In Prendergast's obituary in the *Dominion*, Te Whiti is ascribed the blame for the events of 1881:

> Sir James held the office of Deputy-Governor at the time when it was feared
> Te Whiti's action would occasion war, and, on the advice of his Ministers, he
> authorised the military authorities to march on Parehaka [sic] and arrest the
> troublesome chief.[73]

One of the reasons why Gordon ultimately did not attempt to formally reverse Prendergast's proclamation is that he knew the majority of the colony supported the actions of the Government in seeking to attack Parihaka.[74] Many colonists were glad to see Gordon depart and were thankful to Prendergast for his support of the Hall Government, which had often clashed with Gordon.

As with so many other aspects of Prendergast's career, his actions were supported by most of his contemporaries and most historians writing before the 1970s, while being damned by modern-day historians.[75] However, this cannot stand as a justification for Prendergast's actions, especially given the attitudes of other contemporary leaders such as Gordon, and Prendergast's successor as Chief Justice, Robert Stout. Gordon and Stout proved that it was possible to intellectually justify a position in direct opposition to the popular zeitgeist without sacrificing one's career. Stout wrote to the liberal newspaper, the *Lyttelton Times*:

> I suppose, amidst the general rejoicings at the prospects of a Maori war, it is
> useless for anyone to raise his voice against the present native policy. I do so
> more as a protest than with any hope that any one colonist can ever aid in
> preventing the murder of the Maoris, on which it seems we as a colony are
> bent.[76]

In the Legislative Council, Prendergast's nemesis, Walter Mantell, also questioned Prendergast's actions and demanded to see all relevant memoranda and papers relating to the proclamation.[77] The views of Stout, Gordon and Mantell prove that while Prendergast's views may have been commonly held, it was not a foregone conclusion that he *must* hold these views. This in turn raises the question of why Prendergast held these views while Stout, Gordon and Mantell did not. One reason could be that Prendergast's main cultural encounter with Maori took place in the context of the New Zealand Wars, whereas Stout's and Gordon's did not.

Prendergast's role in the Parihaka invasion cannot be adequately dealt with in a few sentences. The Hall Government in 1881, and in particular John Bryce, wanted to solve the Parihaka question as soon as possible. With Gordon's departure for Fiji, the Government could use Prendergast as Administrator to aid it in this task. The description of Prendergast as 'pliable' in this situation has some accuracy. Gordon definitely took a gamble by leaving New Zealand for an extended period of time and appointing an Administrator in his place during a time of tension on the West Coast. During Prendergast's 24-year career as Chief Justice, this would be the only instance when Prendergast would serve as Administrator during the term of a Governor. The role of the Governor in New Zealand politics in 1881 was far different to that during the period 1840-1870. To a large extent, the Governor was expected to follow the advice of his ministers. Gordon was not consistently doing this and therefore was resented by the Hall Ministry. It seems highly likely that the Hall Government took Gordon's absence as an opportunity to put pressure on Te Whiti and Parihaka. Gordon may have been unable to stop events even if present in New Zealand, but, with his departure, the path to invasion was made smoother.

The events of September and October 1881 wrecked the relationship between Gordon and Prendergast. Distrust and anger best describe their connection after October 1881. Gordon's claim that Prendergast, among others, failed to keep him advised of developments during his absence is unfair. As argued earlier, Murray had been assigned the role of informant during the Administration period. Gordon's claim that Prendergast knew of Gordon's imminent arrival on the afternoon before the signing of the proclamation is again difficult to prove. But Prendergast did know that Gordon could well have been arriving in New Zealand in a matter of days or weeks and, despite this, he agreed to help issue a drastic proclamation that he knew would be against the views of the Governor. Prendergast did not wait for communication from Gordon before making the proclamation. Instead, as with his legal opinions of the late 1860s, the 1869 trials and the decision in *Wi Parata*, he took the path of supporting the colonial settler majority. The question then becomes whether Prendergast was just 'doing his job' or more actively protecting settler interests.

Most of the settler community were behind the Hall Government in its views on native affairs and Prendergast can be seen as part of the ruling establishment transforming those views into action. Recent scholarship on the Parihaka invasion has strongly argued that it was unfair and probably illegal. Therefore, those associated with the period are ascribed blame depending on their level of support of the invasion. Gordon opposed the invasion, Rolleston was uncomfortable about it, Prendergast helped to issue the proclamation allowing it and Bryce led it. But to see the incident as a backroom conspiracy between Bryce, Hall, Whitaker and Prendergast is not necessarily accurate. After Parihaka, the *Lyttleton Times* mused:

> The low cunning, characteristic of the whole proceeding, leads us to suppose that its conception must have originated in the mind of the Attorney-General [Whitaker]. His idea of statesmanship is political thimblerig. What we are surprised at is, that Sir James Prendergast, if he knew the likelihood of the immediate return of the Governor, should have lent himself to such a discreditable piece of finesse behind the Governor's back.[78]

Despite any possible qualifications, Prendergast, as Administrator, had directly aided in beginning a chain of events that would leave Parihaka in ruins and create distrust and bitterness amongst many Maori for generations to come. The invasion of Parihaka was not led by Prendergast, but he definitely did not use his power as Administrator to prevent it. The proclamation which sparked the invasion required the signature of the Queen's representative in New Zealand. Prendergast supplied that signature without any resistance. And, as Administrator in July 1882, Prendergast added insult to injury by assenting to the West Coast Peace Preservation Act,[79] which validated the holding of Te Whiti and Tohu without trial and legally confirmed the Government's policy to dismantle the Parihaka movement. Prendergast's assent in this instance failed to attract public attention.

A Wellington Supreme Court trial in 1886 provides a fitting epilogue to Prendergast's experiences with Parihaka and the New Zealand Wars. His nemeses, Te Whiti and Titokowaru, had been arrested (along with others) on charges of riot, forcible entry upon land and malicious injury to property.[80] Te Whiti had also been charged with inciting the other prisoners. Te Whiti and Titokowaru both pleaded guilty and in a crowded court room on 6 October 1886, Prendergast sentenced them to imprisonment and to pay a fine.[81] When asked if he had anything to say as to why the sentence of the court should not be passed upon him, Te Whiti replied:

> I am the original owner of the land. You, the white-faced people, came in a cloud, or army, and turned me off the land. When I got sufficient courage to re-enter, my hand was put forth again. We and others were expelled from the land. We were not expelled peaceably, but by the guns of the Government. When I rose from the ground the pain of the blow I received was still great, but I still put out my hand. I was then tried by law, but those who turned me from the land were not tried. That is all I have to say to your Honour – not many words.

In sentencing Prendergast responded, "I have nothing to do with any supposed wrong you have against the Crown; all I have to do is to take into account the facts upon which this prosecution are based."[82] With this exchange Prendergast ended his 20-year involvement in resisting Maori independence, refusing to admit any fault, or even participation, in any possible wrongdoing. As shown in this book, Prendergast had much to do with the 'supposed' wrong Te Whiti had against the Crown. As Attorney-General, Administrator and Chief Justice, Prendergast played a key role in separating Maori (including Te Whiti) from their land and culture. Te Whiti's speech had no impact whatsoever on Prendergast. The two men remained as far apart from a meeting of minds as it is possible for two men to be.

With the exception of September and October 1881, Prendergast's role as Administrator of the Colony of New Zealand was successful. He was well liked by large sectors of the public and "the unanimous comment of all is that he again performed these duties to everybody's entire satisfaction".[83] With the obvious exception of Gordon, Prendergast had a positive working relationship with the New Zealand Governors. That he could provide such satisfaction while working concurrently as both Chief Justice and Administrator demonstrates his capacity for a heavy workload and his strong commitment to the colony. It could also show a liking for powerful positions and status.

Prendergast became a fixture as Administrator and some, including Governor Ranfurly, would have desired Prendergast to continue in this role after his retirement as Chief Justice. Being Administrator allowed Prendergast to keep in touch with the powerful political figures of the time. While Chief Justices are of course high-ranking leaders, an 'Acting Governor' arguably has a closer relationship to the ruling Ministry. This led to Prendergast being able to cement his place not only in the legal elite, but also amongst the political elite. While not an especially social figure, Prendergast successfully hosted the various parties and gatherings expected by an Acting Governor. The support of his wife, Mary, and nephew and secretary, Charles Prendergast Knight, was vital in this area of Governorship.

The black mark on Prendergast's career as Administrator is Parihaka. The fact that this incident occurred during the only time Prendergast was administering the colony in the temporary absence of the Governor highlights the difficult role he faced in having to account for his actions to the returning Governor rather than a new one. Prendergast's role as Chief Justice of New Zealand was more than just one quotation, and his role as Administrator was more than just one proclamation. That said, Prendergast's actions during September and October 1881 were at best weak, and at worst deceitful. While he successfully reflected the views of the settler community, Prendergast seemed apathetic to the views of Maori, towards whom he continued to demonstrate a hard-line attitude.

Historians are divided in their views of Prendergast as an Administrator. Recent historians have been highly critical of his actions during 1881 and have not analysed other aspects of his career as Administrator, but many contemporaries were supportive of Prendergast in his role as figurehead of a growing settler society. In many ways, Prendergast's outlook and personality were very much in keeping with New Zealand settler society, making him a popular official. This division between the views of past and present is also apparent when analysing the other roles James Prendergast played in helping to build colonial New Zealand society.

10

'RETIREMENT'
1899–1921

After Prendergast's retirement from the position of Chief Justice in 1899, he continued to live a prosperous and useful life in Wellington. Legally, his most important achievement was representing New Zealand at the 1901 London Conference discussing the Privy Council. He also served as adjudicator in an unhappy controversy at Wanganui Collegiate in 1903. From 1902 to 1907, Prendergast acted as a director of the Bank of New Zealand and was also involved in other directorships. Throughout his judicial career and retirement, Prendergast showed some interest in fine art, music, reading and tennis but his primary concern outside his career and family was his farming interests in the Manawatu. While most of Prendergast's farming exploits occurred before his retirement, they will be discussed in this chapter. An analysis of Prendergast's later life is important in understanding the man beyond the bench and also in understanding how Prendergast became so wealthy.

James Prendergast had no children, but he was committed to his wife and extended family. In describing the life of an eminent political or legal leader it is often easy to ignore the impact or influence of close family and friends. While these figures have received attention in previous chapters, an overall assessment of their influence is provided here.

James Prendergast died in 1921, aged 94. His life spanned almost a century of history, most of it during the reign of Queen Victoria. Only 31 of these 94 years were spent under a different monarch and these were the years of childhood and old age. Living during the height of the British Empire, Prendergast was extremely loyal to Empire and colony, and the political, legal and racial views accompanying those institutions. Prendergast continued to play an important role in New Zealand society after his retirement in 1899, but to a large extent he became a man left over from another century. Popular with the public during the early twentieth century, Prendergast was seen by some as a relic from a bygone age. After playing a pivotal role in the development of colonial New Zealand, Prendergast would have seen the nation come of age during the First World War. But by that stage, Prendergast "was perhaps not much more than a name to the present generation of legal practitioners in the dominion".[1]

1. Post-retirement activities

Mary Prendergast died on 5 March 1899 of endocarditis[2] after struggling with illness for many years. James Prendergast resigned as Chief Justice of New Zealand on 25 May, less than three months later. Robert Stout, who had long desired Prendergast's position, became the colony's fourth Chief Justice. But Prendergast's role in legal affairs was not at an end. The years of experience he had gained as a lawyer, Attorney-General and Chief Justice were highly prized in New Zealand society.

The Judicial Committee of the Privy Council stood at the apex of the New Zealand legal system but has long been a source of controversy. Up until the Supreme Court Act 2003, the Council, which sits in London, had been seen by some commentators as out of touch, inaccessible and irrelevant. Others supported its objectivity, experienced adjudicators and attention to Maori affairs. In 1901, New Zealand was asked to attend a conference considering the question of strengthening the representation of the self-governing colonies on the Privy Council. Joseph Chamberlain, Secretary of State for the Colonies, wrote to Governor Ranfurly: "New Zealand has interests divergent to some extent from those of Australia. His Majesty's Government will be prepared, if it is desired by your Government to receive a separate representative from New Zealand."[3] The matter was considered by Premier Seddon and his Cabinet, and Prendergast was asked to represent the colony: "Sir James has responded that he will be quite willing to place his services at the disposal of the colony."[4]

The conference agenda focused on the question of whether to allow the colonies to be represented on the Judicial Committee, whether a specific colonial Court of Appeal should be established or whether to preserve the status quo. Prendergast asked for opinions from the New Zealand legal community and received a handsome number:[5] "However, the opinion of the majority of the representatives in London, which Prendergast apparently shared, was that 'for the present the existing system had better continue'."[6] Prendergast was reluctant to publicly state his personal opinion but the *Evening Post* reported that:

> agreeing with the majority of the colonial delegates, [Prendergast] considered that the time might arrive at no remote date for the establishment of a new final Court of Appeal for the whole Empire, but he saw no reason for any colonial representation on the Judicial Bench of the Privy Council of colonies whose legal systems were substantially the same as that of England.[7]

Prendergast's failure to effect any changes in London may have disappointed some in New Zealand, especially the current Chief Justice Stout, who was a strong critic of including the Privy Council in the New Zealand legal structure.[8]

The question of the Privy Council became a major New Zealand issue only two years after the conference. In the Privy Council decision of *Wallis v Solicitor-*

General (1903),[9] New Zealand's Court of Appeal was harshly criticised, evoking an indignant defence from New Zealand legal leaders. The Privy Council ruled against the New Zealand Government, stating:

> The proposition advanced on behalf of the Crown is certainly not flattering to the dignity or the independence of the highest Court in New Zealand or even to the intelligence of the Parliament . . . . In the opinion of their Lordships the respondent [Government] has been wrong in every step from first to last.[10]

If the conference had been held after this decision, Prendergast's conservative views on the Privy Council would probably have been unpopular with the New Zealand legal community. A hundred years later, the issue of the Privy Council was still being debated in legal circles in New Zealand.

In London, Prendergast met with some of the leading figures in colonial law and politics, including Chamberlain.[11] This would be Prendergast's last visit to the 'mother country'. He had left London in 1862 as a struggling advocate and returned 39 years later as one of the most respected legal figures in the British Empire. But England had long ceased to be home for Prendergast, and he soon returned to New Zealand, via a train journey across the United States, to enjoy his 'retirement'.

Prendergast's standing as a figure of integrity was again utilised in 1903. The headmaster at the prestigious private boys' school, Wanganui Collegiate, had been accused by a student of sexual abuse. Prendergast was asked to enquire into the affair and, after several days of investigation, exonerated the headmaster, Walter Empson, from any wrongdoing and placed the blame on the teenage boy for making false accusations.[12] Empson was an influential figure in New Zealand's education history and a highly respected institution at Collegiate by 1903.[13] Much trust was placed in Prendergast's hands, as the trustees of the school:

> most wisely determined to seek the assistance of the Honourable Sir James Prendergast, lately Chief Justice of this colony, of whose ripe experience and strict impartiality it is as unnecessary, as it would be impertinent, for me to speak . . . . the decision was to be left to Sir James and to him alone.[14]

The father of the boy making the accusation was not so impressed by Prendergast's experience:

> If, as a perusal of the [Prendergast] decision shows, my boy's story was chiefly disbelieved because it related to something of a nature never before heard of by the judges, then I respectfully affirm it is not so much my lad's veracity as their knowledge, that is at fault.[15]

The father was also disturbed at Empson's lack of involvement in the enquiry proceedings due to ill health. No stranger to controversy, Prendergast had once again found himself in the midst of an argument which has resonance in more recent times. Prendergast also found himself on the side of the establishment, a common occurrence throughout his career.

Land issues continued to dominate New Zealand politics at the beginning of the twentieth century. The debate over ownership of Porirua land, which had led to the 1877 *Wi Parata* case, refused to disappear. A Royal Commission was established in 1905 to report on the Porirua, Otaki, and other School Trusts. Prendergast was one of four commissioners appointed.[16] There were continuing questions over who rightfully owned the land on which an Anglican school was to be built in 1848: the Anglican Church, local Maori or the Crown. The Anglican Church was unhappy with the Commission's proposal to found a school at Otaki with a non-denominational character.[17]

Less controversial was Prendergast's role as a Director of the Bank of New Zealand from 1902 to 1907. Prendergast seems to have played a fairly passive role on the Board of Directors, compared with other directors such as Harold Beauchamp, the father of Katherine Mansfield. The bank's summary of his contribution was, "During the five years that Sir James Prendergast was connected with the Directorate he rendered good service to the Bank."[18] From 1884 to 1903, Prendergast served as a member of the New Zealand University Senate.[19] He was also a director of the Wellington Trust, Loan and Investment Company and the Colonial Mutual Life Insurance Company until his death.[20]

While banking, investment and insurance were key business interests for Prendergast, farming was perhaps the most important. After serving six years as Attorney-General, Prendergast had acquired enough money to purchase land in Manawatu. In 1871, Prendergast acquired 5000 acres of land in both Fitzherbert and Bunnythorpe.[21] The Fitzherbert land was known as the 'Tiritea Estate', and the main campus of Massey University now occupies part of Prendergast's former property. Controversy surrounded the purchase of the Manawatu area from Maori. Prendergast:

> had played an important part in the long litigation over the sale of the Manawatu area, with the Maori tribes disputing the ownership of the land . . . . the case [for Manawatu ownership] was reopened a year later, this time in Wellington; Sir James Prendergast, then Attorney-General, appeared for the Crown.[22]

Therefore Prendergast, who as Attorney-General and Chief Justice would be partly responsible for the alienation of large amounts of Maori land, financially benefited in his personal life from his public actions. The quotation refers to Prendergast's role in representing the Crown during the Native Land Court hearing regarding the 'Manawatu Block'. Prendergast, along with William Fox and others, argued in support of Ngati Apa and allied groups' claims and against the claims of Ngati Raukawa. While this may seem like an inter-tribal dispute, Ngati Apa's interests were closely aligned with the Crown's desire to open up the region to sale and settlement. Prendergast and the Crown emerged victorious. As Boast explains: "What makes this case stand out is the very direct role played by the Crown . . . . The counterclaim was in effect the Wellington Provincial Government."[23]

Prendergast's land was developed and then sold in January 1900, 29 years later, at a significant profit.[24] Prendergast also aided in the administration of farming in the Manawatu: "In his role as a landowner, he played a prominent part in the establishment of the Manawatu and West Coast Agricultural and Pastoral Association, of which he was the first president."[25] During the 1880s, Michael Prendergast, James' nephew, acted as manager of the farm before he became ill. Based at Fitzherbert, Michael regularly provided updates for his uncle on farming developments. The letters sent by Michael to his uncle speak of clearing bush, planting seed, grazing stock and battling fires and floods.[26] Relations between uncle and nephew were not always happy and Michael struggled to please a demanding Prendergast, who was often critical of Michael's financial management: "I fully realise that you have done as much for me as any one could have done for his son, and I will endeavour to merit your confidence."[27]

Prendergast's other main property investment was his house on Bolton Street. Contemporary pictures show the house perched above the central city with a commanding view of the Wellington harbour. Prendergast acquired the property in 1868.[28] There is no evidence to suggest Prendergast ever resided anywhere other than Bolton Street from 1868 onwards, though he took numerous business trips to different locations and spent some time up at his Manawatu properties. Built in the early days of Wellington's development as a city, the large Bolton Street property became a valuable piece of land during the 53 years Prendergast lived there. The house and land were eventually sold in 1922 and subdivided in 1923.[29] In 1879, Prendergast also purchased two plots of newly reclaimed land around the northern part of Lambton Quay.[30] Prendergast's property investments were wise and timely, and helped to make him a very wealthy man.

2. Family matters

In 1852, James had married Mary Hall, the daughter of John Hall and Sarah Hall *née* Kean. John Hall's occupation was listed as 'a gentleman' and the Hall family was Anglican.[31] Therefore, Mary was from a 'respectable' Church of England background like her husband. Little direct evidence remains about Mary Prendergast to provide the historian with insights into her personality, but indirect evidence suggests a patient, loyal and supportive woman. Soon after their marriage, James spent time away from his wife as an 'adventurer' in Victoria. Mary eventually joined her husband, only to return with him to London several months later. She provided James with unwavering support during the trying times before his career flourished in Dunedin.

Mary Prendergast was a popular figure amongst friends and family. In the collection of private and professional letters received by James Prendergast while in Wellington, the vast majority send warm greetings to Mary and enquire after her health.[32] Unfortunately no personal records remain written by Mary. Whether Mary enjoyed the pomp and ceremony of being 'Lady Prendergast' is unclear, but she played a major role in hosting the social functions held by James, especially when he was Administrator of the Colony.[33] While Mary seems to have enjoyed the social aspects of elite Wellington society, she also would have experienced loneliness as a result of James' long periods on circuit.[34] To alleviate this, Mary entertained friends and family at the Prendergast mansion.

While James Prendergast was a career man, his family was very important to him during his time in New Zealand. It was often observed that Prendergast had experienced a meteoric rise up the New Zealand 'legal ladder', but it must be remembered that during this period he had the total support of his dedicated wife, Mary. Though Mary suffered long periods of isolation while her husband attended to business, she remained loyal to him and his career until her death in 1899. In leaving southeast England for colonial New Zealand with her husband, Mary Prendergast showed courage and fortitude. Of the four Prendergast men, Michael Prendergast QC and his three sons, James was easily the most successful and emotionally stable. This was, to a large extent, due to a moderate, disciplined personality and a happy marriage. The death of Mary in 1899 resigned Prendergast to a solitary retirement without the chance to enjoy his final days with his wife.

The closeness of the Prendergast marriage in later years is probably apparent in James' almost immediate resignation as Chief Justice after her death. Mary had been suffering poor health for some time. No evidence exists revealing why the Prendergasts did not have any children. That said, James and Mary effectively adopted James' nephew, Michael, at a young age upon the death of his mother and desertion of his father. The way in which Mary and James supported their nephews, Henry Hall and Charles Prendergast Knight (sons of Mary's siblings), also demonstrates interest of a parental nature. James Prendergast was close to Mary's extended family and, at his death, 22 years after his wife, he left the vast majority of his wealth to the Hall and Knight families.[35]

While the marriage of James and Mary Prendergast was successful, James' nuclear family continued to experience tragedy and hard times. James' brothers, Michael and Philip, had both received first-rate English educations at leading public schools, Cambridge University and Middle Temple. Both had shown ambition and talent in their early careers in London and Victoria, as mentioned in earlier chapters. Yet Michael had become an alcoholic while in Victoria and his wife had left him. During his time in Dunedin during the 1860s, Michael's health and reputation deteriorated and eventually James had to take over the upbringing of Michael's son, Michael junior.[36] Michael senior left Dunedin in c1868 and returned to Australia. After his near-death experience in 1870, Michael seems to have spent the rest of his life in a 'retreat' for the mentally unstable. At one point, he was diagnosed as suffering from dipsomania. Michael's wife, Jane, died in 1864,[37] effectively leaving Michael junior an orphan and under the care of James and Mary Prendergast.

Philip Prendergast also met with tragedy. After returning to London in late 1856 after a largely unsuccessful time in Victoria, Philip qualified as a barrister but shortly after became mentally ill. The cause of the illness was apparently a result of either the fever he caught on the Victorian goldfield or 'intemperance'. Soon after James left London in 1862, Philip's health collapsed and only a few years later he had lost all rationality.[38] Proceeds from the Prendergast family trust, and from James personally, supported Philip in his cousin Henry Manning's lunatic asylum,[39] and he remained in an asylum until his death.[40] He never married. When James visited England with his wife in 1884, he visited Philip in the asylum. The brother whom James had once been so close to did not recognise him. James stopped in Melbourne on his return journey to visit Michael, but no comment on the visit can be found in James' correspondence.[41]

From the late 1820s through to the early 1860s, the Prendergast brothers had been close. The disintegration of this fraternal bond as his brothers succumbed to severe mental illness would certainly have affected James Prendergast's emotional state. His continued success in New Zealand colonial society while his brother's lives deteriorated demonstrates that he responded to tragedy by working harder and concentrating on his career. Whether he felt any guilt at his inability to prevent his brother's suffering is unclear. But unlike colonial leaders such as Harry Atkinson and William Richmond, Prendergast operated in New Zealand without the help of a large, supportive family network. The illness of Philip and Michael provides the historian with insights into the state of mental health in the late nineteenth century. As knowledge of mental health was minimal during the nineteenth century it is hard to know what were the exact causes of the brothers' illnesses. The causes of mental illness were still largely unknown and often the best society could do was house patients in lunatic asylums until they died.[42]

By the late 1860s, of the six members of James Prendergast's immediate family, three were dead and two were suffering from serious mental illness. Prendergast set out to give his brother's son, Michael, the best opportunities money could buy. Michael was sent to England during the 1870s to become an English gentleman and obtain a degree at Oxford University.[43] The colonial boy did not take well to English life and soon returned to New Zealand to pursue life as a farmer. Placed in charge of Prendergast's Manawatu properties, Michael seemed to flourish as a settler. But, like his father before him, tragedy struck in the form of mental illness. By the late 1880s, Michael was unable to continue as his uncle's farm manager and retired from society.

While James Prendergast sometimes demonstrated an unforgiving and ruthless streak while Attorney General and Chief Justice, his commitment to his family showed a more generous side to his personality. The 'adoption' of Michael Prendergast was an impressive example of family loyalty. James also provided financial aid to other relatives during his time in New Zealand.[44] Looking after his nephew, Michael, was often frustrating and troublesome for Prendergast.[45] Committed to his official posts, Prendergast struggled to find ample time to support Michael in his endeavours. The other nephews close to Prendergast, Henry Hall and Charles Prendergast Knight, were a great asset to the Chief Justice. They aided James both professionally and personally, and were rewarded in Prendergast's will.

Prendergast finally died in 1921 of cerebral apoplexy.[46] After a service at St Paul's Cathedral, Prendergast was buried at Karori Cemetery.[47] A range of dignitaries were present at the funeral, including the Prime Minister William Massey, the Attorney-General Francis Bell, Judges Robert Stout and Frederick Chapman, Harold Beauchamp and Michael Myers. Members of Prendergast's extended family were also present.

During his time in New Zealand, James Prendergast had become a wealthy man. When he died the value of his estate was 132,605 pounds.[48] Prendergast spread his wealth amongst his wife's nephews and nieces, though he also provided a legacy for his house staff and his brother Michael's sister-in-law. Henry Hall and Charles Prendergast Knight were the main beneficiaries, receiving 20,000 pounds each. The list of beneficiaries does not include Prendergast's two brothers or his nephew Michael, indicating that they must have died sometime before 1921. Prendergast also gifted his collection of pictures by George Dawe (excepting family portraits) and George Morland to the New Zealand Academy of Fine Arts.[49] In 1921, Prendergast's library was sold at auction. The collection included standard works of poetry, history, classics, music and fiction.[50]

The life of James Prendergast spanned almost a century of change and development. He became a Wellington institution in later years. By all accounts, he kept his mental faculties until his death aged 94. During the period 1899 to 1907, Prendergast continued to play an active role in colonial society. Whether representing New Zealand in London or conducting enquiries into scandals and land disputes, he remained an important figure. Prendergast was totally committed to the development of the New Zealand colony but still remained loyal to British institutions and concepts. Despite his continuing activities, Prendergast's impact on New Zealand history largely finished when he retired as Chief Justice in 1899. As the twentieth century progressed, Prendergast became almost a curiosity from a bygone colonial age.

Like other colonial power brokers, such as Frederick Whitaker and Harry Atkinson, Prendergast's actions in public life benefited his private fortunes. At one point in the late 1850s, the Prendergast family included a high-profile English judge, a Victorian Member of Parliament and two London barristers. Less than ten years later, only James Prendergast remained in the public sphere. The Prendergast family decline would have been painful for James, but he succeeded in spite of it and attempted to aid members of his family in a variety of ways. James Prendergast remained, fulfilling his words written while a gold-digger in Victoria during the 1850s:

> Success I am persuaded must eventually be the end sooner or later to the man who will give himself wholly up to the work. What he will chiefly stand in need of is power of Endurance without he can do nothing . . . . Pluck is the one thing needful. Any man from any class who can bear disappointments and hard fare will make [it].[51]

When Prendergast died he was the oldest ex-Chief Justice within the Empire, and probably also the oldest Knight Batchelor.[52]

Prendergast, the ultimate survivor, had seen New Zealand progress from a colony divided by cultural conflict to a thriving agricultural settlement to a Dominion with a national identity forged through foreign war. In his final years, Prendergast was a solitary figure content to ruminate alone about the events of the past. Prendergast was spotted at a Days Bay picnic in 1908 by a social reporter:

> Nearby the chute, where black swans and pale young ladies disported themselves, in the shade of the old spreading tree, Mr. Justice Prendergast flung himself down at mid-day to cool himself. He looked happy and patriarchal . . . . He had the right tree and a good seat, and he soon had his hat off and was tucking into some fruit. The bag was on the ground between his feet. He is fond of fruit as anyone might see, and he had his picnic on his own, with little sea views and ocean breezes in between the bites.[53]

11

CONCLUSION

James Prendergast played an integral and influential role in the development of the New Zealand legal system. As Attorney-General, Prendergast dominated the drafting of legislation and provision of governmental legal advice for ten years. As Chief Justice, he dominated the judicial branch of government for 24 years. Therefore, for the final 34 years of the nineteenth century, New Zealand's legal development was closely linked to the career of Prendergast. No study of late-nineteenth-century legal history could be complete without substantial reference to the achievements of Prendergast. While not all his contributions were positive, they were contributions nevertheless, and they continue to influence New Zealand in the present day.

The overriding purpose of this book is to argue that James Prendergast was more than just a two-dimensional historical figure, more than just a one-line quotation. On a general level, this book has investigated the problems of judging the past by the standards of the present. The gaping dichotomy between the treatment of Prendergast by his contemporaries and his treatment by modern commentators is obvious. A hero in one century became a villain in the next. It is not the purpose of this book to construct an apology for James Prendergast. The actions and views of Prendergast can be discovered, revealed and interpreted through detailed and informed research. This can provide the basis for a more accurate assessment.

Another key theme in this book is the overwhelming importance of the English legal heritage on the development of the New Zealand legal system. To a large degree, the English legal system was uplifted and planted in New Zealand with little modification. This readymade system was the product of centuries of English trial and error but was not necessarily suited to the New Zealand environment. A conflict between the rules and laws of Britain and those of the Maori people was virtually inevitable. Cultural encounter between Maori and Pakeha is the pivotal theme running through New Zealand history and dominates modern scholarship. Therefore, a figure such as Prendergast is currently remembered for his views and actions in the area of race relations. Thrust into the arena of the New Zealand Wars with little previous experience of other cultures, Prendergast's defensive attitudes and total devotion to the British Empire created a ready example of the colonial imperialist. But history is not about stereotypes, it is about real people, and a biography of a powerful figure such as Prendergast must seek to view the man in context.

A number of important conclusions have been stated in the course of this book. Prendergast was a product of Victorian England and the British Empire. His formative years and early career was centred in London, the heart of Imperial Britain. A loyal son of the Empire, Prendergast sought to recreate British life and British values in his adopted home of New Zealand. Born into an affluent family, Prendergast was provided with opportunities closed to the mass of English people. But, despite the best education and an ambitious and intelligent disposition, Prendergast struggled for success in his early career. Frustrated by the intense competition in England, Prendergast viewed the colonies as the obvious alternative. As with many of New Zealand's leading legal and political figures during the nineteenth century, Prendergast set sail for the colony after a less than prosperous experience in Britain. Although he was unable to break into the London legal elite, the experience gained by Prendergast as a barrister in the English legal system would prove invaluable for his later roles as Attorney-General and Chief Justice.

By the time Prendergast left England with his wife, Mary, the Prendergast family had collapsed. This tragedy did not deter Prendergast and probably strengthened his resolve to succeed. Prendergast was 36 years old when he arrived in New Zealand, young enough to make a new start, but too old to easily alter ingrained attitudes. Prendergast's life and career must be seen in the context of the 'Victorian Frame of Mind'. Traits such as hard work, optimism, devotion to duty and commitment to British superiority are clearly evident in Prendergast's personality. Many of these traits were shared by other leading New Zealand colonists such as Henry Chapman and William Richmond.

In a career as publicly successful as that of James Prendergast, it is easy to brush over apparent failures. Prendergast's three-year adventure in Victoria was *prima facie* a failure. But Prendergast had the ability to transform failure into a valuable learning experience. From his time in Victoria, Prendergast learned harsh truths about colonial life and did not make the same mistakes again in Dunedin. It is during the Victorian experience that Prendergast's defining attribute becomes clear, namely, his endurance.

One of Prendergast's most remarkable achievements was rising from an unknown Otago immigrant in 1862 to Attorney-General of New Zealand only three years later. By a combination of luck, timing, talent and hard work, Prendergast become the legal equivalent of an 'overnight success'. Prendergast wisely chose gold-rush Dunedin as his starting point in New Zealand. Money abounded and, instead of taking the risky path of gold-digging, as in Victoria, Prendergast took the wiser and more secure path of supporting the gold industry as a lawyer. Prendergast was an able lawyer, especially in the areas of special pleading and *in banco* suits. Capable men of Prendergast's experience were in short supply in 1860s New Zealand, and

it was not long before Prendergast's talent was recognised by the New Zealand
Government. With his appointment as Attorney-General in 1865, Prendergast's
focus moved to Wellington. It would be difficult to construct a comprehensive
civic history of Wellington in the late nineteenth century without mention of
James Prendergast. He dominated the legal arena in Wellington for 35 years and
lived in the city for 56 years.

It was as Attorney-General that Prendergast made his first enduring mark on
New Zealand's history. Appointed to this pivotal position in the midst of New
Zealand's only civil war, Prendergast found himself at the centre of a devastating
cultural conflict. From his first days in New Zealand, Prendergast had associated
with power-brokers and he quickly moved to the centre of the New Zealand
political elite as Attorney-General. While his role as a Legislative Counsellor was
limited, Prendergast excelled as a non-political Attorney-General, in particular,
managing the process of drafting new legislation. The huge body of legislation
drafted from 1865 to 1875 is an enduring legacy of James Prendergast. While these
statutes have long since been repealed, they have formed the basis of much of New
Zealand's present legislation, especially in the areas of land law and criminal law.
Statutes such as the Land Transfer Act 1870 are of lasting historical importance. In
no other area of his New Zealand career is the influence of the English legal system
more evident than in Prendergast's statutes. The triumphs and failures of this body
of legislation are primarily a result of successful and unsuccessful importation of
English statutes.

As the Government's legal advisor, Prendergast earned a reputation as an enemy
of the Maori, though his harsh decisions were aimed specifically at Maori leaders in
arms against the Crown. Prendergast demonstrated no mercy in his dealings with
Titokowaru and Te Kooti, and received the overwhelming support of the settler
community. The reputations of these Maori leaders have prospered over the last 40
years, while Prendergast's reputation has been on a downward spiral. The situation
existing in 1860s colonial New Zealand has been turned on its head. Prendergast's
decisions must be seen in the context of a nation at war.

While Attorney-General, Prendergast became a strong supporter of central
government, an institution of which he had become an integral part. While
Prendergast was not a flamboyant public figure, Theodore Roosevelt's famous
maxim 'Speak softly and carry a big stick' would have applied to his outlook
and personality. Prendergast's success as Attorney-General aided him in his next
step up the legal ladder and in 1875 he was appointed New Zealand's third Chief
Justice.

As Chief Justice, Prendergast is now remembered for one statement in one
decision. An entire career is thus condensed into one quotation. Until approximately
40 years ago, Prendergast CJ's peers such as Richmond and Williams enjoyed a
greater historical profile than their nominal leader, but with the recent public

attention given to the Treaty of Waitangi, Prendergast CJ has largely eclipsed these judges in New Zealand historiography. During his Chief Justiceship, Prendergast relied heavily on the support offered by his brother judges, and, in particular, the professional companionship of Richmond J. Prendergast CJ was a cautious judge and took some time to feel secure on the Supreme Court Bench, especially after the Barton affair early in his judicial career. But through endurance and sheer determination, Prendergast CJ became a widely respected and powerful judge. By the 1890s, with the possible exception of Williams J, Prendergast CJ was *the* outstanding legal figure in the colony of New Zealand.

Prendergast CJ was an excellent administrator and excelled as leader of the judiciary. The administration of colonial justice was in capable hands during the period 1875 to 1899. As a jurist, he was pragmatic and able, but demonstrated a number of weaknesses. Prendergast CJ could deliver comprehensive judgments on issues where he had a command of the subject matter, such as real property, the land transfer system and aspects of criminal law. He was also capable of delivering brief, unsubstantial judgments based on sparse legal precedent. Prendergast CJ was a conservative jurist who, despite some assertive and controversial decisions, preferred to apply the existing statute and common law to the fact situation at hand. In keeping with this conservatism, Prendergast CJ preferred a literal approach to statutory interpretation, providing security to his decisions. Many of the statutes Prendergast CJ was called on to interpret were in fact drafted while he was Attorney-General. There was little need to take an assertive approach to interpreting statutes, when the adjudicator had some responsibility for the construction.

Prendergast CJ was usually able to deal with controversial case situations with tact and professionalism. While in cases such as *Wi Parata*, Prendergast CJ could be perceived to be using the law to support established power groups, the general rule in his decisions is one of impartiality. As a judge, Prendergast CJ mixed efficiency with caution. Some of his best judgments created concise and perceptive precedents which are still used in the modern New Zealand legal system. While many of Prendergast CJ's decisions reflect the New Zealand colonial environment, the Chief Justice relied heavily on English precedent to support his legal decisions. Prendergast was a solid, but not inspired, Chief Justice who provided effective leadership on the Supreme Court Bench for over three decades.

A sizeable number of Prendergast CJ's decisions were on matters affecting Maori, and the judgments show a man attempting to grapple with a different cultural outlook. As time went on he matured as a judge, making many of his best decisions in the twilight years of his judicial career. Analysis of his later judgments and his report on problems in the Cook Islands reveals a slightly more tolerant attitude towards indigenous people than during the earlier part of his career. Prendergast CJ was a conservative, wary of change and new directions.

Throughout his career, Prendergast faced controversy and challenging situations. Whether on the Victorian goldfields or the Wellington Supreme Court Bench, Prendergast met conflict head on. Generally, Prendergast showed integrity in these situations, for example, in the awkward affair of Edwards J's void appointment to the Supreme Court Bench. Occasionally, as in the Barton affair, Prendergast lost his composure and made a destructive error of judgement. Many of the well-known figures from late nineteenth-century New Zealand society touched the career of James Prendergast, including criminals such as Minnie Dean and the Sullivan Gang, politicians such as George Grey and Robert Stout, lawyers such as William Travers and Alfred Hanlon, and Maori leaders such as Te Kooti, Te Whiti and Titokowaru. In this kaleidoscope of famous names, Prendergast appears a somewhat retiring figure, prominent but uncomfortable in the limelight. However, he was a powerful force behind the scenes. Many of the famous legal names of later generations would owe some of their success to Prendergast's influence, including Michael Myers, William Downie Stewart and Martin Chapman.

For all the many achievements and disappointments in the career of James Prendergast, only three words continue to be associated with his name: 'a simple nullity'. Greater attention must be paid to Prendergast's other contributions to nineteenth-century New Zealand society. Supported by his peers, damned by many of the present generation of scholars, perhaps Prendergast will be viewed differently again by future New Zealanders. There is little doubt that Prendergast considered judicial impartiality of the utmost importance. It is highly unlikely that the *Wi Parata* decision was a cynically and deliberately 'rigged' judgment by Prendergast CJ and Richmond J to disenfranchise the Maori people. But its legacy has been one of land loss and cultural devastation.

Unfortunately for Prendergast's present reputation, he was involved not only in diminishing the founding document of New Zealand but also in destroying the village of Parihaka, a model of Maori success and independence. While Prendergast has received some of the blame for the destruction of Parihaka, it is John Bryce who has become the obvious villain in this key incident. As with the *Wi Parata* decision, in the context of Prendergast's Chief Justiceship, the Parihaka invasion was one isolated incident in the many brief terms during which Prendergast served as Administrator of New Zealand.

Prendergast carried on public disputes with two men during his career, George E. Barton and Governor Arthur Gordon. Both Barton and Gordon were unpopular with the settler government and both were extremely outspoken. Prendergast ably survived both disputes and enjoyed more consistent success than either man, though history has been kinder to Barton and Gordon than it has to Prendergast.

Upon leaving England in 1862, Prendergast experienced a relatively settled personal life. Aided by his supportive wife, Prendergast superficially separated his personal and private lives, but the reality was a man totally dedicated to his work. Prendergast had no children of his own, devoting his time to the law instead. While career came first, Prendergast was also committed to family. He effectively raised his nephew, Michael, and continued to support his seriously ill brothers.

Prendergast was an example of the Victorian gentleman, patriarchal, moral but also hypocritical. Upon retirement, Prendergast continued to be involved in public life, in particular farming pursuits and various directorships. While he could easily have returned to London to see out his later years at the heart of the Empire, Prendergast chose to stay in New Zealand. By 1899, Prendergast had become totally dedicated to the development of the New Zealand colony. His energy and focus was on New Zealand. New Zealand was his home, the place where he had achieved career success and fortune. Therefore, in condemning James Prendergast, the scholarly community condemns one of modern New Zealand's founding fathers. It cannot be disputed that this founding father had feet of clay and in his dealings with Maori caused much lasting damage. But Prendergast remains a founding father for all that.

When Prendergast arrived in New Zealand in 1862, the Colony of New Zealand was in the throes of war, economic boom and rapid growth. When he died in 1921, the Dominion of New Zealand was experiencing peace and relative prosperity after the destructive, but nation-forming, experience of World War I. During his final few years of life, Prendergast withdrew from the public glare he had been in for so long, but when he died, a number of important official figures gathered at his funeral. While prominent men such as William Massey were present out of official duty, others were there to pay their personal respects to one of the defining figures in New Zealand's legal history. Francis Bell, Robert Stout, Frederick Chapman and Michael Myers had all been influenced by the life and career of James Prendergast. They in turn would continue to develop and administer justice in New Zealand.

There is no more apt nor fitting tribute to Prendergast than that of his old associate and rival, Robert Stout. Prendergast and Stout's careers had intersected and overlapped since those early days in gold-rush Dunedin. On Prendergast's death, Stout accurately predicted his legacy. At times, Stout had disagreed with the actions and decisions of Prendergast, so the ambiguity of his eulogy is fitting:

> I believe he will not be forgotten by our law students and our future race. He is enshrined in the history of our judiciary and his name will be recalled as our students study our case law and our legal history.[1]

NOTES

Chapter 1. Introduction

1   Guy Lennard *Sir William Martin: The Life of the First Chief Justice of New Zealand* (Whitcombe and Tombs, Christchurch, 1961); WH Dunn and ILM Richardson *Sir Robert Stout: A Biography* (AH & AW Reed, Wellington, 1961); DA Hamer "The Law and the Prophet: A Political Biography of Sir Robert Stout 1844–1930" (MA Thesis, University of Auckland, 1960); Peter McKenzie "New Zealand's First Chief Justice: The Rule of Law and the Treaty" (2012) 43 VUWLR 207.

2   This point is supported by Jeremy Finn's survey of New Zealand legal historiography in Jeremy Finn "Sir Kenneth Gresson: A Study in Judicial Decision Making" (1997) 6 Canterbury L Rev 481.

Chapter 2. The creation of a colonial imperialist

1   Baptismal Lists, Guildhall Library, London.

2   "Legal Obituary: M Prendergast Esq QC" *The Law Times* (London, 9 April 1859) at 19, 44–45.

3   Frederic Boase *Modern English Biography, 1851–1900* (Frank Cass, London, 1897, 1965) vol. 2 at 1626 and vol. 6 at 424.

4   Leslie Stephen and Sidney Lee (eds) *The Dictionary of National Biography: From the Earliest Times to 1900* (Oxford University Press, Oxford, 1885 onwards) at 659–660.

5   Robert Barlow Gardiner (ed) *The Admission Registers of St. Paul's School from 1748 to 1876* (George Bell, London, 1884) at 289, 293.

6   AH Mead *A Miraculous Draught of Fishes: A History of St Paul's School 1509–1990* (St. Paul's School, London, 1990) at 138.

7   Mead at 60.

8   Mead at 69.

9   RB Gardiner and John Lupton (eds) *Res Paulinae: The Eighth Half-Century of St Paul's School* (St Paul's School, West Kensington, 1911) at 12.

10   Charles J Robinson *Register of the Scholars admitted into Merchant Taylors' School, From AD 1562 to 1874* (Farncombe & Co, Lewes, 1883) vol. 2 at 182, 256.

11   Gardiner (ed) at 404.

12   St. Paul's School Archival Records.

13   Letter, Michael Prendergast (Father), Norwich, to Caroline Prendergast, London, 30 March c1844, Prendergast Papers, Misc-MS-Papers 735-A, Hocken Library, Dunedin.

14   John Venn *Biographical History of Gonville and Caius College 1349–1897* (Cambridge University Press, Cambridge, 1898) vol. 2 at 271.

15   Letter, James Prendergast, Cambridge, to Michael Prendergast (Father), London, 17 October 1845, Prendergast Papers, MS-Papers 1791, Alexander Turnbull Library, Wellington.

16   Letter, James Prendergast, Cambridge, to Michael Prendergast (Father), London, 3 December 1845, Prendergast Papers, MS-Papers 1791, Alexander Turnbull Library, Wellington.

17   Letter, James Prendergast, Cambridge, to Caroline Prendergast, London, 1845, D.O.W. Hall Papers, MS-Papers 986, Hocken Library, Dunedin.

18   Letter, James Prendergast to Michael Prendergast (Father), c1844/5, D.O.W. Hall Papers, MS-Papers 986.

19   Letter, James Prendergast, Cambridge, to Michael Prendergast (Father), London, 17 October 1845, Prendergast Papers, MS-Papers 1791.

20   Letter to author from University of Cambridge Library, January 2000.

21   Letter, James Prendergast, Cambridge, to Michael Prendergast (Father), London, 3 December 1845, Prendergast Papers, MS-Papers 1791.

22   Judith Bassett "Williams, Joshua Strange" (30 October 2012) Te Ara: The Encyclopedia of New Zealand <www.teara.govt.nz>.

23   Letter, James Prendergast, Cambridge, to Caroline Prendergast, London, 27 December 1845, D.O.W. Hall Papers, MS-Papers 986.

24   Letter to author from University of Cambridge Library, January 2000.

25   Admission, 24 May 1849, Henry F Macgeagh and HAC Sturgess (eds) *Register of Admissions to the Honourable Society of the Middle Temple: Years 1782–1909* (Butterworths, London, 1949) vol. 2 at 512.

26   Administration of Caroline Prendergast's Estate, Prendergast Papers, Misc-MS-Papers 735-A, Hocken Library, Dunedin.

27   Letter, James Prendergast, Bishop's Hull, to Michael Prendergast (Father), London, 1850, Prendergast Papers, MS-Papers 1791.

28   Letter, Michael Prendergast (Father), London, to James Prendergast, Bishop's Hull, 26 September 1850, Prendergast Papers, MS-Papers 1791.

29   Census, 1851.

30   Letter, James Prendergast, Bishop's Hull, to Michael Prendergast (Father), London, 1850, Prendergast Papers, MS-Papers 1791.

31   Census, 1851.

32   Letter, James Prendergast, Bishop's Hull, to Michael Prendergast (Father), London, 1850, Prendergast Papers, MS-Papers 1791.

33   Marriage Certificate, 12 June 1852, MS-Papers 986.

34   AH Manchester *Sources of English Legal History: 1750–1950* (Butterworths, London, 1984) at 133.

35   Ibid.

36   Theodore Plucknett *A Concise History of the Common Law* (5th ed, Butterworths, London, 1956) at 416.

37   Ibid.

38   "Obituary" *Dominion* (Wellington, 28 February 1921) at 4.

39   Daniel Duman *The English and Colonial Bars in the Nineteenth Century* (Croom Helm, London, 1983) at 4.

40   It could be other Prendergasts, or Michael Prendergast senior, who retained a small private practice while a judge (Corporation of London Records), or Philip Prendergast from 1859 onwards.

41   Letters, 1862, D.O.W. Hall Papers, MS-Papers 986.

42   Mark Herber *Legal London: A Pictorial History* (Phillimore, London, 1999) at 68.

43   William Wilks Dalbiac (ed) *The Law List* (V & R Stevens and GS Norton, London, published annually).

44   Letter, Thomas Chitty to Michael Prendergast, London, 1850s, D.O.W. Hall Papers, MS-Papers 986.

45   Letter, Thomas Chitty to James Prendergast, London, 1850s, D.O.W. Hall Papers, MS-Papers 986.

46   Jack IH Jacob *Chitty and Jacob's Queen's Bench Forms* (21st ed, Sweet & Maxwell, London, 1986) at vii.

47   Ibid.

48   The title was changed to *Queen's Bench Forms* and the book altered to incorporate the Common Law Procedure Act 1852.

49   "The Late and the New Chief Justice" in James Macassey (ed) *Colonial Law Journal: being a selection of reports and cases argued in the Supreme Court of New Zealand, 1865–1875 and various*

articles (Henry Wise, Dunedin, 1875) at 24.

50   *The Records of the Honorable Society of Lincoln's Inn* (Lincoln's Inn, London, 1896) vol. 2 at 67.

51   John Venn *Alumni Cantabrigienses* Part II (Cambridge University Press, Cambridge, 1953) vol. 5 at 185.

52   "The Late and the New Chief Justice" in Macassey (ed) at 24.

53   Recorded in the *English Law Reports*.

54   Letters, Prendergast Family, c1840, D.O.W. Hall Papers, MS-Papers 986.

55   Charles Mackie *Norfolk Annals: A Chronological Record of Remarkable Events in the Nineteenth Century* (Office of the Norfolk Chronicle, Norwich, 1901) vol. 1 at 474.

56   Boase at 1625.

57   Patrick Polden *A History of the County Court 1846–1971* (Cambridge University Press, Cambridge, 1999) at 322.

58   G Pitt-Lewis *Commissioner Kerr: An Individuality* (T Fisher Unwin, London, 1903) at 76.

59   1858 Inquiry, Corporation of London Records Office.

60   Pitt-Lewis at 22, 33.

61   Sergeant Ballantine *Some Experiences of a Barrister's Life* (8th ed, Richard Bentley, London, 1883) at 30.

62   Ibid.

63   *Suffolk Literary Chronicle* at 71–72, c1835, MS-Papers 986, Hocken Library, Dunedin.

64   Ballantine at 30 and Pitt-Lewis at 76.

65   Administration of Michael Prendergast's Estate, 1859, Probate Office, London.

66   Letters, Prendergast Family, 1830s, D.O.W. Hall Papers, MS-Papers 986.

67   Letter, Michael Prendergast, Bury St. Edmunds, to Caroline Prendergast, London, 1830s, D.O.W. Hall Papers, MS-Papers 986.

68   Letter, Michael Prendergast, Cambridge, to Caroline Prendergast, London, 24 June 1835, D.O.W. Hall Papers, MS-Papers 986.

69   Letter, Michael Prendergast, Huntingdon, to Caroline Prendergast, London, 22 March 1839, D.O.W. Hall Papers, MS-Papers 986.

70   Letter, Michael Prendergast, Bury St. Edmunds, to Caroline Prendergast, London, c1840, D.O.W. Hall Papers, MS-Papers 986.

71   Letters, Prendergast Family, D.O.W. Hall Papers, MS-Papers 986.

72   Keith Sinclair "Richmond, Christopher William" (15 January 2014) Te Ara: The Encyclopedia of New Zealand <www.teara.govt.nz>.

73   WH Dunn and ILM Richardson *Sir Robert Stout: A Biography* (AH & AW Reed, Wellington, 1961).

74   GH Scholefield (ed) *A Dictionary of New Zealand Biography* (Department of Internal Affairs, Wellington, 1940) at 46 and Family Information, Alexander Turnbull Library, Wellington.

75   AN Wilson *The Victorians* (Arrow Books, London, 2003).

76   As described by Michael Prendergast in his letters to his wife during the 1830s, Prendergast Family, D.O.W. Hall Papers, MS-Papers 986.

77   *Trial By Jury* (Musical) 1875, Text by W.S. Gilbert, Music by Sir Arthur Sullivan.

78   Jeremy Finn "Development of the Law in New Zealand" in Peter Spiller (ed) *A New Zealand Legal History* (Brookers, Wellington, 1995) at 103.

79   Letter, Michael Prendergast (Father), London, to James Prendergast, Bishop's Hull, 26 September 1850, Prendergast Papers, MS-Papers 1791.

80   As seen in *Wi Parata v The Bishop of Wellington* (1877) 3 NZ Jur (NS) SC 72.

81   For a discussion of stadial theory in a New Zealand context see David V Williams *A Simple Nullity? The* Wi Parata *Case in New Zealand Law and History* (Auckland University Press, Auckland, 2011) and Mark Hickford *Lords of the Land: Indigenous Property Rights and the Jurisprudence of Empire* (Oxford University Press, Oxford, 2011).

82   Wilfred Prest *William Blackstone: Law and Letters in the Eighteenth Century* (Oxford University Press, Oxford, 2008).

83   Letter, Michael Prendergast, London, to James Prendergast, Victoria, 3 August 1854, Prendergast Papers, MS-Papers 1791 and Henry John Stephen *New Commentaries on the Laws of England* (Butterworths, London, 1853).

84   "Monday" *Evening Post* (Wellington, 21 May 1921) at 8.

85   William Richmond did not attend university but was called to the bar at Middle Temple in 1847, two years before Prendergast was admitted to Middle Temple.

Chapter 3. Colonial beginnings

1   Thomas Jeffrey, Letter to his father, 22 September 1852, Prendergast, James, MS-Papers 1791, Alexander Turnbull Library, Wellington and *Immigration to Victoria Inward Passenger Lists and Indexes 1852–1923* (Public Record Office, Victoria, 1993).

2   English adult males accounted for 93 of the 135 passengers, or 69 per cent.

3   *Immigration to Victoria Inward Passenger Lists and Indexes 1852–1923.*

4   James Prendergast, Letter to his father, 22 September 1852, Prendergast, James, MS-Papers 1791.

5   Scholefield Collection, MS-Papers 0212, Alexander Turnbull Library, Wellington.

6   Philip Prendergast, Letter to his father, 21 September 1852, Prendergast, James, MS-Papers 1791.

7   James Prendergast, Letter to his father, 22 September 1852, Prendergast, James, MS-Papers 1791.

8   Philip Prendergast, Letter to his father, 21 September 1852, Prendergast, James, MS-Papers 1791.

9   Ibid.

10   James Prendergast, Letter to his father, 22 September 1852, Prendergast, James, MS-Papers 1791.

11   Ibid.

12   Philip Prendergast, Letter to his father, 21 September 1852, Prendergast, James, MS-Papers 1791.

13   "The immigration rush" <http://web.archive.org/web/20080724135849/http://sbs.com.au/sbsmain/gold/story.html?storyid=49>

14   Philip Prendergast, Letter to his father, 21 September 1852, Prendergast, James, MS-Papers 1791.

15   Thomas Jeffrey, Letter to his father, 22 September 1852, Prendergast, James, MS-Papers 1791.

16   Ibid., and *Immigration to Victoria Inward Passenger Lists and Indexes 1852–1923* (Victoria: Public Record Office, 1993).

17   Philip Prendergast, Letter to his father, 23 January 1853, Prendergast, James, MS-Papers 1791.

18   Ibid.

19   James Prendergast, Letter to his father, 13 April 1853, Prendergast, James, MS-Papers 1791.

20   Ibid.

21   Walter E Houghton *The Victorian Frame of Mind* (Yale University Press, New Haven, 1957).

22   Michael Prendergast, Letter to his father, January 1854, Prendergast, James, MS-Papers 1791.

23   Robert P Whitworth *Bailliere's Victorian Gazetter* (FF Bailliere, Melbourne, 1865) at 109.

24   James Prendergast, Letter to his father, 14 January 1854, Prendergast, James, MS-Papers 1791.

25   Ibid.

26   James Prendergast, Letter to his father, 24 May 1854, Prendergast, James, MS-Papers 1791.

27   James Prendergast, Letter to his father, 19 July 1854, Prendergast, James, MS-Papers 1791.

28   Philip Prendergast, Letter to his father, 15 February 1854, Prendergast, James, MS-Papers 1791.

29   James Prendergast, Letter to his father, 28 October 1854, Prendergast, James, MS-Papers 1791.

30   Ibid.

31   Geoffrey Serle *The Golden Age* (Melbourne University Press, Charlton, 1963) at 168.

32   Philip Prendergast, Letter to his father, 27 January 1855, Prendergast, James, MS-Papers 1791.

33   Ibid.

34   Michael Prendergast, Letter to his father, 17 May 1855, Prendergast, James, MS-Papers 1791.

35   Judith Bassett and JGH Hannan "James Prendergast" in WH Oliver and Claudia Orange (eds) *The Dictionary of New Zealand Biography 1769–1869* (Allen & Unwin/Department of Internal Affairs, Wellington, 1990) vol. 1 at 354.

36   Raewyn Dalziel *Julius Vogel: Business Politician* (Oxford University Press, Auckland, 1986) at 24.

37   Scholefield Collection, MS-Papers 0212.

38   James Flett *Dunolly: Story of an Old Gold Diggings* (2nd ed, Hawthorn Press, Melbourne, 1974) map.

39   *Victorian Law List.*

40   Henry F Macgeagh and HAC Sturgess (eds) *Register of Admissions to the Honourable Society of the Middle Temple* (Butterworths, London, 1949) vol. 2 at 512.

41   Bassett and Hannan at 354.

42   Philip Prendergast, Letter to his father, 27 January 1855, Prendergast, James, MS-Papers 1791 and Serle *The Golden Age.*

43   Philip Prendergast, Letter to his father, 15 February 1854, Prendergast, James, MS-Papers 1791.

44   Philip Prendergast, Letter to his father, 7 January 1855, Prendergast, James, MS-Papers 1791.

45   Ibid.

46   Michael Prendergast, Letter to his father, 17 May 1855, Prendergast, James, MS-Papers 1791.

47   Michael Prendergast, Letter to his father, 1856, Prendergast, James, MS-Papers 1791 and *Register of Admissions to the Honourable Society of the Middle Temple: Vol. II* at 523.

48   Michael Prendergast Biographical File, La Trobe Information Centre, Victorian State Library, Australia.

49   Kathleen Thomson and Geoffrey Serle *A Biographical Register of the Victorian Parliament 1851– 1900* (ANU, Canberra, 1972) at 168.

50   Michael Prendergast, Letter to his father, 1856, Prendergast, James, MS-Papers 1791.

51   Jane Prendergast, Letter to Michael Prendergast QC, 28 January 1856, Prendergast, James, MS-Papers 1791 and the Victoria Pioneers Index.

52   Jane Prendergast, Letter to Michael Prendergast QC, 28 January 1856, Prendergast, James, MS-Papers 1791.

53   Philip Prendergast, Letter to his father, 27 January 1855, Prendergast, James, MS-Papers 1791.

54   *The Argus* (Victoria, 17 April 1860) at 4.

55   Thomson and Serle at 168.

56   Ibid.

57   *Inglewood Advertiser* (Victoria, 24 May 1870) at 2.

58   *Inglewood Advertiser* (Victoria, 31 May 1870) at 2.

59   James Bodell in Keith Sinclair (ed) *A Soldier's View of Empire: The Reminiscences of James Bodell 1831–92* (Bodley Head, London, 1982) at 120.

60   Philip Prendergast, Letter to his father, 27 January 1855, Prendergast, James, MS-Papers 1791.

61   Michael Prendergast, Letter to his father, 30 April 1854, Prendergast, James, MS-Papers 1791.

Chapter 4. Return to the colonies

1   *Otago Daily Times* (Dunedin, 21 November 1862) at 4.

2   Kathleen Thomson and Geoffrey Serle *A Biographical Register of the Victorian Parliament 1851– 1900* (ANU, Canberra, 1972) at 168.

3   Michael Prendergast, Victoria, to James Prendergast, c1860–1, Prendergast, James, MS-Papers 1791, Alexander Turnbull Library, Wellington.

4   Michael Prendergast, Victoria, to James Prendergast, c1861, Prendergast, James, MS-Papers 1791, Alexander Turnbull Library, Wellington.

5   Michael Cullen *Lawfully Occupied: The Centennial History of the Otago District Law Society* (Otago District Law Society, Dunedin, 1979) at 23.

6   Iain Gallaway "Otago" in Robin Cooke (ed) *Portrait of a Profession: The Centennial Book of the New Zealand Law Society* (Reed, Wellington, 1969) at 333.

7   *R v SG Isaacs and Daniel Campbell* [1862] NZLostC 258 (12 December 1862).

8   "Supreme Court" in *Otago Daily Times* (Dunedin, 15 December 1862) at 5.

9   Raewyn Dalziel *Julius Vogel: Business Politician* (Oxford University Press, Auckland, 1986) at 47 and James Macassey (ed) *Colonial Law Journal, being a selection of reports and cases argued in the Supreme Court of New Zealand 1865–1875 and various articles* (Henry Wise, Dunedin, 1875) at 25.

10   *Otago Daily Times* (Dunedin, 30 September 1863) at 5.

11   *New Zealand Banking Corporation v Cutten and another* [1864] NZLostC 348 (4 October 1864).

12   Gallaway at 331.

13   *The New Zealand Banking Corporation v Cutten and Vogel* [1864] NZLostC 364 (3 November 1864).

14   "The Late and the New Chief Justice" in James Macassey (ed) *Colonial Law Journal* (Henry Wise, Dunedin, 1875) at 25. This can be confirmed by looking at the Macassey Reports from 1863 to 1865. Prendergast, Barton and Gillies are the most commonly mentioned barristers appearing before the Supreme Court.

15   *Harnetts Dunedin Dictionary* (1864) at lxvii.

16   Gallaway at 345 and "Dissolution of Partnership" (17 April 1867) 476 *Otago Provincial Government Gazette* 99 at 100.

17   Roll of Articled Clerks at Otago (January 1862 to August 1882).

18   Cullen at 49.

19   Cullen at 48.

20   "The Late and the New Chief Justice" in Macassey (ed) at 25.

21   *New Zealand Times* (New Zealand, 4 March 1921).

22   From Macassey's Reports, 38 cases reported from December 1862 to February 1867.

23   *New Zealand Times* (New Zealand, 4 March 1921).

24   An interesting discussion of this phenomenon can be found in Jeremy Finn "The Founders of the New Zealand Legal Profession: The First Cohort of Lawyers 1841–1851" (2012) 25 NZULR 24. See, in particular, the section on 'Office-holding' at 35.

25   "Appointment" (31 August 1863) 263 *Otago Provincial Government Gazette* 337 at 338.

26   "Appointment" (10 August 1865) 381 *Otago Provincial Government Gazette* 187 at 190.

27   "Appointment" (11 November 1865) 394 *Otago Provincial Government Gazette* 257 at 259.

28   "Appointment" (12 June 1866) 425 *Otago Provincial Government Gazette* 121 at 126.

29   *R v William Andrew Jarvey* [1865] NZLostC 97 (13 March 1865).

30   "Supreme Court" *Otago Daily Times* (Dunedin, 12 September 1865) at 5.

31   Sherwood Young *Guilty on the Gallows: Famous Capital Crimes of New Zealand* (Grantham House, Wellington, 1998) and Justice Department Records, NA J1 66/530, National Archives, Wellington.

32   "Appointment" (10 July 1865) 24 *New Zealand Gazette* 221 at 221.

33   "The Late and the New Chief Justice" in Macassey (ed) at 25–26. See also, Letter suggesting appointment of Prendergast as Crown Solicitor for Otago, Provincial Official, Dunedin, to Colonial Secretary, Wellington, 10 August 1865, J1 65/2026, National Archives, Wellington, and Letter acknowledging that Prendergast had been made Crown Prosecutor for Otago, Superintendent's Office, Dunedin, to Colonial Secretary, Wellington, 23 August 1865, J1 66/2214, National Archives, Wellington.

34   WH Dunn and ILM Richardson *Sir Robert Stout: A Biography* (AH and AW Reed, Wellington, 1961) at 21.

35   Dunn and Richardson at 25 and Cullen at 23.

36   Cullen at 22–23.

37   Cullen at 23.

38   Guy H Scholefield (ed) *The Richmond-Atkinson Papers* (RE Owen, Wellington, 1960) vol. 2 at 50–51.

39   Kavanagh was editor of the *New Zealand Law Journal* from 1931 to 1960.

40   Gallaway at 330.

41   *New Zealand Times* (New Zealand, 4 March 1921).

42   "A Cricket Match in Dunedin" in Macassey (ed) at 14.

43   Ibid. at 17.

44   Cullen at 25.

45   Ibid. at 27.

46   Ibid. at 30.
47   "News of the Week" *Otago Witness* (Dunedin, 25 June 1870) at 14.
48   *R v Thomas Yates* [1864] NZLostC 66 (8 March 1864).
49   Thomson and Serle at 10.
50   "Brief Biography of George E Barton" Alexander Turnbull Library, Wellington, MS-Papers-0212-C/04 at 1.
51   Thomson and Serle at 10.
52   "Brief Biography of George E Barton" at 2.
53   Keith Sinclair "Christopher William Richmond" in WH Oliver and Claudia Orange (eds) *The Dictionary of New Zealand Biography: 1769–1869* (Allen & Unwin/Department of Internal Affairs, 1990) vol. 1 at 365.
54   DG Edwards "Henry Samuel Chapman" in Oliver and Orange (eds) at 79.
55   Peter Spiller *The Chapman Legal Family* (Victoria University Press, Wellington, 1992).
56   Spiller at 88.
57   Ibid. at 155, 192.
58   Michael Prendergast, Victoria, to Michael Prendergast QC, London, 17 May 1855, Prendergast, James, MS-Papers 1791, Alexander Turnbull Library, Wellington.
59   Spiller at 60.
60   *New Zealand Mail* (New Zealand, 29 June 1878) at 9.

Chapter 5. Prendergast as Attorney-General

1   "Appointment" (10 July 1865) 24 *New Zealand Gazette* 221 at 221; James Prendergast Papers, MS-Papers 730-B, Hocken Library, Dunedin.
2   James Prendergast Papers, MS-Papers 730-B, Hocken Library, Dunedin.
3   Raewyn Dalziel *Julius Vogel: Business Politician* (Oxford University Press, Auckland, 1986) at 66.
4   Edmund Bohan *Edward Stafford: New Zealand's First Statesman* (Hazard Press, Christchurch, 1994) at 211.
5   (20 October 1865) 1864–1866 NZPD 607.
6   Dalziel at 66.
7   See 1864–1866 NZPD.
8   John McGrath "Principles for Sharing Law Officer Power: The Role of the New Zealand Solicitor-General" (1998) 18 NZULR 197 at 199.
9   "The Late and the New Chief Justice" in James Macassey (ed) *Colonial Law Journal* (Henry Wise, Dunedin, 1875) at 25–26.
10   Julius Vogel (25 August 1865) 1864–1866 NZPD 354.
11   Bohan at 211.
12   Edward Stafford "Correspondence relative to the appointment of the present Attorney-General" [1870] AJHR D32 at 5.
13   "Correspondence relative to the appointment of the present Attorney-General" at 3.
14   "Correspondence relative to the appointment of the present Attorney-General" at 6.
15   James Prendergast to the Colonial Secretary (3 October 1866) Letter AG 67/3311, National Archives, Wellington.
16   Ibid.
17   Ibid.
18   Ibid.
19   Raewyn Dalziel "The Politics of Settlement" in Geoffrey W Rice (ed) *The Oxford History of New Zealand* (2nd ed, Oxford University Press, Auckland, 1992) at 87–111.
20   For more information on the world of Parliament during this period (in particular, the House of Representatives) see John E Martin *The House: New Zealand's House of Representatives 1854–2004* (Dunmore Press, Palmerston North, 2004).

21   Bohan at 212.

22   Bohan at 291–292.

23   "Papers Relative to Occupation of Ministerial Residences" [1869] I AJHR D26.

24   Ibid. at 9.

25   Robin Cooke (ed) *Portrait of a Profession: The Centennial Book of the New Zealand Law Society* (Reed, Wellington, 1969) at 146.

26   Ibid.

27   GB Barton (ed) *The New Zealand Jurist Reports* (Reith and Wilkie, Dunedin, 1876) at 56.

28   Peter Spiller, Jeremy Finn and Richard Boast *A New Zealand Legal History* (Brookers, Wellington, 1995) at 244.

29   For example, William Gisborne *New Zealand Rulers and Statesmen from 1840 to 1897* (Sampson Law, London, 1897) 220.

30   See 1864–1866 NZPD.

31   JC Richmond (1 August 1865) 1864–1866 NZPD 206–207.

32   J Menzies (1 August 1865) 1864–1866 NZPD 206–207.

33   H Tancred (1 August 1865) 1864–1866 NZPD 207.

34   J Prendergast (1 August 1865) 1864–1866 NZPD 208.

35   Indemnity Act 1866. This Act was later repealed and replaced by the Indemnity Act 1868.

36   W Mantell (28 August 1866) 1864–1866 NZPD 901.

37   G Whitmore (28 August 1866) 1864–1866 NZPD 901.

38   J Prendergast (28 August 1866) 1864–1866 NZPD 902.

39   (30 August 1866) 1864–1866 NZPD 909.

40   J Prendergast (18 September 1866) 1864–1866 NZPD 974.

41   J Prendergast (18 September 1866) 1864–1866 NZPD 974, Marine Board Debate.

42   J Menzies (5 October 1866) 1864–1866 NZPD 1043.

43   J Prendergast (7 August 1865) 1864–1866 NZPD 255.

44   J Prendergast (22 August 1865) 1864–1866 NZPD 333.

45   J Prendergast (7 August 1865) 1864–1866 NZPD 255.

46   J Hall (10 October 1865) 1864–1866 NZPD 667.

47   J Menzies (3 October 1866) 1864–1866 NZPD 1029.

48   J Prendergast (3 October 1866) 1864–1866 NZPD 1030.

49   Chris Maclean "Wellington Region – Population" (13 July 2012) Te Ara: The Encyclopedia of New Zealand <www.teara.govt.nz>.

50   H Tancred (26 October 1865) 1864–1866 NZPD 720.

51   J Prendergast (26 October 1865) 1864–1866 NZPD 721.

52   Bohan at 207, 213.

53   J Prendergast (4 July 1866) 1864–1866 NZPD 753.

54   J Prendergast (19 July 1866) 1864–1866 NZPD 786.

55   S Peacocke (7 September 1866) 1864–1866 NZPD 930.

56   R Stokes (7 September 1866) 1864–1866 NZPD 931.

57   J Prendergast (7 September 1866) 1864–1866 NZPD 931.

58   J Prendergast (15 August 1866) 1864–1866 NZPD 883.

59   Law Practitioners Amendment Act 1866, s 3.

60   J Prendergast (18 September 1866) 1864–1866 NZPD 974–975.

61   J Prendergast (20 September 1866) 1864–1866 NZPD 984.

62   (1888) 7 NZLR 235 (SC).

63   (1888) 7 NZLR 288 (CA).

64   See for example; JGA Pocock *Barbarism and Religion: Barbarians, Savages and Empires* (Cambridge University Press, Cambridge, 2008) vol. 4; RW Kostal *A Jurisprudence of Power: Victorian Empire and the Rule of Law* (Oxford University Press, Oxford, 2005); PG McHugh *Aboriginal Societies and the Common Law* (Oxford University Press, Oxford, 2004); Mark Hickford *Lords of the Land: Indigenous Property Rights and the Jurisprudence of Empire* (Oxford University Press,

Oxford, 2011).

65   Williams notes in relation to *Wi Parata*, "The 1877 judges, without any reflective theorising, took it for granted that British civilisation was superior to that in all other social formations and that Maori were toward the lower end of the 'steps' in the scales of civilisation from naked savagery to European enlightenment." David V Williams *A Simple Nullity? The* Wi Parata *case in New Zealand law and history* (Auckland University Press, Auckland, 2011) at 230.

66   See James Belich *The New Zealand Wars and the Victorian Interpretation of Racial Conflict* (Penguin, Auckland, 1986).

67   (1 August 1865) 1864–1866 NZPD 208.

68   Waitangi Tribunal *Ngati Awa Raupatu Report* (Wai 46, 1999) at 71.

69   See Kostal's discussion of this debate.

70   Waitangi Tribunal *Ngati Awa Raupatu Report* at 72 and Letters, Prendergast to Stafford, 23 and 28 December 1865, JC22-3A AG65/1992, Archives New Zealand, Wellington.

71   These trials were covered by the *Daily Southern Cross* on 17 March and 5–6 April 1866. Five Maori were charged with Volkner's murder, three were hanged, one sentenced to prison and one aquitted. Sixteen were charged with the murders of Fulloon and seaman Ned, all were found guilty and one was hanged (Waitangi Tribunal *Ngati Awa Raupatu Report* at 72).

72   Graham and Susan Butterworth "Indigenous Insurrection and British Law: Anatomy of a Trial" (2005) ANZLHS E-Journal 141. On page 147 the article provides an incorrect reason as to why Prendergast chose not to prosecute, based on a misunderstanding of the role of Attorney General during 1865–1875.

73   "Southern Telegrams" *Daily Southern Cross* (Auckland, 28 December 1871) at 3.

74   Peter Wells, *Journey to a Hanging: The events that set New Zealand race relations back by a century* (Vintage, Auckland, 2014). Wells makes a number of inaccurate biographical statements relating to Prendergast, for example, that he graduated from "Temple Bar" (at 268).

75   Wells at 186.

76   "Despatch, Granville to Bowen, 26 February 1869" [1869] I AJHR A1a at 26. At least this is how Stafford interpreted this correspondence in James Prendergast "Opinion of the Attorney-General as to the legal status of the Maoris now in arms as regards their rights as 'belligerents', 30 June 1869" [1869] I AJHR A14 at 3.

77   Stafford was Colonial Secretary until 28 June 1869 when he was replaced by William Fox, who in turn was replaced by William Gisborne on 2 July 1869.

78   James Prendergast "Opinion of the Attorney-General as to the legal status of the Maoris now in arms as regards their rights as 'belligerents', 30 June 1869" [1869] I AJHR A14 at 3.

79   James Prendergast "Opinion of the Attorney-General on legal questions raised in Earl Granville's Despatch, September 1870" [1870] I AJHR A23.

80   However it is consistent with his 1 August 1865 Legislative Council speech.

81   Paul McHugh "The aboriginal rights of New Zealand Maori at common law" (PhD thesis, University of Cambridge, 1987) at 270.

82   James Belich *'I Shall Not Die': Titokowaru's War 1868–1869* (2nd ed, Bridget Williams, Wellington, 2010) at 194–195.

83   The same conditions also applied to the capture of Te Kooti ("Stafford memo to Bowen, 21 May 1869" [1869] I AJHR A1 at 78–79). A similar reward existed for Kereopa Te Rau, though in 1867 an attempt to increase this reward by way of a parliamentary resolution failed (20 August 1867) 1 NZPD 508.

84   Belich *The New Zealand Wars* at 240. See also Belich *'I Shall Not Die'* at 262 and Tony Sole *Ngati Ruanui: A History* (Huia, Wellington, 2005) at 343.

85   In April 1869, Granville also questioned the alleged actions of Native Minister, James Richmond, in creating minimal rewards for the capture of Te Kooti's followers, dead or alive. This allegation turned out to be untrue ("Despatch, Granville to Bowen, 20 April 1869" [1869] I AJHR A1a at 31).

86   Emer de Vattel *The Law of Nations, Or, Principles of the Law of Nature, Applied to the Conduct and*

Affairs of Nations and Sovereigns (1st English edition, translated from original French edition 1758, GG and J Robinson, London, 1797) at 348.

87   James Prendergast "Opinion of the Attorney-General as to the legal status of the Maoris now in arms as regards their rights as 'belligerents', 30 June 1869" [1869] I AJHR A14 at 4.

88   While it is usually applied to twentieth-century conflicts, many historians argue that 'total war' was first demonstrated in the American Civil War (1861–1865).

89   James Prendergast "Opinion of the Attorney-General as to the legal status of the Maoris now in arms as regards their rights as 'belligerents', 30 June 1869" [1869] I AJHR A14 at 3.

90   "Despatch, Granville to Bowen, 4 November 1869" [1870] I AJHR A-1b at 60–61.

91   The New Zealand Government had resisted pronouncing martial law, as Prendergast pointed out, during the 1865 Bay of Plenty trials.

92   James Prendergast "Opinion of the Attorney-General on legal questions raised in Earl Granville's Despatch, September 1870" [1870] I AJHR A23.

93   Ibid.

94   Ibid.

95   (16 June 1869) 5 NZPD 126.

96   Ibid. at 125.

97   *Evening Post* (Wellington, 10 September 1869) at 2.

98   Dom Felice Vaggioli *History of New Zealand and its Inhabitants* translated by John Crockett (University of Otago Press, Dunedin, 2000, first published 1896).

99   Williams at 147.

100 Ibid.

101 James Prendergast "Opinion of the Attorney-General on Indemnity, 29 October 1868" [1870] I AJHR A1 at 11.

102 This debate is comprehensively explored in Kostal.

103 The Waitangi Tribunal's Taranaki Report specifically blamed the Government for starting the Taranaki Wars, including Titotokowaru's campaign (Waitangi Tribunal *The Taranaki Report: Kaupapa Tuatahi* (Wai 143, 1996)).

104 Seventy-eight of these prisoners were from "Titokowaru's party" ("Supreme Court: Criminal Settings – Thursday, Sept. 30" *Wellington Independent* (Wellington, 2 October 1869) at 5), and five were from Te Kooti's forces ("Execution of Hamiora Pera [sic]" *Wellington Independent* (Wellington, 18 November 1869) at 3).

105 For information on similar actions taken during earlier episodes in the New Zealand Wars see LH Barber "The Treatment of Maori Prisoners taken in the New Zealand Wars" [1979] NZLJ 324.

106 Premier William Fox outlined the drafting history of the Bill in the House of Representatives on 17 August 1869 (6 NZPD 483). The original bill was drafted by Prendergast and focused on the creation of courts-martial. When Fox took power in mid-1869 Prendergast was instructed to revise the bill. The Legislative Council then argued for the deletion of the courts-martial clauses. This argument was eventually accepted by the Government.

107 Disturbed Districts Act, ss 22 and 23. See also David Clark and Gerard McCoy *Habeas Corpus: Australia, New Zealand and the South Pacific* (Federation Press, Sydney, 2000).

108 (20 August 1869) 6 NZPD 603.

109 Johnston J's summation to the jury was highly complimentary to all counsel in the trial. Johnston clearly had no empathy for the causes of Te Kooti and Titokowaru, but he made an obvious effort to divide his praise between prosecution and defence ("'Mr Justice Johnston's Charge on the High Treason Cases' – Enclosure in despatch from Bowen to Granville, 28 October 1869" [1870] I AJHR A1 at 51–54).

110 "Supreme Court: Criminal Settings – Thursday, Sept. 30" *Wellington Independent* (Wellington, 2 October 1869) at 5.

111 "Despatch from Bowen to Granville, 28 October 1869" [1870] I AJHR A1 at 49–50.

112 "Trial of the Maori Prisoners", Justice Department Records, NA J1 1873/586, Archives New

Zealand, Wellington.

113 Waitangi Tribunal *Turanga Tangata Turanga Whenua: The Report on the Turanganui a Kiwa Claims* (Wai 814, 2004).

114 Ibid. at 623.

115 Maurice Shadbolt *Season of the Jew* (Hodder and Stoughton, Kent, 1986); Witi Ihimaera *The Matriarch* (Heinemann, Auckland, 1986). Shadbolt's fictional accounts of Te Kooti and Titokowaru are critiqued in Ralph Crane "Tickling History: Maurice Shadbolt and the New Zealand Wars" (1991) 9 Journal of New Zealand Literature 59.

116 Shadbolt at 441.

117 Shadbolt at 448.

118 Shadbolt at 459.

119 Shadbolt at 464.

120 Ibid; Waitangi Tribunal *Turanga Tangata Turanga Whenua*; CAL Treadwell "The Trial of Hamiora Pere" (1934) 9(4) NZ Railways Magazine; Rosemary Lyon "A Casualty of Conflict" in Ray Knox (ed) *New Zealand's Heritage: The Making of a Nation* (Hamlyn House, Wellington, 1971) vol. 8.

121 The Waitangi Tribunal also reached this conclusion in the *Turanga Tangata Turanga Whenua* Report. In assessing the Government's response it should be noted that Te Kooti also carried out a massacre at Mohaka in April 1869 leaving approximately 60 Maori and 7 Europeans dead (Waitangi Tribunal *Mohaka ki Ahuriri Report* (Wai 201, 2004) at 415).

122 "Supreme Court: Criminal Settings – Monday, Sept. 27" *Wellington Independent* (Wellington, 28 September 1869) at 3.

123 "Supreme Court: Criminal Settings – Thursday, Sept. 28" *Wellington Independent* (Wellington, 30 September 1869) at 3.

124 In "Despatch, Bowen to Granville, 24 November 1869" [1870] I AJHR A1 at 54–57.

125 Giselle Byrnes *The Waitangi Tribunal and New Zealand History* (Oxford University Press, Auckland, 2004) at 122.

126 "Opinion of the Attorney-General on Imperial Legislation" [1867] I AJHR A1a at 84.

127 James Prendergast "Opinion of the Attorney-General on the Vice-Admiralty Courts" [1867] I AJHR A1a at 80.

128 James Prendergast "Opinion of the Attorney-General on the Dunedin Disputed Land Reserves" [1868] I AJHR F4 at 14–15.

129 *R v Macandrew* (1869) 1 CA 172.

130 Williams at 159–160.

131 James Prendergast "Opinion of the Attorney-General on the Appointment of Members of the Legislative Council" [1868] I AJHR D6 at 3–5.

132 James Belich *Making Peoples: A History of the New Zealanders from Polynesian Settlement to the End of the Nineteenth Century* (Penguin, Auckland, 1996).

133 James Prendergast "Opinion of the Attorney-General on the Validity of Provincial Ordinances" [1871] I AJHR at A7.

134 Iain Gallaway "Otago" in Cooke (ed) at 332.

135 Gallaway at 332.

136 James Prendergast "Opinion of the Attorney-General on the *R v Barton* affair, 3 April 1871" [1871] I AJHR A1 at 91–92.

137 Guy H Scholefield and E Schwabe (eds) *Who's Who in New Zealand and the Western Pacific, 1908* (Gordon & Gotch, Wellington, 1908) at 139.

138 James Prendergast "Opinion of the Attorney-General on the Power of the University of Otago to Confer Degrees" [1872] I AJHR G45.

139 Appointment, James Prendergast Papers, MS-Papers 730.

140 Legal Opinion by James Prendergast for Walter Lawry Buller, 15 June 1869, Buller Papers, Micro-MS-Coll-0048, Alexander Turnbull Library, Wellington.

141 Justice Department Records, Archives New Zealand.

142 *R v Thomas Kelly and Richard Burgess* [1862] NZLostC 84 (21 May 1862).

143 Letter from James Prendergast, Dunedin, Justice Department Records, J1 66/2678.

144 Sherwood Young *Guilty on the Gallows: Famous Capital Crimes of New Zealand* (Grantham House, Wellington, 1998) at 47.

145 David W McIntyre and WJ Gardner (eds) *Speeches and Documents on New Zealand History* (Clarendon Press, Oxford, 1971) at 74.

146 Justice Department Records.

147 James Prendergast "Opinion of the Attorney-General on the Wanganui Bridge Tolls" [1872] I AJHR G19 at 6.

148 *"Attorney-General v Bunny"* [1874] I AJHR A4.

149 "Opinion of the Attorney-General on the Power of the General Assembly to abolish Provinces" [1875] I AJHR A8.

150 Ibid.

151 The New Zealand Lost Cases Project (which relies heavily on newspaper reports) is also very helpful up until 1869, the end date of the project.

152 These figures were obtained from the *Evening Post* (Wellington Supreme Court), Johnston's Court of Appeal reports (Court of Appeal), and the New Zealand Lost Cases Project database (Dunedin Supreme Court).

153 March 1874, SC, and June 1874, CA.

154 May 1872, CA.

155 *R v William Larkin and John Manning and others* [1868] NZLostC 121 (18 May 1868).

156 Ibid.

157 Neil Vaney "Manning, John" (30 October 2012) Te Ara: The Encyclopedia of New Zealand <www.teara.govt.nz>; David McGill *The Lion and the Wolfhound* (Grantham House, Wellington, 1990).

158 In his entertaining book on the controversy, McGill disagrees in respect of Richmond, arguing that he was openly anti-Home Rule and effectively ended up prosecuting the case (McGill, chapters 10–12).

159 Leases and Sales of Settled Estates Act 1865, s3.

160 Parliamentary Counsel Office website, <www.pco.parliament.govt.nz>.

161 Immigration and Public Works Loan Act 1873.

162 Gisborne at 221.

163 GH Scholefield (ed) *A Dictionary of New Zealand Biography* (Department of Internal Affairs, Wellington, 1940) at 184.

164 *Journals of the Legislative Council.*

165 JB Ringer *An Introduction to New Zealand Government* (Hazard Press, Christchurch, 1991) at 180.

166 *Evening Post* (Wellington, 11 February 1868) at 2.

167 J Millen *The Story of Bell Gully Buddle Weir, 1840–1990* (Bell Gully, Wellington, 1990) at 53.

168 *Wellington Independent* (Wellington, 1 November 1872) at 2.

169 Millen at 57.

170 Millen at 56.

171 "City Election: Mr. Travers for Wellington" *Evening Post* (Wellington, 27 January 1871) at 2.

172 For a brief time New Zealand adopted the British approach of a political Solicitor-General. JH Harris was a member of Stafford's Ministry in this capacity from 1867 to 1868 (see John McGrath "Principles for Sharing Law Officer Power: The Role of the New Zealand Solicitor-General" (1998) 18 NZULR 197).

173 Anonymous letter to the editor, *Evening Post* (Wellington, 1 June 1875) at 2.

174 PA Cornford "Crown Law Office – Early History" (1964) 18 NZLJ 423 at 424.

175 *Journals of the Legislative Council*, 1865.

176 *Journals of the Legislative Council*, 1866.

177 Jeremy Finn "Development of the Law in New Zealand" in Spiller, Finn and Boast (eds) *A New Zealand Legal History* at 103.

178 Long Title, Criminal Law Procedure Act 1866.
179 Finn at 103.
180 Finn at 110.
181 Gisborne at 221.
182 Peter Spiller *Butterworths New Zealand Law Dictionary* (4th ed, Butterworths, Wellington, 1995) at 298.
183 Preamble to the Act.
184 Immigration and Public Works Amendment Act 1871 and Immigration and Public Works Act 1872.
185 Donald McLean to James Prendergast, August 1868, McLean Papers, MS-Papers 0032, Alexander Turnbull Library, Wellington.
186 Letter, Thomas Jeffrey to James Prendergast, 22 November 1869, D.O.W. Hall, MS-Papers 986, Hocken Library, Dunedin.
187 Letter, Thomas Jeffrey to James Prendergast, 17 February 1866, D.O.W. Hall, MS-Papers 986.
188 Letter, Charles Manning junior to James Prendergast, 21 October 1875, D.O.W. Hall, MS-Papers 986, Hocken Library, Dunedin.
189 Letter, Charles Manning junior to James Prendergast, 17 January 1867, D.O.W. Hall, MS-Papers 986.
190 Letter, Thomas Jeffrey to James Prendergast, 22 November 1869, D.O.W. Hall, MS-Papers 986.
191 Letter, Charles Manning to James Prendergast, 1 May 1872, D.O.W. Hall, MS-Papers 986.
192 Letter, Charles Manning junior to James Prendergast, 7 January 1874, D.O.W. Hall, MS-Papers 986.
193 Letter, Charles Manning junior to James Prendergast, 24 December 1874, D.O.W. Hall, MS-Papers 986.
194 *Evening Post* (Wellington, 3 August 1872) at 2.

Chapter 6. Chief Justice Prendergast

1 The Wellington Supreme Court judgments analysed in the New Zealand Law Reports featured Prendergast: sitting alone (71 per cent); sitting with Richmond, Prendergast delivering (13 per cent); sitting with Richmond, both delivering (7 per cent); sitting with Richmond, Richmond delivering (5 per cent); other (4 per cent).
2 GH Scholefield (ed) *A Dictionary of New Zealand Biography* (Department of Internal Affairs, Wellington, 1940) at 439.
3 Ibid.
4 Johnston J to the Colonial Secretary "Changes in Distribution of Judges of Supreme Court" [1875] I AJHR H28 at 2.
5 Henry Hall, Wellington, to James Prendergast, Britain, 28 May 1884, D.O.W. Hall Papers, MS-Papers 986, Hocken Library, Wellington.
6 Diary, Charles Prendergast Knight, 1895, Prendergast Papers, MS-Papers 1791, Alexander Turnbull Library, Wellington.
7 "Changes in Distribution of Judges of Supreme Court" [1875] I AJHR H28.
8 Hugh Rennie "Thomas Bannatyne Gillies" in WH Oliver and Claudia Orange (eds) *The Dictionary of New Zealand Biography 1769–1869* (Allen & Unwin/Department of Internal Affairs, Wellington, 1990) vol. 1 at 149.
9 Seen in his *Mangakahia v New Zealand Timber Company* (1881) 2 NZLR (SC) 345 judgment in which Gillies states that the Treaty of Waitangi is "no such 'simple nullity', as it is termed in *Wi Parata*."
10 "Changes in Distribution of Judges of Supreme Court" [1875] I AJHR H28.
11 "The Retiring Chief Justice" *New Zealand Mail* (New Zealand, 1 June 1899) at 41.
12 Judith Bassett "Joshua Strange Williams" in Oliver and Orange (eds) at 580.
13 "A Legal Ceremony" *New Zealand Mail* (New Zealand, 12 October 1899) at 36.

14   Judith Bassett "Edward Conolly" in Claudia Orange (ed) *The Dictionary of New Zealand Biography: 1870–1900* (Bridget Williams Books/Department of Internal Affairs, 1993) vol. 2 at 97.

15   Scholefield (ed) at 201.

16   Bernard Brown "Worley Bassett Edwards" in Claudia Orange (ed) *The Dictionary of New Zealand Biography: 1901–1920* (Auckland University Press, Auckland, 1996) vol. 3 at 146.

17   GP Barton "William Martin" in Oliver and Orange (eds) at 277.

18   Scholefield (ed) at 19.

19   David Hamer "Robert Stout" in Orange (ed) *The Dictionary of New Zealand Biography* vol. 2 at 486.

20   "Changes in Distribution of Judges of Supreme Court" [1875] I AJHR H28 at 5.

21   Rennie at 149.

22   Daniel Pollen "Changes in Distribution of Judges of Supreme Court: The Hon the Colonial Secretary to His Honour Chief Justice Prendergast" [1875] I AJHR H28 at 7.

23   Waldo Hilary Dunn and Ivor LM Richardson *Sir Robert Stout: A Biography* (AH & AW Reed, Wellington, 1961) at 162.

24   Departmental Indexes, 1875–1899, Justice Department Records, National Archives, Wellington.

25   "The Retiring Chief Justice" *New Zealand Mail* (New Zealand, 1 June 1899) at 41.

26   William Gisborne *New Zealand Rulers and Statesmen from 1840 to 1897* revised and enlarged edition (Sampson Low, London, 1897) at 221.

27   *New Zealand Times* (New Zealand, 4 March 1921).

28   Ibid.

29   *New Zealand Free Lance* (Wellington, 13 April 1907).

30   *New Zealand Free Lance* (Wellington, 2 March 1921).

31   Hamer at 486.

32   "The Retiring Chief Justice" *New Zealand Mail* (New Zealand, 1 June 1899) at 41.

33   Ronald Jones "James Prendergast" in AH McLintock (ed) *An Encyclopedia of New Zealand* (RE Owen, Wellington, 1966) vol. 1 at 862.

34   JF Jeffries "Sir James Prendergast" in Robin Cooke (ed) *Portrait of a Profession: The Centennial Book of the New Zealand Law Society* (Reed, Wellington, 1969) at 44.

35   *New Zealand Times* (New Zealand, 4 March 1921).

36   See note 1. The Court of Appeal judgments analysed in the New Zealand Law Reports featured Prendergast: sitting, all judges delivering (49 per cent); sitting, and delivering for the court (29 per cent); sitting, and not delivering (22 per cent).

37   Survey from Peter Spiller, Jeremy Finn and Richard Boast (eds) *A New Zealand Legal History* (Brookers, Wellington, 1995) at 255–256.

38   *R v Potter* at 92.

39   *R v Potter* at 96.

40   *R v Te Kira* at 267.

41   *R v Rogers* at 168.

42   *Nankivell* at 61.

43   In *Auckland Regional Council v Holmes Logging Limited and Holmes* HC Auckland CIV-2009-404-35, 17 June 2010 at [101], Prendergast's *Nankivell* decision is mentioned within a quotation from Fisher J's decision.

44   *McKenzie* at 238.

45   Ibid.

46   *Picturesque Atlas Publishing Company* at 352.

47   *Picturesque Atlas Publishing Company* at 350.

48   *Young* at 86.

49   Twenty-three per cent of all Prendergast's cases published in the *Evening Post* from 1875 to 1881 were bankruptcy cases.

50   *Re Cairns* at 42.

51   *Re H.* at 241.

52 *Paraone* at 750.

53 *Housing Corporation of New Zealand* at 680.

54 *Re Stewart & Co.* at 748.

55 *Re Stewart & Co.* at 745. The Court of Appeal differed on semble in *Piripiri te Maari v Stewart* (1892) 11 NZLR 205.

56 *Re Mrs Jackson's Claim* at 152–153.

57 *Bradley* at 50.

58 *Merrie* at 127–128.

59 HC Auckland CIV- 2007-404-6806, 20 December 2007.

60 *In re Aldridge* (1893) 15 NZLR 361.

61 *Re Campbell's Application* at 202–203.

62 *Rangimoeke* at 481.

63 *Wellington City Election* at 458.

64 *Wellington City Election* at 462.

65 *Wellington City Election* at 465.

66 *R v Woodgate* (1876) SC, Unreported Judgment, Justice Department Records, NA J1 77/731.

67 CAL Treadwell "Famous New Zealand Trials: The Trial of Tuhiata" (1933) 8 NZ Railways Magazine.

68 "The Child Murder Case" *Wanganui Chronicle* (Wanganui, 1 May 1883) at 2.

69 Ibid.

70 "The Child Murder Case" *Wanganui Chronicle* (Wanganui, 2 May 1883) at 2.

71 "The Late Criminal Session" *Wanganui Herald* (Wanganui, 7 May 1883) at 2.

72 Ibid.

73 "Public Opinion" *Star* (Canterbury, 16 July 1889) at 3.

74 *Timaru Herald* (Timaru, 25 September 1889) at 2.

75 "Suicide of Louis Chemis" *Evening Post* (Wellington, 24 October 1898) at 5.

76 For example, Lynley Hood *Minnie Dean: Her life and crimes* (Penguin, Auckland, 1994).

77 *R v Dean* (1895) 14 NZLR (CA) at 272.

78 Hood at 189.

79 *R v Dean* at 283.

80 *Smith v MacKenzie* (1880–1881) 1 NZLR 1 CA.

81 *The Attorney-General v Mr Justice Edwards* (1891) 9 NZLR 321.

82 *Bell v Finn* (1896) 14 NZLR 447.

83 *The Wellington City Election Petition* (1897) 15 NZLR 454.

84 "Sympathetic Miners" *Thames Advertiser* (Thames, 7 August 1897) at 2.

85 Ibid.

86 "The Retiring Chief Justice" *New Zealand Mail* (New Zealand, 1 June 1899) at 41.

87 *Fanzelow* at 664.

88 *Attorney-General v Edwards* at 359.

89 *Barton* at 48.

90 *Tarry* at 467.

91 *Tarry* at 474.

92 *Tarry* at 475.

93 *Hocking* at 534. In particular, see *Corbett v Social Security Commission* [1962] NZLR 878 (CA).

94 *Bell* at 453.

95 *Robinson and Morgan-Coakle v Behan* [1964] NZLR 650, 661–662.

96 Peter Spiller *The Chapman Legal Family* (Victoria University Press, Wellington, 1992) at 98.

97 "So what was rule 28 [of the 1844 Rules] intended to do? It seems that it did two things: first, it radically modified some aspects of English common law procedure – in particular the abolition of most of English special pleading . . ." in Shaunnagh Dorsett "Reforming Equity: New Zealand 1843–56" (2013) 34 JLH 285 at 292.

98 *R v Hall* (1887) 5 NZLR 93 (CA), NB. Johnston J delivered the Court of Appeal's judgment.

99   *R v Hall* at 102.

100   Hood at 188.

101   Hood at 189.

102   *Jenkins* at 125. See also Municipal Corporations Act 1886, s 227: "Every person having any estate or interest in any land or buildings so taken, or suffering any damage by the exercise of powers hereby given, shall be entitled to full compensation."

103   *Arihi* at 415.

104   *R v Vowles* at 112.

105   *Piripi Te Maari* at 209.

106   *Doyle* at 573–574.

107   *Lower Hutt City* at 77–78.

108   *Victory Park Board* at 746.

109   *Olsen* at 715.

110   *Russell (No.2)* at 788.

111   *Coomber* at 685.

112   *Blaymires* at 570.

113   *Rural Banking and Finance Corporation of New Zealand Ltd* at 355.

114   *Low* at 58.

115   *Re Proudfoot* at 284.

116   [1960] NZLR 577.

117   *Rira Peti* at 235.

118   *Rira Peti* at 239.

119   Paul McHugh *The Maori Magna Carta: New Zealand Law and the Treaty of Waitangi* (Oxford University Press, Auckland, 1991) at 95.

120   Nan Seuffert "Shaping the Modern Nation: Colonial Marriage Law, Polygamy and Concubinage in Aotearoa New Zealand" (2003) 7 Law Text Culture 186 at 198.

121   Seuffert at 195.

122   "Obituary" *Dominion* (Wellington, 28 February 1921) at 4.

123   *Broughton v Donnelly* (1888) 7 NZLR 288 (CA) 295.

124   *Re McGregor* at 243.

125   *Jull* at 516.

126   *Jull* at 517.

127   "Reid's Case" *Evening Post* (Wellington, 6 April 1876) at 2.

128   For example, the claim made in the *New Zealand Free Lance* (Wellington, 2 March 1921) at 32.

129   *New Zealand Law Reports*, vol. 14.

130   "The Chief Justice's New Examination Papers" in James Macassey (ed) *Colonial Law Journal* (Henry Wise, Dunedin, 1875) at 34.

131   Ibid. at 34–35.

132   Guy H Scholefield (ed) *The Richmond-Atkinson Papers* (RE Owen, Wellington, 1960) vol. 2 at 432.

133   "The Chief Justice's New Examination Papers" in Macassey (ed) at 34–35.

134   See John Austin *The Province of Jurisprudence Determined* edited by Wilfrid E Rumble (Cambridge University Press, Cambridge, 1995, first published 1832).

135   See Walter E Houghton *The Victorian Frame of Mind* (Yale University Press, New Haven, 1957).

136   Departmental Indexes, 2 January 1877, Justice Department Records, J1 77/52.

137   Department Indexes, Justice Department Records. Hall continued to support Prendergast in administration throughout his term as Chief Justice.

138   Department Indexes, Justice Department Records.

139   Prendergast wanted a telephone connection from work to home in 1892.

140   Grand Jurors, Wellington, to Prendergast CJ, July 1877, Justice Department Records, J1 77/2914.

141 Henry Hall to Colonial Architect's Office, 1877, Justice Department Records, J1 77/2914.

142 Grand Jurors, Picton, to Prendergast CJ, July 1875, Justice Department Records, J1 75/1860.

143 Prendergast CJ to Colonial Secretary, 21 June 1875, Justice Department Records, J1 77/1649.

144 Prendergast CJ to Colonial Secretary, 28 June 1877, Justice Department Records, J1 77/2493.

145 Justice Department Records, J1 77/601.

146 "The Retiring Chief Justice" *New Zealand Mail* (New Zealand, 1 June 1899) at 41.

147 Ibid.

148 Brown at 146. While Edwards J was the most controversial during his lifetime, Prendergast CJ would have a claim to be the most controversial from a modern perspective.

149 Ibid.

150 "Papers Relating to the Appointment of Mr. WB Edwards" [1891] I AJHR H13 at 3.

151 James Prendergast "Papers Relating to the Appointment of Mr WB Edwards: His Honour the Chief Justice to His Honour Mr. Justice Denniston" [1891] I AJHR H13 at 4.

152 William Richmond "Papers Relating to the Appointment of Mr. WB Edwards: Mr. Justice Richmond to His Honour the Chief Justice" [1891] I AJHR H13 at 5.

153 Frederick Whitaker "Papers Relating to the Appointment of Mr WB Edwards: The Hon Sir F Whitaker to the Hon the Premier" [1891] I AJHR H13 at 5.

154 James Prendergast "Papers Relating to the Appointment of Mr WB Edwards: His Honour the Chief Justice to the Hon the Premier" [1891] I AJHR H13 at 7.

155 James Prendergast and John Ballance "Papers Relating to the Appointment of Mr WB Edwards" [1891] I AJHR H13 at 14–15.

156 "Papers Relating to the Appointment of Mr WB Edwards" [1891] I AJHR H13 at 18–19.

157 "Letter, Prendergast CJ to John Ballance, 28 February 1891" [1891] I AJHR H13 at 25.

158 "Letter, Prendergast CJ to John Ballance, 10 April 1891" [1891] I AJHR H13 at 30.

159 "Correspondence Relating to the Case of WB Edwards" [1892] I AJHR H28 at 3.

160 James Prendergast "Further Papers Relating to the Appointment of Mr. WB Edwards: Telegram from His Honour the Chief Justice to WB Edwards [1891] I AJHR H13a at 1–2.

161 "Strained Relations, British Resident, Rarotonga: Sir James Prendergast to hold inquiry" [1898] I AJHR A1 at 10.

162 Rarotonga had been a protectorate since 1890, the same year Moss was appointed.

163 James Prendergast "Cook Islands: Correspondence Relating to Requests for Removal of FJ Moss" [1898] I AJHR A3 at 15.

164 James Prendergast "His Honour Sir James Prendergast to his Excellency the Governor, 24 January 1898" [1898] I AJHR A3 at 16.

165 Ibid. at 24–25.

166 Barrie MacDonald "Frederick Moss" in Orange (ed) at 338.

167 James Prendergast "His Honour Sir James Prendergast to His Excellency the Governor, 24 January 1898" [1898] I AJHR A3 at 24.

168 JB Ringer *An Introduction to New Zealand Government* (Hazard Press, Christchurch, 1991) at 317.

169 "Letters Patent, Commission of Inquiry into the Constitution, Practice and Procedure of the Supreme Courts and other Courts" [1880] I AJHR A10 at 1–2.

170 Ibid.

171 Spiller, Finn and Boast (eds) at 194.

172 "Interim Report of the Law Procedure Commission" [1881] I AJHR A6 at 5.

173 "Final Report of the Commission of Inquiry into the Constitution, Practice and Procedure of the Supreme Court and other Courts" [1882] I AJHR A3 at 4.

174 *New Zealand Free Lance* (Wellington, 13 March 1907).

175 *Thames Observer* (Thames, 4 July 1896) at 18.

176 Diaries, Charles Prendergast Knight, 1890s, Prendergast Papers, MS-Papers 1791, Alexander Turnbull Library, Wellington.

177 "To help the boys" *Evening Post* (Wellington, 3 July 1896) at 4.

178 "Cathedral Fund" *Evening Post* (Wellington, 22 February 1896) at 2.

179 "St John's Presbyterian Church" *Evening Post* (Wellington, 15 May 1885) at 2.

180 Henry Hall, Wellington, to James Prendergast, Britain, 1 March 1884, D.O.W. Hall Papers, MS-Papers 986.

181 'Rads' being political 'radicals' such as George Grey; Henry Hall, Wellington, to James Prendergast, Britain, 20 June 1884, D.O.W. Hall Papers, MS-Papers 986.

182 Henry Hall, Wellington, to James Prendergast, Britain, 18 November 1884, D.O.W. Hall Papers, MS-Papers 986.

183 Charles Manning, Dublin, to James Prendergast, Wellington, 16 February 1886, D.O.W. Hall Papers, MS-Papers 986.

184 Henry Hall, Wellington, to James Prendergast, Britain, 24 November 1884, D.O.W. Hall Papers, MS-Papers 986.

185 Marchant, Purvis and Benwell (law firm), London, to James Prendergast, Wellington, 15 June 1883, D.O.W. Hall Papers, MS-Papers 986.

186 *Evening Post* (Wellington, 25 May 1899) at 6.

Chapter 7. The Barton affair

1 *Gillon v MacDonald* (1878) 3 NZ Jur (NS) 27 (SC). Much of the reporting of the events in question appears in *The New Zealand Jurist*, which served as both a legal magazine and a law report series during the 1870s.

2 Case details appear in "Otago" *Hawkes Bay Herald* (Napier, 8 November 1864) at 2 and "The Libel Case" *Otago Witness* (Dunedin, 5 November 1864) at 11 and (12 November 1864) at 7.

3 *Re GE Barton* (1876) 2 NZ Jur (NS) 13 (SC) at 14 (in relation to the first contempt charge).

4 *Re GE Barton* (1876) 1 NZ Jur (NS) 109 (SC) at 110 (earlier hearing).

5 James' references to the Irish in Victoria are more oblique, for example, he mentions a "mean little Irish Barrister appointed Police Magistrate and altogether unfit for his place". James Prendergast, "Letter sent from Melbourne to his father in London", Alexander Turnbull Library, Wellington, MS-Papers 1791, 28 October 1854.

6 "Mr GE Barton's Petition" (1877) 2 NZ Jur (NS) 163 at 166.

7 Robin Cooke "Wellington" in Robin Cooke (ed) *Portrait of a Profession: The Centennial Book of the New Zealand Law Society* (AH & AW Reed, Wellington, 1969) at 395.

8 Barton's movements between 1874 and 1876 are unclear.

9 "Brief Biography of George E Barton", Alexander Turnbull Library (ATL), Wellington, MS-Papers-0212-C/04 (Guy Scholefield's letters relating to the *Dictionary of New Zealand Biography*). There is no stated author for this document but it appears to be written by one of Barton's sons for the purposes of the dictionary.

10 *Re GE Barton* (1876) 1 NZ Jur (NS) 109 at 110.

11 *New Zealand Times* (Wellington, 4 March 1921).

12 "Supreme Court This Day" *Evening Post* (Wellington, 10 October 1876) at 2. Barton refers to the defendant as Jacob Pune.

13 *Re GE Barton* (1876) 2 NZ Jur (NS) 13 (SC) at 13–14.

14 Ibid. at 13.

15 Ibid. at 17–18.

16 The key cases cited by Barton are; *Corporation of Wellington v CW Schultze, Gillon v MacDonald, Peters v Joseph, Pole v Tonks, Leach v Johnston, Doherty v Education Board,* and *Buckridge v Wardell*: "Mr Barton's Charges Against Judges of the Supreme Court" [1879] AJHR A4 at 2. Details of all the cases are included in the AJHR document, while reported judgments can be found for some of the cases: *Gillon v MacDonald* (1878) 3 NZ Jur (NS) 27 (SC); *Peters v Joseph* (1878) 3 NZ Jur (NS) 142; *Pole v Tonks (reported as Poll, ex parte, in re Tonks)* (1877) 3 NZ Jur (NS) 1; *Doherty v Education Board* (1878) 4 NZ Jur (NS) 78.

17 "Petition from Barton to the Colonial Secretary, 22 August 1877" Archives New Zealand, Wellington, [ANZ] J1 1877/3334; "Mr GE Barton's Petition" (1877) 2 NZ Jur (NS) 163.

18 This principle is now enshrined in the Constitution Act 1986, ss 23–24. The 1986 Act stipulates that dismissal can only occur on grounds of misbehaviour or incapacity. This Act repealed s 7 of the Judicature Act 1908 which used the term "good behaviour". The process for dismissal is instigated by the executive and in our present system by the Attorney-General (Judicial Conduct Commissioner and Judicial Conduct Panel Act 2004). The House of Representatives makes the final decision but has never dismissed a judge in New Zealand's history. In 1877 the prevailing statute was the Supreme Court Act 1862, which repealed ss 3 and 4 of the Supreme Court Judges Act 1858. Under the 1862 Act, judges continued in office during good behaviour, with provision for the Queen to remove a judge upon the address of both Houses of Parliament.

19 See for example reports in: the *Evening Post* (Wellington, 10, 21 and 23 August 1877); the *West Coast Times* (West Coast, 15, 18 and 30 August 1877); and the *Grey River Argus* (Greymouth, 15, 18 and 30 August 1877).

20 "Mr GE Barton's Petition" (1877) 2 NZ Jur (NS) 163 at 166.

21 "Mr Barton, Solicitor" *West Coast Times* (West Coast, 18 August 1877) at 2.

22 Untitled (1877) 2 NZ Jur (NS) 195.

23 "Prendergast's reply to Barton's claims, 27 August 1877" Justice Department Records, J1 77/3361, ANZ.

24 "Judge to challenge conduct panel move" *The Dominion Post* (Wellington, 1 June 2010) at A5.

25 "Mr GE Barton's Petition" (1877) 2 NZ Jur (NS) 184 at 184.

26 Ibid. at 188.

27 (29 August 1877) 25 NZPD 99–101.

28 (30 August 1877) 25 NZPD 133–139.

29 "Supreme Court This Day" *Evening Post* (Wellington, 15 January 1878) at 2.

30 Ibid.

31 "Wellington" *North Otago Times* (Oamaru, 17 January 1878) at 2.

32 "Journalistic Fracas" *Thames Star* (Thames, 19 January 1878) at 2.

33 *Gillon v MacDonald* at 28.

34 "Letter from William Richmond to the Colonial Secretary regarding Barton's complaints, 3 October 1878" [1878] AJHR A6.

35 *Gillon v MacDonald* at 27.

36 Ibid. at 28.

37 *Spence v Pearson* (1878) 3 NZ Jur (NS) 25 (CA) at 26.

38 Ibid.

39 "Contempt of Court" (1878) 3 NZ Jur (NS) 16 at 16–18.

40 *Smith v The Justices of Sierra Leone* (1841) 3 Moo 361 (PC); *Smith v The Justices of Sierra Leone* (1848) 7 Moo 174 (PC); *Rainy v The Justices of Sierra Leone* (1852) 8 Moo 47 (PC); *Ex parte Pater* (1864) 5 B & S 299; *Re Pollard and the Chief Justice of Hong Kong* (1868) 2 LR 106 (PC).

41 "Contempt of Court" at 17.

42 Case referred to in "Contempt of Court" (1878) 3 NZ Jur (NS) 39 at 40.

43 "More Contempt" (1877) 2 NZ Jur (NS) 193 at 194.

44 *Re GE Barton* (1876) 2 NZ Jur (NS) 13 at 16 (SC).

45 During the parliamentary debates relating to the 1878 Judicial Commission Bill, several Members of Parliament referred to the unique nature of the penalty, and in particular, the length of the prison sentence. See for example: Frederick Moss (30 September 1878) 29 NZPD 429.

46 *Re Pollard and the Chief Justice of Hong Kong* (1868) 2 LR 106 (PC).

47 Recent textbooks provide a much superior summary of the law than contemporary textbooks and often provide historical context. Of the contemporary textbooks, the following confirm the legality of Prendergast's actions, though they are not particularly helpful in deciding whether his ruling could be seen as unreasonable in the circumstances: Henry John Stephen *New Commentaries on the Laws of England (partly founded on Blackstone)* (5th ed, Butterworths, London, 1863); Charles Johnston Edwards *The Law of Execution upon Judgments and Orders of the Chancery and Queen's Bench divisions of the High Court of Justice* (Stevens and Sons, London,

1888); Matthew Bacon *A New Abridgment of the Law* (T & JW Johnson, Philadelphia, 1876); James Paterson *Commentaries on the liberty of the subject and the laws of England relating to the security of the person* (MacMillan, London, 1877); Charles Greenstreet Addison *Wrongs and their remedies: being a treatise on the law of torts* (5th ed, Stevens and Sons, London, 1879); Henry Coleman Folkard *The Law of Slander and Libel: Founded upon the Treatise of the late Mr. Starkie* (4th ed, Butterworths, London, 1876). Folkard's summary is the most useful in this case.

48   Gordon Borrie and Nigel Lowe *Borrie and Lowe's Law of Contempt* (2nd ed, Butterworths, London, 1983) at 321.

49   David Eady and ATH Smith *Arlidge, Eady and Smith on Contempt* (3rd ed, Sweet and Maxwell, London, 2005) at 702.

50   "Contempt of Court" at 18.

51   Borrie and Lowe at 30 referring to Peter Butt "Contempt of Court in the legal profession" [1978] Crim LR 463 at 467.

52   Robert Stout was the Attorney-General under the Grey Ministry, which lasted from 13 October 1877 to 8 October 1879. Frederick Whitaker was Attorney-General under the Atkinson Ministry which preceded it. Therefore Whitaker was Attorney-General during the first set of parliamentary debates relating to the feud while Stout was Attorney-General during the second set.

53   (30 September 1878) 29 NZPD 419.

54   No specific references are provided in the parliamentary debates, but Stout could have been referring to the texts by Henry John Stephen (based on Blackstone) and Henry Coleman Folkard (Starkie). Blackstone's original text contains limited information on contempt.

55   Including *Carus Wilson's case* (1845) 115 ER 759 (QB); *Ex parte Fernandez* (1861) 142 ER 349.

56   (30 September 1878) 29 NZPD 439.

57   Whitaker argued that there were a number of examples of English lawyers being punished for contempt and that he had observed committals for contempt. It is important to note that he did not provide a specific example of where a *lawyer* has been *committed* for contempt. (30 September 1878) 29 NZPD 440.

58   *Re George Elliot Barton* (1878) 3 NZ Jur (NS) 67 (SC).

59   *New Zealand Mail* (Wellington, 29 June 1878) at 9–10.

60   "Contempt of Court" (1878) 3 NZ Jur (NS) 16 at 16–18.

61   Ibid. at 17.

62   "The case of Mr Barton" *Evening Post* (Wellington, 19 February 1878) at 2.

63   "The Nomination" *Evening Post* (Wellington, 16 February 1878) at 2.

64   "Supreme Court Sittings in Banco This Day" *Evening Post* (Wellington, 9 April 1878) at 2.

65   "Supreme Court Sittings in Banco This Day" *Evening Post* (Wellington, 12 April 1878) at 2.

66   Ibid.

67   *Gillon v MacDonald* (1878) 3 NZ Jur (NS) 137 (SC).

68   "Supreme Court Sittings in Banco This Day" *Evening Post* (Wellington, 21 August 1878) at 2.

69   "Wellington This Day" *Thames Star* (Thames, 20 August 1878) at 2.

70   "Letter from Barton to Whitmore, 16 December 1878" [1879] AJHR A4 at 32.

71   "Mr Barton and the Judges" *New Zealand Mail* (Wellington, 29 June 1878) at 9–10.

72   "Mr Barton and the Judges" *Timaru Herald* (Timaru, 5 November 1878) at 8. Also found in (18 October 1878) 30 NZPD 914–921.

73   "Letter from William Richmond to the Colonial Secretary regarding Barton's complaints, 3 October 1878" [1878] AJHR A6; *New Zealand Mail* (Wellington, 12 October 1878) at 12–13.

74   "Letter from William Richmond to the Colonial Secretary regarding Barton's complaints, 3 October 1878" [1878] AJHR A6.

75   Ibid.

76   Ibid.

77   "Mr GE Barton's Case" (1878) 3 NZ Jur (NS) 139 at 139. Also found in (18 October 1878) 30 NZPD 918. The judges' notebooks of Richmond and Prendergast are located in Archives New

Zealand and contain references to a number of the cases mentioned in this article, including *Gillon v MacDonald*. The *Gillon* references do not include further important details, that is, they reflect what can be found in the case reports.

78 A good discussion of this Bill is found in "Mr Barton and the Judges" *Timaru Herald* (Timaru, 5 November 1878) at 8. The introduction of the Bill is found in (12 September 1878) 29 NZPD 135.

79 Judicial Commission Bill as found in (1878) 3 NZ Jur (NS) 112.

80 "Parliament: House of Representatives: Yesterday" *Evening Post* (Wellington, 1 October 1878) at 2.

81 Ibid.

82 For the most part, newspaper editorial comment relating to the feud was restrained and often descriptive but, as demonstrated in "Mr Barton and the Judges" *Timaru Herald* (Timaru, 5 November 1878) at 8, editorial support for Barton had begun to wane by the later stages of the saga, "It surely will never be permitted that a member of Parliament shall slander the highest judicial officers in the country with impunity. Every consideration of justice and expediency alike demands that, as, if the charges are proved, the Judges must quit the Bench, so, if they are not proved, Mr Barton must quit both the House and the Bar."

83 (18 October 1878) 30 NZPD 921–928.

84 "Letter from Barton to Whitmore, 26 October 1878" [1879] AJHR A4 at 1.

85 "Letter from Whitmore to Barton, 29 October 1878" [1879] AJHR A4 at 1.

86 "Letter from Barton to Whitmore, 5 November 1878" [1879] AJHR A4 at 2; "Letter from Whitmore to Barton, 12 December 1878" [1879] AJHR A4 at 6.

87 "Letter from Barton to Whitmore, 16 December 1878" [1879] AJHR A4 at 33.

88 "Letter from Whitmore to Barton, 20 December 1878" [1879] AJHR A4 at 34.

89 "Letter from Barton to Whitmore, 16 December 1878" [1879] AJHR A4 at 32. As mentioned above, Stout voted against the Judicial Commission Bill. Grey voted for the Bill and launched a vociferous defence of Barton during the parliamentary debates. (1 October 1878) 29 NZPD 458.

90 "Barton, George Elliott" in GH Scholefield (ed) *Dictionary of New Zealand Biography* (Department of Internal Affairs, Wellington, 1940) at 46.

91 "Judge to challenge conduct panel move" *Dominion Post* (Wellington, 1 June 2010) at A5 and "Top Judge quits with a year's pay plus costs" *Dominion Post* (Wellington, 22 October 2010) at A5. The alleged misconduct revolved around whether Justice Wilson properly disclosed information about this relationship. Justice Wilson's argument – that the process should cease because the alleged misconduct could not justify removal even if proved – echoes Prendergast's argument in his letter to the Colonial Secretary, "Prendergast's reply to Barton's claims, 27 August 1877".

92 Janet November *In the footsteps of Ethel Benjamin: New Zealand's first woman lawyer* (Victoria University Press, Wellington, 2009).

93 See "Seniority at the bar" (1877) 2 NZ Jur (NS) 89.

94 See for example "Contempt of Court" at 17; "Parliament: House of Representatives: Yesterday" *Evening Post* (Wellington, 1 October 1878) at 2.

95 Williams disagrees with this argument in *A Simple Nullity: The Wi Parata case in New Zealand law & history* (Auckland University Press, Auckland, 2011) at 154–159.

96 (30 September 1878) 29 NZPD 431.

Chapter 8. The Treaty is a simple nullity

1 (1877) 3 NZ Jur (NS) 72 (SC).

2 George Grey, Governor of New Zealand, Crown Grant of Porirua land to George Augustus Selwyn, Bishop of New Zealand, 28 December 1850, MS-Papers-5449-2 *Wi Parata versus the Bishop of Wellington, and others* – Papers [1898–1905] found under Church of the Province of New Zealand, Wellington Diocese: Further records (89–008), Alexander Turnbull Library, Wellington.

3   *Wi Parata* at 72.

4   Frederika Hackshaw "Nineteenth Century Notions of Aboriginal Title and their Influence on the Interpretation of the Treaty of Waitangi" in IH Kawharu (ed) *Waitangi: Maori and Pakeha Perspectives of the Treaty of Waitangi* (Oxford University Press, Auckland, 1989) at 110.

5   *Wi Parata* at 72–73.

6   Grant Morris "James Prendergast and the Treaty of Waitangi: Judicial Attitudes to the Treaty During the Latter Half of the Nineteenth Century" (2004) 35 VUWLR 117.

7   See principally early New Zealand historians such as Saunders, Rusden and Miller, but also contemporaries such as William Martin and Octavius Hadfield. Richmond's critics are answered and his conduct defended in William Downie Stewart *Mr. Justice Richmond and the Taranaki War of 1860: A Great Judge Vindicated* (Whitcombe & Tombs, Wellington, 1945) especially 7–9.

8   Keith Sinclair outlines Richmond's views in WH Oliver and Claudia Orange (eds) *Dictionary of New Zealand Biography 1769–1869* (Allen & Unwin/Department of Internal Affairs, Wellington, 1990) vol. 1 at 364: "Richmond wanted to destroy what he called the 'beastly communism' of Maori society by introducing private property in land . . . . Richmond knew almost nothing about Maori culture or land tenure. He simply believed that it was necessary to 'civilise' the Maori, that is, to lead them to adapt British habits and practices." While Native Minister, Richmond attempted to overthrow Crown pre-emption, thus challenging Article Two of the Treaty.

9   David V Williams *A Simple Nullity? The* Wi Parata *case in New Zealand law and history* (Auckland University Press, Auckland, 2011) at 148.

10   Hohepa Solomon "Wiremu Te Kakakura Parata" in Claudia Orange (ed) *The Dictionary of New Zealand Biography 1870–1900* (Bridget Williams/Department of Internal Affairs, Wellington, 1993) vol. 2 at 375.

11   *Wi Parata* at 72–73.

12   Solomon at 375.

13   Winsome Shepherd "William Thomas Locke Travers" in Oliver and Orange (eds) at 547.

14   Robin Cooke (ed) *Portrait of a Profession: The Centennial Book of the New Zealand Law Society* (Reed, Wellington, 1969) at 146.

15   GH Scholefield (ed) *A Dictionary of New Zealand Biography* (Department of Internal Affairs, Wellington, 1940) at 431.

16   Scholefield (ed) at 431.

17   (1900–01) NZPCC 371.

18   (1902–03) NZPCC 730.

19   Warren E Limbrick "George Augustus Selwyn" in Oliver and Orange (ed) at 388.

20   *Wi Parata* at 78–79.

21   *Wi Parata* at 78.

22   Phrase from James Belich *Making Peoples: A History of the New Zealanders from Polynesian Settlement to the End of the Nineteenth Century* (Penguin, Auckland, 1996).

23   Funds would be applied as near as possible to the application specified by the donor: Peter Spiller *Butterworths New Zealand Law Dictionary* (4th ed, Butterworths, Wellington, 1995) at 80.

24   *Wi Parata* at 83.

25   Loosely translated as 'treasures'.

26   From the Texts of the Treaty of Waitangi (Text in English, Maori and Translation of Maori text by Kawharu) in IH Kawharu (ed) at 316–321.

27   EJ Haughey "A vindication of Sir James Prendergast" (July 1990) NZ Law Journal 230–1.

28   (1847) NZPCC 387 per Chapman J.

29   *Wi Parata* at 78.

30   *Wi Parata* at 80.

31   Peter Spiller "Chapman J and the *Symonds* Case" (1990) 4 Canterbury L Rev 257 at 264.

32   *Wi Parata* at 77.

33   *Wi Parata* at 79.

34   *Nireaha Tamaki v Baker* at 382.

35   Williams at 171.

36   21 US (8 Wheat) 543, 5 L Ed 681 (1823) per Marshall CJ.

37   5 Peters, US Rep 1 (1831) per Marshall CJ.

38   (1847) NZPCC 387.

39   *Wi Parata* at 76–77.

40   *Wi Parata* at 78.

41   *Wi Parata* at 79.

42   *Wi Parata* at 77.

43   *Wi Parata* at 78.

44   *Wi Parata* at 82.

45   Paul McHugh "The Aboriginal Rights of the New Zealand Maori at Common Law" (PhD
      Thesis, University of Cambridge, 1987) at 271.

46   Guy Chapman "The Treaty of Waitangi – Fertile Ground for Judicial (and Academic) Myth-
      Making" (July 1991) NZLJ 228 at 231.

47   Williams at 3–4.

48   See Williams.

49   Most comprehensively in PG McHugh *Aboriginal Societies and the Common Law: A History of
      Sovereignty, Status, and Self-Determination* (Oxford University Press, Oxford, 2004) and PG
      McHugh *Aboriginal Title: The Modern Jurisprudence of Tribal Land Rights* (Oxford University
      Press, Oxford, 2011).

50   Mark Hickford *Lords of the Land: Indigenous Property Rights and the Jurisprudence of Empire*
      (Oxford University Press, Oxford, 2011).

51   Haughey at 231.

52   *Re the Bed of the Wanganui River* [1962] NZLR 600.

53   *Re Ninety-Mile Beach* [1963] NZLR 461.

54   *Nireaha Tamaki* at 382.

55   *Nireaha Tamaki* at 383–384.

56   (1901) 19 NZLR 665.

57   Protest of Bench and Bar re *Wallis v Solicitor-General*, Appendix (1903) NZPCC 730 at 744.

58   Protest of Bench and Bar re *Wallis* at 756.

59   (1902) 21 NZLR 655.

60   This section legislated that native title could not undermine a Crown grant.

61   [1941] NZLR 590 (PC).

62   [1986] 1 NZLR 680.

63   Paul McHugh "From Sovereignty Talk to Settlement Time" in Paul Havemann (ed) *Indigenous
      Peoples' Rights in Australia, Canada, & New Zealand* (Oxford University Press, Auckland, 1999)
      at 458.

64   Paul McHugh "Constitutional Theory and Maori Claims" in Kawharu (ed) at 51.

65   [1987] 1 NZLR 641.

66   *New Zealand Maori Council* at 667 per Cooke P.

67   *New Zealand Maori Council* at 715 per Bisson J.

68   (1992) 66 Australian Law Journal Reports 408.

69   Waitangi Tribunal *Report of the Waitangi Tribunal on the Orakei Claim* (Wellington, 1987) s 4.6.

70   *Orakei Claim*, s 4.6.

71   *Nireaha Tamaki* at 384.

72   Waitangi Tribunal *Report of the Waitangi Tribunal on the Kaituna River Claim* (Wellington, 1984)
      s 5.6.10.

73   Waitangi Tribunal *Report of the Waitangi Tribunal on the Ngai Tahu Sea Fisheries Claim*
      (Wellington, 1992) s 5.14.

74   Treaty of Waitangi Acts 1975 and 1985.

75   *Ngati Apa and others v Attorney-General and others* [2003] 3 NZLR 643 at 663.

76   Paul McHugh *The Maori Magna Carta: New Zealand Law and the Treaty of Waitangi* (Oxford University Press, Auckland, 1991) at 113–114.

77   PG McHugh "A History of Crown Sovereignty in New Zealand" in Andrew Sharp and Paul McHugh (eds) *Histories, Power and Loss: Uses of the Past – A New Zealand Commentary* (Bridget Williams, Wellington, 2001) at 189–211.

78   See McHugh *Aboriginal Title*.

79   Paul McHugh *Aboriginal Societies and the Common Law: A History of Sovereignty, Status and Self-Determination* (Oxford University Press, Oxford, 2004) at 173.

80   RP Boast "The Law and the Maori" in Peter Spiller, Jeremy Finn and Richard Boast (eds) *A New Zealand Legal History* (Brookers, Wellington, 1995) at 127.

81   Stuart C Scott *The Travesty of Waitangi: Towards Anarchy* (The Campbell Press, Dunedin, 1995) at 25.

82   Walter Christie *New Zealand Education and Treatyism* (Wyvern Press, Auckland, 1999) at 28.

83   Jonathan Lamb "The Idea of Utopia in the European Settlement of New Zealand" in Klaus Neumann, Nicholas Thomas and Hilary Ericksen (eds) *Quicksands: Foundational Histories in Australia & Aotearoa New Zealand* (UNSW Press, Sydney, 1999) at 80.

84   Ranginui Walker *Ka Whawhai Tonu Matou: Struggle Without End* (Penguin Books, Auckland, 1990) at 158.

85   Martin was criticised from some quarters for his support of the Maori cause and emphasis on the importance of the Treaty, as discussed by GP Barton in Oliver and Orange (eds) at 279.

86   See for example, Edmund Bohan *To Be a Hero: Sir George Grey: 1812–1898* (HarperCollins, Auckland, 1998).

87   "Obituary" *Dominion* (Wellington, 28 February 1921) at 4; "Obituary" *Evening Post* (Wellington, 28 February 1921) at 6; "The Retiring Chief Justice" *New Zealand Mail* (New Zealand, 1 June 1899) at 41; "Presentation to Sir James Prendergast" *New Zealand Mail* (New Zealand, 27 January 1883) at 189.

88   Orange at 202; Walker at 158.

89   Michael King *The Penguin History of New Zealand* (Penguin, Auckland, 2003) at 325.

90   Williams at 240.

91   Hone Harawira "Ngapuhi's settlement role critical to future of Treaty" (6 February 2014) *New Zealand Herald* <www.nzherald.co.nz>.

92   Tariana Turia, Speech, "Wiremu Parata Waipunahau" (Wiremu Parata Waipunahau Te Kakakura Exhibition, 2 October 2006).

Chapter 9. Prendergast as 'Acting Governor'

1   "Letters Patent, Instructions, and Commission of His Excellency Sir Hercules Robinson, GCMG" [1879] AJHR A1 at 1–6.

2   William Gisborne *New Zealand Rulers and Statesmen, From 1840 to 1897*, revised and enlarged edition (Sampson Low, London, 1897) at 220.

3   *New Zealand Mail* (New Zealand, 6 February 1907) at 1.

4   Ibid.

5   Ibid.

6   Gavin McLean *The Governors: New Zealand's Governors and Governors-General* (Otago University Press, Dunedin, 2006) at 51.

7   Letter, Governor Ranfurly, Wellington, to Joseph Chamberlain, Secretary of State for the Colonies, London, 7 July 1899, Hocken Library.

8   McLean at 155.

9   McLean at 156.

10   Letter, Governor Gordon to James Prendergast, 23 June 1881, James Prendergast Papers, MS-Papers 730, Hocken Library, Dunedin.

11 Letter, Governor Gordon to James Prendergast, 8 September 1881, James Prendergast Papers, MS-Papers 730.

12 Gordon McLauchlan (ed) *Bateman New Zealand Encyclopedia* (6th ed, Bateman, Auckland, 2005) at 487.

13 Ibid. at 270.

14 Ibid. at 494.

15 Ibid. at 264.

16 Ibid. at 553. Dates from Bryce Fraser (ed) *The New Zealand Book of Events* (Reed Methuen, Auckland, 1986) at 244–245.

17 *New Zealand Times* (New Zealand, 19 January 1883) at 2–3.

18 Diary of Charles Prendergast Knight, 15 February 1892, at 53, James Prendergast Papers, MS-Papers 1791, Alexander Turnbull Library, Wellington.

19 Diary of Charles Prendergast Knight, 17 February 1892, at 55, James Prendergast Papers, MS-Papers 1791.

20 Diary of Charles Prendergast Knight, 13 May 1892, at 102, James Prendergast Papers, MS-Papers 1791.

21 Diary of Charles Prendergast Knight, 24 May 1892, at 103–104, James Prendergast Papers, MS-Papers 1791.

22 Newspaper report in Diary of Charles Prendergast Knight, 24 May 1892, at 104, James Prendergast Papers, MS-Papers 1791.

23 Diary of Charles Prendergast Knight, 19 July 1892, at 118, James Prendergast Papers, MS-Papers 1791.

24 Diary of Charles Prendergast Knight, 8 August 1893, at 8, James Prendergast Papers, MS-Papers 1791.

25 Letter, Governor Ranfurly, Wellington, to Joseph Chamberlain, Secretary of State for the Colonies, London, 7 July 1899, Hocken Library.

26 "The Longhurst Case" *Evening Post* (Wellington, 8 January 1883) at 2.

27 *Evening Post* (Wellington, 21 November 1882) at 2.

28 This is primarily due to the 35-year gap between Parihaka and Maungapohatu. Parihaka occurs relatively soon after Te Kooti's 'truce'. The 1881 date is supported in Peter Adds "Te Muru me te Raupatu" in Kelvin Day (ed) *Contested Ground: Te Whenua I Tohea: The Taranaki Wars 1860–1881* (Huia, Wellington, 2010). At 267, Parihaka is described as "the last armed military engagement in New Zealand".

29 WPN Tyler "Arthur Hamilton Gordon" in WH Oliver and Claudia Orange *The Dictionary of New Zealand Biography 1870–1900* (Department of Internal Affairs/Bridget Williams, Wellington, 1993) vol. 2 at 173.

30 When leaving for Fiji in 1881, Gordon did not even meet with Prendergast: "I am sorry not to have had the pleasure of meeting you before leaving for Fiji, but I do not know that I had anything to say which cannot be said equally well on paper." Letter, Governor Gordon to James Prendergast, 8 September 1881, James Prendergast Papers, MS-Papers 730.

31 Letter, Governor Gordon to James Prendergast, 23 June 1881, James Prendergast Papers, MS-Papers 730.

32 Ibid.

33 Letter, Governor Gordon to James Prendergast, 8 September 1881, James Prendergast Papers, MS-Papers 730.

34 Letter, Governor Gordon to James Prendergast, 13 September 1881, James Prendergast Papers, MS-Papers 730.

35 Letter, Governor Gordon, Fiji, to James Prendergast, Wellington, 7 October 1881, James Prendergast Papers, MS-Papers 730.

36 Letter, Governor Gordon, Wellington, to James Prendergast, 24 October 1881, James Prendergast Papers, MS-Papers 730.

37 Hazel Riseborough *Days of Darkness: Taranaki 1878–1884* (Allen and Unwin, Wellington,

1989) at 155–156.

38   James Prendergast, Administrator of the Government "A Proclamation" No 83 (19 October 1881) *New Zealand Gazette Extraordinary* vol. 2 at 1300. Also signed by William Rolleston, Native Minister.

39   Ibid.

40   John Hall "Memo from Hall to Prendergast, 19 October 1881" [1882] I AJHR A8b at 1.

41   Tyler at 173.

42   Riseborough at 157.

43   Tyler at 173.

44   Dick Scott *Ask that Mountain: The Story of Parihaka* (Reed/Southern Cross, Auckland, 1975) at 123.

45   Ibid.

46   See personal correspondence between Prendergast and Bryce in ATL.

47   Letters from Michael Prendergast junior, Manaia, to James Prendergast, Wellington, 9 November 1881, D.O.W. Hall, MS-Papers 986/17, Hocken Library, Dunedin.

48   Riseborough at 197. The chain of events leading to the proclamation was also examined in *Bryce v Rusden* [1886] 2 Times LR 435 (QB), the case in which Bryce successfully sued Rusden for libel appearing in Rusden's *History of New Zealand* (Chapman and Hall, London, 1883). In the trial transcript, Prendergast is mentioned only in passing. In Rusden's *History*, Prendergast plays a key role in the Parihaka machinations and is described as "of the cabal if not formally a member"(at 282). As the *Bryce* decision shows, Rusden's book is full of historical errors and can only be used as evidence of Rusden's opinions, not of facts.

49   Memorandum, James Prendergast to Governor Jervois, 27 January 1883 at 1, Governor's Papers, Archives New Zealand, Wellington.

50   Ibid. at 2.

51   Ibid. at 3.

52   Ibid. at 4.

53   The steamer *Southern Cross* carried communications from Auckland to Fiji monthly. Prendergast wrote to Gordon on 16 September and the letter left Wellington for Auckland on 23 September. A few days later, the *Southern Cross* carried both Prendergast's letter and Murray's communications to Fiji, arriving 4 October. Prendergast did not keep a copy of his letter but remembered it being brief, as he stated that Murray would provide a more detailed account of happenings in New Zealand (ibid. at 7). Prendergast argues that he could not send any further communications to Gordon before the middle of October, when the next steamer left New Zealand. By that time, Gordon would have left Fiji to travel around the Western Pacific (ibid. at 8). The *Southern Cross* steamer voyage in late September was effectively the only opportunity of communicating with Gordon, and both Murray and Prendergast sent information on that steamer. Riseborough (at 145) argues that Prendergast could have penned a further letter to Gordon between 16 and 23 September as tension increased between Te Whiti and the Government.

54   Ibid. at 5.

55   Ibid. at 6.

56   Ibid. at 9.

57   Ibid. at 11–12.

58   Ibid. at 14.

59   Ibid. at 18.

60   Riseborough at 154.

61   Dom Felice Vaggioli *History of New Zealand and Its Inhabitants* translated by John Crockett (University of Otago Press, Dunedin, 2000, first published 1896) at 290.

62   Riseborough at 157.

63   Letter, Governor Gordon to James Prendergast, 23 May 1881, James Prendergast Papers, MS-Papers 730, Hocken Library, and Kimberley Papers, 4 May 1881, Alexander Turnbull Library,

Wellington.

64 Waitangi Tribunal *The Taranaki Report: Kaupapa Tuatahi* (Wai 143, 1996) at 5–6.

65 Riseborough at 130.

66 Ibid. at 145.

67 Scott at 100.

68 Ranginui Walker *Ka Whawhai Tonu Matou: Struggle Without End* (Penguin Books, Auckland, 1990) at 158.

69 JK Chapman *The Career of Arthur Hamilton Gordon: First Lord Stanmore 1829–1912* (University of Toronto Press, Toronto, 1964).

70 WJ Hunter "New Zealand Legal Portraits" (1959) MS-Papers 1777-02 at 125, Alexander Turnbull Library, Wellington.

71 DK Fieldhouse "Sir Arthur Gordon and the Parihaka crisis, 1880–1882" (1961) 10 Historical Studies: Australia and New Zealand 30 at 37.

72 Ibid. at 42.

73 "Obituary" *Dominion* (Wellington, 28 February 1921) at 4.

74 McLean at 103.

75 Works that focus on Parihaka but not the legal machinations behind the invasion include; Te Miringa Hohaia, Gregory O'Brien and Lara Strongman (eds) *Parihaka: The art of passive resistance* (Victoria University Press, Wellington, 2001); Rachel Buchanan *The Parihaka Album* (Huia, Wellington, 2009) and Kelvin Day (ed) *Contested Ground: Te Whenua I Tohea: The Taranaki Wars 1860–1881* (Huia, Wellington, 2010). A fictional account which does address Prendergast's role is John Hinchcliff *Parihaka* (Steele Roberts, Wellington, 2004).

76 Scott at 101.

77 (14 June 1882) 41 NZPD 426.

78 Memorandum, James Prendergast to Governor Jervois, 27 January 1883, at 17, Governor's Papers, Archives New Zealand, Wellington.

79 Riseborough at 193.

80 "Supreme Court. Criminal Sessions. This Day" *Evening Post* (Wellington, 4 October 1886) at 2.

81 Te Whiti was sentenced to three months' imprisonment in the Terrace Gaol and to pay a fine of 100 pounds, Titokowaru to one month's imprisonment and to pay a fine of 20 pounds ("The Maori Rioters in Court" *Evening Post* (Wellington, 6 October 1886) at 2).

82 Ibid. This episode is also recounted in Scott at 151–153 and Tony Sole *Ngati Ruanui: A History* (Huia, Wellington, 2005) at 2–3. Sole states that Prendergast was "clearly not remotely interested in the justice of this case".

83 JF Jeffries "Sir James Prendergast" in Robin Cooke (ed) *Portrait of a Profession: The Centennial Book of the New Zealand Law Society* (Reed, Wellington, 1969) at 44.

Chapter 10. 'Retirement'

1 *Otago Daily Times* (Dunedin, 1 March 1899) at 4.

2 A heart disease, Death Certificate, Mary Prendergast, 1921.

3 Joseph Chamberlain, Secretary of State for the Colonies, London, to Governor Ranfurly, Wellington, 15 February 1901, MS-730-B, Hocken Library, Dunedin.

4 *New Zealand Times* (New Zealand, 7 March 1901) at 33.

5 Sir James Prendergast Papers, MS-Papers 730, Hocken Library, Dunedin.

6 Robin Cooke (ed) *Portrait of a Profession: The Centennial Book of the New Zealand Law Society* (Reed, Wellington, 1969) at 153.

7 "The Suggested Final Court of Appeal" *Evening Post* (Wellington, 23 September 1901) at 5.

8 Cooke (ed) at 153.

9 (1902–1903) NZPCC 23.

10 *Wallis* at 35.

11   *Illustrated London News* (London, 20 July 1901) at 83.

12   Empson Enquiry – Summary by Bishop of Wellington Wallis (September 1903), Riddiford Family, MS-Papers 5714-045, Alexander Turnbull Library, Wellington.

13   PB Mackay "Empson, Walter" (7 June 2013) Te Ara: The Encyclopedia of New Zealand <www.teara.govt.nz>.

14   Empson Enquiry Decision – Sir James Prendergast, July 1903, Riddiford Family, MS-Papers 5714-045.

15   Empson Enquiry – Letter from John M.L. Davies, accuser's father, 1 September 1903, Riddiford Family, MS-Papers 5714-045.

16   Letter of the Lord Primate (Church of England), 4 September 1905, *Wi Parata v Bishop of Wellington*, MS-Papers 5449, Alexander Turnbull Library, Wellington.

17   David V Williams *A Simple Nullity: The* Wi Parata *Case in New Zealand Law and History* (Auckland University Press, Auckland, 2011) at 196.

18   *Bank of New Zealand: Reports of Proceedings at the Ordinary, Half Year and Special General Meeting of Proprietors from August 1900 to June 1920* (Whitcombe & Tombs, Wellington, 1920) at 120.

19   Guy H Scholefield and E Schwabe (eds) *Who's Who in New Zealand and the Western Pacific, 1908* (Gordon & Gotch, Wellington, 1908) at 139.

20   "Obituary" *Dominion* (Wellington, 28 February 1921) at 4.

21   Scholefield Notes, Scholefield, Guy Hardy, MS-Papers 0212, Alexander Turnbull Library, Wellington.

22   Dorothea Joblin *Behold the Plains: The Story of the Old Houses of Massey* (Longman Paul, Auckland, 1970) at 46.

23   Richard Boast *The Native Land Court: A Historical Study. Cases and Commentary 1862–1887* (Brookers, Wellington, 2013) at 565.

24   *New Zealand Mail* (New Zealand, 8 February 1900) at 17. See also Lucy Marsden "A Sound Investment: Sir James Prendergast and his Fitzherbert Estate" (2013) 9 The Manawatu Journal of History 41.

25   Ronald Jones "James Prendergast" in AH McLintock (ed) *An Encyclopedia of New Zealand* (RE Owen, Wellington, 1966) vol. 1 at 862.

26   Letters from Michael Prendergast junior, Fitzherbert, to James Prendergast, Wellington, 1880s, D.O.W. Hall, MS-Papers 986/17, Hocken Library, Dunedin.

27   Letter from Michael Prendergast junior, Fitzherbert, to James Prendergast, Wellington, 30 July 1881, D.O.W. Hall, MS-Papers 986/17.

28   D.O.W. Hall, MS-Papers 986.

29   Margaret H Alington *Unquiet Earth: A History of the Bolton Street Cemetery* (Wellington City Council/Ministry of Works, Wellington, 1978) at 111.

30   "First Thorndon Reclamation" *Evening Post* (Wellington, 8 February 1915) at 16.

31   Death Certificate, Mary Prendergast, 1899.

32   Letters to James Prendergast, 1865–1899, D.O.W. Hall, MS-Papers 986.

33   Diary of Charles Prendergast Knight, early 1890s, Prendergast, James, MS-Papers 1791, Alexander Turnbull Library, Wellington.

34   Letters, 1865–1899, D.O.W. Hall, MS-Papers 986.

35   Probate, James Prendergast, 1921.

36   Letters, 1865–1899, D.O.W. Hall, MS-Papers 986.

37   Jane Prendergast died 1864 aged c31 at Meat.(could be short for Meatian which is near Swan Hill and Lalbert Vic.) Certificate no. 6766, Father – Lawrence Smyth, Mother – Ellen Maria Ryan.

38   Letters, D.O.W. Hall, MS-Papers 986.

39   Ibid.

40   Date of death unknown for Philip, Michael senior and Michael junior.

41   Letters, D.O.W. Hall, MS-Papers 986.

42   See the work of Catharine Coleborne, especially *Madness in the Family: Insanity and Institutions in the Australasian Colonial World 1860–1914* (Palgrave Macmillan, Melbourne, 2009).

43   Letters, D.O.W. Hall, MS-Papers 986.
44   Ibid.
45   Ibid.
46   Death Certificate, James Prendergast, 1921.
47   *New Zealand Times* (New Zealand, 3 March 1921).
48   Probate, James Prendergast, 1921. This is approximately equivalent to $11 million today (using the Reserve Bank inflation calculator <www.rbnz.govt.nz> as a very rough guide).
49   Codicil to the Will of James Prendergast, New Zealand Academy of Fine Arts, MS-Papers 1372, Alexander Turnbull Library, Wellington.
50   "Monday" *Evening Post* (Wellington, 21 May 1921) at 8.
51   James Prendergast, Letter to his father, 13 April 1853, Prendergast, James, MS-Papers 1791.
52   "Obituary" *Dominion* (Wellington, 28 February 1921) at 4.
53   *New Zealand Free Lance* (Wellington, 22 February 1908) at 4.

Chapter 11. Conclusion

1   *New Zealand Times* (New Zealand, 4 March 1921).

BIBLIOGRAPHY

PRIMARY

Unpublished

A. Private Papers

NEW ZEALAND

1. Alexander Turnbull Library, Wellington

Ballance, John, MS-Papers 0025
Buller, Walter Lawry, Micro-MS-Coll 0048
Domett, Alfred, MS-Papers 0377
Gladstone, William Ewart, Micro-MS-Coll 20
Gordon, Arthur, Micro-MS-Coll 20
McLean, Donald, MS-Papers 0032
New Zealand Academy of Fine Arts, MS-Paper 1372
New Zealand Legal Portraits, MS-Papers 1777
Prendergast, James, MS-Papers 1791
Reeves, William Pember, MS-Papers 0129
Riddiford, Family, MS-Papers 5714
Rolleston, Family, MS-Papers 0446
Scholefield, Guy Hardy, MS-Papers 0212
Seddon, Family, MS-Papers 1619
Vogel, Family, MS-Papers 0178
Vogel, Julius, MSY-1334
Wi Parata v Bishop of Wellington, MS-Papers-5449

2. Hocken Library, Dunedin

Hall, D.O.W., MS-Papers 986
Prendergast, Sir James, MS-Papers 730

AUSTRALIA

1. Victoria State Library, Melbourne

GREAT BRITAIN

1. British Library, London

B. Official Papers

NEW ZEALAND

1. National Archives, Wellington

Governor's Records
Justice Department Records

AUSTRALIA

1. Public Record Office, Victoria

GREAT BRITAIN

1. Inns of Court, London
Admission Registers

2. Corporation of London Records Office/Guildhall Library, London
Baptismal Records
Corporation Records

3. Norfolk Record Office
City Records

4. Public Record Office, London
Assize Records
Colonial Office Records
Family Records, Islington Centre

Published

A. Official

1. NEW ZEALAND
Appendices to the Journals of the House of Representatives
Appendices to the Journals of the Legislative Council
New Zealand Gazette
New Zealand Parliamentary Debates
Otago Provincial Government Gazette

2. AUSTRALIA
Victoria. Parliamentary Debates

3. GREAT BRITAIN
British Parliamentary Papers on Australia and New Zealand, 1800–1899 (Irish University Press, Shannon, 1974)
William Wilks Dalbiac (ed) *The Law List* (V&R Stevens and GS Norton, London, published annually)

B. Newspapers

1. NEW ZEALAND
Daily Southern Cross (Auckland)
Dominion (Wellington)
Evening Post (Wellington)
Free Lance (Wellington)
Grey River Argus (West Coast)
Hawke's Bay Herald
Lyttleton Times
New Zealand Herald (Auckland)
New Zealand Mail
New Zealand Times
North Otago Times
Otago Daily Times
Otago Witness
Thames Advertiser
Thames Star

Timaru Herald
Wanganui Chronicle
Wanganui Herald
Wellington Independent
West Coast Times

2. AUSTRALIA
The Age (Victoria)
The Argus (Victoria)
Inglewood Advertiser (Victoria)

3. GREAT BRITAIN
The City Press (London)
Manchester Guardian
The Times (London)

C. Contemporary Books, Pamphlets and Articles

Addison, Charles Greenstreet *Wrongs and their remedies: being a treatise on the law of torts* (5th ed, Stevens and Sons, London, 1879).

Austin, John *The Province of Jurisprudence Determined* edited by Wilfrid E Rumble (Cambridge University Press, Cambridge, 1995, first published 1832).

Bacon, Matthew *A New Abridgment of the Law* (T & JW Johnson, Philadelphia, 1876).

Ballantine, Sergeant *Some Experiences of a Barrister's Life* (8th ed, Richard Bentley, London, 1883).

Bank of New Zealand: Reports of Proceedings at the Ordinary, Half Year and Special General Meetings of Proprietors from August 1900 to June 1920 (Whitcombe & Tombs, Wellington, 1920).

Barton, GB (ed) *The New Zealand Jurist Reports* (Reith and Wilkie, Dunedin, 1870s).

Boase, Frederic *Modern English Biography, 1851–1900* (Frank Cass, London, 1897, 1965).

Crockford's Clerical Directory for 1860 (Crockford's, London, 1860).

The Cyclopedia of New Zealand: Volume 1 – Wellington Provincial District (Cyclopedia Company, Wellington, 1897).

Edwards, Charles Johnston *The Law of Execution upon Judgments and Orders of the Chancery and Queen's Bench Divisions of the High Court of Justice* (Stevens and Sons, London, 1888).

Folkard, Henry Coleman *The Law of Slander and Libel: Founded upon the Treatise of the late Mr. Starkie* (4th ed, Butterworths, London, 1876).

Foster, Joseph *Alumni Oxonienses* (James Parker, Oxford, 1891).

Foster, Joseph *Men-at-the-Bar* (2nd ed, Hazell, Watson and Viney, London, 1885).

Gardiner, Robert Barlow (ed) *The Admission Registers of St. Paul's School, from 1748 to 1876* (George Bell, London, 1884).

Gisborne, William *New Zealand Rulers and Statesmen, 1840 to 1885* (Sampson Low, London, 1886).

Gisborne, William *New Zealand Rulers and Statesmen from 1840 to 1897* (Sampson Low, London, 1897).

Haydn, Joseph *The Book of Dignities* (3rd ed, WH Allen, London, 1894).

Macgeagh, Henry F and Sturgess, HAC (eds) *Register of Admissions to the Honourable Society of the Middle Temple* (Butterworths, London, 1949).

Mackie, Charles *Norfolk Annals: A Chronological Record of Remarkable Events in the Nineteenth Century* (Office of the Norfolk Chronicle, Norwich, 1901).

Paterson, James *Commentaries on the Liberty of the subject and the laws of England relating to the security of the person* (MacMillan, London, 1877).

Pitt-Lewis, G *Commissioner Kerr: An Individuality* (T Fisher Unwin, London, 1903).

The Records of the Honorable Society of Lincoln's Inn (Lincoln's Inn, London, 1896).

Roxburgh, Ronald (ed) *The Records of the Honorable Society of Lincoln's Inn: The Black Books* (Lincoln's Inn, London, 1968).

Robinson, Charles J *Register of the Scholars admitted into Merchant Taylors' School, From AD 1562 to 1874* (Farncombe & Co, Lewes, 1883).

Romilly, Joseph *Graduati Cantabrigienses* (Deighton, Bell, Cambridge, 1856).

Rusden, GW *History of New Zealand* (Chapman and Hall, London, 1883).

Scholefield, Guy H and Schwabe, E (eds) *Who's Who in New Zealand and the Western Pacific 1908* (Gordon & Gotch, Wellington, 1908).

Stephen, Henry John *New Commentaries on the Laws of England* (Butterworths, London, 1863).

Stephen, Sir Leslie and Lee, Sir Sidney (eds) *The Dictionary of National Biography: From the Earliest Times to 1900* (Oxford University Press, Oxford, 1885 onwards).

Stones Wellington Directory (Stone & Son, Dunedin, ongoing).

Vaggioli, Dom Felice *History of New Zealand and Its Inhabitants* translated by John Crockett (University of Otago Press, Dunedin, 2000, first published 1896).

Venn, John *Alumni Cantabrigienses, Part II* (Cambridge University Press, Cambridge, 1953).

Venn, John *Biographical History of Gonville and Caius College 1349–1897* (Cambridge University Press, Cambridge, 1898).

Whishaw, James *A Synopsis of the Members of the English Bar* (Stevens, London, 1835).

Whitworth, Robert P *Bailliere's Victorian Gazetter* (FF Bailliere, Melbourne, 1865).

Wises NZ Post Office Directory (H Wise, Dunedin, ongoing).

D. Edited collections of primary documents

Bell, Kenneth N and Morrell, WP (eds) *Select Documents on British Colonial Policy, 1830–1860* (Clarendon Press, Oxford, 1928).

McIntyre, David W and Gardner, WJ (eds) *Speeches and Documents on New Zealand History* (Clarendon Press, Oxford, 1971).

Scholefield, GH (ed) *The Richmond-Atkinson Papers* (RE Owen, Wellington, 1960).

E. List of Cases

1. NEW ZEALAND:

Anna Kapara v Mair (1885) 4 NZLR 216.

Arihi Te Nahu v Locke (1887) 5 NZLR 408.

Attorney-General v Bunny [1874] I AJHR A4.

Attorney-General v Edwards (1891) 9 NZLR 321 (CA).

Auckland City v Auckland Metropolitan Fire Board [1967] NZLR 615.

Auckland City Council v Wotherspoon [1990] 1 NZLR 76.

Auckland Regional Council v Holmes Logging and Holmes HC Auckland CIV-2009-404-35, 17 June 2010.

Barton v Allan (1878) 3 NZ Jur NS 46.

Beecham Group Ltd v Bristol-Myers Co (No. 2) [1979] 2 NZLR 629.

Bell v Finn (1896) 14 NZLR 447.

Bishop of Wellington v Solicitor-General (1901) 19 NZLR 214.

Blaymires v Ewing (1890) 9 NZLR 567.

Bradley v Attorney-General [1978] 1 NZLR 36.

Broughton v Donnelly (1888) 7 NZLR 288 (CA).

Bunt v Hallinan [1985] 1 NZLR 450 (CA).

Chan v Lower Hutt City Corporation [1976] 2 NZLR 75.

Commercial Union Assurance Co of NZ Ltd v Lamont [1989] 3 NZLR 187 (CA).

Coomber v Birkenhead Borough Council [1980] 2 NZLR 681.

Corbett v Social Security Commission [1962] NZLR 878 (CA).

Corunna Bay Holdings v Gracie Dean [2002] 2 NZLR 186 (CA).

Dodwell v Bishop of Wellington (1886) 5 NZLR 263.

Doherty v Education Board (1878) 4 NZ Jur (NS) 78.

Doyle v Edwards (1898) 16 NZLR 572.

Echolands Farms Ltd v Powell [1976] 1 NZLR 750.

Fanzelow v Kerr (1896) 14 NZLR 660.

Gifford v Police [1965] NZLR 484 (CA).

Gillon v MacDonald (1878) 3 NZ Jur (NS) 27 (SC).

Goodall v Te Kooti (1890) 9 NZLR 26 (CA).

Hadfield v Armstrong (1894) 12 NZLR 476.

Harris v Fitzmaurice [1956] NZLR 975.

Hawera County Council v Standard Insurance Co (1889) 7 NZLR 268.

Hickford v Tamaki [1962] NZLR 786.

Hoani Te Heuheu Tukino v Aotea District Maori Land Board [1941] NZLR 590.

Hocking v Attorney-General [1963] NZLR 513.

Hohepa Wi Neera v Bishop of Wellington (1902) 21 NZLR 655 (CA).

Housing Corporation of New Zealand v Maori Trustee [1988] 2 NZLR 662.

Innes v Ewing [1989] 1 NZLR 598.

Instant Funding Ltd v Greenwich Property Holdings HC Auckland CIV-2007-404-6806, 20 December 2007.

Jenkins v Mayor, Councillors and Citizens of the City of Wellington (1896) 15 NZLR 118.

Johns v Westland District Licensing Committee [1961] NZLR 35.

Jull v Treanor (1896) 14 NZLR 513.

Light v Milton (1883) 2 NZLR 214.

Low v Hutchinson (1893) 13 NZLR 55.

Lower Hutt City v Attorney-General [1965] NZLR 65 (CA).

Mangakahia v New Zealand Timber Company (1881) 2 NZLR (SC) 345.

Mawley v Masterton Road Board (1889) 7 NZLR 649.

McCabe v Cassidy [1966] NZLR 115.

McCrae v Wheeler [1969] NZLR 333.

McKenzie v Couston (1898) 17 NZLR 228.

McKenzie v Risk [1974] 2 NZLR 214.

Merrie v McKay (1897) 16 NZLR 124.

Nankivell v O'Donovan (1893) 13 NZLR 60.

Nelson City Corporation v Nelson College (1896) 14 NZLR 507.

New Zealand Maori Council v Attorney-General [1987] 1 NZLR 641 (CA).

Ngati Apa and others v Attorney-General and others [2003] 3 NZLR 643.

Nireaha Tamaki v Baker (1900–01) NZPCC 371.

Olsen v Bailey (1888) 6 NZLR 713.

Paraone v Matthews (1888) 6 NZLR 744.

Parsons v Young Swan Morison McKay [1986] 2 NZLR 204.

Payze v Everitt [1959] NZLR 423.

Peters v Joseph (1878) 3 NZ Jur (NS) 142.

Picturesque Atlas Publishing Company v Harbottle (1891) 10 NZLR 348.

Piripi Te Maari v Stewart (1892) 11 NZLR 205.

Poll, ex parte, in Re Tonks (1877) 3 NZ Jur (NS) 1.

R v Dean (1895) 14 NZLR 272 (CA).

R v Hall (1887) 5 NZLR 93 (CA).

R v Macandrew (1869) 1 CA 172.

R v Mason [2012] 2 NZLR 695.

R v Pennell [2003] 1 NZLR 289.

R v Potter (1887) 6 NZLR 92.

R v Rogers [2006] 2 NZLR 156.

R v SG Isaacs and Daniel Campbell [1862] NZLostC 258 (12 December 1862).

R v Symonds (1847) NZPCC 387.

R v Te Kira [1993] 3 NZLR 257 (CA).

R v Thomas Kelly and Richard Burgess [1862] NZLostC 84 (21 May 1862).

R v Thomas Yates [1864] NZLostC 66 (8 March 1864).

R v Tuhiata [1880] NZLostC 4 (13 December 1880).

R v Vowles (1885) 3 NZLR 111.

R v William Andrew Jarvey [1865] NZLostC 97 (13 March 1865).

R v William Henry Woodgate [1876] NZLostC 3 (5 December 1876).

R v William Larkin and John Manning and others [1869] NZLostC 121 (18 May 1868).

Rangimoeke v Strachan (1895) 14 NZLR 477.

Re Aldridge (1893) 15 NZLR 361.

Re the Bed of the Wanganui River [1962] NZLR 600.

Re Campbell's Application (1891) 10 NZLR 197.

Re Cairns, Ex parte NZ Land Mortgage Co Ltd (1888) 7 NZLR 42.

Re GE Barton (1876) 1 NZ Jur (NS) 109 (SC).

Re GE Barton (1876) 2 NZ Jur (NS) 13 (SC).

Re George Barton (1878) 3 NZ Jur (NS) 67 (SC).

Re H (A Bankrupt) [1967] NZLR 263.

Re H (A Bankrupt) [1968] NZLR 231 (CA).

Re Mrs Jackson's Claim (1890) 10 NZLR 148.

Re A Lease, Whakarare to Williams (1894) 12 NZLR 494.

Re the Lundon and Whitaker Claims Act 1871 (1872) 2 NZCA 41.

Re M's application [1973] 2 NZLR 169.

Re McGregor; Ex parte McGregor (1888) 7 NZLR 241.

Re Ninety Mile Beach [1963] NZLR 461.

Re Proudfoot, A Bankrupt, Ex parte Ballins Breweries (New Zealand) Ltd [1961] NZLR 268 (CA).

Re The Puhatikotiko No. 1 Block (1893) 12 NZLR 131.

Re Reimer, Ex parte Official Assignee (1896) 15 NZLR 198.

Re Rickman, Ex parte The Bank of New Zealand (1890) 8 NZLR 381.

Re Selwyn County Council (1887) 5 NZLR (CA) 163.

Re Stewart & Co, Ex parte Piripi Te Maari (No 2) (1892) 11 NZLR 745.

Re Roche (1888) 7 NZLR 206.

Re Te-Au-O-Tonga Election Petition [1979] 1 NZLR S26 (Cook Islands HC).

Re Wellington Central Election Petition, Shand v Comber [1973] 2 NZLR 470.

Reid v Official Assignee of McCallum (1886) 5 NZLR 68.

Retaruke Timber Co Ltd v Rodney County Council [1984] 2 NZLR 129.

Rira Peti v Ngaraihi Te Paku (1888) 7 NZLR 235.

Robinson and Morgan-Coakle v Behan [1964] NZLR 650.

Rural Banking and Finance Corporation of New Zealand Ltd v Official Assignee [1991] 2 NZLR 351.

Russell v Minister of Lands (1898) 17 NZLR 241 and 780; 1 GLR 15 and 195.

Sargood v Corporation of the City of Dunedin (1888) 6 NZLR 489.

Scott v Broadlands Finance Ltd [1972] NZLR 268.

Shand v Comber [1973] 2 NZLR 470.

Smith v McKenzie (1880–1881) 1 NZLR 1 (CA).

Solicitor-General v Bishop of Wellington (1901) 19 NZLR 665.

Spence v Pearson (1878) 3 NZ Jur (NS) 25 (CA).

Strongman Electric Supply Co Ltd v Thames Valley Electric Power Board [1964] NZLR 592.

Sulco Ltd v E.S. Redit and Co Ltd [1959] NZLR 45.

Superior Lands Ltd v Wellington City Corporation [1974] 1 NZLR 240.

Sutherland v McGimpsey (1898) 17 NZLR 431; 1 GLR 28.

Sutton v O'Kane [1973] 2 NZLR 304 (CA).

Takamore v Clarke [2012] 1 NZLR 573.

Tarry v Taranaki County Council (1894) 12 NZLR 467.

Te Weehi v Regional Fisheries Officer [1986] 1 NZLR 680.

The New Zealand Banking Corporation v Cutten and Vogel [1864] NZLostC 364 (3 November 1864).

Victory Park Board v Christchurch City [1965] NZLR 741.

Waimiha Sawmilling Co Ltd v Waione Timber Co Ltd [1926] AC 101; NZPCC 267 (CA).

Wallis v Solicitor-General (1902–03) NZPCC 23.

Protest of Bench and Bar re *Wallis v Solicitor-General*, Appendix (1903) NZPCC 730.

Webber v Finnimore (1880) 1 OB & F (SC) 150.

Wellington City Corporation v Public Trustee [1921] NZLR 423.

Wellington City Council v Victoria University of Wellington [1975] 2 NZLR 301.

Wellington City Election Petition (1897) 15 NZLR 454.

Wilson and King v Brightling (1885) 4 NZLR 4.

Wi Parata v The Bishop of Wellington & the Attorney-General (1877) 3 NZ Jur (NS) SC 72.

Wotherspon v Dobson (1893) 11 NZLR 283.

Young v Hill, Ford and Newton (1883) 2 NZLR 62 (CA).

2. AUSTRALIA

The Borough of Bathurst v MacPherson 4 App Cas 256 (PC).

Mabo v Queensland (No.2) (1992) 66 Australian Law Journal Reports 408 (High Court of Australia).

3. GREAT BRITAIN

Bryce v Rusden [1886] 2 Times LR 435 (QB).

Carus Wilson's Case (1845) 115 ER 759 (QB).

Central Criminal Court: Minutes of Evidence (London: George Herbert, ongoing).

The English Reports (1820s–1862).

Ex parte Fernandez (1861) 142 ER 349.

Ex parte Pater (1864) 5 B & S 299.

4. UNITED STATES

Cherokee Nation v The State of Georgia 5 Peters, US Rep 1 (1831) per Marshall CJ.

Johnson v M'Intosh 21 US (8 Wheat) 543, 5 L Ed 681 (1823) per Marshall CJ.

5. OTHER

Rainy v the Justices of Sierra Leone (1852) 8 Moo 47 (PC).

Re Pollard and the Chief Justice of Hong Kong (1868) 2 LR 106 (PC).

Smith v the Justices of Sierra Leone (1841) 3 Moo 361 (PC).

Smith v the Justices of Sierra Leone (1848) 7 Moo 174 (PC).

F. List of Statutes

1. NEW ZEALAND

Abolition of the Provinces Act 1875.

Accessories Act 1867.

Affirmation in Lieu of Oaths in Criminal Proceedings Act 1866.

Aliens Act 1866.

Arbitration Act 1890.

Armed Constabulary Act 1867.

Assault on Constables Act 1873.

Attorney-General's Act 1866.

Attorney-General's Act 1876.

Highways Act 1867 (Auckland).

Bankruptcy Act 1867.

Bankruptcy Act 1885.

Coinage Offences Act 1867.

Commencement of Acts Act 1865.

Confiscated Lands Act 1867.

Constitution Act 1986.

Court of Appeal Act 1882.
Criminal Law Amendment Act 1872.
Criminal Law Procedure Act 1866.
Debtors and Creditors Act 1875.
Debtors and Creditors Act 1876.
District Courts Amendment Act 1865.
District Courts Jurisdiction Extension Act 1866.
Disturbed Districts Act 1869.
Divorce and Matrimonial Causes Act 1867.
Employment of Females Act 1873.
English Laws Act 1858
Forgery Act 1867.
Immigration Act 1868.
Immigration and Public Works Act 1870.
Immigration and Public Works Act 1872.
Immigration and Public Works Amendment Act 1871.
Immigration and Public Works Loan Act 1870.
Immigration and Public Works Loan Act 1873.
Indemnity Act 1866.
Indemnity Act 1868.
Indictable Offences Repeal Act 1867.
Injuries by Dogs Act 1865.
Innkeepers Liability Act 1866.
Intestate Estates Amendment Act 1866.
Judicature Act 1908.
Judicial Conduct Commissioner and Judicial Conduct Panel Act 2004.
Juries Act 1868.
Justices of the Peace Act 1866.
Justice of the Peace Acts Repeal Act 1866.
Justices Protection Act 1866.
Larceny Act 1867.
Land Transfer Act 1870.
Land Transfer Act 1885.
Law Amendment Act 1882.
Law Practitioners Act 1861.
Law Practitioners Amendment Act 1865.
Law Practitioners Amendment Act 1866.
Leases and Sales of Settled Estates Act 1865.
Licensing Act 1881.
Lunatics Act 1866.
Malicious Injury to Property Act 1867.
Maori Affairs Act 1953.
Maori Representation Act 1867.
Municipal Corporations Act 1886.
Native Lands Act 1865.
Native Land Act 1873.
Native Land Act 1909.
Native Rights Act 1865.
Native Schools Act 1867.
New Zealand Constitution Act 1852.
New Zealand Law Society's Act 1869.
New Zealand Settlements Amendment and Continuance Act 1865.

New Zealand Post Office Amendment Act (No. 2) 1866.
New Zealand University Act 1874.
Offences Against the Person Act 1866.
Offences Against the Person Act 1867.
Otago Provincial Public Offices Site 1865.
Otago Waste Lands Act 1865.
Partnership Law Amendment Act 1866.
Punishment of High Treason Act 1870.
Sale and Lease of Settled Estates Act 1865.
Sale of Poisons Act 1866.
Summary Procedure on Bills Amendment Act 1866.
Supreme Court Act 1862.
Supreme Court Act 1882.
Supreme Court House Site Act 1865.
Supreme Court Judges Act 1858.
Supreme Court Practice and Procedure Amendment Act 1868.
Treason-Felony Act 1868.
Treaty of Waitangi Act 1975.
Treaty of Waitangi Amendment Act 1985.
Fencing Act 1867 (Wellington).
West Coast Peace Preservation Act 1882.

2. AUSTRALIA
South Australian Land Transfer Act 1858.

3. GREAT BRITAIN
Judicature Acts 1873/1875.

G. List of contemporary law journals

James Macassey (ed) *Colonial Law Journal, being a selection of reports and cases argued in the Supreme Court of New Zealand 1865–1875 and various articles* (Henry Wise, Dunedin, 1875).
Edward Cave (ed) *The Gentleman's Magazine and Historical Review* (Henry & Parker, London).
The Law Journal (London).
The Law Times (London).
The New Zealand Jurist (Dunedin).

SECONDARY

A. Books

Alington, Margaret H *Unquiet Earth: A History of the Bolton Street Cemetery* (Wellington City Council/Ministry of Works, Wellington, 1978).
Alphers, Antony and Baker, Josephine (eds) *Confident Tomorrows: A Biographical Self-Portrait of OTJ Alphers* (Godwit Press, Auckland, 1993).
Bade, James N (ed) *The German Connection: New Zealand and German-Speaking Europe in the Nineteenth Century* (Oxford University Press, Auckland, 1993).
Baker, JH *An Introduction to English Legal History* (3rd ed, Butterworths, London, 1990).
Bassett, Judith *Sir Harry Atkinson, 1831–1892* (Auckland University Press/Oxford University Press, Auckland, 1975).
Belich, James *'I Shall Not Die': Titokowaru's War 1868–1869* (2nd ed, Bridget Williams, Wellington, 2010).
Belich, James *Making Peoples: A History of the New Zealanders from Polynesian Settlement to the End of the Nineteenth Century* (Penguin, Auckland, 1996).

Belich, James *The New Zealand Wars and the Victorian Interpretation of Racial Conflict* (Penguin, Auckland, 1986).

Boast, Richard *The Native Land Court: A Historical Study. Cases and Commentary 1862–1887* (Brookers, Wellington, 2013).

Bohan, Edmund *Edward Stafford: New Zealand's First Statesman* (Hazard Press, Christchurch, 1994).

Bohan, Edmund *To Be A Hero: Sir George Grey: 1812–1898* (HarperCollins, Auckland, 1998).

Borrie, Gordon and Lowe, Nigel *Borrie and Lowe's Law of Contempt* (2nd ed, Butterworths, London, 2005).

Brookfield, FM *Waitangi and Indigenous Rights: Revolution, Law and Legitimation* (Auckland University Press, Auckland, 1999).

Brown, Bernard "Sir James Prendergast" in AWB Simpson (ed) *Biographical Dictionary of the Common Law* (Butterworths, London, 1984).

Buchanan, Rachel *The Parihaka Album* (Huia, Wellington, 2009).

Burdon, RM *King Dick: A Biography of Richard John Seddon* (Whitcombe & Tombs, Christchurch, 1955).

Byrnes, Giselle *The Waitangi Tribunal and New Zealand History* (Oxford University Press, Auckland, 2004).

Catran, Ken *Hanlon: A Casebook* (BCNZ Enterprises, Auckland, 1985).

Chapman, JK *The Career of Arthur Hamilton Gordon: First Lord Stanmore 1829–1912* (University of Toronto Press, Toronto, 1964).

Chappell, NM *New Zealand Banker's Hundred: a history of the Bank of New Zealand, 1861–1961* (Bank of New Zealand, Wellington, 1961).

Christie, Walter *New Zealand Education and Treatyism* (Wyvern Press, Auckland, 1999).

Christie, Walter *Treaty Issues* (Wyvern Press, Christchurch, 1997).

Clark, David and McCoy, Gerard *Habeas Corpus: Australia, New Zealand and the South Pacific* (Federation Press, Sydney, 2000).

Coates, Ken S and McHugh, PG (eds) *Living Relationships/Kokiri Ngatahi: The Treaty of Waitangi in the New Millenium* (Victoria University Press, Wellington, 1998).

Coleborne, Catharine *Madness in the Family: Insanity and Institutions in the Australasian Colonial World 1860–1914* (Palgrave Macmillan, Melbourne, 2009).

Cooke, Robin (ed) *Portrait of a Profession: The Centennial Book of the New Zealand Law Society* (Reed, Wellington, 1969).

Cullen, Michael *Lawfully Occupied: The Centennial History of the Otago District Law Society* (Otago District Law Society, Dunedin, 1979).

Dalziel, Raewyn *Julius Vogel: Business Politician* (Oxford University Press, Auckland, 1986).

Day, Kelvin (ed) *Contested Ground: Te Whenua I Tohea: The Taranaki Wars 1860–1881* (Huia, Wellington, 2010).

Denniston, ED *Memoir of Sir John Edward Denniston: Judge of the Supreme Court of New Zealand* (Gaskell, Christchurch, 1926).

Downie Stewart, William *Mr. Justice Richmond and the Taranaki War of 1860: a Great Judge Vindicated* (Whitcombe & Tombs, Wellington, 1945).

Downie Stewart, William *Portrait of a Judge: Sir Joshua Williams P.C.* (Whitcombe & Tombs, Wellington, 1945).

Duman, Daniel *The English and Colonial Bars in the Nineteenth Century* (Croom Helm, London, 1983).

Duman, Daniel *The Judicial Bench in England 1727–1875: The Reshaping of a Professional Elite* (Royal Historical Society, London, 1982).

Dunn, WH and Richardson, ILM *Sir Robert Stout: A Biography* (AH & AW Reed, Wellington, 1961).

Eady, David and Smith, ATH *Arlidge, Eady and Smith on Contempt* (3rd ed, Sweet and Maxwell, London, 2005).

Fargher, Ray *The Best Man Who Ever Served the Crown? A Life of Donald McLean* (Victoria University Press, Wellington, 2008).

Flanagan, Thomas "From Indian Title to Aboriginal Rights" in Louis A Knafla (ed) *Law & Justice in a*

New Land: Essays in Western Canadian Legal History (Carswell, Toronto, 1986).

Flett, James *Dunolly: Story of an Old Gold Diggings* (2nd ed, Hawthorn Press, Melbourne, 1974).

Flett, James *Maryborough, Victoria: Goldfields History* (Poppet Head Press, Glen Waverly, 1975).

Foden, NA *New Zealand Legal History, 1642–1842* (Sweet & Maxwell, Wellington, 1965).

Frame, Alex *Salmond: Southern Jurist* (Victoria University Press, Wellington, 1995).

Fraser, Bryce (ed) *The New Zealand Book of Events* (Reed Methuen, Auckland, 1986).

Gardiner, RB and Lupton, John (eds) *Res Paulinae: The Eighth Half-Century of St. Paul's School* (St. Paul's School, West Kensington, 1911).

Graham, Jeanine *Frederick Weld* (Auckland University Press/Oxford University Press, Auckland, 1983).

Havemann, Paul (ed) *Indigenous Peoples' Rights in Australia, Canada, and New Zealand* (Oxford University Press, Auckland, 1999).

Herber, Mark *Legal London: A Pictorial History* (Phillimore, London, 1999).

Hickford, Mark *Lords of the Land: Indigenous Property Rights and the Jurisprudence of Empire* (Oxford University Press, Oxford, 2011).

Hinchcliff, John *Parihaka* (Steele Roberts, Wellington, 2004).

Hodgson, Judy (ed) *The English Legal Heritage* (Oyez Publishing, London, 1979).

Hohaia, Te Miringi, O'Brien, Gregory and Strongman, Lara (eds) *Parihaka: The Art of Passive Resistance* (Victoria University Press, Wellington, 2001).

Holborn, Guy *Sources of Biographical Information on Past Lawyers* (British and Irish Association of Law Librarians, Warwick, 1999).

Hood, Lynley *Minnie Dean: Her life and crimes* (Penguin, Auckland, 1994).

Houghton, Walter E *The Victorian Frame of Mind* (Yale University Press, New Haven, 1957).

Hutchinson, Sidney C *The History of the Royal Academy: 1768–1968* (Chapman & Hall, London, 1968).

Ihimaera, Witi *The Matriarch* (Heinemann, Auckland, 1986).

Jacob, Jack IH *Chitty and Jacob's Queen's Bench Forms* (21st ed, Sweet & Maxwell, London, 1986).

Joblin, Dorothea *Behold the Plains: The Story of the Old Houses of Massey* (Longman Paul, Auckland, 1970).

Kawharu, IH (ed) *Waitangi: Maori and Pakeha Perspectives of the Treaty of Waitangi* (Oxford University Press, Auckland, 1989).

Kelsey, Jane *A Question of Honour? Labour and the Treaty 1984–1989* (Allen & Unwin, Wellington, 1990).

Kiernan, VG *Colonial Empires and Armies 1815–1960* (Sutton Publishing, Sutton, 1998).

King, Michael *The Penguin History of New Zealand* (Penguin, Auckland, 2003).

Knapland, Paul *Gladstone and Britain's Imperial Policy* (Allen & Unwin, London, 1927).

Knox, Ray (ed) *New Zealand's Heritage: the making of a nation* (Hamlyn House, Wellington, 1971).

Kostal, RW *A Jurisprudence of Power: Victorian Empire and the Rule of Law* (Oxford University Press, Oxford, 2004).

Lennard, Guy *Sir William Martin: The Life of the First Chief Justice of New Zealand* (Whitcombe and Tombs, Christchurch, 1961).

Lewis, JR *The Victorian Bar* (Robert Hale, London, 1982).

Manchester, AH *Sources of English Legal History: 1750–1950* (Butterworths, London, 1984).

Martin, John E *The House: New Zealand's House of Representatives 1854–2004* (Dunmore Press, Palmerston North, 2004).

McDonnell, Michael FJ *A History of St. Paul's School* (Chapman and Hall, London, 1909).

McGill, David *The Lion and the Wolfhound* (Grantham House, Wellington, 1990).

McHugh, PG *Aboriginal Societies and the Common Law: A History of Sovereignty, Status and Self-Determination* (Oxford University Press, Oxford, 2004).

McHugh, PG *The Maori Magna Carta: New Zealand Law and the Treaty of Waitangi* (Oxford University Press, Auckland, 1991).

McHugh, PG *Aboriginal Title: The Modern Jurisprudence of Tribal Land Rights* (Oxford University Press, Oxford, 2011).

McIvor, Timothy *The Rainmaker: A Biography of John Ballance* (Heinemann Reed, Auckland, 1989).

McKinnon, Malcolm *Bateman New Zealand Historical Atlas* (Bateman/Department of Internal Affairs, Wellington, 1997).

McLauchlan, Gordon (ed) *Bateman New Zealand Encyclopedia* (6th ed, Bateman, Auckland, 2005).

McLean, Gavin *The Governors: New Zealand's Governors and Governors-General* (Otago University Press, Dunedin, 2006).

McLintock, AH *Crown Colony Government in New Zealand* (Government Printer, Wellington, 1958).

McLintock, AH (ed) *An Encyclopedia of New Zealand* (RE Owen, Wellington, 1966).

Mead, AH *A Miraculous Draught of Fishes: A History of St. Paul's School 1509–1990* (St. Paul's School, London, 1990).

Millen, J *The Story of Bell Gully Buddle Weir, 1840–1990* (Bell Gully, Wellington, 1990).

Neuman, Klaus, Thomas, Nicholas and Ericksen, Hilary (eds) *Quicksands: Foundational Histories in Australia and Aotearoa New Zealand* (University of New South Wales Press, Sydney, 1999).

November, Janet *In the Footsteps of Ethel Benjamin: New Zealand's First Woman Lawyer* (Victoria University Press, Wellington, 2009).

Oliver, WH and Orange, Claudia (eds) *The Dictionary of New Zealand Biography: 1769–1869* (Allen & Unwin/Department of Internal Affairs, Wellington, 1990).

Orange, Claudia (ed) *The Dictionary of New Zealand Biography: 1870–1900* (Bridget Williams/ Department of Internal Affairs, Wellington, 1993).

Orange, Claudia (ed) *The Dictionary of New Zealand Biography: 1901–1920* (Auckland University Press, Auckland, 1996).

Orange, Claudia *The Treaty of Waitangi* (Allen & Unwin, Wellington, 1987).

Osborn, Betty and DuBourg, Trenear *Maryborough: A Social History 1854–1904* (Maryborough City Council, Maryborough, 1985).

Phillips, Jock (ed) *Biography in New Zealand* (Allen & Unwin, Wellington, 1985).

Plucknett, Theodore *A Concise History of the Common Law* (5th ed, Butterworths, London, 1956).

Pocock, JGA *Barbarism and Religion: Barbarians, Savages and Empires* (Cambridge University Press, Cambridge, 2008).

Pocock, JGA *Politics, Language and Time: Essays on Political Thought and History* (Methuen, London, 1972).

Polden, Patrick *A History of the County Court, 1846–1971* (Cambridge University Press, Cambridge, 1999).

Prest, Wilfred *William Blackstone: Law and Letters in the Eighteenth Century* (Oxford University Press, Oxford, 2008).

Rice, Geoffrey W (ed) *The Oxford History of New Zealand* (2nd ed, Oxford University Press, Auckland, 1992).

Ringer, JB *An Introduction to New Zealand Government* (Hazard Press, Christchurch, 1991).

Riseborough, Hazel *Days of Darkness: Taranaki 1878–1884* (Allen and Unwin, Wellington, 1989).

Round, David *Truth or Treaty: Commonsense questions about the Treaty of Waitangi* (Canterbury University Press, Christchurch, 1998).

Sainty, Sir John *A List of English Law Officers, King's Counsel and Holders of Patents of Precedence* (Selden Society, London, 1987).

Schofield, AB *Dictionary of Legal Biography 1845–1945* (Barry Rose Law, Chichester, 1998).

Scholefield, GH (ed) *A Dictionary of New Zealand Biography* (Department of Internal Affairs, Wellington, 1940).

Scott, Dick *Ask that Mountain: The Story of Parihaka* (Reed/Southern Cross, Auckland, 1975).

Scott, Stuart C *The Travesty of Waitangi: Towards Anarchy* (The Campbell Press, Dunedin, 1995).

Scott, Stuart C *Travesty after Travesty* (Certes Press, Christchurch, 1996).

Serle, Geoffrey *The Golden Age* (Melbourne University Press, Charlton, Victoria, 1963).

Shadbolt, Maurice *Season of the Jew* (Hodder and Stoughton, Kent, 1986).

Sharp, Andrew and McHugh, Paul (eds) *Histories, Power and Loss: Uses of the Past – A New Zealand Commentary* (Bridget Williams, Wellington, 2001).

Shore, W Teignmouth (ed) *Trial of James Blomfield Rush* (William Hodge, Edinburgh, 1928).

Sinclair, Keith *A History of New Zealand* (4th revised ed, Penguin, Auckland, 1991).

Sinclair, Keith (ed) *A Soldier's View of Empire: The Reminiscences of James Bodell 1831–92* (Bodley Head, London, 1982).

Sole, Tony *Ngati Ruanui: A History* (Huia, Wellington, 2005).

Spiller, Peter *Butterworths New Zealand Law Dictionary* (4th ed, Butterworths, Wellington, 1995).

Spiller, Peter *The Chapman Legal Family* (Victoria University Press, Wellington, 1992).

Spiller, Peter, Finn, Jeremy and Boast, Richard *A New Zealand Legal History* (Brookers, Wellington, 1995).

Spiller, Peter, Finn, Jeremy and Boast, Richard *A New Zealand Legal History* (2nd ed, Brookers, Wellington, 2001).

Thomson, Kathleen and Serle, Geoffrey *A Biographical Register of the Victorian Parliament 1851–1900* (Australian National University, Canberra, 1972).

Vattel, Emer de *The Law of Nations, Or Principles of the Law of Nature, Applied to the Conduct and Affairs of Nations and Sovereigns* (1st English edition, GG and J Robinson, London, 1797).

Walker, Ranginui *Ka Whawhai Tonu Matou: Struggle Without End* (Penguin Books, Auckland, 1990).

Ward, Alan *A show of justice: racial 'amalgamation' in nineteenth century New Zealand* (Auckland University Press, Auckland, 1974).

Ward, Louis E *Early Wellington* (Whitcombe & Tombs, Wellington, 1929, 1975).

Webb, EA *The Records of St. Bartholomew's Priory and of the Church and Parish of St. Bartholomew the Great, West Smithfield* (Humphrey Milford, London, 1921).

Wells, Peter *Journey to a Hanging* (Vintage, Auckland, 2014).

Williams, David V *A Simple Nullity? The* Wi Parata *case in New Zealand law and history* (Auckland University Press, Auckland, 2011).

Williams, David V *'Te Kooti tango whenua': The Native Land Court 1864–1909* (Huia Publishers, Wellington, 1999).

Wilson, AN *The Victorians* (Arrow Books, London, 2003).

Wood, GA *Studying New Zealand History* (2nd ed, University of Otago Press, Dunedin, 1992).

Young, Sherwood *Guilty on the Gallows: Famous Capital Crimes of New Zealand* (Grantham House, Wellington, 1998).

B. Articles

Barber, LH "The Treatment of Maori Prisoners taken in the New Zealand Wars" (1979) NZLJ 324.

Boast, RP "Lawyers, Historians, Ethics and the Judicial Process" (1998) 28 VUWLR 87.

Butt, Peter "Contempt of Court in the Legal Profession" [1978] Crim LR 463.

Butterworth, Graham and Susan "Indigenous Insurrection and British Law: Anatomy of a Trial" [2005] ANZLHS E-Journal 141.

Chapman, Guy "The Treaty of Waitangi – fertile ground for judicial (and academic) myth-making" (July 1991) NZLJ 228.

Cornes, Richard "A point of stability in the life of the nation: The office of Chief Justice of New Zealand – Supreme Court judge, judicial branch leader, and constitutional guardian & statesperson" [2013] NZ L Rev 549.

Cornford, PA "Crown Law Office – Early History" (1964) 18 NZLJ 423.

Crane, Ralph "Tickling History: Maurice Shadbolt and the New Zealand Wars" (1991) 9 Journal of New Zealand Literature 59.

Dorsett, Shaunnagh "Reforming Equity: New Zealand 1843–56" (2013) 34 JLH 285.

Fieldhouse, DK "Sir Arthur Gordon and the Parihaka Crisis, 1880–1882" (1961) 10 Historical Studies: Australia and New Zealand 30.

Finn, Jeremy "Sir Kenneth Gresson: A Study in Judicial Decision Making" (1997) 6 Canterbury L Rev 481.

Finn, Jeremy "The Founders of the New Zealand Legal Profession: The First Cohort of Lawyers 1841–1851" (2012) 25 NZULR 24.

Gerritsen, Nick "The Treaty of Waitangi: 'Do I dare, Disturb the universe?'" (April 1991) NZLJ 138.

Haughey, EJ "A vindication of Sir James Prendergast" (July 1990) NZLJ 230.

Havemann, Paul "'The Pakeha Constitutional Revolution?' Five Perspectives on Maori Rights and Pakeha Duties" (1993) 1 Waikato L Rev 53.

Hutchinson, Charles "The origin of the legal system in New Zealand" (December 1988) NZLJ 427.

James, Colin "The treaty: a compact of (dis)honour" (December 1988) National Business Review Weekend Review W1.

Marsden, Lucy "A Sound Investment: Sir James Prendergast and his Fitzherbert Estate" (2013) 9 The Manawatu Journal of History 41.

McGrath, John "Principles for Sharing Law Officer Power: The Role of the New Zealand Solicitor-General" (1998) 18 NZULR 197.

McHugh, Paul "Constitutional myths and the Treaty of Waitangi" (September 1991) NZLJ 316.

McHugh, Paul "Law, History and the Treaty of Waitangi" (1997) 31 NZJH 38.

McHugh, Paul "Sovereignty this Century – Maori and the Common Law Constitution" (2000) 31 VUWLR 187.

McKenzie, Peter "New Zealand's First Chief Justice: The Rule of Law and the Treaty" (2012) 43 VUWLR 207.

Millen, J "The Legal Profession in Wellington: a historical perspective" (1991) 360 LawTalk 23.

Morris, Grant "James Prendergast and the Treaty of Waitangi: Judicial Attitudes to the Treaty During the Latter Half of the Nineteenth Century" (2004) 35 VUWLR 117.

Orange, Claudia "The Treaty of Waitangi – A Historical Overview" (1988) 11 Public Sector 2.

Rikys, Pita "Trick or Treaty" (October 1991) NZLJ 370.

Spiller, Peter "Chapman J and the Symonds Case" (1990) 4 Canterbury L Rev 257.

Spiller, Peter "Realism reflected in the Court of Appeal: The value of the oral tradition" (1998) 2 Yearbook of New Zealand Jurisprudence 31.

Seuffert, Nan "Shaping the Modern Nation: Colonial Marriage Law, Polygamy and Concubinage in Aotearoa New Zealand" (2003) 7 Law Text Culture 186.

Treadwell, CAL "Famous New Zealand Trials: The Trial of Tuhiata" (1933) 8 New Zealand Railways Magazine.

Treadwell, CAL "The Trial of Hamiora Pere" (1934) 9(4) New Zealand Railways Magazine.

Upston-Hooper, K "Slaying the Leviathan: Critical Jurisprudence and The Treaty of Waitangi" (1998) 28 VUWLR 683.

Williams, Joe "Chapman is wrong" (October 1991) NZLJ 373.

C. Unpublished Papers, Theses and Research Essays

Hamer, DA "The Law and the Prophet: A Political Biography of Sir Robert Stout 1844–1930" (MA thesis, University of Auckland, 1960).

McHugh, Paul "The aboriginal rights of the New Zealand Maori at common law" (PhD thesis, University of Cambridge, 1987).

D. Reports of the Waitangi Tribunal

Kaituna River Claim (Wai 4, 1984).

Mohaka ki Ahuriri Report (Wai 202, 2004).

Ngai Tahu Sea Fisheries Claim (Wai 27, 1992).

Ngati Awa Raupatu Report (Wai 46, 1999).

Orakei Claim (Wai 9, 1986).

Rangiteaorere Land Claim (Wai 32, 1990).

Taranaki Report – Kaupapa Tuatahi (Wai 143, 1996).

Te Roroa Claim (Wai 38, 1992).

Turanga Tangata Turanga Whenua: The Report on the Turanganui a Kiwa Claims (Wai 814, 2004).

E. Other

Internet Materials

"Dictionary of New Zealand Biography" Te Ara: The Encyclopedia of New Zealand <www.teara. govt.nz>.

Interviews

Lord Robin Cooke of Thorndon (18.2.99)

Sally Hobbs, descendant of Henry Hall (19.2.99)

William Knight, descendant of Charles Prendergast Knight (19.2.99)

Music

"Trial By Jury" (Musical) 1875, Text by WS Gilbert, Music by Sir Arthur Sullivan

Speeches

Tariana Turia "Wiremu Parata Waipunahau" (Wiremu Parata Waipunahau Te Kakakura Exhibition, 2 October 2006).

INDEX

JP refers to James Prendergast.

aboriginal title, enforceability of, 157–71
Acland, John, 57
Acting Governorship/Administrator *see*
　Prendergast, James
Aeneid (Virgil), 124
Aeschylus, 7
alcohol licensing, 121
Aldridge, Re (1893), 103, 130
Alison, Archibald, 125
Allan, William, 66, 140
Anglesea (ship), 26
Anglican Church, 19, 92, 126, 135, 154, 157,
　191, 192
Antigone (Sophocles), 124
The Argus, 28
Arihi Te Nahu v Locke (1887), 114
Arney, George, 1, 3, 20, 70, 74, 89, 91, 92, 93
Atkinson, Arthur Richmond, 104–5, 108
Atkinson, Harry, 1, 17, 51, 104, 128, 129, 135,
　136, 157, 176, 194, 195
Atkinson, Mr (JP's secretary), 126
Attorney-General v Bunny [1874], 74, 75–76
Attorney-General v Mr Justice Edwards (1891), 92,
　105, 110, 130
　see also Edwards, Worsley Bassett
Attorney-Generalship *see* Prendergast, James
Auckland City Council v Wotherspoon [1990], 98
Auckland City v Auckland Metropolitan Fire Board
　[1967], 114
Austin, John, 17, 18, 19, 125, 160, 162

Ballance, John (and Ministry), 128, 129, 149,
　175, 176
Ballantine, William, 13
Bank of New Zealand, 191
Bankruptcy Act 1867, 82
bankruptcy cases, 100, 120
Baragwanath J, 98
Barry, Redmond, 27
Barton, George B ('long Barton'), 71–72
Barton, George Elliott ('little Barton'), 3, 28,
　30, 34, 35, 41, 71, 109, 201
　background, 16
　feud with judiciary, 43, 130, 138–53, 201
　　background, 138–42, 153
　　Barton praised by Stout, 140

　　effect of feud on *Wi Parata* claim, 138, 141,
　　　152, 153, 157, 171
　　events following *Gillon,* 148–51
　　Gillon and contempt ruling, 138, 140, 142–48
　　insights into nature of legal profession,
　　　151–52
　　judges' pre-1876 relationship with Barton,
　　　139
　　Re GE Barton, 140, 141
　　legal career, 37, 38, 39, 139
　　Wi Parata see Wi Parata (1877)
Barton and Fitzherbert (firm), 140, 156
Barton v Allan (1878), 111, 124
Bassett, Judith, 1, 26
Beattie J, 101
Beauchamp, Harold, 191, 195
Bed of the Wanganui River, Re the [1962], 163
Beecham Group Ltd v Bristol-Myers Company (No 2)
　[1979], 104
Bell, Francis, 50, 95, 108, 122, 140, 157, 195
Bell Gully (firm), 157
Bell v Finn (1896), 112
Benjamin, Ethel, 2, 151
Bentham, Jeremy, 11, 17, 18, 19
Bern, R v (1895), 124
Bigelow on Estoppel, 124
Bishop's Hull (Somerset), 9
Bisson J, 165
Blackstone, 19, 125
Blackwell (ship), 25
Blaymires v Ewing (1890), 111
Boast, Richard, 2, 162, 168, 192
Bodell, James, 28–29
Boer War, 16
Bohan, Edmund, 1
The Borough of Bathurst v Macpherson, 111, 112
Bowen, George, 50, 62, 63, 68, 72
Bradley v Attorney-General [1978], 102
Brandon, Messrs (Wellington lawyers), 140
British Empire, 16–17, 18, 21
Broom, Herbert, 125
Brougham, Henry, 11, 17
Broughton v Donnelly (1888), 59, 119–20
Brunner mine disaster compensation, 109
Bryce, John, 46, 59, 129, 172, 176, 177, 179, 180,
　184, 185, 201

Buchanan (a prisoner), 127
Buckley, Patrick, 91, 92
Edwards J affair, 128–30
Buller, Walter, 72, 140
Bunny, Henry, 74
Bunny case [1874], 74, 75–76
Bunnythorpe land, 191
Bunt v Hallinan [1985], 103
Burgess, Richard, 73
Burgess Gang, 72–73
Byrnes, Giselle, 69

Cairns, Re (1888), 100
Cambridge University, 5, 6, 7–9, 12, 18, 20
Campbell, Daniel, 33
Campbell case (1862), 33, 34
Campbell's Application, Re (1891), 103–4
Canterbury customs revenue, 54
Captivi (Plautus), 6
Carisbrook (Victoria), 25
Carlyle, Thomas, 17
Catholic Church, 76–77
cause célèbre cases, 76–77, 89, 107, 138
Cayley, Arthur, 8
Chamberlain, Joseph, 173–74, 189, 190
Chan v Lower Hutt City Corporation [1976], 101
Chapman, Frederick, 40, 75, 122, 137, 195, 202
Chapman, Guy, 161
Chapman, Henry, 27, 35, 36, 37, 40, 41, 91,
   124, 132, 140, 159, 166, 169, 198
Chapman, James, 183
Chapman, Martin, 104, 122, 130, 132, 137, 201
The Chapman Legal Family (Spiller), 1, 2
Chapman Tripp (firm), 140
Chemis, Louis, 107
Chemis, R v (1889), 106, 107–8
Cherokee Nation v The State of Georgia (1831),
   160
Chief Justiceship see Prendergast, James
Chile (ship), 32
Chitty, Joseph, 124, 156
Chitty, Thomas, 11–12, 20, 124
Christie, Walter, 168
Churchill, John, 6
Chute, Major-General, 52
Cicero, 124
Cleary J, 118
Colet, John, 6
Colonial Law Journal, 34–35, 36–37
Colonial Mutual Life Insurance Company, 191
Commentaries on the Laws of England
   (Blackstone), 19
Commercial Union Assurance Co of NZ Ltd v
   Lamont [1989], 110
common law procedure, adaptation of, 132–33

Conolly, Edward, 91–92, 99, 104, 108, 110, 117,
   118, 123
Edwards J affair, 129, 130
Royal Commission of 1881, 132–33
constabulory, 82
Constitutional History (Hallam), 125
constitutional issues
controversial appointments, 71
Governor's powers and jurisdiction, 71
provincial system, 73–76, 84
Cook, George, 37
Cook Islands, 200
Moss affair, 130–31
Re Te-Au-O-Tonga Election Petition [1979], 105
Cooke, Robin
decisions referencing JP's judgments, 103, 105,
   116
as jurist, 95
NZ Maori Council v Attorney-General case, 165
Portrait of a Profession (ed), 2, 96
Coomber v Birkenhead Borough Council [1980], 117
Cooper, Theophilus, 130
Coote, Major, 53
corporal punishment, 121–22
Corunna Bay Holdings Ltd v Robert Gracie Dean
   Ltd [2002], 103
court constitution and procedure, 132–33
Court of Appeal
Bench members, 1875–99, 123
conflict with Privy Council, 164, 165, 189–90
disagreement among members, 123
JP as Chief Justice see Prendergast, James
JP's advocacy role as Attorney-General, 75–77
Court of Appeal Reports (Vols I–II), 97
Creighton, Robert, 63–64
Crimean War, 16, 17
criminal law
codification, 18, 44, 56, 78, 81
key statutes, 56, 81–82, 83, 84
procedure, 81
Criminal Law (Chitty), 124
Cropp, Frederick, 22–24
Crown Law Office, 48, 79–80

Dalziel, Raewyn, 1, 26, 34
Darwin, Charles, 18, 19
Davey, Lord, 163–64
Davison CJ, 104
Dawe, Caroline see Prendergast, Caroline (née
   Dawe) (JP's mother)
Dawe, George, 6, 195
Dawe, Henry, 20
Dawe, Phillip, 6
Dawson, 30–31
De Lautour, Cecil Albert, 150

Dean, Minnie (and 1895 case), 89, 106, 108, 113, 201

Denniston, John, 91, 92, 99, 100, 108, 109, 110, 111, 112, 117, 118, 123, 136
  Edwards J affair, 128, 129, 130

Department of Justice, 48, 79

Devore, A E T, 132

Dickens, Charles, 17

The Dictionary of New Zealand Biography 1769-1869 (1990), 1, 26

Dictionary of New Zealand Biography (Scholefield, 1940), 1

divorce law, 82

Dobie, Mary, 106

Domett, Alfred (and Ministry), 20, 48, 53, 56

Dominion, 10, 119, 183–84

Dormant Commission, 172–74

Doyle v Edwards (1898), 94–95, 102, 115–16, 122, 137

Dunedin Bar, 37–40
  decline of city as centre of legal profession, 42
  see also Prendergast, James

Dunolly (Victoria), 26

Echolands Farms v Powell [1976], 99

Edinburgh, Duke of, 76

Edwards, Worsley Bassett, 89, 91, 92, 108, 114, 117, 136
  appointment to Supreme Court Bench, 92, 105, 110, 128–30, 140, 201
  Court of Appeal/Privy Council conflict, 164, 165
  judicial activism, 123

Eichelbaum J, 99–100, 111

Eldon, Lord, 95

Elements (Euclid), 7

Elephant Bridge (Victoria), 25

Elias CJ, 166–67

Employment of Females Act 1894, 84

Empson, Walter, 190

English law, application in New Zealand, 70

English legal system
  criminal law reform, 81
  influence on New Zealand system, 15–19
    legislation, 44, 53–54
  oversupply of practitioners, 10, 17–18
  philosophical approaches, 19
  reform and change, 11, 17
  special pleading in, 10, 11

English Reports, 10–11

Euclid, 7, 125

Eureka diggings (and stockade tragedy), 22, 25, 26, 28, 30, 40, 76

Evening Post, 48, 64, 75, 86, 177, 189

reports of JP's decisions, 88

'Examinations for Barristers and Solicitors', 124–25

Eyre, Governor, 65

Falloon, James, 60

Fanzelow v Kerr (1896), 110

Fargher, Ray, 1

female employment law, 84

Fieldhouse, D K, 104

Finn, Jeremy, 2

Fisher, George, 104, 105

Fisher J, 98, 117

FitzGerald, William, 140

Fitzherbert, Henry S, 140

Fitzherbert, William, 74

Fitzherbert land ('Tiritea Estate'), 191–92

foreshore and seabed case, 166–67

Forms of Practical Proceedings to the Court of King's Bench, Common Pleas and Exchequer of Pleas (Chitty), 11

Fountain, John, 79

Fox, William (and Ministry), 20, 45, 47, 48, 49, 54, 66–67, 71, 73, 93, 121, 191

Frame, Alex, 2

Francis Henty (ship), 22–23, 29

Frederick Weld (Graham), 1

Gifford v Police [1965], 121

Gilbert, W S, 17–18

Gillies, Thomas, 35, 37–38, 39, 90, 91, 93, 123
  Royal Commission of 1881, 132–33

Gillon v MacDonald (1878), 138, 140, 142–48
  see also Barton, George Elliott ('little Barton')

Gisborne, William, 67, 78, 95, 97, 132

Glasgow, Governor (Earl of Glasgow), 175, 177

Glasgow, Lady, 177

gold rush
  Otago, 32, 33, 37, 40, 42, 54
  Victoria, 23–24, 42

Gordon, Arthur, 156, 170, 172, 174, 175, 177, 178–79, 180, 181–87, 201

Governor
  constitutional issue, 71
  JP as Administrator/Acting Governor *see* Prendergast, James

Graham, Jeanine, 1

Grant, James, 34

Granville, Earl, 61, 62, 63, 64

Gray, Alexander, 80

Gray, Wilson, 37

Gresson, Henry Barnes, 33, 74, 91

Grey, George (and Ministry), 48, 55, 56, 73, 136, 201
  abolition of provinces debate, 73–74

Barton affair, 150–51
biography, 1
issue of Crown grant to Bishop of Wellington, 154, 157
and JP, 74, 136
appointment to Legislative Council, 45
relationship with Maori, 157, 170
Gully, Hugh, 121, 122, 140

H. (A Bankrupt), Re [1968], 100
Hackshaw, Frederika, 154–55
Hadfield, Alexander, 126
Hadfield, Octavius (Bishop of Wellington), 157
see also Wi Parata (1877)
Hadfield v Armstrong (1894), 100
Haggitt, Bryan Cecil, 33, 36, 37, 38, 50
Haines, W C, 27
Hall, Henry (JP's nephew), 85, 90, 93, 126, 127, 133, 134, 135, 193, 195
Hall, John (and Ministry), 17, 46, 54, 113, 174, 175, 179, 180, 183, 184, 185
Hall, John (Mary Prendergast's father), 192
Hall, Mary Jane *see* Prendergast, Mary (née Hall)
Hall, R v (1886–87), 113
Hall, Sarah (née Kean), 192
Hall, Thomas, 113
Hallam, Henry, 125
hangings
Jarvey, 36
Kereopa Te Rau, 61
Minnie Dean, 108
Punishment of High Treason Act 1870, 83
Hanlon, Alfred, 108, 201
Hannan, J G H, 26
Harawira, Hone, 171
Harris, J H, 36
Harris v Fitzmaurice [1956], 103
Harrison, Henry, 64
Hart, Robert, 72, 79
Haughey, E J, 159
Haultain, Theodore, 46, 50, 62
Hawera County Council v Standard Insurance Company (1889), 115
Hawkins, Thomas, 107
Heredotus, 124
Hickford, Mark, 162
'Hilary Rules', 10
History of England (Macauley), 19
History of Europe (Alison), 125
History of New Zealand (Rusden), 64
HMS *Torch*, 130
Hoani Te Heuheu Tukino v Aotea District Maori Land Board [1941], 165
Hobbes, Thomas, 162

Hocking v Attorney-General [1963], 112
Hohepa Wi Neera v Bishop of Wellington (1902), 165
Hokitika, 73, 75
Holborn (London), 5
Homer, 7, 124
Hopkins, William, 8
Horace, 7
Hosking and Cook (firm), 34
Hotham, Charles, 25
Houghton, Walter E, 125
Housing Corporation of New Zealand v Maori Trustee [1988], 101
Howorth, Henry, 36
Howorth, James, 36, 38
Hunter, William, 183
Hutchinson J, 119

Ihimaera, Witi, 67
Iliad (Homer), 124
Immigration and Public Works Act 1870, 83
Imperial law, application in New Zealand, 70
industrial revolution, 17
Inglewood Advertiser, 28
Innes v Ewing [1989], 100
Inns of Court, 8, 38
Instant Funding Limited v Greenwich Property Holdings Limited (2007), 103
Introduction to the Principles of Morals and Legislation (Bentham), 19
Ireland, Robert, 76
Irish judges, Manning's view of, 86
Irish nationalist protest trials, 76–77
Irish settlers, JP's brothers' views, 25–26, 27
Izard, Charles, 66, 122, 140, 156, 157

Jackson's Claim, Re Mrs (1890), 102
Jamaican Rebellion (1865), 63
Jarvey, Catherine, 36
Jarvey, William, 36
Jeffrey, Thomas (cousin), 22–24
Jeffrey, Thomas (uncle), 84, 85
Jenkins v The Mayor, Councillors, and Citizens of the City of Wellington (1896), 114
Jervois, William, 172, 175, 176, 177, 181
John Taylor (ship), 30
Johns v Westland District Licensing Committee [1961], 118
Johnson v McIntosh (1823), 160
Johnston, Alexander, 61, 66, 68, 74, 75, 89, 90, 91, 93, 100, 106, 113, 136
acting Chief Justice, 173
Royal Commission of 1881, 132–33
Journal of the Legislative Council, 80

Journey to a Hanging (Wells), 61
Julius Vogel (Dalziel), 1, 26
Jull v Treanor (1886), 121
juror payments, 56–57
Justice Department, 48, 79
Justices of the Peace, 81

Kaituna River Claim report (Waitangi
  Tribunal), 166
Karahere, Pera, 68
Kaupapa Tuatahi (Waitangi Tribunal), 183
Kavanagh, Paul, 38
Kean, Sarah (later Hall), 192
Kelly, Thomas, 73
Kelvin, Lord, 8
Kenyon, Edmund Pell, 33, 36, 37
Kenyon and Hosking (firm), 34
Kereopa Te Rau, 60–61
King, Michael, 170
Knight, Charles Prendergast (JP's nephew), 85,
  126, 131, 133–34, 176, 187, 193, 195
  diaries, 134
Kynaston, Herbert, 6

Lamb, Jonathan, 169
Lambton Quay land, 192
land
  JP as judge, 98–99, 103
  JP's legal opinions as Attorney-General, 70–71
  Land Transfer Act 1870, 83
  Royal Commission of 1905, 191
  see also Maori land
Larkin, William, 75, 76–77
Larnach, William, 108
The Law of Nations (Vattel), 62, 156
Law Society, 38, 45, 50
Lease, Whakarere to Williams, Re A (1894), 114
Lee, George, 58
legal system/ profession *see* English legal system;
  New Zealand legal system
legislation, 71, 77–84
  abolition of provinces, 84
  Assistant Law Officer's role, 77, 79
  bankruptcy, 82
  constabulory, 82
  criminal law codification, 18, 44, 56, 78, 81
  criminal procedure, 81
  criminal statutes, 56, 81–82, 83, 84
  Crown Law Office's drafting responsibility,
    79–80
  divorce, 82
  employment of females, 84
  JP's contribution and role as Attorney-
    General, 44, 56, 77

Justices of the Peace, 81
  Land Transfer Act 1870, 83
  landmark statutes, 78–79, 83
  Maori affairs, 78, 83
  public works, 83
  punishment of high treason, 83
  reliance on Imperial legislation, 78
  university system, 84
Legislative Council
  abolition, 51
  Bills introduced, 79, 80–81
  elitism, 56, 58
  importance, 58
  issues, 44
    English law, 53–54
    juror payments, 56–57
    Maori representation, 51–52
    New Zealand Wars, 52–53
    parliamentary dissolution, 55–56
    provincial matters, 54–55
    regulation of legal profession, 57–58
  JP's membership, 36, 44, 45–48, 51–58
  JP's roles, generally, 58
  JP's speeches, 51
  limitation of number of Councillors, 56
Levy, Phil, 73
Lewis, George Henry, 13
Lewis, Mr (Wellington lawyer), 140
libel cases, 34, 39, 71–72, 77
Light v Milton (1883), 116
liquor licensing, 121
livestock protection, 120
Livy, 124
Longhurst, George, 177
Low v Hutchinson (1893), 118
Lower Hutt City v Attorney-General [1965], 116
"The Lundon and Whitaker Claims Act 1871", In
  re, 76
Lyttelton Times, 181, 184, 185

Mabo v Queensland (No 2) (1992), 166
Macadam, John, 36
Macandrew, R v (1869), 70–71
Macassey, James, 37
Macassey Law Reports, 35, 40
Macauley, Thomas, 17, 19
McCarthy J, 100
McCrae v Wheeler [1969], 103
McGechan J, 101
McGrath, John, 46
McGregor, Re (1888), 100, 120–21
McHugh, Paul, 161, 162, 165, 166, 167–68
McKenzie, Jock, 176
McKenzie v Couston (1898), 99

MacLachlan, R J, 117
McLean, Donald, 1, 46, 68, 84
McLean, Gavin, 173, 174
McMullin J, 103
Magna Carta 1297, 60
Makin, R v, 113
Mana Party, 171
Manawatu and West Coast Agricultural and
    Pastoral Association, 192
'Manawatu Block' hearing, 191
Manawatu properties, 191–92, 194
'Manchester Martyrs', 76
Manning, Charles, 15, 85
Manning, Charles (junior), 15, 85–86, 135
Manning, Henry, 15, 85, 194
Manning, John, 75, 76–77
Mansfield, Katherine, 191
Mantell, Walter, 52–53, 55, 67, 184
Maori
    Grey and, 157, 170
    invasion of Parihaka, 46, 49, 54, 59, 67, 90–91,
        101, 113, 156, 172, 177–87, 201
    JP's approach to Maori affairs, 44, 51–53,
        58–69, 119–20, 158, 169–70
    Maori-Pakeha relations in modern times, 154,
        168–69
    parliamentary representation, 51–52, 78–79, 83
    regulation of society by statute, 78, 83
    Selwyn and, 157
Maori customary law
    fishing rights, 165
    marriage, 59, 119
    native title doctrine differentiated, 159
    wills, 59
Maori land
    enforceability of native customary title,
        157–71
    *In re "The Lundon and Whitaker Claims Act
        1871",* 76
    Manawatu alienations, 191–92
    'Princes St Reserves', 70–71
    see also New Zealand Wars; *Wi Parata* (1877)
Martin, William, 1, 89, 91, 92, 113, 166, 169,
    170
Maryborough (Victoria), 25, 26, 27, 28
Mason, R v [2012], 167
Massey, William, 195, 202
Massey University campus land, 191
Matawhero massacre, 67, 68
Maungatapu murder trials, 73
Maxwell, James Clerk, 8
Menzies, James, 51–52, 53, 55
Merchant Taylors' School (London), 6, 12
Merrie v McKay (1897), 94–95, 102–3, 122, 137

Middle Temple, 9, 10, 16, 27
Mill, John Stuart, 17
Milton, John, 6
Minister of Justice, 47, 48
Ministry of Justice, 79
Moller J, 99
Moorhouse, Mr (Wellington lawyer), 140
Morland, George, 195
Moss, Frederick, 128, 131–32, 150, 153
Murray, Mr (Gordon's private secretary),
    178–79, 181, 182, 185
Muston, Charles, 72
Myers, Michael, 137, 195, 201, 202

Nankivell v O'Donovan (1893), 98, 121
Napoleonic Wars, 16
native customary title, enforceability of, 157–71
Nelson City Corporation v Nelson College (1896),
    114
New Zealand Academy of Fine Arts, 195
New Zealand Banking Corporation case, 34
New Zealand Celt, 77
New Zealand Education and Treatyism (Christie),
    168
New Zealand Gazette, 46
New Zealand Herald, 171
New Zealand Jurist, 72, 97, 140, 141, 149, 150
New Zealand Law Reports, 97, 109, 114, 122,
    123, 155
    Leading Cases series, 103
New Zealand Law Society, 38, 45, 50
A New Zealand Legal History (Spiller, Boast and
    Finn), 2
New Zealand legal system
    adaptation of common law procedure, 132–33
    application of Imperial legislation, 70
    Dunedin Bar, 37–40
        decline of city as centre of legal profession,
            42
    English influence, 15–19
    legislation, 44, 53–54
    Gillon saga's insights into nature of legal
        profession, 151–52
    regulation of legal profession, 38, 57–58
        Law Society, 38, 45, 50
        regional law societies, 38
    Supreme Court *see* Supreme Court
    Vice-Admiralty Courts, 70
        see also constitutional issues; Court of Appeal;
        legislation; Legislative Council; Parliament;
        Supreme Court
New Zealand Mail, 91
New Zealand Parliamentary Debates, 4, 46, 51,
    58, 140, 142, 150

New Zealand Times, 149
New Zealand University Senate, 72, 191
New Zealand Wars, 16
  end date, 177
  invasion of Parihaka, 46, 49, 54, 59, 67, 90–91,
    101, 113, 156, 172, 177–87, 201
  JP's actions, generally, 45
  JP's first experience of war, 17
  JP's role as Attorney-General, 58–69
  legal opinions, 60–66
    interpretation of Crown-Maori relations, 62
  Legislative Council debate, 52–53
  treason trials, 66–69
Newman, Cardinal, 17
Ngai Tahu, 70–71, 158
Ngai Tahu Sea Fisheries Claim report (Waitangi
  Tribunal), 166
Ngati Apa, 191–92
Ngati Apa v Attorney-General [2003] (foreshore
  and seabed case), 166–67
Ngati Raukawa, 191
Ngati Toa land *see Wi Parata* (1877)
Ninety-Mile Beach, Re [1963], 163, 167
Nireaha Tamaki v Baker (1900-01), 157, 160, 163,
  166
Normanby, Marquis of, 174–75
North J, 112, 121
November, Janet, 2
NZ Maori Council v Attorney-General [1987], 165

Offences Against the Person Acts, 56, 77, 79,
  81, 82
Ollivier, Bell and Fitzgerald's Reports (1878-80),
  97
Ollivier, Frank Morton, 132, 140
Olsen v Bailey (1888), 116–17
*On the Origin of the Species by Means of Natural
  Selection* (Darwin), 18
Onslow, Earl of, 175, 176
Onslow, Lady, 176
Orakei Claim report (Waitangi Tribunal), 166
O'Regan J, 102
Otago Daily Times, 32, 33, 34, 35, 39, 71
Otago gold rush, 32, 33, 37, 40, 42, 54
Otago Provincial Council, 39, 41, 150
Otago University degrees, 72
Otago Witness, 35
Oxford University, 6, 15, 20, 194

Papers Past, 4, 88
Paraone v Matthews (1888), 101
Parata, Wiremu, 39, 180
  presence at invasion of Parihaka, 156
  see also Wi Parata (1877)

Parihaka invasion, 46, 49, 54, 59, 67, 90–91, 101,
  113, 156, 172, 177–87, 201
Parliament, 51
  dissolution issue, 55–56
  Select Committee for Standing Orders, 56
  see also Legislative Council
parliamentary politics, generally, 48–50
Parsons, Thomas, 38
Parsons v Young Swan Morison McKay [1986], 111
Paterson, James, 46
Payze v Everitt [1959], 120
Peacocke, Colonel, 53, 55, 56–57
Pennefather J, 99
Pennell, R v [2003], 98
Pepys, Samuel, 6
Pere, Hamiora, 67–68
Perry J, 102
Petition of Right 1627, 60
Pharazyn, William, 56, 79
*The Picturesque Atlas Publishing Company (Limited) v
  Harbottle* (1891), 99–100
Piripi Te Maari v Stewart (1892), 115
Plautus, 6
Plunket, Governor, 173, 174
political backdrop to JP's Attorney-Generalship,
  45–50
Pollen, Daniel, 93
Pollen, Hugh, 173
Portrait of a Profession (Cooke), 2, 96
Potter, R v (1887), 97–98
Prendergast, Caroline (JP's sister), 12, 14, 15, 20
Prendergast, Caroline (née Dawe) (JP's mother),
  6, 7, 8, 12, 14, 15, 20
Prendergast, James
  1826-62: EARLY YEARS, 5–21
    academic interests, 7–8
    academic success, 6, 8
    cultural influences, 16–17, 21
    employment as special pleader, 10–11
    family origins, 6
    impact of experiences on future career, 19–21
    intellectual influences, 18–19
    legal apprenticeship, 11–12
    legal training at Middle Temple, 9, 10
    political leanings, 17
    privilege and opportunities, 5, 6, 17
    school teaching in Somerset, 9–10
    St Paul's School, 5, 6–7
    University of Cambridge, 5, 6, 7–9, 18, 20
  1852-55: VICTORIA, 22–31
    clerical work, 25–26
    emigration, 18, 22–23
    family relationships, 27–29
    gold mining, 22–24

impact of experiences on future career,
  29–31
near death experience, 24
return to London, 25–26
supposed connection with Vogel, 26
1862-67: DUNEDIN, 32–43
  Acting Provincial Solicitor and Crown
    Solicitor, 36–37, 41, 45
  admission to Bar, 33
  advocacy talent, 34–35
  appearances before Richmond, 40
  appearances in Supreme Court, 35
  arrival, 32–33
  called to Legislative Council, 36
  case load, 35
  connection with Vogel, 33–34
  Conveyancing Counsel, 36
  cricket skills, 38
  domestic life, 42
  first case, 33
  impact of experiences on future career,
    40–43
  Jarvey case, 36
  key contacts made, 41
  law firm, 34
  leaders of the Bar, 37–40
  political life, 35
  prominence (and rise) in legal profession,
    34, 36–37, 41–42
  social life, 35, 38
1865-75: ATTORNEY-GENERAL, 44–87
  advocacy role, 44, 66–69, 75–77
  approach to Maori affairs, 44, 51–53,
    58–69
  Burgess Gang trial, 72–73
  on changing nature of office and argument
    for Minister of Justice, 47–48
  conflicts of interest, 72
  drafting of legislation, 77–84
  legacy/influence, 44, 86–87, 197, 199
  legal adviser and legal opinions, 44, 60–66,
    69–74
  Legislative Council, 36, 44, 45–48, 51–58
  Manning and Larkin trial, 76–77
  move to Wellington, 45, 47, 84
  nature of role, 45–50
  New Zealand Wars, 45, 58–69
  non-political office and tenure, 47, 49
  personal affairs, 84–86
  political backdrop, 45–50
  political life, 44
  political office, 45–47, 48
  President of Law Society, 45, 50
  private practice, 48

qualities and ability shaped by earlier
  experience, 40–41
regulation of legal profession, 38, 45, 50,
  57–58
roles, generally, 44–45
Select Committee for Standing Orders, 56
speeches in Legislative Council, 51
success, 85, 86–87
views on abolition of provinces, 73, 74
Westland Court involvement, 73
workload, 85, 86
1875-99: 'ACTING GOVERNOR', 134,
  172–87
  Dormant Commission, 172–74
  invasion of Parihaka, 46, 49, 54, 59, 67,
    90–91, 101, 113, 156, 172, 177–87, 201
  periods of service as Administrator, 174–77
  social life, 176–77
1875-99: CHIEF JUSTICE, 88–137
  abilities as judge, 95–96, 97–110
  abilities as judicial administrator, 94,
    126–27, 136
  alcohol licensing, 121
  appointment, 41, 47, 93
  approach to Maori affairs, 90–91, 158,
    169–70
  bankruptcy cases, 100, 120
  brevity of judgments, 97
  case analysis, 94–123
  conflicts of interest, 137
  conservatism, 111–15
  controversial cases, 127–31
  corporal punishment, 121–22
  Court of Appeal Bench, 123
  decisions reflecting colonial environment,
    120–22
  dissenting judgments in Court of Appeal,
    109–10
  Edwards J affair, 92, 105, 110, 128–30
  'Examinations for Barristers and Solicitors',
    124–25
  head of Court of Appeal, 88
  influence of, and relationship with brother
    judges, 96, 136
  influence of Richmond, 96, 108, 123
  interpretation of own legislation/use of past
    experience, 101–4
  jurisprudential influences and approach, 19,
    20, 123–25
  land law, 98–99, 103
  legacy/influence of judgments, 88–89, 96,
    122–23, 136–37, 199–201
  management of high-profile cases, 104–9
  Maori issues, 119–20

Moss affair, 130–31
nature of position, 89–94
overseas visits, 134, 135
personal affairs, 133–36
relationship with Johnston, 89–90
relationship with Richmond, 90, 108, 136
relationships with legal and political elite, 135
reliance on English precedent, 111–13
resignation, 137
Royal Commission of 1881, 132–33
sources of judgments, 88, 97
success, 92
support of the establishment, 113–15
Supreme Court, Wellington District, 93–94
Supreme Court Bench, 90–92, 122–23
tort law relating to farming practice, 120
treatment of legal issues, 97–100, 115–17
vagueness of judgments, 117–18
view of, in *Portrait of a Profession*, 96
weak judgments/overturned decisions, 118–19
weaknesses as judge, 115–20
Wi Parata case *see Wi Parata* (1877)
1899-1921: RETIREMENT, 188–96
    adjudicator at Wanganui Collegiate, 188, 190–91
    directorships, 191
    family matters, 192–96
    farming interests, 191–92
    London Conference on Privy Council, 188, 189–90
    New Zealand University Senate, 72, 191
    Royal Commission of 1905, 191
and Atkinson, 136
and Barton *see* Barton, George Elliott ('little Barton')
birth, 5, 12
and Bowen, 72
and Chapman, 40
death, 15, 189, 195
    beneficiaries of will, 195
    estate, 15
    funeral, 195
    obituaries, 10, 119, 183–84
    Stout's eulogy, 38, 140, 202
death of wife, 137, 193
domestic life, 42, 193
    Bolton St property, 84, 192
family bonds, 8, 20
    nephews as assets, 195
    nepotism, 85, 93, 126
    support of brothers, 194, 202

support of nephew Michael, 15, 85, 193, 194–95, 202
support of nephews Henry and Charles, 193
and Gordon, 174, 201
and Grey, 45, 74, 136
influence/legacy, 4, 19–20, 44, 197–202
    as Administrator, 201
    as Attorney-General, 44, 86–87, 197, 199
    as Chief Justice, 88–89, 96, 122–23, 136–37, 199–201
influences on JP
    brothers, 8
    Chitty, 11–12, 20
    extended family, 15
    father, 5, 12–15, 20–21
    Henry Chapman, 40
    Manning, 15
    Richmond, 96, 108
    Routledge, 20
    uncles, 20
knighthood, 183, 196
letters suggesting desire to leave New Zealand, 135
letters to parents, 7, 8, 9, 14
loyalty to Empire and colony, 21, 188, 201
marriage, 9, 192
patronage, 134–35
personality, 14, 15, 21, 29, 43
President of Wellington Boys' Institute, 134–35
racial views, 19, 59–60, 64, 188
religion, 19, 135
and Richmond, 35, 41, 42, 50, 90, 136, 200
rumour about health, 135
and Sewell, 86
social life
    as Administrator, 176–77
    as Attorney-General, 84
    as Chief Justice, 133, 134
    Days Bay picnic, 196
    Dunedin, 35, 38
and Stafford, 49, 86
and Stout *see* Stout, Robert
talents as advocate, 34–35
temper, 14, 24, 29
tenacity, 24, 30, 40
Victorian frame of mind, 17, 21, 24, 125, 202
and Vogel, 26, 33–34, 41, 42, 45, 86, 93, 139
and Williams, 91
Prendergast, Jane (née Smyth), 28, 29, 85, 193, 194
Prendergast, Joseph, 6, 9, 20
Prendergast, Kenyon and Maddock (firm), 34
Prendergast, Leonard, 26

Prendergast, Mary (née Hall), 9, 22, 25, 26, 32,
    84, 85, 133, 137, 187–88, 198, 201
Prendergast, Michael (JP's brother)
    alcoholism, 13, 28–29, 39, 43, 85, 121, 193
    anti-Irish sentiment, 26, 139
    and Barton, 39, 139
    birth, 12
    death of wife, 85
    education, 6, 8
    emigration, 18, 22, 24
    encourages JP to come to Dunedin, 33
    Eureka trial, 76
    on JP's career and return to England, 26
    legal career
        admission to Dunedin Bar, 33
        decline, 28–29, 42–43, 45, 85, 87
        defence of Kelly and Burgess, 72–73
        Dunedin, 28, 37, 38–39
        lack of success, generally, 20
        Melbourne, 27–29, 30, 41
        relationship with, and views about, Henry
            Chapman, 40
        training and admission to Bar, 9
    marriage and birth of son, 28
    mental illness, 29, 39, 133, 194
        committed to lunatic asylum, 1870, 85
    personality, 29, 43
    settlement in Otago region, 33
    Victorian Legislative Assembly, 22, 27, 40
    visited by JP, 1884, 135
Prendergast, Michael (JP's father), 7, 9, 19, 40,
    139, 193
    alcoholism, 121
    contact with political figures, 17
    death, 12, 14, 20
    death of daughter, 12, 14, 15
    death of wife, 14, 15
    education, 8, 12
    family bonds, 14
    family origins and social mobility, 6
    and JP
        early expectations of JP, 7
        impressed by JP's skills as special pleader, 10
        influence on JP, 5, 12–15, 20–21, 108
        letters, 7, 8, 9, 14
    legal career
        appointment as QC, 12
        Chitty's support, 11
        as counsel in London, 12
        dishevelment and disorganisation, 13
        impact of developments in legal profession,
            17, 18
        integrity and sense of justice, 13–14
        judge at Old Bailey, 18

    judge of the Sheriff's Court, 11, 12
    Norfolk Circuit, 14–15
    performance as judge, 12–13
    prominence/success, 5, 18
    Recorder for Norwich, 12
    reputation as lawyer, 13
    Sergeant, 11
    letters to wife, 14
    marriage and birth of children, 6, 12
    personality, 14, 15
Prendergast, Michael (JP's grandfather), 6, 12, 15
Prendergast, Michael (JP's nephew), 15, 28, 85,
    180, 192, 193, 194–95
    as temporary secretary to JP, 126, 134
Prendergast, Philip (JP's brother)
    admission to Middle Temple, 27
    alcoholism, 121, 194
    anti-Irish sentiment, 25–26, 27, 139
    career in Victoria, 27
    education, 6, 8
    emigration, 22–23
    gold mining, 22–24
        near death experience, 24
    on his brothers' personalities, 27
    on JP's career and return to England, 25–26
    legal career
        decline, 45, 87
        lack of success, generally, 20
        London, 11
    on Melbourne, 23
    mental illness, 11, 15, 85, 133, 194
    return to England, 27, 30
Prichard J, 116
'Princes St Reserves' (Dunedin), 70–71
Privy Council
    1901 London Conference, 188, 189–90
    conflict with New Zealand Court of Appeal,
        164, 165, 189–90
Prometheus Bound (Aeschylus), 7
Proudfoot, A Bankrupt, Re [1961], 118–19
The Province of Jurisprudence Determined (Austin), 19
Provincial Council Ordinances, validity of, 71
provincial issues facing Legislative Council,
    54–55
provincial system, 73–76
    abolition of provinces, 73–74, 84
Puhatikotiko No. 1 Block, Re The (1893), 108–9
Punishment of High Treason Act 1870, 83

Quick, Mr (Wellington lawyer), 140

R v Bern (1895), 124
R v Chemis (1889), 106, 107–8
R v Dean (1895) (Minnie Dean), 89, 106, 108, 113

R v Hall (1886-87), 113
R v Macandrew (1869), 70–71
R v Makin, 113
R v Mason [2012], 167
R v Pennell [2003], 98
R v Potter (1887), 97–98
R v Rogers [2006], 97, 98
R v SG Isaacs and Daniel Campbell (1862), 33, 34
R v Symonds(1847), 159, 160, 169
R v Te Kira [1993], 97, 98
R v Tuhiata (1880), 106
R v Veitch (1883), 106–7
R v Vowles (1885), 115
R v Woodgate (1876), 106
Ranfurly, Governor, 131, 173–74, 175, 177, 187, 189
Rangimoeke v Strachan (1895), 104, 124
Re A Lease, Whakarere to Williams (1894), 114
Re Aldridge (1893), 103, 130
Re Cairns; Ex parte New Zealand Land Mortgage Company (Limited) (1888), 100
Re Campbell's Application (1891), 103–4
Re GE Barton (1876), 140, 141
Re H. (A Bankrupt) [1968], 100
Re McGregor; Ex parte McGregor (1888), 100, 120–21
Re Mrs Jackson's Claim (1890), 102
Re Ninety-Mile Beach [1963], 163, 167
Re Proudfoot, A Bankrupt, Ex parte Ballins Breweries (New Zealand) Limited [1961], 118–19
Re Reimer, Ex parte The Official Assignee (1896), 118, 119
Re Rickman, Ex parte The Bank of New Zealand (1890), 117–18
Re Roche (1888), 100
Re Stewart & Co., Ex parte Piripi Te Maari (No. 2) (1892), 102
Re Te-Au-O-Tonga Election Petition [1979], 105
Re the Bed of the Wanganui River [1962], 163
Re "The Lundon and Whitaker Claims Act 1871", 76
Re The Puhatikotiko No. 1 Block (1893), 108–9
Re Wellington Central Election Petition, Shand v Comber [1973], 105
Read, Gabriel, 32
Reeves, William Pember, 176
regional law societies, 38
Reid, Thomas (a young offender), 121–22
Reid, Walter, 79, 80, 84, 132
Reid v Official Assignee of McCallum (1886), 100
Reimer, Re (1896), 118, 119
Retaruke Timber Co Ltd v Rodney County Council [1984], 116

Richardson J, 98, 110
Richmond, Christopher William, 32, 51, 75, 104, 176, 194, 198
  background, 16
  and Barton *see* Barton, George Elliott ('little Barton')
  death, 39, 90, 92, 108, 118, 123
  and JP, 35, 40, 41, 42, 50, 90, 136, 137, 200
    influence on JP, 96, 108
  legal career
    admission to Dunedin Bar, 33
    alliance with JP, 41
    Broughton appeal, 120
    Bunny case, 74
    chances of becoming Chief Justice, 93
    Court of Appeal decisions, 115
    Court of Appeal judge, 123
    Dunedin, 37, 39, 92
    Edwards J affair, 129, 130
    influence of JP, 137
    JP's appearances before, 40
    Manning and Larkin trials, 76–77
    Minnie Dean appeal, 108
    move to Wellington, 90
    profile, 199–200
    Royal Commission of 1881, 132–33
    speed of career success, 42
    Supreme Court costs decision, 117
    Supreme Court judge, 39, 41, 88, 90, 94, 100, 123
    talents, 136
    Tarry case, 111–12
    Wi Parata case *see Wi Parata* (1877)
    views on Maori affairs, 91
    views on quality of Dunedin lawyers, 37
Richmond, Henry Robert, 125
Richmond, James Crowe, 50, 51, 54
Richmond-Atkinson families, 50, 105, 129
Rickman, Re (1890), 117–18
Rira Peti v Ngaraihi Te Paku (1888), 59, 119
Riseborough, Hazel, 182, 183
Robinson, Hercules, 132, 175
Robinson and Morgan-Coakle v Behan [1964], 112
Roche, Re (1888), 100
Rogers, R v [2006], 97, 98
Rolleston, William, 20, 185
Roosevelt, Theodore, 199
Routledge, William, 9, 20
Royal Commission of 1881, 132–33
Royal Commission of 1905, 191
Rua Kenana, 177
Rural Banking and Finance Corporation of New Zealand v Official Assignee [1991], 117
Rusden, G W, 64

Ruskin, John, 17
Russell, Andrew, 46, 50, 53
Russell v The Minister of Lands (1898) and *(No.2)*
    (1899), 117

St John's Presbyterian Church (Wellington), 135
St Bartholomew's (London), 5
St Paul's School (London), 5, 6–7
Salmond, John, 95, 103, 124, 165
Salmond: Southern Jurist (Frame), 2
Schnell, Antonio, 177
Scholefield, G H, 1, 26, 78, 89
Scott, Dick, 183
Scott, Stuart C, 168
Scott v Broadlands Finance Limited [1972], 102
Season of the Jew (Shadbolt), 61, 67–68
Seddon, Richard, 105, 121, 174, 176, 189
Selwyn, George Augustus (Bishop of
    Wellington), 157
Sergeants' Inn, 11
Seuffert, Nan, 119
Sewell, Henry (and Ministry), 37, 41, 45–46, 47,
    48, 49, 54, 56, 86
SG Isaacs and Daniel Campbell, R v (1862), 33, 34
Shadbolt, Maurice, 61, 67–68
Simons family, 24
A Simple Nullity? (Williams), 1, 155, 160,
    161–62, 167, 171
Sir Harry Atkinson (Bassett), 1
Skerrett, Charles, 95, 98, 104, 121, 122, 137
Sleath, John, 6
Smith, James, 38
Smyth, Jane (later Prendergast), 28, 29, 85, 193,
    194
Solicitor-General v Bishop of Wellington (1901), 164
Sophocles, 124
Southern Cross (ship), 179
special pleading in English legal system, 10, 11
Speight J, 117
Spencer, Herbert, 17, 19
Spiller, Peter, 1, 2, 159
Stafford, Edward (and Ministry), 1, 20, 37, 41,
    45, 46, 47, 48, 49, 50, 55–56, 61, 63, 70, 73, 86
Stephen, Henry John, 19
Stewart, William Downie, 34, 37, 201
*Stewart & Co., Ex parte Piripi Te Maari, Re (No.
    2)* (1892), 102
Stokes, Robert, 57
Stout, Robert, 1, 32, 75, 150, 201
    as articled clerk, 34
    background, 16
    career in Dunedin, 37, 38
    as Chief Justice
        appointment, 91, 189
        conflict of interests, 137

    judgments, 92–93
    profile, 89, 94
    tenure, 88, 92
    Court of Appeal/Privy Council conflict, 164,
        165
    and Deputy-Governor/Administrator roles,
        174
    Edwards J affair, 130
    funeral of JP, 195
    eulogy, 38, 202
    praise of Barton in eulogy, 140
    influence of JP, 137
    on JP's social and political life, 35
    on JP's talents as special pleader, 35
    overturned Supreme Court decisions, 122
    relationship with JP, 42, 74, 136
    Royal Commission of 1881, 132–33
    rumour about JP's health, 135
    speed of career success, 42
    view of JP as judge, 96
    view of native policy, 184
    views on Privy Council within NZ legal
        structure, 189
Sugden on Powers (8th ed), 124
Sullivan, Joseph (Burgess Gang), 73, 201
Supreme Court
    Barton feud *see* Barton, George Elliott ('little
        Barton')
    JP as Chief Justice *see* Prendergast, James
    JP's advocacy role as Attorney-General, 75
        New Zealand Wars cases, 66–69
    Vice-Admiralty judges, 70
Supreme Court Rules (1844), 113
Sutton v O'Kane [1973], 103
Symonds case (1847), 159, 160, 169

Takamore v Clarke [2012], 167
Tamararo, Wi, 68
Tancred, Henry, 52, 55
Taranaki report (Waitangi Tribunal), 183
Tarry v The Taranaki County Council (1894),
    111–12
Taylor on Evidence, 124
Te-Au-O-Tonga Election Petition, Re [1979], 105
Te Kira, R v [1993], 97, 98
Te Kooti, 50, 59, 60, 64, 66, 67, 68, 177, 199, 200
Te Maari, Piripi, 102
    Piripi Te Maari v Stewart (1892), 115
    *Re Stewart & Co., Ex parte Piripi Te Maari (No.
        2)* (1892), 102
Te Weehi v Regional Fisheries Officer [1986], 165,
    166
Te Whiti o Rongomai, 172, 178, 179, 180,
    183–84, 185, 186, 201
Thames Advertiser, 109

The Argus, 28
Thomas, Arthur Allan, 107
Tipping J, 103
'Tiritea Estate', 191–92
Titokowaru, 50, 59, 60, 61, 62–64, 66, 68, 177, 180, 186, 199, 201
Todhunter, Isaac, 8
Tohu Kakahi, 178, 186
Torrens, Robert Richard, 83
Torrens system, 79, 83, 101
tort law relating to farming practice, 120
Travers, Ollivier, and Co. (firm), 156
Travers, William, 50, 74, 75, 79, 122, 132, 140, 151, 201
    on Court of Appeal/Privy Council conflict, 164–65
    death, 165
    Wi Parata see Wi Parata (1877)
The Travesty of Waitangi (Scott), 168
Treadwell, C A L, 106
Treaty of Waitangi
    articulation of principles in NZ Maori Council case, 165
    modern debate, 154, 168–69, 170
    see also Waitangi Tribunal; Wi Parata (1877)
Tsong Tsi (a prisoner), 127
Tuhiata, R v (1880), 106
Turanganui a Kiwi report (Waitangi Tribunal), 67
Turia, Tariana, 171
Turner J, 103, 116, 121, 167
Turton, Hanson, 34, 38

University of Cambridge, 5, 6, 7–9, 12, 18, 20
university system, 84

Vaggioli, Felice, 64, 182–83
Vattel, Emer de, 62, 64, 156
Veitch, Phoebe, 106–7
Veitch, R v (1883), 106–7
Venning J, 103
Vice-Admiralty Courts, 70
Victoria, Queen, 176, 188
The Victorian Frame of Mind 1830-1870 (Houghton), 125
Victorian gold rush, 23–24, 42
Victorian Legislative Assembly, 22, 27, 39, 40
Victory Park Board v Christchurch City Council [1965], 116
Virgil, 124
Vogel, Julius (and Ministry), 26, 32, 33–34, 46, 48, 70, 74, 93
    appointment of JP as Chief Justice, 41, 47, 93
    biography, 1
    borrowing schemes, 50, 83

and JP, 26, 33–34, 41, 42, 45, 86, 93, 139
    toll collection at Wanganui Bridge, 73
Volkner, Carl, 60–61
Vowles, R v (1885), 115

Waimiha Sawmilling Co Ltd v Waione Timber Co Ltd [1926], 103
Waitangi Tribunal
    controversy, 168
    Pere trial in Turanganui a Kiwa report, 67
    reports referencing Wi Parata, 166
    Taranaki report criticism of JP, 183
    see also Treaty of Waitangi
Walker, Ranginui, 169, 183
Wallis v Solicitor-General (1902-03), 157, 163, 164, 166, 189–90
Wanganui Collegiate sexual abuse inquiry, 188, 190–91
Wanganui Herald, 107
Webber v Finnimore (1880), 120
Weld, Frederick (and Ministry), 1, 20, 37, 45–46, 48–49, 51, 54, 55, 56
Wellington as seat of government, 49, 54–55
Wellington Boys' Institute, 134–35
Wellington Cathedral Fund, 135
Wellington Central Election Petition, Shand v Comber, Re [1973], 105
Wellington City Corporation v Public Trustee [1921], 103
Wellington City Council v Victoria University of Wellington [1975], 116
The Wellington City Election Petition (1897), 104–5
Wellington Trust, Loan and Investment Company, 191
Wells, Peter, 61
Westland, 73
Whakarere to Williams, Re A Lease (1894), 114
Whitaker, Frederick (and Ministry), 37, 46, 48, 54, 76, 129, 132, 142, 146, 150, 176, 179, 181, 185, 195
Whitmore, George Stoddart, 52, 53, 57, 150
Wi Parata (1877), 39, 62, 63, 67, 69, 71, 103, 104, 105, 116, 131, 154–71
    academic opinion of JP's role, 167–71
    advocates
        Barton for Parata, 39, 138, 156
        Izard for Attorney-General, 156, 157
        Travers for Bishop of Wellington, 138, 156, 157
    authority of, 94
    background to fact situation, 154–55
    criticism, generally, 136
    criticism in NZ Maori Council case, 165
    as early decision in JP's career, 122, 136

effect of Barton's feud with judiciary, 138, 141, 152, 153, 157, 171
JP's ties with Travers, 171
judgment of JP and Richmond, 62, 157–63
  dismissal of statutory references to Maori custom, 119
  joint responsibility, 1, 155–56
  Treaty of Waitangi and the 'simple nullity' statement, 1, 158–59, 171
key players in decision, 155–57
legacy/influence of judgment, 163–67, 201
  anti-Treaty works, 168
  in later Court of Appeal/Privy Council conflict, 164–65
  modern courts, 102, 137, 165, 166–67
legal sources canvassed, 124
motivation of Parata to bring case, 154–55
practical effect on retention of Maori land, 124
reference to US law, 112
as test case, 154
Waitangi Tribunal reports referencing, 166
Williams on, 1, 155, 160, 161–62, 167, 171
Williams, David V
  on JP's advocacy role as Attorney-General, 70–71
  on JP's wartime opinions, 64–65
  A Simple Nullity?, 1, 155, 160, 161–62, 167, 171

Williams, Joshua, 90, 93, 95, 99, 110, 111, 112, 124
  Cambridge education, 8, 20
  career struggles in London, 8
  on Court of Appeal/Privy Council conflict, 164
  Edwards J affair, 129, 130
  and JP, 91
  Minnie Dean trial, 108
  profile, 199–200
  Royal Commission of 1881, 132–33
  writings used in examinations, 125
Williamson, Hudson, 80
Williamson J, 165
wills, Maori, 59
Wilson, Bill, 142, 151
Wilson, James, 73
Wilson and King v Brightling (1885), 103
Wilson J, 116
womens' employment law, 84
Woodgate, R v (1876), 106
Woodgate, Susan, 106
Woodgate, William, 106
Woodhouse J, 103
World War I, 16
Wotherspon v Dobson [1893], 112
Wren, Christopher, 6

Young v Hill, Ford and Newton (1883), 100